D0497996

WITHDRAWN
UTSA LIBRARIES

JEAN TOOMER

Jean Toomer

Race, Repression, and Revolution

BARBARA FOLEY

UNIVERSITY OF ILLINOIS PRESS
URBANA, CHICAGO, AND SPRINGFIELD

© 2014 by the Board of Trustees
of the University of Illinois
All rights reserved
Manufactured in the United States of America
C 5 4 3 2 1

∞ This book is printed on acid-free paper.

Library of Congress Cataloging-in-Publication Data
Foley, Barbara, 1948- author.
Jean Toomer : Race, Repression, and Revolution / Barbara Foley.
pages   cm
Includes bibliographical references and index.
ISBN 978-0-252-03844-0 (hardback)
ISBN 978-0-252-09632-7 (ebook)
1. Toomer, Jean, 1894–1967—Criticism and interpretation. 2.
Modernism (Literature)—United States. 3. Harlem Renaissance.
I. Title.
PS3539.O478Z636   2014
813'.52—dc23   2013050781

Library
University of Texas
at San Antonio

To David

CONTENTS

ACKNOWLEDGMENTS

My abiding interest in Jean Toomer has indebted me to many scholars, informants, and friends over the years. The late Robert B. Jones first piqued my interest in Toomer. Kent Anderson Leslie was of great assistance in ferreting out biographical information, securing permission to publish Toomer family photographs, and supplying me with helpful genealogical charts. Nathan Grant's and Charles Scruggs's astute readings of the manuscript for the University of Illinois Press were very helpful as I revised the text for publication. Other scholars who have assisted me are Esme Bhan, Rudolph P. Byrd, Lee Ann Caldwell, Edward Cashin, Russell Eliot Dale, Timothy Dayton, Maria Onita Estes-Hicks, Cynthia Franklin, Peter Gardner, Angus Gillespie, Marcial González, David Hoddeson, Cynthia Earl Kerman, Charles Larson, Nellie Y. McKay, Adam McKible, Gregory Meyerson, Carlton Morse, David G. Nicholls, Gino Michael Pellegrini, Carla Peterson, Kathleen Pfeiffer, Lola Richardson, Frederik L. Rusch, Gerald J. Smith, Claudia Tate, Paul Beekman Taylor, Mark Whalan, Belinda Wheeler, and Jon Woodson.

I am grateful to the many members of the staff at Yale's Beinecke Library who have patiently assisted me over the years, including Sara Azam, Nancy Kuhl, and Patricia C. Willis. I wish to thank L. Malcolm Morris of the Division of Archives of the State of Louisiana; Andrea Jackson of the Atlanta University Center; Joellen ElBashir and Robin Van Fleet of the Moorland-Spingarn Research Center, Howard University; Brenda Square of the Amistad Research Center, Tulane University; Sandra Stelts of the Rare Books Room, Van Pelt Library, University of Pennsylvania; Judith Gray of the Library of Congress; Ann Allen Shockley of the Special Collections Division at the Fisk University Library; Lori N. Curtis of the Special Collections division of the University of Tulsa; and Muriel McDowell, Genealogy Librarian of the Middle Georgia Regional Library.

Several local historians and current or former residents of Middle Georgia provided valuable information relevant to Toomer's family history and the making of *Cane*. These include Colin Campbell, Dr. Jimmy Carter, George L. Gardiner, Gertrude (Trudy) Lewis, Josephine Richardson, John W. Rozier, Dr. Guy Braswell Sheftall, and Forrest Shivers. Harrell Lawson and LaVerne Lawson-Jack made it possible for me to interview some dozen Sparta residents. I am especially grateful to them for introducing me to Katy Hunt, the 106-year-old granddaughter of Spencer Beasley, Johm Cain's coconspirator in the 1863 Sparta slave revolt; and George ("Snap") Ingram, who once worked at Sparta's Old Rock Shop and recalled a woman with two Negro sons who lived between the railroad tracks and the Culverton Road, evidently the prototype of Toomer's Becky.

Special thanks must go to members of the Toomer and Dickson families: Fannie and George Toomer of Perry, Georgia; Sharon Toomer of New York; Margery Toomer Latimer of Doylestown, Pennsylvania; and Jean Jackson of Annapolis, great-granddaughter of Amanda America Dickson.

Two grants from the National Endowment for the Humanities and two grants from the Rutgers Research Council provided valuable time and funds that enabled me to complete this project.

The University of Illinois Press provided me with splendid support in bringing this book into being. I wish especially to thank Willis Regier, director of the press, for guidance going back to the press's 2003 publication of *Spectres of 1919: Class and Nation in the Making of the New Negro*, which was originally conceived as the first part of this study of Jean Toomer. Dustin Hubbart, the art director, did an outstanding job of producing the book's illustrations. Deborah Oliver performed the work of copyediting with expert precision and subtlety. Thanks also go to Jennifer Clark for her speedy and efficient work, as well has her patient response to my last-minute request for revisions.

I especially thank my children, Adam Stevens and Margaret Stevens, for the humor and patience with which they have heard me talk about Jean Toomer over many years. Peter Gardner, who read early drafts of various chapters, cheered me on with astute advice and loving support.

This book is dedicated to my dear brother, David Ross Foley, who has a passion for literature, politics, and history.

TOOMER GENEALOGICAL CHARTS

These three genealogical charts will help the reader untangle Jean Toomer's complicated family history. The first maps Toomer's ancestry, beginning with his maternal grandfather, P. B. S. Pinchback. The second outlines the three marriages of Nathan Toomer, Jean Toomer's father. The third sets forth the family tree of Nathan Toomer's second wife, Amanda America Dickson, said to be in 1891 "the wealthiest colored woman in the world." The Toomer Genealogy and the African American Dickson Genealogy are reproduced with permission from Virginia Kent Anderson Leslie, *Woman of Color, Daughter of Privilege: Amanda America Dickson, 1849–1893* (Athens: University of Georgia Press, 1995), 148 and 147.

The Pinchback Genealogy

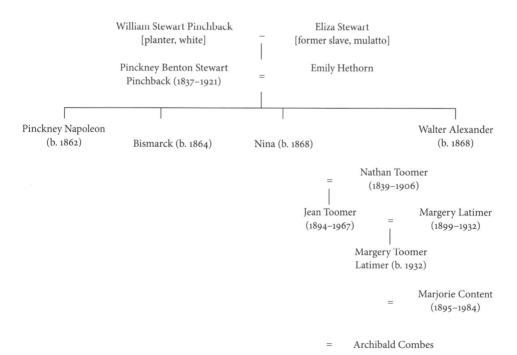

The Toomer Genealogy

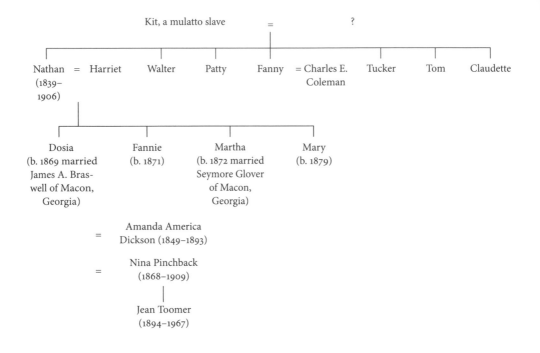

The African American Dickson Genealogy

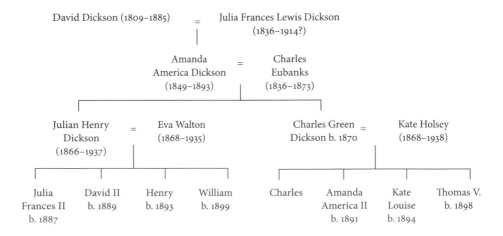

Introduction

In the literature of the Socialist movement in this country there is to be found a rational explanation of the causes of race hatred and, in the light of these, a definite solution, striking at the very root of the evil, is proposed. It is generally established that the causes of race prejudice may primarily be found in the economic structure that compels one worker to compete against another and that furthermore renders it advantageous for the exploiting classes to inculcate, foster, and aggravate that competition. . . . Demagogues may storm and saints may plead, but America will remain a grotesque storm center torn by passion and hatred until our democratic pretensions are replaced by a socialized reality.

—Jean Toomer, "Reflections on the Race Riots"

It is a symptom of weakness when one must bring God, equality, liberty, and justice to one's support. It follows that the working classes, particularly the dark-skinned among the working classes, are still weak. Witness Russia. The Bolsheviks no longer say, "We do this because it is just, but because it is just under the circumstances, i.e., expedient. Because it furthers our purpose, this purpose being to remain in power—at whatever cost."

If the workers could bellow, "We Want Power," the walls of capitalism would collapse. They are as yet too weak for that. They give cat-mews for "freedom." . . . If the Negro, consolidated on race rather than class interests, ever becomes strong enough to demand the exercise of Power, a race war will occur in America.

—Jean Toomer, journal, 1922–23

As I vaguely glimpse and feel it, it seems tremendous: this whole black and brown world heaving upward against, here and there mixing with the white. The mixture, however, is insufficient to absorb the heaving, hence it but accelerates and fires it. This upward heaving is to be symbolic of the proletariat or world upheaval. And it is likewise to be symbolic of the subconscious penetration of the conscious mind.

—Jean Toomer to Horace Liveright, 9 March 1923

Readers routinely scan rapidly through the epigraphs to critical studies, assuming that the chunks of quotation highlight key features of the argument to come.

When we reencounter these quoted passages, we experience a flash of recognition that affirms both their original importance and their subsequent centrality to the argument in process. Epigraphs thus conventionally—and somewhat redundantly—gesture toward presence, rather than absence, toward typicality, not anomaly. I ask readers to glance back over the three quotations reproduced above. The first is taken from an article Jean Toomer published in the Socialist *New York Call* in the wake of the race riots in Washington, DC, and Chicago during the "red summer" of 1919. The second appeared in the journal he kept while he was creating *Cane*. The third, written to Toomer's publisher Horace Liveright while *Cane* was awaiting publication, describes the novel gestating in Toomer's mind. Bracketing the period during which he conceived and birthed *Cane*, these statements indicate that the writer who penned the first major text associated with the New Negro (later Harlem) Renaissance admired the Bolsheviks and held high hopes for world revolution, even as he despaired at the racial divisions in the U.S. working class.

The Toomer we hear in these epigraphs is not familiar to most readers of *Cane* and Toomer's other *Cane*-era writings. He does not enthuse about "America" as the site of cultural pluralism or future racial amalgamation; rather, it is victory in the class struggle against capitalism and imperialism, the attainment of "power" in a "socialized reality," that will put an end to racial division. Whether the "black and brown world heaving upward" will manage to "mix" with the white in a "proletariat or world revolution" is, it would seem, at least as much a matter of political alliance as of biological fusion. While it could be argued that the cluster of left-inflected utterances reproduced above is reflective of a political standpoint that was only tenuously connected to the consciousness that produced *Cane*, I propose that Toomer's 1923 masterwork cannot be understood apart from the upsurge of postwar antiracist political radicalism and its aftermath. The violent class struggles that signaled 1919 as a possible revolutionary conjuncture, coupled with the compensatory ideological paradigms adopted by various political actors and cultural producers as insurgency devolved into quietism, supply not just the context, but the formative matrix, from which Toomer's text emerged. The expectations and desires that were aroused and then quashed in the wake of the Great War and the Russian Revolution, I argue, constitute a spectre haunting the world of *Cane*.

Because scholars of Toomer's work have either marginalized or simply overlooked the evidence of his early radicalism, most of the influential readings of *Cane* fail to grapple with the text's crucially important historical dimension. This neglect has occurred in part because scholars have often not taken with the necessary grain of salt Toomer's rhapsodic descriptions of his Georgia experiences in letters to the various writers, critics, and editors whose support he needed to publish the various texts that would eventually be gathered as *Cane*. There has also been an overreliance on the often distorted retrospective accounts that Toomer himself supplied of the *Cane* years in several of his unpublished autobiographies. The tendency to read the Toomer who produced *Cane* from the standpoint of the Toomer of later years has been compounded by the apparent about-face of his post-*Cane* life: his activism as an acolyte of the mystic George Gurdjieff, his increasing disavowal of his African American heritage. This study seeks to redress the balance by reconstructing Toomer's choices in the pre-*Cane* and *Cane* periods, emphasizing the options that were available to him, as a writer and a political being, in an era of revolution and reaction. In various respects a sequel to my 2003 *Spectres of 1919: Class and Nation in the Making of the New Negro*, this book hopes to contribute not only to the scholarship on an important and still little understood writer but also to literary histories situating the Harlem Renaissance—and, more generally, American modernism—in the crucible of the postwar global upsurge.[1]

In asserting the importance of leftist politics to an understanding of Toomer's work, I do not wish to bend the stick too far in the opposite direction. While Toomer evidently embraced key elements of a Marxist class analysis during the *Cane* years, he was hardly a systematic thinker; his radicalism would assert itself through fragments, through fits and starts, rather than through a cogently formulated alternative to the hegemonic ideologies of his day. Moreover, both the impetus for and the constraints on Toomer's leftism need to be viewed within the context of the principal political and cultural formations by which Toomer was influenced: American socialism, the New Negro Movement, and Young America. It was the limitations and potentialities of these larger movements, in combination with Toomer's distinct insertion within them, that produced the highly contradictory ideological matrix—at once evolutionist and revolutionist, idealist and materialist, nationalist and internationalist—from which *Cane* would emerge. Although recognition of Toomer's attraction to leftist ideas and programs is fundamental to my approach to *Cane*, I am most interested by the ways in which Toomer's politically charged hopes and doubts are secreted in the corners of his texts.

History, Geography, and Biography

The upsurge of 1919, marked in the United States by militant class struggles on the one hand, violent race riots and state repression on the other, constitutes a clear instance of a historical "conjuncture"—that is, as formulated by Antonio Gramsci, a moment when a long-standing structural ("organic") crisis combines with a series of occurrences and situations of a more "accidental" nature in a way that opens up a terrain on which the "forces of opposition" can "seek to demonstrate that the necessary and sufficient conditions already exist to make possible, and hence imperative, the accomplishment of certain historical tasks." While resulting in a qualitatively new set of historical potentialities, however, a conjuncture

does not necessarily result in forward movement for the "forces of opposition."
As Gramsci observed, "The point is to see whether in the dialectic of revolution/
restoration it is the element of revolution or of restoration that prevails, since it
is certain that in the movement of history there can be no turning back ever."
The occurrences and situations immediately bringing the conjuncture into being
thus do not necessarily assume the status of "events," which have been variously
defined as "happenings that transform structures" (William Sewell) and as "beginnings that authorize re-beginnings" (Alain Badiou). That is, it is only from
the standpoint of hindsight that one knows whether a conjuncture has resulted
in a major historical turning-point or simply a deepening of the organic crisis
that underlay its appearance.[2]

People inhabiting a given conjuncture, glimpsing (with either fear or hope)
a possible future in the present, characteristically name various occurrences in
the anticipation that they will emerge from the conjuncture as events, endow-
ing these occurrences with the "will have been" markers of as yet unrealized
possibilities. Hence the Seattle General Strike was dubbed the "Seattle Soviet";
hence "Bogalusa"—the site of a 1919 Louisiana lumber strike during which white
workers lost their lives defending an African American labor organizer—became
a symbol of potential multiracial solidarity in the postwar labor movement. At
times the past is invoked as a guide to interpretation of the present and prophecy
of the future: Richard B. Moore of the African Blood Brotherhood, for example,
declared, "We dare hope that the sacrifice of Bogalusa holds as great significance
for the 15,000,000 black freedmen . . . and for their white fellow-citizens . . . as
held the sacrifice of Harper's Ferry for the chattel slaves of the South and the free
laborers of the North." If a potential event does not fulfill such hopes, however,
it loses its future-perfect status; the dialectic of historical development appears
to have been arrested. The necessity of oscillating between the poles of antinomy
supersedes the possibility of negating and sublating the poles of contradiction:
Walter Benjamin proposed the centrality of this perception of historical blockage
to the project of modernism in his influential 1935 formulation of the image as
embodying "dialectics at a standstill." History does not, of course, actually grind
to a halt: as Gramsci grimly observed, "The crisis consists precisely in the fact
that the old is dying and the new cannot be born; in this interregnum a great
variety of morbid symptoms appear." But forward movement is prevented; the
fact that the "arrested dialectic" is more apparent than real does not reduce its
impact upon the observer-participant's experience of confusion and loss.[3]

Uneven geographical development was crucially involved with the connection
between historical conjuncture and arrested dialectic. The anticipation that, in
the United States, the intense class struggles of 1919 might usher in a new era of
working-class power was indissolubly tied to the emerging consolidation of the
Russian Revolution. If the dispossessed masses in the semi-industrialized zones of
the Russian Empire could establish and maintain the rule of the hammer and the

sickle, could not their peasant and proletarian counterparts in the United States enact a comparable change? While failing to establish workers' power elsewhere, the global anticapitalist upsurge—from Germany to Hungary, from Egypt to Persia, from Mexico to Trinidad, from South Africa to India—further inspired radicals in the United States. If the restive brown, yellow, and black masses elsewhere in the world could arouse in capitalists, statesmen, and pundits fears of a "rising tide of color"—the phrase made famous by the anticommunist nativist Lothrop Stoddard—might not the possibilities for resistance to racism be greatly expanded at home? The hoped-for prophetic status of both the Seattle Soviet and Bogalusa—sites of historical possibility designated on the basis of location—drew sustenance from events occurring half a world away. Moreover, the Leninist call for conjoining anticolonial struggles in the periphery with anticapitalist struggles in the core rescued the globe's populations of color from the status of "non-historical people"; they could be crucial actors in the creation of a better world. Geographically dispersed insurgencies could be viewed as differentiated but synchronous moments in a worldwide assault on existing social hierarchy; the world-historical dialectic of class struggle was played out across both time and space.[4]

But when the global anticapitalist upsurge ended in massive postwar defeats in Europe, in brutal suppression in the colonies, and in the repression of the movements for industrial democracy and against lynching in the United States, the dominant discourses of the day reconfigured the geographical designation of sites of class struggle. This meant, in the United States, that the nation's regions, rather than denoting locales of transformative political activism, came to signify "sectional" cultures: the reconfiguration of uneven revolutionary geographical development as federalist localism was central to the postwar liberal pluralist project. As I propose in *Spectres of 1919*, the doctrine of "metonymic nationalism"—positing a signifying chain connecting folk with soil with region with nation—offered a paradigm wherein spatially (and often racially) segmented populations could be said to "stand for" the nation from which they were otherwise excluded. For New Negro artists and critics bent on featuring African Americans as integral to the body politic, the figure of the rural African American, rooted in the rich loam of the South and contributing the "gift" of the spirituals and folklore to the nation, was one vital means by which this claim to representative status could be made. That this claim was often embodied in an organic trope saturated in what I call hyper-materiality—that is, a near-obsessive insistence upon the identification of the Negro with the soil—suggests the strain at times involved in proposing the signifying chain of metonymic nationalism. For the political price of this aspiration to cultural pluralism was the conversion of the sharecropping "peasant"—a potentially revolutionary figure when analogized with its Soviet counterpart—into the culture-bearing "folk." Similarly, proletarianized migrants to northern urban areas invited representation not as the gun-bearing radicals of 1919, but—in the influential description offered in Alain Locke's 1925 anthology, *The New Negro: An Interpretation*—as "pioneers," validated as citizens through their participation in the American project of pushing ahead the frontier. The spatially grounded poetics of sectional art thus reinforced the imperatives of a revitalized and hegemonic capitalism that codified uneven geographical development not as an inspiration to global revolution, but instead as a central component of the nation's economy and culture. The struggle within *Cane* over the meaning and significance of "Georgia," we shall see, registers the intense conflict in Toomer's consciousness between a quietistic cultural pluralism and a class-conscious critique of racist super-exploitation.[5]

Biography figures centrally in this book—and not simply because it focuses on the work of a single writer. *Pace* linguistic doctrines proposing either the "intentional fallacy" or the "death of the author," texts are composed by individuals uniquely inserted into the larger movements shaping their times and places. History can be written with both a capital H and a small h; to study the life and oeuvre of an author is at once to connect a text with the dynamics of an overarching "History" and to explore its location in a "history" individually lived. Knowledge of the distinct particularity of a given author's experience—from inherited familial traumas to conflicted adult relationships, from avoidance to engagement in relation to defining debates and confrontations of the time—is essential to the analysis of the ideas and attitudes embedded in a given text. *Cane*, I argue, cannot be fully understood without reference to the general political ideas and attitudes, widely shared by radicals of his day, voiced in the epigraphs at the beginning of this introduction. But Toomer's text also cannot be understood without reference to the author's specific insertion in time and place. As we shall see, this insertion involved, on the one hand, his occluded relationship to such important happenings as the Palmer Raids and the 1919 Washington race riot, and, on the other, his contradictory feelings toward his friend and mentor Waldo Frank, his complicated identity as a member of Washington's mulatto aristocracy, and his ambivalent response to a tangled web of family secrets. Everything that Toomer poured into the creation of *Cane* is, in one register or another, "political." But in order to grasp these registers both separately and in their interconnection, investigation of Toomer's connection to specific places and occurrences—both his assertions and his denials, his encounters and his evasions—is required. In an examination of the dialectics of literary production, biography supplies the particulars enabling us to grasp the writer's relationship to the general, between repression as a broadly social phenomenon and repression as experienced in the recesses of the individual psyche.[6]

Appreciation of the theoretical centrality of biography to a materialist literary history requires, further, that we attempt to study a text in the process of its formation—a methodology that I call reading forward. As the famous formulator of communism-as-spectre reminds us, people "make their own history, but they do not make it just as they please [or] under circumstances chosen by themselves."

Authors, too, shape their texts by choosing among alternatives at once opened up and constrained by their moment and their place. Every social process unfolding in time and space is—as another well-known writer has noted—a series of roads taken and not taken: if we wish to understand how a given text came into being, it is important to recreate not just the context but also, insofar as is possible, the history of its production. As we shall see, reading forward through an examination of the roads taken and not taken in the composition of *Cane* is indispensable to an understanding of the text's connections with history—and History. This procedure also helps to uncover the workings of the text's political unconscious.[7]

The Politics of the Political Unconscious

This book is to a significant degree indebted to Fredric Jameson's seminal 1981 work, *The Political Unconscious: Narrative as a Socially Symbolic Act*, which is to date the most ambitious attempt to explore the connections between and among history, ideology, and text. History, for Jameson, constitutes the latent cause of which the literary text is the manifest symptom; the "history [that] hurts" is the Real, the rock against which Dr. Johnson strikes his foot to confirm the existence of a reality beyond language. Because history can be known only in textual form, however, it constitutes a kind of "absent cause" that must be inferred from the literary work's "symbolic acts," which at once gesture toward and suture over painful social contradictions that are inaccessible to direct representation. One crucial mediation between history and symbolic action is, for Jameson, the "ideologeme," which he defines as the "smallest intelligible unit of the essentially antagonistic collective discourses of social classes." As expressions of class interest, ideologemes typically mask the social contradictions for which they purportedly supply ethically cogent explanations: both the text's implied assertions and its "structured silences" are shaped by notions of politically charged common sense requiring no interrogation. At the same time, the text displays its connection with history at the level of genre. Using the term "cultural revolution" to designate the clashing between and among the different modes of production that are simultaneously present in any given social formation, Jameson proposes that the totality of the text's form replicates the tensions informing the moment of its production.[8]

This book makes substantial use of some key features of Jameson's model. The concept of the ideologeme figures prominently in my formulation of the role played—in 1920s cultural pluralism generally and in *Cane* specifically—by the encompassing notion of metonymic nationalism; its cognate ideologemes range over a spectrum from "America," "the South," and "sectional art" to the "labor movement," "Socialism," and the "New Negro." My discussion of the key tropes guiding Toomer's representation of black modernity in *Cane* draws on Jameson's analysis of symbolic action; the *combinatoire* of terms comprising the organic trope and a secondary cluster of images associated with the Machine together function to propose "formal resolution[s] in the aesthetic realm . . . to real social contradictions, insurmountable in their own terms." Finally, I propose that *Cane*'s dramatically experimental form be seen as a response on the level of literary genre to the possibility for world revolution glimpsed, however briefly, in the aftermath of the Great War and the Russian Revolution. Drawing together in a single text images of a goat path in Africa, a lynched Georgia sharecropper burning under a "red nigger moon," an alienated urban working-class mortgage holder, and powerful underground races half a world away erupting under the streetcar tracks in Washington, DC, the modernist montage that is *Cane* embodies the "cultural revolution" embodied in the shifting tectonics of the global social formation, even as its rounded form testifies to the "arrested dialectic" of social revolution.[9]

At the same time, I have found it necessary to revise and extend Jameson's model to confront various issues raised by Toomer's text. Perhaps because the case studies invoked in *The Political Unconscious* involve writers who had little interest in subverting the status quo, Jameson's formulation of the ideologeme presupposes a notion of ideology as by its nature obfuscatory and legitimating—that is, as dominant ideology. In my analysis of Toomer and his texts, at least some ideologemes are sites of struggle. The "New Negro" can be construed in either confrontational or quietist terms; even "America" remains open to contestation, especially when contrasted with competing contemporaneous nativist doctrines of "100% Americanism" and the "rising tide of color." Moreover, Jameson's formulation of the political unconscious privileges texts featuring a tortuous and reifying bourgeois consciousness, one that of necessity occludes knowledge of the social totality. By this token, however, texts that attempt to break through the mask, so to speak, appear not to have much of a political unconscious at all—whether these be "Third World" texts undertaking "national allegory" or texts composed at a "conjuncture (and at the outer limit a polarizing, revolutionary situation) [that] causes the (usually liberal) ideological system of defenses to crumble . . . confront[ing] [the writer] with the anxiety of choice and commitment." *Cane*, we shall see, enacts a confrontation with "anxieties of choice and commitment"; its political unconscious, while rife with repressed contradictions, occupies a radical rather than a bourgeois terrain. Yet by no means does the text shrug off the trailing mists of bourgeois ideology or evade reification.[10]

Indeed, the main areas where I have reworked Jameson's theorization of the political unconscious have been in relation to the twin issues of repression and reification. In Jameson's schema, repression is inherent in narrative; it is a function of history as it bears down on—or erupts upward through—representation. The specifics of a writer's insertion in this process are, however, relatively incidental: the political unconscious is a property of broadly social rather than individual experience. My attention to biography—not simply as a source of information, but as a theoretical component of literary production—alerts me to potential drawbacks of this approach. Jean Toomer's ambivalence toward key programs and figures in the socialist, New Negro, and Young American movements produced a complex admixture of skepticism and allegiance—a pattern of cognitive dissonance—that, repeated in various spheres of his life, was distinctly individual, and not simply reflective of his era. Further, his probable discovery of troubling hidden family secrets while he was composing *Cane* willy-nilly implicated him in a private history that hurt, one that linked his very existence to a sordid past of slavery and Jim Crow in which no heroes, but only villains and victims, were to be found. The anxieties produced by these experiences and discoveries were compounded, I propose, by Toomer's own retreat from engagement with the class struggle at key moments when state power and racist vigilante violence were being brought down on the resisters to the status quo with whom he wished to be aligned. His visit to the Deep South in 1921, moreover, revealed to him not just the soulfulness of the Negro peasantry but also the threat of lynch terror that brooded over rural black existence. The repression displayed throughout *Cane* is thus a multilayered phenomenon, indicating the inseparability of personal trauma from social nightmare, private guilt and shame from public oppression and violence.[11]

Moreover, *Cane*'s complex engagement with the historical-cum-geographical matrix of 1919 complicates Jameson's designation of reification as the principal debilitating effect of capitalist modernity. Toomer's text contains a powerful commentary on the effects of what Georg Lukács called the contemplative attitude—that is, the separation of the monadic self from a commodified world seen as fragmented and impervious to change. Particularly central to the portraits of northern urban alienation in part II, this commentary also undergirds the depiction, in part I, of various narrators and poetic personae who, only semi-ironized, insist upon conflating the folk with the soil through culture rather than exploring labor as the key mediation between the peasantry and the land. The text can thus be seen at once to critique and to reproduce reification as a phenomenon of consciousness: the fragmented and fragmenting immediacy that cannot relate part to whole, self to world. On the other hand, in its traumatic encounter with the figures of murdered sharecroppers and childless madonnas in the Deep South, especially in "Kabnis," *Cane* also testifies to reification as the brutal "thingification" of human flesh. The totality to which this "thingification" corresponds—the regime of debt peonage and sharecropping sustained by racial terrorism—is transparently visible: immediacy consists not in the occlusion of totality, but in the bearing down of history as a present, not an absent, cause. The challenge is not just to grasp this totality, but to change it. Where Jameson's formulation of reification resides largely in the realm of epistemology, Toomer's insistently links seeing with knowing and doing.[12]

Reading Forward to *Cane*

The organization of this book facilitates a layered and sequential exploration of its central concerns—historical, biographical, and literary. The first three chapters in part I examine Toomer's engagement with key political and cultural movements of the late 1910s and early 1920s; while refraining from glancing ahead to *Cane*, these chapters touch on some important pre-*Cane* journalistic and imaginative texts that illuminate the 1923 masterwork. Chapter 1, "Touching Naked Reality," takes issue with the view, prevailing to this day, that Toomer's interest in class-conscious radical politics was at best transitory and immature. Drawing on his early left-wing journalism, correspondence, handwritten 1936 autobiography, and psychoanalytic records from the late 1940s, I argue that Toomer not only held strongly left-wing views during the *Cane* period but also remained in some respects a man of the left throughout his life. Indeed, I propose that his social constructionist view of race, usually attributed to his situation as a light-skinned black man able to "pass," is also traceable to his awareness of race as a product of capitalist exploitation and state-sanctioned racial violence, ideas that are allegorically displayed in his poem "Banking Coal," which appeared in the *Crisis* in June 1922. While aspects of Toomer's early affiliation with leftist politics have previously been analyzed—with particular effectiveness by Charles Scruggs and Lee VanDemarr—I emphasize the extent to which Toomer both criticized and reproduced some of the shortcomings—reformist, economist, nationalist, and intermittently racist—of the contemporaneous left, even as he was energized by the prospect of multiracial proletarian revolution and envisioned a classless society as the site where race would disappear. In his socialist-inspired writings, we shall see, the signifier "the labor movement" lacks a clear referent, functioning less as a descriptor than as an ideologeme comprising a range of conflicting assessments of the place of the U.S. proletariat in the process of worldwide revolutionary social transformation. Both Toomer's affirmations and his doubts, I argue, cannot be understood apart from an analysis and assessment of the radical politics to which he had access.[13]

In chapter 2, "The Tight Cocoon," I argue that Toomer was more intimately involved with the New Negro Movement than he was wont to acknowledge either in his early 1920s correspondence with white modernists or in the autobiographies written the following decade. Toomer was particularly influenced, I propose, by a circle of African American women he had known from his youth, and whose writings—which were significantly influenced by postwar leftist debates—would shape Toomer's representations of womanhood and motherhood in *Cane*. Moreover, although attracted from 1920 onward—indeed, to the end of his life—by the notion of an "American race" transcending racial binaries, during the entire *Cane* period Toomer had no qualms about identifying himself as a Negro under conditions of his own choosing. His short play "Balo," written in

1922, explores the psychology of the Old Negro from the standpoint of a New Negro; his unpublished essay "The Negro Emergent"—composed in response to the *Survey Graphic* version of *The New Negro* that appeared in early 1925—limns his critique of the culturalism that pervades the book version of the anthology that Alain Locke would publish later that year. I argue that Toomer's presumed discomfiture with Locke's unauthorized publication of parts of *Cane* in *The New Negro*, as asserted in his 1934 autobiography, has been mistakenly taken as evidence of his reluctance to define himself as a Negro in the *Cane* period. At the same time, the terms "Negro," "New Negro," and "American race" are marked by multiple slippages in Toomer's writings, depending on whether he is stressing the political, economic, biological, or cultural features of their presumed referents; like "the labor movement," these terms, in his usage, encompass the range of contradictory meanings they possessed in contemporaneous progressive social and cultural movements. As with Toomer's views on class politics, however, it is imperative to read forward through his early writings in order to determine the ideas about race that shaped the composition of *Cane*; reading backward from Toomer's later positions produces only confusion.

"The Experiment in America," chapter 3, explores Toomer's relationship with the early 1920s modernists dubbing themselves "Young America"—above all with Waldo Frank, whose influential *Our America* (1919) vigorously advocated a pluralistic and experimental program for national cultural renewal. In this program, the notion of sectional art figured as a highly contradictory ideologeme, at once promising a strategy for including the nation's marginalized peoples and papering over the reasons for their exclusion. While it is routinely proposed that Toomer retreated from Young America because of his distress at Frank's allusions to Toomer's African American ancestry in his foreword to *Cane*, I argue that Toomer's growing skepticism about the possibility that cultural pluralism could produce social change, rather than a lack of willingness to identify himself as a Negro, is what supplied the primary cause of his eventual break with Frank's project—even though his personal indebtedness to Frank set up a situation of considerable internal conflict, particularly after their trip into the Deep South together in September 1922. Querying the extent to which the Negro would be allowed to stand for an increasingly nativist and racist nation, Toomer found in the doctrine of sectional art only provisional solace. The challenge to contemporaneous discourses of race and nation in his 1922 short story "Withered Skin of Berries," as well as in the vague but ambitious 1923 outlines for his post-*Cane* novel, testify to his continuing restlessness with the metonymic nationalism embedded in the federalist doctrines of Young America. "America"—the endpoint of the signifying chain toward which its component parts presumably led—was the ideologeme that, more than any other, both tempted and troubled Toomer throughout the composition of *Cane* and beyond. That he eventually proved unable to formulate a more satisfactory substitute testifies more to the arrested dialectic of the international revolutionary movement in the early 1920s than to any particular patriotism Toomer felt toward the nation of his forebears.

I involve myself in a quite different kind of critical and scholarly enterprise in chapter 4, "All the Dead Generations." Here I engage in an exploratory discussion of information that Toomer appears to have gleaned about his family's history while he was conceiving and creating *Cane*. This material features the fabulous fortune gained and lost by his father, Nathan Toomer, on the death of his second wife, the Georgia heiress Amanda America Dickson, said to be the "richest colored woman in America"; it also involves a near-Gothic narrative of attempted seduction and rape of his half-sister, Mamie Toomer, by her stepbrother, Charles Dickson. This buried family history gave rise, I propose, to a complex admixture of shame and guilt that compounded Toomer's already conflicted consciousness as a pro-socialist radical born into Washington's light-skinned Negro aristocracy. I argue that various scenes, characterizations, and wordplays in Toomer's 1922 play *Natalie Mann* indicate the strong likelihood that this familial narrative was on Toomer's mind throughout the time when he was composing *Cane*. In this chapter I lay the basis for my later claim that the haunting figures of the young girl desired by men who would ripen her too soon in "Karintha" and of her virginal counterpart in the Carrie Kate Halsey of "Kabnis" both have their basis in the class, race, and gender matrix enclosing the figure of Toomer's never-encountered half-sister. Extending our notion of the political unconscious into the realm of sexuality and the family that is the particular purview of Freud, this investigation does not abandon the terrain of Marx: the foundation of Amanda Dickson's huge fortune in the surplus extracted from slave and sharecropper labor—with the correlative implications for the sexual fates of women of African descent under slavery and Jim Crow—is never far from view.

Throughout the first four chapters I attempt to determine as accurately as possible the parameters within which Toomer's ideas and attitudes at any given point can be ascertained, or at least estimated. This has been no small task. As I note above, Toomer's unpublished autobiographies—written at different phases of his post-*Cane* career as an apostle, sometimes dedicated, sometimes skeptical, of the proto–New Age cult leader George Gurdjieff—are notoriously unreliable. Containing mutually contradictory accounts of crucial incidents and situations— his encounter with socialism, his two-week stint in a New Jersey shipyard, his inquiries into his racial ancestry, even the experience in Georgia that gave rise to *Cane*—these overlapping texts, many of them handwritten, frustrate the researcher attempting to reconstruct the "real" Jean Toomer. They contain, indeed, a number of outright lies: Toomer's retrospective accounts of his breaks with both Frank and Locke, while widely taken as accurate testaments to the inability of his colleagues to understand the complexity of his racial philosophy, are sufficiently inaccurate as to constitute deliberate untruths. Toomer's contemporaneous writings—his letters, journals, and journalistic writings of the late 1910s and early

1920s—more reliably register his thoughts and feelings; but these too, on close examination, contain gaps and evasions. While it is widely acknowledged that all nonfictional texts are hardly lacking in invention, this truism applies with particular force to Toomer's oeuvre.[14]

There was, nonetheless, a "real" Jean Toomer who authored *Cane*, and the ideas and attitudes that motivated his text were anchored in a concrete, and largely knowable, historical reality. In my attempt to reconstruct key features of Toomer's biography in part I of this book, I have occasionally triangulated among various bits of evidence in order to establish what appears to be the most probable scenario, in the process indicating which features of my analysis I consider to be more or less grounded in verifiable evidence. The difficulty of this reconstructive task renders it no less urgent. Indeed, the project of uncovering the political unconscious of *Cane* is all the more tantalizing because of the barriers set up by the author himself.

Reading Forward through *Cane*

Part II of this book, comprising chapters 5 through 7, treats *Cane*. A prefatory comment is needed regarding the order of my discussion. Most studies of *Cane* treat the text in the sequence supplied by its three parts: first, the portraits of women and poems set in Sempter, Toomer's fictional representation of Sparta, Georgia; next, the portraits of men and the poems mostly located in the nation's capital; finally, the closet drama depicting the experiences of the would-be poet Ralph Kabnis back in Sempter. In these analyses, the closing "Kabnis" section is usually treated as indicative either of Toomer's attempt to resolve issues raised in the earlier sections or of his decision to leave the text open-ended. The few studies of *Cane* that depart from this sequential treatment usually are structured thematically—examining, for instance, the notions of gender, race, or trauma shaping the text—or generically—examining, for instance, the range of literary forms constituting Toomer's experimental montage. While many critics have discussed Toomer's famous December 1922 letter to Frank in which he described the text as a circuit beginning with "Bona and Paul," "plunging" into "Kabnis," "rising" to "Karintha" and "pausing" at "Harvest Song," "Kabnis" generally supplies the terminus, not the beginning, of most critical analyses of *Cane*.[15]

My interest in reading forward through Toomer's life leads me to read forward through *Cane*, as well: I begin with a consideration of "Kabnis" in chapter 5, "In the Land of Cotton." Composed in rough draft before Toomer left Middle Georgia in November 1921 and finished before the end of that year, "Kabnis"—even after some significant revision a year later—reflects Toomer's sense of felt urgency to reproduce his Georgia experiences with a combination of lyric intensity and journalistic precision. In "Kabnis," more than elsewhere in *Cane*, history is felt as present cause; the text's unambiguous references to notorious documented episodes of lynching, accounting for Kabnis's tortured preference for "split-gut" over "golden" words, testify to the dilemma confronting the artist who would grapple with the Real of Jim Crow violence. Prominently featured in "Kabnis," too, are a range of images of black women—as nurses, lynchees, madonnas, virgins, prostitutes—whose fates limn the conditions of production and reproduction in the rural Deep South. These women's various relationships to motherhood—from pregnancy to lactation to infanticide to having an unborn child ripped from the womb—not only display, on the level of historical causality, the reification wrought by Jim Crow but also suggest, on the level of allegory, the impossibility of a new world being birthed out of the womb of the old, so long as such violence and degradation persist. That this section of *Cane* contains the clearest evidence of Toomer's haunting by the repressed history of his own family—and in particular of the pursuit of his barely adolescent half-sister by her pedophile adult stepbrother—illustrates the complex causality accompanying the creation of the text.

Chapters 6 and 7 address, respectively, parts I and II of *Cane*. Since part I of *Cane* focuses on prose sketches of rural southern women and poems about labor and the land, my chapter 6, "Georgia on His Mind," continues the consideration of production and reproduction in the Jim Crow South that was begun in the previous chapter. Chapter 7, "Black and Brown Worlds Heaving Upward," focuses largely on the treatment of reification in the urban section of *Cane*, where possibilities for radical social transformation are shown to be largely vitiated by the pressures of consumerism, status seeking, and privatized daily life. In both of these chapters I continue to stress the order in which their component elements were composed. Most of the sketches and poems appearing in the opening sections of both parts I and II of *Cane*—that is, the texts extending from "Karintha" through "Fern" in the former, from "Seventh Street" through "Calling Jesus" in the latter—were written in the winter and spring of 1922, when Toomer began to recollect his Georgia experiences in the relative tranquility of his Washington home. The poems and short stories appearing toward the ends of the first two sections, however—"Esther" through "Blood-Burning Moon" in *Cane* part I, "Theater" through "Bona and Paul" in part II—were for the most part written, or substantially revised, after Toomer's trip to the Deep South with Waldo Frank in the fall of 1922. While there is clearly an overlap between the pre- and post-trip texts, in both subject matter and style, and Toomer continued to work on some of the earlier texts up to the time he submitted the book for publication, the more complex stories and poems appearing toward the ends of both parts I and II in *Cane* signal a subtle but significant shift in Toomer's approach to both politics and aesthetics. Toomer's renewed experience of the harshness of the Jim Crow South in the fall of 1922, I propose, coupled with his direct exposure to the ideological limitations of his traveling companion, Waldo Frank, moved him to confront more critically the shortcomings of a program for social transformation premised on culturalist metonymic nationalism. Moreover, the insurrectionary aspirations voiced through the character of Dan Moore in "Box Seat"—the last story completed in the creation of *Cane*—indicate that, even as he was putting the finishing touches on his book and preparing to enter the world of modernist New York, Toomer had by no means abandoned the revolutionary outlook expressed in his radical journalism of 1919.

I had several goals in writing this book. My focus on a single writer has enabled me to extend the examination of the radical roots of the Harlem Renaissance that I began in *Spectres of 1919*. Always attracted by the challenge of articulating Marx with Freud, I have taken this opportunity to theorize and test a notion of the political unconscious that draws on both broadly historical and specifically personal notions of repression. Recent trends in literary and cultural study have further motivated this work. While skeptical of the explanatory power of the notion of a "spatial dialectic" isolated from temporality, I explore the ways in which attention to uneven geographical development can enhance the traditional emphasis on history in Marxist literary criticism. Provoked, moreover, by the critique of symptomatic reading by literary scholars recently issuing a call for "surface reading," I have sought to enact a critical practice that newly legitimates what Paul Ricoeur called the "hermeneutics of suspicion." So long as the organization of social existence under capitalism creates conditions of subjectivity that foster repression, evasion and subterfuge—and there is no reason to suppose that such conditions will not exist for some time to come—the notion of the political unconscious will have enduring utility as a tool of literary and cultural analysis.[16]

Finally, a comment on my long-standing fascination with Toomer, as well as my decision to devote a lengthy book to the modest body of his oeuvre ending with the publication of *Cane*. Although I published in the 1990s a series of articles on Toomer and *Cane*, the theoretical concerns I address here, reinforced by additional archival research, have prompted me to think through and past enough of my earlier work to warrant a refocused and expanded study. That this project has led me to alter some of my earlier readings of *Cane* will be evident to anyone familiar with these earlier articles. My further motivation in devoting all this effort and attention to Toomer, however, has been largely political—a statement that may be somewhat surprising, since Toomer was hardly among the most "political" writers of either the New Negro Movement or, more generally, American modernism. His ties with the major political movements of his time were relatively tenuous; even at his most impassioned he remained on their margins. But it is precisely this "fringe" aspect of Toomer that I find most interesting. After all, for every writer who has entered the lists of social struggle and directly confronted what Jameson calls the "anxieties of choice and commitment," there are dozens who, like Toomer, have remained more or less as observers on the sidelines of revolutionary movements. That their texts should register both the shock of a conjuncture and its failure to "authorize re-beginnings" indicates the extent to which every life is affected by history's seismic shifts. By examining the multiple ways in which Toomer's 1923 text both acknowledges the world-historical impact of the Russian Revolution and grieves its unfulfilled U.S. aftermath, we can, perhaps, gain a fuller understanding of how people—not just creative artists, but ordinary citizens of the world—register the hopes and doubts raised at moments when it appears that the earth may rise on new foundations. Given the continuing need for such new foundations to be laid, this insight can carry a value that goes beyond the merely literary.

PART I

CHAPTER 1

Touching Naked Reality
Socialism, the Labor Movement, and the Embers of Revolution

It is the historic mission of the working class to do away with capitalism.
—IWW constitution preamble, 1905

I recognized as never before the *need* of socialism, the *need* of a radical change of the conditions of human society.
—Jean Toomer, untitled 1936 autobiography

The scholarship on Jean Toomer has largely overlooked the substantial evidence indicating his serious early interest in leftist politics, as well as his abiding leftist conscience. Toomer's publications in the Socialist press, when taken into account at all, have been routinely interpreted as expressions of a youthful romanticism soon abandoned. His two-week-long experience working in a New Jersey shipyard in December 1919, which presumably proved to him the proletariat's indifference to its own exploitation, is often cited as the terminus of his fascination with socialism. The 1998 publication of Charles Scruggs and Lee VanDemarr's *Jean Toomer and the Terrors of American History*, which argues persuasively for the impact of a leftist politics on *Cane*, has not substantially altered the depoliticized paradigms through which the majority of scholars continue to view Toomer and his 1923 masterwork.[1]

Toomer himself, it should be added, played no small role in setting the terms of this agenda. The unpublished autobiographies of his adult years that he composed during his years as a disciple of Gurdjieff—"The Outline of an Autobiography" (1931) and "On Being an American" (1934)—largely effaced the evidence of his radical political involvements. Darwin Turner's reliance on these typewritten texts in patching together the autobiographical narrative published in *The Wayward and the Seeking* (1980) has strongly influenced the terms in which scholars and general readers have construed the meaning and shape of Toomer's life up to and through the writing of *Cane*. Although in 1936 Toomer composed an account that contradicts the 1931 and 1934 narratives in crucial respects, this autobiography remains unpublished and only available in archives; its inaccessibility limits its reference in the great majority of critical commentaries on *Cane*.[2]

My principal goal here is to demonstrate that Toomer's early commitment to socialism was neither superficial nor temporary. In the wake of the Russian Revolution, he entertained strong hopes for a workers' revolution in the United States; when the conjuncture of 1919 failed to materialize as an event, his disappointment was deep and lasting. Toomer was hardly an engaged participant in radical political movements. His direct ties with members of the Socialist Party of America (SPA) appear to have been few, most likely formed through his frequent visits to the SPA-affiliated Rand School in 1918–20 and his contacts at the *New York Call*. There is, moreover, no clear evidence that, other than through his acquaintance with the *Liberator*, he was acquainted with members of the fledgling Communist Party during the *Cane* period. In many ways an astute observer and analyst of the wartime and postwar left-wing upsurge, Toomer carried forward from his observations and experiences not only an appreciation of the violent repression visited on rebels against the capitalist regime but also an understanding of the role played by racism in hamstringing the working-class movement. Optimistic—for a period—about the possibilities for revolutionary change, he was alert to some of the limitations of American Socialism, uncritical of others. But the complex amalgam of views expressed in Toomer's early political writings would carry over into the composition of *Cane*; Toomer's 1923 text cannot be understood apart from the hopes and pressures generated by the radical upsurge of 1919.

"An intelligible scheme of things":
The 1931 and 1934 Accounts of Finding Socialism

Toomer's various accounts of his encounter with socialism emphasize quite different features of its appeal. "The Outline of an Autobiography" offers a largely dismissive assessment:

> I had been, I suppose, unconsciously seeking—as man must ever seek—an intelligible scheme of things, a sort of whole into which everything fit, or seemed to fit, a body of ideas which held a consistent view of life and which enabled me to see and understand as one does when he sees a map. Socialism was the first thing of this kind I had encountered. . . . It was not so much the facts or ideas, taken singly, that aroused me. . . . More it was the *body*, the *scheme*, the order and inclusion. These evoked and promised to satisfy all in me that had been grasping for form amid the disorders and chaos of my personal experiences.

Widely cited in commentary on Toomer, this account suggests that he was attracted not so much by the content of socialist doctrine as by its formal structure and therapeutic holism.[3]

Describing his dizzying wanderings over the next four years—including short stints at the University of Wisconsin, the University of Massachusetts, the American School of Physical Culture (Chicago), the University of Chicago, New York University, and Columbia University—the 1931 autobiography records Toomer's early attraction to leftist politics and leftist people. In Chicago, for instance, he established a friendship with a serious-minded young woman, Eleanor Davis— "the first girl of my own age who could meet me in terms of understanding and interest in the ways of life"—with whom he shared an interest in socialism. The 1931 text tends to downplay Toomer's interest in Bolshevism, however, noting that when he began to attend classes at New York's Rand School in the spring of 1918, he was "still a socialist in my political and economic and sociological views—but now it was a compound of ideas of Lester F. Ward and Bernard Shaw." After working at an East Side settlement house and intensively studying music in the fall of 1918, Toomer wrote, he experienced a breakdown and went upstate to an unspecified site in Ellenville—"a place I knew of in the mountains"—where he was "seized by a passion for writing" and composed "long letters which usually dealt with world-matters as I saw them." Returning to Washington, DC, the following spring, he made a temporary truce with his despairing grandparents, only to depart once again to bum around upstate New York with a friend from his Wisconsin days, returning to Washington in the late summer. His grandparents' frustration became too much for him, however, and within a few months Toomer was on the road again, hitchhiking toward New York City on December 20 and arriving the next evening.[4]

According to the 1931 autobiography, the next day Toomer started work in a New Jersey shipyard:

> The work was hard, harder than I ever thought work could be. The steel of the half-finished ships was terribly cold. Just to touch it was enough to freeze you. . . . All day long I had to cramp myself under heavy plates, in small compartments, and work the holes so that bolts could be slid in from the top. I was called a fitter. I got $22.00 a week. After ten days of it, I quit. And that, by the way, finished socialism for me. The men who worked in those yards—and they were realistic workmen—had two main interests: playing craps and sleeping with women. Socialism? Well, it was for people like Shaw and Sidney Webb. . . . It was the way they saw social life. But as for working a great betterment in the lives of the proletariat—this was a pipe dream only to those who had never really experienced the proletariat.

Relegating the "pipe dream" appeal of socialism to Fabian intellectuals, this passage—reproduced in *The Wayward and the Seeking* and widely quoted in the scholarship on Toomer—proposes that to "experience the proletariat" is to grant the harshness of its conditions of labor but acknowledge its imperviousness to higher things.[5]

"On Being an American," the 1934 autobiography, offers a still more truncated view of Toomer's youthful leaning toward the left:

Readings of Darwin and Haeckel, the evolutionists, the materialists, and the atheists, stripped me of all religious belief; and, though my mind was greatly stimulated, my emotions were such that for a time I felt as if the bottom of the world had dropped from under, leaving me dangling like a man being hung.

Socialism stripped me of my republican aristocratic notions; and I felt myself to be a comrade of the mass of men of no destiny whose life is caught and thwarted in the injustices and stupidities of an acquisitive society.

Life ripped at my props and stays until they toppled. All things tore at my ego until I seemed to have none left, until I felt myself as pulp, sunken, prostrate, doomed to failure.

Toomer concludes, "I worked in a shipyard and therefore could no longer idealize the proletariat." Although more self-critical here—he admits his past elitism—he posits a reader who will agree that direct experience with the working class will of necessity ("therefore") produce disillusionment.[6]

"Naked I touched naked reality": The Encounter with Socialism in the Mid-1930s Autobiographies

The 1931 and 1934 autobiographies were written when Toomer was deeply involved in the Institute for the Harmonious Development of Man. As the leader of a Gurdjieff group based in Chicago, he was interacting primarily with the movement's well-heeled white acolytes: the implied reader invoked in these texts, while liberal, would hardly have been a partisan of workers' revolution. By 1935, however, when Toomer had retreated from Gurdjieff and revived his contacts on the left, he authored an autobiography that offers a significantly different slant on his first encounter with socialism. The working-class men he encountered in Chicago were "not free and equal citizens of a democracy. . . . They were futureless, anything but masters of their own lives." Himself unemployed, he "realized that, like myself, there were countless numbers of people out of work . . . pounding the pavements from place to place. . . . It was appalling." In this account, Toomer's growing sense of identification with the needs of the working class, more than his personal alienation, is what sparks his interest in socialism. Of the large numbers of families sleeping on Grand Boulevard's grassy median strip on hot summer evenings, he wrote, "Chicago in summer gave the impression . . . that the workers' revolution had already taken place and that the city belonged not to the few but to the many." Finding himself "in the midst of Chicago's radical and liberal movements," he was formally introduced to socialist doctrine by one Farrell, an instructor at the American College of Physical Culture:

Then and there, hemmed in by the lockers, with fellows standing around, he presented to me the cardinal ideas of what he understood to be socialism. The economic division of society into three main classes, capitalist, bourgeois, and workers. That contemporary society was organized and maintained for the benefit of the capitalists as against the workers. That opportunity was a myth. . . . That rich men get rich because they exploit natural resources and human labor, defrauding the workers of a just portion of the wealth which they, the workers, help bring into existence. That the state should take over the main industries upon which everyone was dependent. That there should be an equitable distribution of wealth. . . . That the workers, now the slaves of the parasites, would come into their rightful inheritance only on the condition that they organized themselves and in some way stripped the parasites of their power.

The young Toomer initially rejected Farrell's message: "I was a member of the ruling class. . . . [If] a revolution came and slaves were victorious . . . I'd proudly repeat the way of the aristocrats during the French revolution and ride . . . to the guillotine with my head up." Soon, however, he "acknowledged that the main ideas [Farrell] voiced were . . . true to justice and humanity and a fair full life for all, necessary to myself as I outgrew myself and stepped beyond my ego-prison to become a social being, invaluable to me in my efforts to understand and orient myself to the larger scheme of things, now breaking upon me, of which I was but a part." The "larger scheme" of socialism is portrayed here not as a structuring idea, imposed upon reality from without, but as an attribute of actual social relations.[7]

According to the untitled 1936 autobiography, once Toomer arrived in New York in 1918, he did all he could to enter and expand "my chosen world" by regularly attending lectures at the Cooper Union and the Rand School and cultivating the acquaintance of such prominent literary leftists as the poet Lola Ridge and the *Dial* editor Lewis Mumford. Socialism was "germinating in the subsoil of my common human feelings," he recalled. "[M]y roots began to push down and find fastening." Working with working-class youth at an East Side settlement house, he was "outraged . . . that these young people, if left to themselves to acquire the 'ideals' that were floating around in their environment, would grow up and devote their lives to obtaining just the falsities of a civilization which our best minds had learned to condemn and reject." Toomer's politics caused a stir: "One or two of my fellow residents demanded that a stop be put to my activities, charging that I was a 'radical' bent on undermining not only the Settlement but all American institutions."[8]

Where the 1931 and 1934 autobiographies convey the impression that in early 1919 Toomer recuperated from stress and overwork in a state of glorious isolation in the Catskills, the 1936 text indicates that his hosts, Lide and Charles Goldsmith, were a politically progressive farming couple who nurtured—and perhaps humored—their "paying guest." "I began talking, . . . [T]hey responded and I talked more," Toomer recalled. "Now I wanted to reach more people." He and his hosts on one occasion trudged several miles through snowdrifts to a gathering of neighbors "on another mountain," where he held forth. "It was quite a meeting, if only to the three of us," Toomer recalled. "One or two others got something from what I said.

The rest, as I learned later, mostly puzzled or wondered." While at the Goldsmiths'
farm, Toomer "subscribed to several magazines" and William Randolph Hearst's
New York American, delighting in George Bernard Shaw's sardonic commentary
on the secret prewar treaties among the imperialist powers. With his "interest in
the outside world revived," Toomer began writing—and presumably distributing—mimeographed letters that "sprang straight from my inner life in a molten
lucid state, straight from my need to put in words what I had to say"; these letters
"constituted my social life, my 'propaganda,' my practice in writing, all in one."
Although the Goldsmiths' guest had hardly shrugged off his youthful narcissism,
he evidently took his leftist education far more seriously—and passionately—than
is indicated in the 1931 and 1934 texts. He also appears to have had no qualms
about discussing his mixed racial ancestry with his hosts; as with Eleanor Davis
in Chicago, the context of radical politics enabled him to be transparent about
his family background.[9]

Since Toomer's supposed debacle with the shipyard workers in Elizabeth, New
Jersey, is usually viewed as the terminus of his political leftism, the version of this
episode in the 1936 autobiography—consisting of more than thirty handwritten
pages—warrants particular notice. Toomer recounts the long, cold predawn com-
mute from Manhattan and then the harshness of labor in the "freezing inferno,"
where he manipulated "the holes . . . the bolts . . . the nuts . . . down in the zero
hell and dark of what was to be the hold of a ship." Even worse than the physical
hardship of the work itself was its numbing effect on mind and spirit: "Each day,
if possible, I had lost more of myself and become just another doomed body on
the train, in the yards, going through with it in utter identification as if I had
no past but this, no future but this, this pitiless compression, of my life between
plates of steel." The "ravaged" faces of his coworkers "haunted" him—"not their
faces only, not their eyes only, but their spirits crucified in life, up against it and
nailed there." Toomer was occasionally "thrilled aesthetically by the purity and
perfect functioning of that slender [crane's] arm as delicate as an etching and
yet so powerful. So, I told myself, so a perfect mind might lift the bulk of knowledge and deposit it for mankind to build a world." He gained sustenance from
the thought that the ship he was building would be used, and that, seeing it in
the future, he might think, "I worked on you, ship, I helped make you." But he
feared losing his larger sense of purpose, seeing that "[what] happens to others
began to happen to me from the first day I went on the job." The foremen were
like "slavedrivers," and the

> so-called work in the yard was in truth a sort of grim game played by slaves and
> masters who matched wits, the one to do as little work as possible and yet get
> a pay check, the other to exact and extract all work possible not for ships but
> for profits. Ships? How ironical. . . . To the workers, it was a salary-yard essen-
> tially undistinguishable from the thousands of salary-yards spread all over the

kingdom of industry and finance. To the owners it was a profit-yard, similarly undistinguished.

The workers experienced no interest in the product of their labor: "[T]hat ships were being built by them—this meant absolutely nothing to them." Toomer's description displays a more than passing acquaintance with the Marxist discussion of the abstraction and alienation of labor.[10]

In the 1936 text, Toomer traces the phlegmatic behavior of his fellow workers to their estranged relation to production. On the train taking them to work, most were "gloomy men [who] sat silent, not asleep, but in a brooding, weighted consciousness." The few "raucous" ones were "young fellows with animal bodies bent on raising hell, until even hell was taken out of them by the wheels that grind and take it all from the body and all from the mind." Only the black workers "seemed to be weathering it: they were huge-bodied fellows who took their job with a laugh, got fairly good pay as riveters, and had the good sense to loaf and enjoy themselves at least one solid week every month. . . . The rest were pale, drawn, embittered and beaten men." The workers' gambling symptomatically displaced their need for freedom: "For the chance of a day off they . . . were willing to risk having to work many additional days. Moreover, they seemed to take to [gambling] as if it were their one chance at excitement in a dull day, their one time to do what they wanted in a life controlled by others." Initially regarding the "entrepreneurial" worker who set up the gambling games as a "bird of prey," he came to view this "predation" as a reflection of the "new savagery" fostered by the labor practices that "round-up . . . rootless nomadic men" and "corral . . . them within fences of economic fear." Citing anthropological work by Marquis W. Childs contrasting the "'ancient integration'" and "'fundamental coherence'" accompanying primitive communalism with modern "cohesion by coercion," Toomer concluded that the capitalist labor process produces a "general pattern and similar traits, stamped on owners and workers alike."[11]

Toomer's designation of the shipyard as a site of predation may simply reflect his acquaintance with contemporaneous anticapitalist discourses equating exploitation with bloodletting. His use of the phrase "birds of prey" suggests, however, that there echoed in the back of his mind Claude McKay's sonnet "Birds of Prey," which had appeared in the December 1919 issue of the *Messenger*. Published by two SPA-affiliated young black radicals, A. Philip Randolph and Chandler Owen, the *Messenger* was at the time the most militant and class-conscious of the black radical publications in the United States, linking racism with capitalism, condemning lynching, and calling for multiracial unity in the labor movement. These politics were forcefully conveyed in McKay's poem, which described capitalists as huge predatory birds that "swoop down . . . fasten[ing] in our bleeding flesh their claws . . . and stuff[ing] our gory hearts into their maws." In the version of the poem featured in the *Messenger*, McKay especially stressed the multiracial composition of the class of "toilers"—"We may be black or yellow, brown or white"—who take shape as a composite Promethean figure. Toomer's use of the phrase "birds of prey" suggests that, as he contemplated the situation of the shipyard workers—both at the time and some seventeen years later—his imagination was jogged by the unabashed imagery of class struggle deployed by the most noted black Marxist poet of the day.[12]

Where the 1931 and 1934 autobiographies offer no motivation for Toomer's decision to work in the shipyard, the 1936 text makes it clear that he went there to get a political education:

> I had expected to experience not only the "real worker" but also the labor movement. Not a sign of this movement. Not a union. Not a socialistic idea or view. On one occasion I asked my crap-shooting entrepreneur if no one had tried to form a union. His answer was, that if I wanted to keep my job I'd better not ask about that. . . . On another occasion I asked one of my team-mates if no one in the yards ever talked about socialism. He said, bluntly and briefly, that only a few had tried—and that they had gone one way out of the gate. . . .
>
> They talked about women and whoring and drinking and gambling freely and at every opportunity. They talked of nothing else. The labor movement simply was not in their minds except . . . (1) that it wasn't prudent to mention it, and (2) that they had a faintly superior and contemptuous attitude toward it.

His designation of the different behaviors of the black and white workers, more-over, suggests that he was alert to the different expectations of the recently pro-letarianized migrants from the South and their native urban counterparts. Given the recent class struggles in Bogalusa, Toomer's disappointed description of the attitudes and actions of both groups suggests that he may have been hoping for a greater display of solidarity. Toomer sadly concluded that the actual workers he met, whom "my readings had taught me to think of as the real workers of the world," were "not the workers of the labor movement." What he had seen was "not only a violation of my own values and those of socialism, it was a violation of the traditional American valuation of good work and hard workers. . . . America was betraying herself."[13]

Despite his deep disappointment, however, Toomer came away from the shipyard experience more convinced than ever of the necessity of abolishing capitalism. "That I was disillusioned with these workers did not mean that I was disillusioned with socialism," he wrote. "On the contrary . . . I realized as never before the *need* of socialism, the *need* of a radical change of the conditions of human society. Whereas before, socialism had been for me a reasoned and a felt *value*, now it became more deeply rooted in me, as *the* most urgent need of life for the majority of living people" (original emphasis). Moreover, it was not only blue-collar workers in a "freezing inferno" who needed to live in a different social order. The clerical workers at his subsequent job were similarly "doomed," fearful of layoff, working in a "hopeless man-breaking grind." One correlate of Toomer's

antipathy to capitalism was a profound pessimism: "Of one thing I was certain.
. . . that the underlying conditions of human experience were ruthless and terrible beyond anything written in books. . . . This is what the shipyard experience
had done to me—and done for me. Naked I touched naked reality." Another
correlate was a distinct sense of shame: "I could give [the workers] nothing."
This was not an easy realization. "I suffered for them. I suffered because of them.
An agonizing suffering that would never leave me, so it seemed. They haunted
me, these men, they and their plight. . . . I wonder[ed] if I were committing a
betrayal, and ask[ed] myself in all possible sincerity if my 'deep knowing' were
not merely a rationalization of on the one hand my dislikes and inadequacies
in the proletarian world, and, on the other hand, any preferences and ego urges
for the middle class." He concluded, "The conditions of man's life were terrible. I
could not change them. They were too much for any one man, for any one group
unless this group grew to millions in membership and developed greater wisdom
and driving force than any group I knew of had."[14]

The 1936 autobiography ends with Toomer's drawing near-Darwinian lessons
from his shipyard experience: "I too must become a killer in my way and for my
purpose—a destroyer of whatever impeded me. . . . I was alone . . . to struggle and
survive, or struggle and die." As he changed course, his energies would hence-
forth be devoted to "the struggle of values against the valueless, the contest of
the normal against the abnormal, construction against destruction, love against
hate, life itself against living death. The worm had turned." Now living in the great
metropolis, he would "use this colossus [New York] . . . for all it was worth." He
concluded, "Back there in the New York of 1920, some deep center of me came
awake for the first time, gave its birth cry, looked about." This finale portrays
Toomer's turn away from the working class in somewhat self-serving terms:
the struggle of labor against capital morphs into the artist-hero's heroic struggle
for survival in a hostile universe. But the overall effect of the 1936 narrative is
to depict Toomer's decision to leave the shipyard—the turning of the worm in
his own life—as a wrenching one. Where the 1931 and 1934 accounts portray the
workers as brutalized and apolitical, omitting any mention of the repression encountered by radicals attempting to organize in the shipyards, the 1936 narrative
links the workers' dissipation with their defeat. Where the earlier accounts are
self-congratulatory, applauding Toomer's wisdom in relinquishing his illusions
about the working class, the 1936 narrative is profoundly self-critical, lamenting
its author's solitariness and inability to stay the course.[15]

The information supplied in the mid-Depression-era narratives thus places in
larger historical and political context the motivations of the young Toomer who
for two weeks performed hard labor in the freezing ship hulls. His decision to
seek the "labor movement" in an Elizabeth, New Jersey, shipyard was not the naive
project many scholars have described. Shipyard workers had been in the lead of
the wave of wartime strikes; there had been a militant shipbuilders' strike right

in Newark Bay in 1917. Moreover, shipyard workers in Seattle had sparked the general strike of February 1919 that was dubbed the Seattle Soviet, which in turn inspired Seattle longshoremen in December 1919 to refuse to load ships bearing matériel to be used in the postwar Allied attempt to crush the Russian Revolution. Commentaries on Bogalusa were frequently appearing in the left press, hailing the November 1919 self-sacrifice of the southern white lumber workers in defense of their Negro American Federation of Labor organizer comrade as a possible harbinger of a coming era of multiracial anticapitalist militancy. While evidently based more on his reading of leftist literature than on any personal ties with the organized left, Toomer's desire to experience at first hand the revolutionary potential of the working class was, in its context, hardly implausible. The "labor movement" was an ambiguous ideologeme, signifying situations ranging from explicitly anticapitalist worksite activity to the actual state of class struggle and union organizing in a wide variety of settings.[16]

Even as Toomer's 1935 and 1936 autobiographies give a largely sympathetic account of his political radicalism from Chicago onward, they expose fault lines within the working-class movement in the mid- to late 1910s. Of some of these limitations Toomer was apparently cognizant: his comment that the "terrible . . . conditions of man's life" could not be changed by any "one group" unless that group "grew to millions in membership and developed greater wisdom and driving force than any group I knew of had" suggests a skeptical assessment of the SPA, the principal organization on the left with which his contacts at the Rand School had made him acquainted. Of other shortcomings, however, he evinced less critical awareness. Although Farrell's locker room tutorial made Toomer aware that capitalists were "parasites" and workers "slaves," it also reflected the SPA's economist bent, as well as its ambiguous analysis of the class nature of the state. The nationalization of industries would presumably restore to the proletariat its "just portion of the wealth," its "rightful inheritance"; the process by which this transfer would occur ("in some way") was, however, apparently not addressed. Toomer's conclusion that the bosses' inhumane treatment of the shipyard laborers was a "violation of the traditional American valuation of hard work and good workers" suggests, moreover, his acceptance of the American exceptionalist doctrine that class antagonism was somehow un-American. Although his recognition that his agitation among youth at the East Side settlement was perceived as "un-American" indicates his awareness of the centrality of patriotic rhetoric to ideological control and state repression, Toomer appears to have been of two minds regarding the ideologeme "America." In this ambivalence Toomer was hardly alone: the opposition of nationalism to internationalism, often linked with the opposition of reform to revolution, was the major bone of contention in the wartime debates within the SPA that culminated in the split occurring in the very month Toomer went to work in the shipyard. Toomer's uncertainty about how to view "America" in relation to its "proletariat" reflects a legacy of early-twentieth-century Socialism that would carry over into the creation of *Cane*.[17]

While indicating his interest in the possibility of building multiracial solidarity, Toomer's description of the different behaviors of Negro and white laborers suggests a standpoint reflective of the limitations of the SPA's approach to the fight against racism. Indeed, the particularly harsh conditions facing black shipyard workers had contributed to the leading role they had played during some of the wartime shipyard strikes. Yet the SPA's sporadic antiracism in the workplace was characteristically confined to the call for black-white labor unity without attention to the need for all workers actively to oppose racism: the doctrine of "class first" often ignored the particularities of race-based discrimination and super-exploitation. Toomer's description of the black workers' ability to take "their job with a laugh [and] . . . to loaf and enjoy themselves" valorizes them in Whitmanesque terms but evades analysis of the segregated conditions in the shipyards. Indeed, his retrospective account suggests that he conversed only with white workers. While he had sought direct contact with the "labor movement," Toomer's brief stay in the shipyard did not enable him to query the economism and racism that hampered the ability of the SPA to promote multiracial solidarity in the ranks of the working class.[18]

Although it hints at significant political shortcomings—in the contemporaneous left, in Toomer himself—the 1936 autobiography unambiguously reveals that the young Jean Toomer was eagerly anticipating the event of workers' revolution when he entered the New Jersey shipyard in December 1919. His intense personal disappointment cannot be separated from the larger demoralization experienced by many on the left as it became clear that, at least in the foreseeable future, the aftermath of the Russian Revolution in the United States would witness the recession of the revolutionary tide. For all its value in reconstructing Toomer's early encounter with socialism, however, the 1936 text is possibly—indeed, probably—disingenuous on one count. In all three versions of his autobiography, Toomer would have us think that the only reason for his quitting the shipyard after two weeks was the disillusionment he experienced there—whether primarily with the workers or with himself. Scrutiny of the dates of his employment supplied by his 1931 autobiography indicates, however, that he may well have had another reason for leaving with such dispatch. If he traveled from Washington to New York on the weekend of December 20–21 and began his ten-day work stint in the New Jersey shipyard on Monday, December 22, 1919, then his last day of work would have been Friday, January 2, 1920. What Toomer neglects to mention is that January 2 was the date of the second Palmer Raid, when thousands of radicals, including hundreds in the New York metropolitan area, were arrested in a nationwide nighttime sweep by federal agents; there was a second roundup on Monday, January 5. As a result of the raids, the Communist Party and the Communist Labor Party—embryonic left-wing formations emerging from the recent split of the SPA—would both be driven underground.[19]

Toomer could not have been unaware of this activity. Even if the New Jersey shipyard where he worked remained unaffected, his Ninth Street apartment in Greenwich Village was close to the Twelfth Street office of the Communist Party, which was invaded by Palmer's men. A frequent visitor at the Rand School, Toomer would have known that radical New York was buzzing over the weekend of January 2–4, 1920. The prospect of returning to work on Monday in the shipyard—where radicals had clearly been surveilled in the recent past—may have been highly unappealing for reasons other than the turning of an internal worm. Toomer makes no mention of the Palmer Raids in any of his autobiographies. Nonetheless, it is noteworthy that he gave up talking about socialism with shipyard workers at exactly the moment when the possible consequences of such talking had become patently clear. The repression of a personal memory was more than incidentally linked to the state's repression of the left; an absent cause was an absented cause.

"America will remain a grotesque storm center": Toomer as Radical Journalist

The greater reliability of the untitled 1936 autobiography in relation to Toomer's early interest in socialism is affirmed by his earliest published works, which amply document his leftist political passions. Toomer's first published writing was a letter to the *Nation* on "Present-Day Socialism." Toomer took issue with a March 29, 1919, editorial titled "Self-Government and Decentralization" arguing that the recently instated Socialist governments in Berlin and Petrograd were anomalous for their degree of local self-government. "Socialism, a political concept, contemplating the highest-powered organization of the political means, tends to centralization," opined the *Nation* editors. "[I]ndeed, centralization is its postulate."[20]

Writing from Ellenville the day after May Day 1919, Toomer defended current experiments with workers' self-government in the light of "orthodox socialist theory." Characterizing "present-day socialism" as a "filtration of previous theory" by historical actors "vigorous . . . in support of Soviet Russia and . . . the ascendancy of the socialist ideal," Toomer declared, "In the writings of these men . . . I fail to find the slightest basis for the contention that the postulate of socialism is centralization." Indeed, "as early as 1912, five years before the Russian revolution, even as orthodox a Marxist as John Spargo, in frankly advocating decentralization whenever practicable, wrote, 'Where capitalist production has developed national organization, the Socialist State will start with that form, continue it if it seems best to do so, abandon it and adopt a process of gradual decentralization if that seems best.'" Toomer's reference to Spargo is strategic: even the non-Bolshevist Spargo, he implies, can be cited in support of the political outlook guiding current revolutionary movements. Toomer presents himself, however, as an unabashed partisan of the contemporaneous revolutionary movements he has been reading about in the *New York American*. At a time when the postwar European workers' governments in Munich, Berlin, and Budapest, as well as the Soviet Union, were coming under intense attack, and U.S. radicals were being accused of throwing bombs—and attempting to overthrow the government—Toomer's statement locates him squarely on the left. While temporarily sequestered in the Catskills, he projected a political being fully engaged with the current conjuncture.[21]

Toomer's first journalistic publication appeared a month later, in the SPA's *New York Call*. A short Gothic parable about war profiteers, "Ghouls" describes a quasi-human monster scouring the pockets of bodies stretched out on a battle-field. Moving with "an almost machine-like . . . precision," the ghoul hesitates only once, when the "luminous eyes" of a dying man plead with him not to "jerk [away] a heart-shaped locket." There is a sudden "flash and a sharp report," and the ghoul falls among "his helpless prey." The scene then shifts to a group of "war profiteers," with full cheeks and "eyes glow[ing] with the light of conquest," who sit at a table. Slaves enter and deposit "heaps of coins" before them—"coins stained with the tears of children, coins wrung from the breasts of mothers." The slaves pile on more gold coins, "red and gory with the blood of men," but finally enter—"with a peculiar light in their eyes"—and deposit a bundle. They stay and watch as the profiteers, grabbing for the bag, "recoil, afraid, for they had touched there the hearts of men." The burden-bearing slaves, it is strongly implied, will not continue in their work for much longer.[22]

"Ghouls" draws on a number of possible influences: the horror tales of Edgar Allan Poe; symbolic vignettes in the *New York Call*'s "Wanderer" series; W. E. B. Du Bois's moral-political parables in the *Crisis*. It may specifically echo Scott Nearing's 1918 *Messenger* condemnation of U.S. munitions makers, "War Shouters and War Contracts," which proclaims, "Profiteers! Profiteers! digging gold out of ground that is soaked with the blood of other men—Profiteers!" In its correlation of the scavenging ghoul in the first paragraph with the conversion of money into bloodied flesh in the second, the sketch's political allegory suggestively recalls Marx's description of capital as "dead labor, which, vampire-like, lives only by sucking living labor, and lives the more, the more labor it sucks." The narrative comments not only on the Great War and the Paris Peace Conference—where, even as Toomer wrote, the leaders of the victorious nations were sitting in the Sun King's palace at Versailles and dividing up the spoils of war—but also on proletarian resistance. The battlefield killing of the ghoul may refer to the Russian Revolution, which not only produced the Treaty of Brest-Litovsk—the "separate peace" liberating Russian workers and peasants from the horror of the war—but also the death of "vampire capital" itself. The impending revolt of the burden bearers may also have a more general global implication. The burden bearers are not racially identified; the only colors in the sketch are, notably, red and gold. Yet the repeated designation of them as "slaves," coupled with their figuring as the source of superabundant profits, suggests an allusion to the colonial masses of Africa and Asia whose lands and labor—as Du Bois was pointing out in the *Crisis*, and Randolph and Owen in the *Messenger*—furnished the principal prize of the war. The behavior of the slaves who stalk into the room "with a peculiar light in their eyes," confronting the rulers with irrefutable evidence of their criminality, intimates the numbered days of the regime that keeps them in thrall. We are reminded that the first Pan-African Congress was concurrent with the redivisions of empire occurring at Versailles, and that strikes and rebellions in Africa, India, Mexico, Central America, and the Caribbean were revealing the global reach of the postwar upsurge. Despite the sentimentality attaching to the central heart-locket image, "Ghouls" is a parable not just of the victimization of the innocent but also of the coming revenge of the dispossessed.[23]

Toomer followed up "Ghouls" a month later in another *New York Call* publication titled "Reflections on the Race Riots," a commentary on the significance of the July 18–22, 1919, race riot in Washington, DC. Noting that the "recent series of race riots" manifests in the Negro "an essentially new psychology, characterized by a fighting attitude," Toomer observes that this new militancy, spurred by the world war, is now directed "against the iniquities of the white man in the United States." He warns that "[i]mmediate steps toward co-operative relations are imperative. It now confronts the nation, so voluble in acclamation of the democratic ideal, so reticent in applying what it professes, to either extend to the Negro (and other workers) the essentials of a democratic commonwealth or else exist from day to day never knowing when a clash may occur, in the light of which the Washington riot will diminish and pale. . . . This is essentially a time for action." Toomer discerns among the population at large three types of responses to the current strife. One group—"deep in the pit of prejudice"—would "eliminate racial differences by increasing the very acts which immediately caused them"; they would "have the fist of the white man educate the brain of the black," and, when necessary, resort to "lynching-bees and burning-fests." A second group, "deplor[ing] the Negro's fighting psychology," would "limi[t] its suggestions to the worn-out method of 'constitutional rights for the Negro'"—even though in Chicago, where "Negroes enjoy political privileges," race riots "are prevalent." Members of this group, he remarks, have no quarrel "with fight *per se* (a war with Mexico would meet their hearty approval)," but only with "the Negro (or any other worker), who displays an active unwillingness to submit to injustices. Such a Negro is difficult to exploit."[24]

Toomer prefers to address a third group, with whose belief that "physical resistance or aggression, as a means to an end, [is] a discredited institution," he has a measure of sympathy. Cautioning, however, that the situation in Washington required Negroes to resist—"If a man would shoot you, and there be no one to prevent him, you must shoot first"—he urges the need to understand "the fundamental and determining causes which have irresistibly drawn the Negro to his present position. To do this brings one adjacent to the thought and action of the labor movement." The article's closing paragraph—from which the first epigraph to this study's introduction is drawn—warrants quoting in full:

In the literature of the Socialist movement in this country there is to be found a rational explanation of the causes of race hatred and, in the light of these, a definite solution, striking at the very root of the evil, is proposed. It is generally established that the causes of race prejudice may primarily be found in the economic structure that compels one worker to compete against another and that furthermore renders it advantageous for the exploiting classes to inculcate, foster, and aggravate that competition. If this be true then it follows that the nucleus of race co-operation lies in the substitution of a socialized community for a competitive one. To me it appears that nothing less than just such an economic readjustment will ever bring concord to the two races; for, as long as there are governing classes, and as long as these classes feel it to their gain to keep the masses in constant conflict, just so long will a controlled press and educational system incite and promote race hatred. Where there is advantage to be secured by racial antagonisms, heaven and hell will be invoked to that purpose. Demagogues may storm and saints may plead, but America will remain a grotesque storm center torn by passion and hatred until our democratic pretensions are replaced by a socialized reality.[25]

Written nearly five months before Toomer would go to work in the shipyards, "Reflections on the Race Riots" shows him fully conversant with the analysis of the causes of racial conflict presented in "the literature of the Socialist movement." His assertion that "the causes of race prejudice may primarily be found in the economic structure that . . . renders it advantageous for the exploiting classes to inculcate, foster, and aggravate" competition between the races indicates his agreement with the Socialists' contention that the basis of racial antagonism is based not in biology or culture but in labor competition. Evidently, too, Toomer shared the Socialists' view that only the "economic readjustment" entailed by the "substitution of a socialized reality" can remedy the situation: to "strike at the very root" of "race hatred," he contends, one must do away with the soil from which it derives nourishment. Deploying the organic trope in its structural register, "root" here signifies material cause; Toomer metaphorically signals the base/superstructure paradigm guiding his theorization that the "controlled press and educational system," as well as of the "passion and hatred" stirred up among workers, are grounded in the exploitation of one class by another. Toomer presented himself to readers of the *New York Call* as not just a partisan of the militant New Negro and a critic of liberal nostrums, but a conscious Marxist. Indeed, the three identities are interchangeable.[26]

In some respects, indeed, Toomer's politics situate him in the vicinity of the left wing of the Socialist movement. His disparaging remarks on voting—"mere suffrage"—indicate a skeptical attitude toward the electoral politics that remained the centerpiece of the right wing's strategy for bringing a "socialized reality" into being. His caustic commentary on the call for "the extension of constitutional rights"—that "[t]o fit a worn-out coat on the Negro will not alter the essential character of things"—voices impatience not just with timid liberals, black and white, but with any proponent of the view that expanding civil liberties will in itself remedy social inequality. His double-edged use of the term "democracy" contrasts the socialist "democratic commonwealth" with the "democratic pretensions" of those supporting the existing state apparatus. His insistence upon equating "the Negro" with "any other worker," moreover, breaks with the view prevalent in much of the Second International that Negroes constituted "nonhistorical people," backward in both culture and location within the capitalist mode of production.[27]

Besides insisting upon the proletarian character of the urban migrants, Toomer hints at an ideological dimension to the notion of race absent in Socialist discourse. In characterizing the most virulent racists as those who "would eliminate racial differences by increasing the very facts which immediately caused them," Toomer suggests that "racial differences" do not preexist racist categorization and violence, but in fact are generated by them. Even as he treats "white" and "Negro" as descriptors having self-evident referents, his assertion that racial violence produces the very categories that it apparently reflects implies a social constructionist view of race based in materialist social analysis. Indeed, the implication of his argument is that socialism would abolish not only racial antagonism but race itself.

Even as he commends the militancy of Negro rebels, condemns the brutality of gutter racists, criticizes the inadequacies of liberals, and argues for socialism as the antidote to racism, Toomer's statement reflects an uncritical acceptance of certain problematic features of contemporaneous Socialism. The rhetorical slippage between "the Negro" and "any other worker who displays an active unwillingness to submit to injustices" blurs the connection between race and class even as it asserts the Negro's identity as a proletarian. Although workers of any demographic group who manifest a "fighting psychology" and "refuse to submit to injustices" are indeed "harder to exploit," the "injustices" sparking their "fighting psychology" may vary considerably—as the race riots themselves display. This confusion is compounded by Toomer's references to the "American white" and the "white man" as the Negro's antagonist. Although Toomer apparently exempts from this monolithic categorization those workers of European descent active in the "labor movement," he was doubtless aware that the Washington race riot, while sparked by incendiary stories of black-on-white rape in the "controlled press," had nonetheless been initiated by working-class white former servicemen on the rampage—that is, racist white "workers," and not just any white "men." But because he embraced the SPA analysis that the basis for racism in the urban working classes was "primarily the economic structure that compels one worker to compete against another," rather than an extension of the racialized imperatives of capitalist class rule that also produced "lynching bees and burnings fests" in the rural South, he did not adequately acknowledge the role played by racist ideology in organizing white workers to engage in acts of terroristic violence against their working-class comrades of a different hue. As in his 1936 autobiographical recollection, the term "labor movement," presumably signifying those workers involved in SPA-led struggles for unionization, functioned in Toomer's *New York Call* piece as an ideologeme papering over the racial divisions precluding working-class unity; its historical referent was hazy at best. Indeed, the term "socialism" was also a contested ideologeme, especially when its capitalized encodation as the doctrine of the Socialist Party was counterposed with the range of meanings associated with its lower-case spelling. Toomer seems to have been aware of certain aspects of this contestation and to have sloughed over others.

Related to Toomer's somewhat vague formulation of exactly how the "labor movement" was going to transform social relations is his uncertain presentation of the process by which the desired "socialized reality" would be "substituted" for the "democratic pretensions" of U.S. capitalism. His use of the word "until"— "America will remain a grotesque storm center torn by passion and hatred until our democratic pretensions are replaced by a socialized reality"—reveals his conviction that the situation of racial polarization can and will change. And his critical comments on the inadequacies of movements calling for "constitutional rights for the Negro" suggest that the "democratic commonwealth" cannot simply be voted in. Neither, however, does he proclaim the necessity for a revolutionary overthrow of the current state, even though he approves the use of force in self-defense. This hesitancy to designate the state as an organ of class rule, rather than a neutral terrain potentially inhabited by the working class, exhibits his contradictory attitude toward the über-ideologeme "America." At times Toomer deploys the words "America" and "Americans" ironically—as when he sardonically refers to the "everyday American brutishness" resulting in racial violence, or when he chides liberals for their misplaced confidence in "the essential goodness of all Americans." Yet his closing appeal is directed to "the nation." He makes mention of the "masses" being divided along lines of race by the "exploiting classes," but the agent of change whom he addresses is an undifferentiated enlightened "we," apparently transcending class, who can act to save the nation before it is too late. For all his stated doubts about the efficacy of "our democratic pretensions," Toomer does not forthrightly propose a class-based view of the state or a fissured view of the body politic. The "press" and the "educational system" may be "controlled," but Toomer—like many others in the orbit of the SPA—apparently does not decisively apply his materialist analytical paradigm to the ideology of progressive nationhood, which sutures over in the realm of politics the stark antinomies displayed in the Socialist analysis of economics.

One other feature of "Reflections on the Race Riots" bears notice. As Scruggs and VanDemarr point out in their examination of the differing chronologies contained in Toomer's different autobiographies, the 1931 text asserts that Toomer spent the entire summer of 1919 in upstate New York with a college friend. The 1936 text, however, indicates that Toomer was away from Washington, DC, for only one month toward the end of the summer—"until fall came"—making it very possible that he was actually in Washington at the time of the riot. When we consider that the apartment where his grandparents lived, at 1371 U Street, was located half a block from the hub of the riot, it becomes difficult indeed to account for Toomer's omission of any reference to having felt anxiety about his grandparents' welfare—if indeed he had not been huddled at home with them at the time. The fact that Toomer published the article only a week after the riot's end and evinced "rather specific" knowledge of its particulars further suggests his proximity to the site of its occurrence. If Toomer did indeed evade mention of his presence in Washington in late July 1919, this omission invites comparison with his occlusion of any reference to the Palmer Raids in connection with his quitting work in the shipyard. Toomer was enough of a radical to explore key sites and moments of social struggle, but not enough of one, perhaps, to place his personal welfare in jeopardy by venturing into situations of direct state repression.[28]

Toomer's 1919 *New York Call* journalism affirms the 1936 autobiography's portrait of the author as a young radical; it also affirms the extent to which his radicalism was cast in the mold of contemporaneous SPA doctrine. That Toomer enjoyed an ongoing congenial relationship with the editors of the *New York Call* is displayed not only in the friendliness of their correspondence but also in his option to publish in its pages, over a year after "Reflections on the Race Riots," "Americans and Mary Austin" (October 1920), an impassioned defense of Waldo Frank's *Our America*. The connection continued past the publication of *Cane*, as is shown in the proposed publication in the *New York Call* of an anonymous review essay, authored by Toomer, titled "The South in Literature," which juxtaposed *Cane* with Waldo Frank's *Holiday*. Although the review was never published, it is noteworthy that Toomer continued to envision the SPA-affiliated press as an appropriate publication venue for his work. The worm might have turned, but Toomer's interaction with the Socialist movement evidently persisted through and beyond the publication of *Cane*.[29]

"To declare openly his solidarity with the oppressed Negroes": Toomer and the *Liberator*

Even as Toomer was cultivating and maintaining his ties with the SPA's most prominent journalistic organ, he was approaching the editors at the *Liberator*, the premier postwar radical cultural journal. Ecumenical in its conception of leftist culture but distinctly allied after late 1919 with the Communist Party, the *Liberator* had announced its antiracist stance in its opening editorial, where Crystal and Max Eastman declared that their journal, true to the abolitionist echoes in its name, would "assert the social and political equality of the black and white races, oppose every kind of racial discrimination, and conduct a remorseless publicity campaign against lynch law." Although produced primarily by white radicals, the *Liberator* was coedited by Mike Gold and Claude McKay for seven months in 1922. It published a substantial number of texts authored by African Americans, including over two dozen by McKay alone. As McKay recalled, during his tenure as coeditor a meeting of "black reds" was held in the office of the *Liberator* to discuss how to make Marcus Garvey's United Negro Improvement Association (UNIA) "more class-conscious." Even before he departed from Sparta in late November 1921, Toomer sent to the *Liberator* a short story titled "Georgia Night," apparently an early version of "Kabnis." His choice of a publishing venue for the first draft of material that would appear in *Cane* speaks volumes about his political proclivities at the time.[30]

Toomer vigorously pursued publication in the premier left-wing literary journal of the day; "Carma" and "Georgia Dusk" appeared in September 1922; "Becky" in October. He attempted to establish a personal friendship with McKay, praising particular poems and *Harlem Shadows*, addressing him as "Brother," and inviting him to visit Washington (McKay gracefully declined). Writing to Toomer in July 1922, McKay referred to work he had sent previously: "I remember very well some of your things that used to come to the Liberator, and parts of them still stand out boldly in my mind for their bright local coloring and individual poetic power. However, none ever seemed to carry clear through from beginning to end in [*sic*] a high level and we had some lively discussions about them in the office." McKay's use of the plural ("some of your things") suggests that "Georgia Night" may not have been Toomer's only previous submission.[31]

In his frequently quoted August 1922 letter to the *Liberator*, written to supply background for a biographical sketch accompanying his forthcoming publications, Toomer introduces himself as the grandson of P. B. S. Pinchback, stressing his grandfather's humble origins, Civil War military service, and Reconstruction-era political prominence. Featuring his own racial identity as an amalgam of "seven blood mixtures," he declares that he had "lived equally amid the two race groups. Now white, now colored. From my own point of view I am naturally and inevitably an American." Noting that he had "striven for a spiritual fusion analogous to the fact of racial intermingling," he asserts that "my growing need for artistic expression has pulled me deeper and deeper into the Negro group." His recent visit to Georgia "was the starting point of almost everything of worth that I have done. I heard folk-songs come from the lips of Negro peasants. . . . [and] a deep part of my nature, a part that I had repressed, sprang suddenly to life. Now I cannot conceive of myself as aloof and separated." Toomer stresses his experience as a jack-of-all-trades: "Personally, my life has been torturous and dispersed. The comparative wealth which my family once had, has now dwindled away to almost nothing. We, or rather, they, are in the unhappy position of the lowered middle-class. . . . I have worked, it seems to me at everything: selling papers, delivery boy, soda clerk, salesman, shipyard worker, librarian-assistant, physical director, school teacher, grocery clerk, and God knows what all."[32]

The self-portrait offered here bears more than a trace of the Whitmanesque portrait of the artist as young proletarian sketched by Gold in his February 1921 *Liberator* manifesto, "Toward Proletarian Art." Toomer conjoins his experiences as a mental and a manual laborer and traces his former "repression" of racial solidarity to his illusory sense of class entitlement. While he notes the multiple strains in his ancestry and gestures toward his theory of a multiracial "American" race, he does not deny that, in the United States, there exist "two race groups." And while he claims to have drawn inspiration from "the folk-songs" of "Negro peasants," he does not rhapsodize about the tang of the soil or planting seeds within himself as he would in letters to Waldo Frank and Sherwood Anderson. The young author introducing himself to the editors of the revolutionary cultural magazine viewing itself as heir to abolitionism takes care to stress credentials that are at once class- and race-conscious.[33]

This letter may have been followed by others now lost. In his 1936 autobiography, *An American Testament*, former *Liberator* editor Joseph Freeman writes that Toomer's introductory letter consisted of "some twenty pages [of] vibrant and lucid prose" and recalled that its author "said he was partly Negro, but his color was so light that he had 'passed. He was now employed in the civil service; but a visit to the South on a vacation had suddenly confronted him with the miseries and cruelties inflicted on the race whose blood flowed in his veins. He decided to throw off the mask, to declare openly his solidarity with the oppressed Negroes, to write about their lives." If Freeman is referring here to Toomer's August 1922 letter, his memory is clearly flawed; there is nothing in that letter about going South on vacation, working for the civil service, or—at least explicitly—"passing." Moreover, the August 1922 letter is hardly twenty pages long. Perhaps Freeman, impressed by the letter's contents, simply erred in his memory of its length; or perhaps "Georgia Night" was included in the twenty pages. It is possible, however, that in 1921–22 Toomer wrote other letters to the *Liberator* in which he said more about the "miseries and cruelties inflicted on the race whose blood flowed in his veins," and that these made up a file of some bulk. This speculation is supported by Freeman's claim that, while he never met the young author face to face, he corresponded with Toomer "for a while." There is, unfortunately, no way of determining the facts, since Freeman claims that, hearing that "the police were going to raid all radical publications, the *Liberator* included . . . tore up everything in my desk, Toomer's manuscripts and letters too. Later his stories appeared in a book called *Cane*." Freeman notes, however, that Toomer was included in a "tentative list of contributors" to the *Liberator*'s successor, the *New Masses*—a list containing "roster of the most progressive American writers and artists of the period." A survey of *New Masses* mastheads reveals, indeed, that from its first issue in May 1926 until January 1927, Toomer is listed as a contributing editor. Toomer's outreach to the *Liberator* was integral to an interest in leftist politics that would last significantly beyond the publication of *Cane*.[34]

"The masters know . . . my solitude": Toomer's *Cane*-Era Journal

While Toomer's correspondence with the editors of the *Liberator* might be read as opportunistic self-fashioning, the journal that he kept in 1922–23 reveals him engaging in a serious—indeed anguished—contemplation of the political landscape.

> It is a symptom of weakness when one must bring God, equality, liberty, and justice to one's support. It follows, that the working classes, particularly the dark skinned among the working classes, are still weak. Witness Russian [*sic*]. The Bolsheviks no longer say, "We do this because it is just but because it is just under the circumstances, i.e., expedient. Because it furthers our purpose, this purpose being to remain in power—at whatever cost."
>
> If the workers could bellow, "We Want Power," the walls of capitalism would collapse. They are as yet too weak for that. They give cat-mews for "freedom." The I.W.W., however, want control of industry. Capitalists recognize their strength.
>
> If the Negro, consolidated on race rather than class interests, ever becomes strong enough to demand the exercise of Power, a race war will occur in America. [. . .]
>
> [T]he masters know that little or nothing that I will ever say will have much effect upon the masses. They permit my exsistence [*sic*] because they (the sharpest amongst them) are confident of my solitude. It is evidence of weakness that men like myself are not forced into the service of the governing class, or exiled, or murdered. I should say, it is evidence of a *recognition* of weakness. The masters know . . . my solitude.[35]

This entry exhibits a Toomer who is significantly less optimistic than the op-ed *New York Call* commentator writing in the heady days of 1919. His earlier warning that the nation would continue to be rocked by race riots unless it moved into a "socialized reality" has metamorphosed into gloomy prophecy: the future will bring either workers' power or race war. His understanding of racial division has sharpened: while "darker skinned" workers have interests in common with the rest of the working class, his earlier equation of "the Negro" with "any worker" has been superseded. Where previously Toomer wrote of the "labor movement" as a monolith, here he distinguishes between the Industrial Workers of the World (IWW), which he views as a serious contender for power, and those elements that "give cat-mews for 'freedom'" and invoke the discourse of patriotism and "rights." The unnamed object of critique here is almost certainly the SPA: criticized for years by the IWW for its reformist and divisive trade union politics, by 1922 the SPA was being steadily drummed in the pro-Bolshevik press for its newfound patriotism and antipathy to the Soviet Union. Toomer's own support of the USSR indicates his positioning in current debates: where his May 1919 letter to the *Nation* had expressed admiration for what he saw as the "decentralized" nature of the emerging Soviet governments, here he supports the Bolsheviks' determination to "remain in power."[36]

Toomer's *Cane*-era journal entry conveys a contradictory assessment of political possibilities. His gloomy estimate that race war is as likely as class war indicates his concurrence with other black radicals who were observing the failure of the white working class, even when organized as the "labor movement," consistently to fight for multiracial solidarity. W. A. Domingo, editor of the short-lived revolutionary journal the *Emancipator*, observed in 1919 that because "American radicals . . . share the typical white psychology towards negroes," African Americans could readily be used as strikebreakers. "The failure to make Negroes class-conscious is the greatest potential menace to the establishment of Socialism in the United States." McKay declared in the *Liberator* in August 1922 that "[the] racial question may be eventually the monkey wrench thrown into the machinery of American revolutionary struggle. . . . [The Negroes in the United States] might remain a reactionary fact, distrustful of the revolutionary activities of the white working class. They might remain the tool of the ruling class, to be used effectively, as in the past, against radical labor. And in that event the black workers will suffer—the white workers will lose—the ruling class will win." Where Marx had warned that, failing to achieve revolution, the class struggle would result in the "common ruin of the contending classes," Toomer feared that the result would be the common ruin of the contending races. At the same time, Toomer, like McKay, was all the more convinced of the need for the walls of capitalism to collapse. The emphasis he placed throughout the journal entry on power, strength, and weakness reflects an unsentimental recognition of political necessity. His use of "if"—"If the workers could bellow, 'We Want Power,' the walls of capitalism would collapse"—indicated a conditional that he fervently wished to become actual. These are not the meditations of a Fabian socialist.[37]

But where McKay ended his polemic with the declaration, "Let the Black Red speak out!" Toomer appeared less confident of his ability as a writer to influence the course of history. His assertion that "the sharpest [among the masters] know my solitude" is somewhat self-aggrandizing; he has hardly done anything to warrant surveillance by the powers that be, much less "exile" or "murder." But he evidently views this "solitude"—which he equates with his inability to have an "effect on the masses"—as debilitating. The weakness of the writer in communicating with the working class correlates with the weakness of the working class in its struggle against the "governing class." In a letter to his lover, Margaret Naumberg, in August 1923, Toomer continued to mull the relationship of the writer to the workers' movement:

> The mass, distrusting on the economic plane any leadership other than their own, have carried this attitude, quite naturally and in most [crossed out, "many" added] cases with a limited [added] justice, into those phases of life where the pure intellect and spirit are concerned. Thus along with economic self-government, they will more and more tend to a worker's science and art, and a proletarian philosophy. The question is: will these values at any point coincide

with those of individual genius. If so, then the genius will still have an immediate social function. If not, genius will become [outcast], removed from temporal happening, and democratically ostracized.

Toomer evidently envisioned himself as one such "genius" inhabiting the realm of "pure intellect and spirit." But he took seriously not only the need for "the mass" to engage in "economic self-government" but also their right to "a worker's science and art and a proletarian philosophy." That he would prefer having "an immediate social function" to being "removed from temporal happening and democratically ostracized" is clear.[38]

Toomer's use of a Marxist terminology in his nonfictional writings and correspondence, as well as his active cultivation of relationships with the *New York Call* and the *Liberator*, lead one to ponder the nature and extent of his acquaintance with Marxism. His autobiographies make no mention of his having read Marx before or during the *Cane* period. But his writings suggest that, in addition to being familiar with the discourse of contemporaneous radical movements, he had more than a passing acquaintance with certain key Marxist tropes and concepts. His description of the alienation of labor in the New Jersey shipyard suggests that he may have read Marx's commentaries on the working day and machinery and large-scale industry in volume 1 of *Capital*. His comparison of capitalists with bloodsucking vampires in his first published *New York Call* piece—a motif that he would reiterate in "Seventh Street" in *Cane*—indicates not just his familiarity with Socialist designations of war profiteers as "blood-suckers" but also an awareness of Marx's use of this trope to describe the relationship between dead and living labor. His discussion of the role of the state and its legitimating institutions in "Reflections on the Race Riots" displays an awareness of the base-superstructure relationship set forth in such writings as *The German Ideology* and Marx's preface to *A Contribution to the Critique of Political Economy*. While Toomer was clearly not a sophisticated student of Marxist philosophy and political economy, it would appear that he was more fully acquainted with the language and key concepts of Marxism than he would later care to admit.

"One grand flare": "Banking Coal" and the Repression of Revolution

The conflicting impulses informing Toomer's political outlook during the time when he was conceiving *Cane* are poignantly set forth in "Banking Coal," a poem that appeared in the *Crisis* in June 1922. The allegorical strategy of the poem requires that it be presented in its entirety:

> Whoever it was who brought the first wood and coal
> To start the Fire, did his part well;
> Not all wood takes to fire from a match,

Nor coal from wood before it's burned to charcoal.
The wood and coal in question caught a flame
And flared up beautifully, touching the air
That takes a flame from anything.

Somehow the fire was furnaced,
And then the time was ripe for some to say,
"Right banking of the furnace saves the coal."
I've seen them set to work, each in his way,
Though all with shovels and with ashes,
Never resting till the fire seemed most dead;
Whereupon they'd crawl in hooded night-caps
Contentedly to bed. Sometimes the fire left alone
Would die, but like as not spiced tongues
Remaining by the hardest on till day would flicker up,
Never strong, to anyone who cared to rake for them.
But roaring fires never have been made that way.
I'd like to tell those folks that one grand flare
Transferred to memory tissues of the air
Is worth a life, or, for dull minds that turn in gold,
All money ever saved by banking coal.[39]

Invoking Robert Frost in its overlay of philosophical meditation on home economics, "Banking Coal" can be read as a generalized commentary on the costs of
conservation: what looks like cautious husbandry of energy results in a tamping
down of the flame of life. But the sustained trope involving the controlled building
and suppression of the fire invites interpretation of the poem as an extended allegorical reflection on the contemporaneous conjuncture. Fire was, after all, adduced
as one of the principal symbols of revolution in the era of 1919. John Reed, who
feared at first that the Russian Revolution would fail, remaining only an inspirational
"pillar of fire" for succeeding generations, would conclude before his death in 1920
that "In spite of all that has happened, the Revolution lives, burns with a steady
flame, licks at the dry, inflammable framework of European capitalist society." A
Messenger editorial proclaimed in September 1920 that the world was "ablaze with
Bolshevism . . . from Armenia to Arabia . . . into Egypt and into the heart of Africa."
Theresa S. McMahon, reporting on the Seattle Soviet for the liberal magazine *Survey*,
wrote that "the spark that kindled the smouldering fire, culminating in the general
strike, was the grievances of the shipyard workers." Claude McKay in "Baptism" used
the fire trope to signify the strength gained from fighting oppression: the process of
entering a furnace and being "transform[ed] into the shape of flame" yields up "a
stronger soul within a finer frame." In "The Night Fire," McKay compared a burning
building with the destruction of the old regime: "The fire leaps out and licks the
ancient walls, / And the big building bends and twists and groans." The leftist poet
and *Broom* editor Lola Ridge, in her poem "Reveille," designated two meanings of
fire: as basis of industry—

Let the fires go cold—
Let the iron spill out, out of the troughs—
Let the iron run wild
Like a red bramble on the floors

—and of revolution: "Let us meet the fire of their guns / With a greater fire."[40]

"Banking Coal" is plausibly read as a reflection on the hopes aroused and then quashed in the "red summer" of 1919. Scruggs and VanDemarr propose that the poem comments on "the repression of radicalism in the United States during the postwar years and, in particular, the decline of the New Negro radicals"; the poem's "one grand flare," they propose, "refers to the Russian Revolution or to African-American resistance during the Washington riots." The poem's intricate allegory invites expansion on this reading. The wood signifies white workers, not readily aroused to engage in rebellion ("take to fire from a match"); the coal signifies black workers, hesitant to respond to the call of whites unless proven trustworthy in the struggle ("before . . . burned to charcoal" themselves). Indeed, the capacity of wood to be transformed into charcoal suggests the non-fixity of racial identities: under conditions of class struggle, "whiteness" may disappear. The conditions for revolt are, moreover, always present: the air, presumably because of its oxygenic content, "takes a flame from anything." When blacks and whites manage to unite—to "ca[tch] a flame"—they "flar[e] up beautifully": Toomer may have in mind Bogalusa, widely celebrated in the black and left press. But when the movement dies down ("somehow the fire was furnaced"), the misleaders go to work, "each in his way." Some declare that African Americans will benefit from a lessening of militancy: "Right banking of the furnace saves the coal." Toomer may allude here to conservative black nationalists like Marcus Garvey, who were advising black workers to stay out of unions. Such African American sell-outs work in league with other figures who, after shoveling ashes over the fire, put on "hooded night-caps," a suggestive reference to the Ku Klux Klan. That these misleaders then "crawl contentedly to bed"—presumably with one another—can be taken as an allusion to the notorious fall 1921 alliance between the Garveyites and the KKK, which had been widely denounced in the African American press. In the aftermath of this betrayal there would occasionally "flicker up" some "spiced tongues" of revolt, discoverable by those who "car[e] to rake for them." But those with "dull minds that turn in gold," who are concerned with "saving money by banking coal," have won the day. The viewpoint of the poem's speaker emerges passionately in the final lines. He feels that "roaring fires" will never emerge from embers buried in ashes. But, in a startling image, he proposes that the air—the oxygen-bearing potential of a common social life—has "memory tissues." To convey to the world historical knowledge of the "flare" of revolution—to keep the flame alive, as it were—is in itself "worth a life": perhaps his own. The class struggles of 1919 may have been repressed, but Toomer's speaker persists, at least in poetry, in keeping the flame alive.[41]

Toomer's poem conveys a deep disappointment that the conjuncture of 1919 has not constituted a "beginning [that] authorizes [a] re-beginning," in Badiou's phrase. Notably, however, Toomer does not deploy the trope of fire to signify another proposition that appeared with some frequency in the discourse of the black left—namely, the equation of smothered coals with the always-present potentiality for racial violence. A *Messenger* editorial of July 1921, calling for the boycott of *The Birth of a Nation*, noted that the embers of a potential riot were "smouldering" in New York: screening the film might well blow them into flame. This metaphor gained historical resonance from recent race riots in which fires had figured prominently—from East St. Louis in 1917, when white women notoriously tossed a black baby into the flames, singing "Rock-A-Bye Baby," to Tulsa in 1921, when large portions of the black community were burned down by white rioters. Toomer's decision to use the trope of fire to signify the possible inception of a multiracial workers' uprising, and in this allegory to insist upon the catalytic role played by "air," signals his hope that the revolution with which elsewhere "the world is ablaze" may supply the needed oxygen to the struggle going on in the United States. However tamped down, the embers described in the poem are those of potential multiracial proletarian revolt, not of abiding racial enmity. The capacity of wood to be transformed into charcoal, moreover, suggests that, in a revolutionary situation, racialization can be reversed. As in "Reflections on the Race Riots," Toomer suggests that race is a function rather than a cause—or at least a necessary cause—of social practice.[42]

Toomer's own comments on the role of the image in literary representation indicate that he was well-acquainted with debates over the relationship between aesthetics and politics in the *Dial* and other little magazines. Toomer was far from committed to a realist notion of mimesis; his stipulation that a sense of "mystery cannot help but accompany a deep, clear-cut image," as well as his declaration that "[i]n my reflective moments I desire the profound image saturated in its own lyricism," imply quite the opposite. Nonetheless, he repeatedly asserted the need for "extra-artistic consciousness in works of art," declaring that "anything vital in the way of writing must be the cause of effects that lie outside the province of pure art." In a discussion of the aesthetic theory set forth by the Imagist poet Richard Aldington, Toomer criticized formalist critics "whose eyes are so charmed and fascinated by the gem, by its outward appearance, by its external form, that the spirit behind the gem is not perceived. An exquisite image is preferred to a rousing message." Denying that this view had majority status among "Western poets or their readers," Toomer wrote, "These are certainly remarkable times we are living in. Transformations occur that leave the nature which produced a fish eye from nothing aghast." Even biological evolution, in other words, is overshadowed by the changes rocking the social world. He continues: "Overnight our voice and our hearing have not shrunk into an eye. The deduction is that 'messages' are now as always measured by their merit; that a fine message beautifully expressed, or a strong message vigorously expressed, will be accepted and appreciated now as much as in any former time." "Banking Coal" exemplifies a melding of Toomer's stated aspirations. Its metaphor of furnacing contains more than a hint of "mystery"; at the same time, it tantalizes the reader with veiled references to a Real beyond metaphor. Even as the poem thematizes the arrested historical dialectic, it signals the role of art in engaging with—and analyzing—the processes holding back revolutionary change."[43]

"The proletariat or world upheaval": Toomer's Unwritten Revolutionary Novel

Even before *Cane* appeared in the fall of 1923, Toomer was mulling plans for his next literary projects. One was to be a collation of three works, most likely "Withered Skin of Berries," *Natalie Mann*, and a third as yet unwritten work. The other was to be a novel that he described to both Liveright and Frank: "As I vaguely glimpse and feel it, it seems tremendous: this whole black and brown world heaving upward against, here and there mixing with the white. The mixture, however, is insufficient to absorb the heaving, hence it but accelerates and fires it. This upward heaving is to be symbolic of the proletariat or world upheaval. And it is likewise to be symbolic of the subconscious penetration of the conscious mind." The clear implication is that Toomer intended to write a novel treating the global intensification of antiracist working-class struggle. Where his journal entry about the need for the workers to "bellow, 'We Want Power!'" stressed the "weakness" of the U.S. proletariat—especially of its "dark-skinned" component—here Toomer envisions the "brown and black world" taking the lead in revolutionary social transformation. The participation of whites "accelerates and fires" the revolt but cannot fully "absorb" its impact; no longer figuring as historical vanguard, the predominantly white "labor movement" has a secondary role to play in what is now envisioned as a global upsurge, "the proletariat or world upheaval." Indeed, it is noteworthy that the phrase "labor movement" does not appear here at all: instead "proletariat" (here evidently functioning as an adjective, not a noun) is rendered equivalent to "world," which has previously been modified by "brown and black": together they modify "upheaval." Clearly, the unionized white working class was, for Toomer, no longer the principal agent of social transformation.[44]

Challenging rather than finessing the view of people of color as "non-historical" that had predominated in the theorizing of the SPA, Toomer appeared to be conversant with the emergent movement of left-led anticolonial rebellion that was arousing fears of a "rising tide of color" among defenders of the global status quo but gaining increasing attention in the discourse of the black left. Despite his skepticism about the ability of U.S. Socialists to give the requisite antiracist leadership, Domingo exulted, "Millions of oppressed people are flocking to the banner of international socialism. . . . [E]very oppressed group of the world is

today turning from Clemenceau, Lloyd George and Wilson to the citadel of Socialism, Moscow." The *Crusader*, published by the African Blood Brotherhood
(ABB), offered an ongoing analysis of the significance of the postwar upsurge of
colonized peoples. While the ABB initially espoused an Afrocentrist worldview
and kept its distance from a politics of class struggle, by 1921 it was firmly in
the Leninist camp. Praising the Soviet Union for its support of movements for
self-determination and its relinquishment of the Czarist claims of the Russian
empire, the *Crusader* condemned imperialism as "the child and protégé of capitalism" and held up socialism as "the antithesis to capitalism and the destroyer
of imperialism." While noting the repression of radicals and rebels in the United
States, the editors wrote, "Bolshevism in its international phase is feared by the
capitalist-imperialist powers even more than they fear Bolshevism in its domestic
operations." The "rising wave" of "political awakening" was sweeping over the
"colored races of the world," from the demand for "complete autonomy" in Egypt
and India to uprisings in "Negro America, West Indies, West Africa, Persia, Af-
ghanistan, Mesopotamia, Syria, Morocco, and Native South Africa." Conjoining
the tropes of rising waters and revolutionary fires, the *Crusader* house poet Ben
Burrell wrote of "The Coming Conflict,"

> I should not sing of war, but yet I hear
> From the Far East, the Darker Races come
> . . . . I see them swarm the mountains, range on range,
> A hurricane of war, a flaming tide.[45]

In addition to its passionate antiracism, this anticolonial discourse drew on
contemporaneous developments in political practice and anthropological theory.
The agrarian aspirations of the short-lived Hungarian Soviet Republic—which
took steps to move directly toward the collectivization of agriculture, bypassing
the stage of distributing private plots of land—repudiated myths about the intrin-
sically backward nature of the peasantry. As the Hungarian Communist leader
Béla Kun noted in a 1920 interview in the *Liberator*, "We proved the possibility
of conserving large-scale agricultural production, along with expropriation. The
conception of the 'anti-collectivist mind of the peasant' was thus relegated to the
realm of Kautskyite fiction." The establishment of socialism in the largely agricultural Soviet Union, moreover, confirmed that, as Melville Herskovits observed,
"it is nothing short of fantastic to talk of the predetermined failure of the Russian
revolution because Russia skipped a step in the fixed economic development of
nations." In the light of recent work in anthropology, he went on, "Our greater
understanding of the organisation, industry and ideas of primitive communities,
makes it difficult to speak of 'stages' of development, of 'higher' or 'lower' cultures.
The biological unity of the human race, the equal potentialities of racial groups,
stands out sharply." Applying such arguments to their analysis of Africa, the *Cru-*

sader editors condemned not only the colonial oppression of the imperialists but also the Socialists' accession to the "destruction of African institutions and assent to the conversion of African cultivators and farmers into wage-slaves . . . content with the thought that in the fullness of time the wage-slaves would themselves evolve the Socialist African State." They quoted from E. D. Morel's recently published *The Black Man's Burden* (1920): "The form of Socialism which Russia has evolved . . . approximates closely to the social conditions of an advanced tropical African community. . . . The corporate character which the Soviet system imparts to all economic activities is substantially identical with the African social system. It seems a strange anomaly to laud advanced Socialism in Europe, and to assent to its destruction in Tropical Africa." In the crucible of 1919, uneven geographical development did not prevent revolutionaries from viewing the world as a unified system; indeed, it permitted them to glimpse the seeds of the future in the past and the present.[46]

Toomer's aligning of the "world upheaval" with the "subconscious penetration of the conscious mind" could be read as a primitivist equation of the dark-skinned masses with a global Id, rising up against the Superego of the West. But we should recall Toomer's earlier association of his own "repressed" racial identity with his former class-based "aloofness" in his August 1922 letter to the *Liberator*. His linking of a black- and brown-led "proletariat or world upheaval" with the intrusion of the "subconscious" into the "conscious mind" suggests that he is paralleling psychic transformation with world-historical movements for liberation rather than simply rendering them equivalent to one another. Although his formulation is rudimentary, it is of no small significance that Toomer described the global proletariat's coming liberation from capitalism by means of a metaphor that connects social revolution with the liberation of repressed impulses and desires, and that both modes of liberation are portrayed through metaphorical equation with an earthquake. Literature—in the form of his projected novel—is envisioned as playing a vital role in both representing and emancipating the political unconscious.[47]

Toomer never wrote the novel he sketched to Liveright and Frank in early 1923; the considerably more detailed outline he produced a few months later would gesture toward the "universal" but remain largely anchored to concerns confined to the U.S. context. Nonetheless, his stated plan to write about "the proletariat or world upheaval" even before he had put the finishing touches on the manuscript of *Cane* suggests that the consciousness that produced his 1923 masterwork was continuing to contend actively with the political passions accompanying his awakening to the "need for socialism" some seven years before. However buried under the banked coal of the postwar United States, these passions remained alive, waiting to "flicker up" should there be a rising of the global tide. The mixing of metaphors here—intentional on my part—anticipates some of the key tropes of *Cane*.[48]

"The whole place is surrounded":
Class as Conscience in Toomer's Later Writings

Traces of Toomer's early class-conscious radicalism would continue to manifest themselves, if sporadically, in later years. Even as he deepened his involvement with the Gurdjieff movement, Toomer remained drawn to a class analysis of the roots of racism. In his 1929 article "Race Problems in Modern Society," he maintained that "whenever two or more races (or nationalities) meet in conditions that are mainly determined by acquisitive interests, race problems arise as by products [sic] of economic issues. The desire for land, the wish to exploit natural resources, the wish for cheap labor—wherever these motives have dominated a situation involving different races, whether the races are set in rivalry, or with one dominant and the other dominated, race problems also have sprung up." The Soviet Union is free from the "race problems" besetting most of the globe, he argued, because "the economic and political causes of race problems either no longer exist or are being removed, the minority races and peoples being guaranteed similar rights, the children of all peoples being taught that all races are similar." In this essay, Toomer explores the notion of "racial stock" from a eugenicist standpoint, arguing that only racial amalgamation, of the "best" elements of all racial groups, would put an end to racial hierarchy and conflict; this was hardly a revolutionary proposition. In its tribute to the USSR as a site where the problem of racial division had been resolved, however, the essay clearly endorses the view he had asserted in his discussion of the postwar race riots a decade before: that capitalism is the source of racism, and socialism its cure.[49]

Elements of a class analysis of the causes and consequences of racism occasionally crept into other Gurdjieff-era writings. In a discussion of "psychic binding," for example, Toomer wrote,

> Negro and white or whoever is so held, both feel that they are being held to their detriment. Both feel the damaging effects of the binding force. But neither, of course, understand [sic] that it is precisely a force that is holding them. Therefore they do not and indeed cannot truly get together to overcome their common enemy. No, each separatistically blames the other. . . . You cannot resolve the problems of separation by operating within the force of separatism. Nor can you genuinely break from slavery by opposing people who are as much its victims as you yourself are.
> Oppose the force, not the man.

Toomer's terminology here draws primarily on the discourse of humanism; the source of the "force" producing "slavery" is not specified in political economy. In both substance and rhetoric, however, the statement that Negro and white need to "get together to overcome their common enemy" indicates the continuing impact of Marxist categories of analysis.[50]

Toomer's view of the role of the artist in society remained deeply ambivalent. No longer so eager for the walls of capitalism to collapse or for the "genius" to have an "immediate social function," in the mid-1930s he expressed distaste at the prospect of submitting to the discipline of a workers' state. "I would consider it as unfortunately [*sic*] and enslaving," he wrote, "to be dictated to by a proletarian as by a policeman or a top sergeant or an old fashioned tyrant of a monarch." No longer so ready to endorse the use of force against the "governing class," he stated, "I am not a revolutionary, at least not in the physical force meaning of this term. I am a spiritual revolutionary. I believe, not in class-consciousness, but in *conscience* as the true constructive lever of human behavior. I am of and for mankind as a whole. My position is not one of class but of humanity."

As fascism threatened and the class struggle sharpened in the mid-1930s, however, Toomer predicted

> [a] moral as well as an economic collapse of "the system." A world that you and I have known and lived in is evidently decadent. Its culture is running down to the level of sensationalism. Its education is a trap. Its institutions are asylums.
>
> There are moral individuals in all classes and groups; but the only social body that manifests morality is the body of the workers.
>
> I see embattled nations and classes, a riot or near riot of passions malicious, revengeful, as destructive as holocausts. A mass-meeting of the vicious calling themselves ideal, evangelic, heroic. A parade of destruction masquerading as salvation. . . . The workers press and organize under stronger repressive measures by the bosses. Strikes are larger and more frequent. A riot in Harlem, a riot in Gallup, New Mexico, riots here and there all over the country, symptomatic of the dynamite coming to explosion among all the unemployed and destitute everywhere. Certain aspects of 1917 are about to be repeated. A recurrence of the gag-measures in force during the late war.

Noting that the movement was moving past a "working class snobbery which would view me as a bourgeois intellectual," he heralded "leaders within the working class movement [who] . . . are opening the way for fruitful contact between the workers and people like myself." In this context, "It is not necessary that we become Marxian or communists [but] it is necessary that we understand what Marxism and communism is about." Invoking the trope of birthing that had figured centrally in *Cane*, Toomer continued, "It is necessary that we see the life struggling to birth under the leadership of communism." Even as he continued to proclaim the need for "spiritual revolution," Toomer evidently viewed capitalism as a failed system. His foregrounding of the riots in Harlem and Gallup, as well as his mention of "gag-measures," reveal his abiding concern with antiracist resistance and state repression. It would appear that Toomer had not abandoned his conclusion on leaving the shipyard in early 1920: "I realized as never before the *need* of socialism, the *need* of a radical change of the conditions of human society."[51]

The working-class spectre haunting Toomer's conscience also made its way into his dreams. In 1949–50, Toomer underwent a period of psychoanalysis during which, as an obedient Jungian analysand, he transcribed his dreams on awaking. Toomer's by then well-established practice of racial passing was the principal zone of repression that his therapy addressed. One dream, however, reveals Toomer's ongoing anxieties about his class identification and allegiance. He recalls:

> I am on the ground floor of a large modern plant or factory that employs many people. Some few of the employees are in the building, but most are outside. I learn that those outside are on strike, and may make a violent mass-attack on the building. I see some of the inside men quickly closing doors to make it more difficult for the angry strikers to break in.
>
> It would seem that I neither own this factory nor am employed in it; yet the very fact that I am within the building groups me with the inside people and would subject me to violence should the strikers storm the place and force entrance. . . . Though I personally am not at odds with the strikers, nor they with me personally, I feel threatened by them because of my position which associates me with those against whom the strikers have a grievance.
>
> I see one of the inside men (he could be the owner) going towards a door as if he does not know that the mob may storm the building any minute. I warn him of the danger, and he keeps inside of the closed doors. I chance to glance out of a window and see a crowd of strikers milling through a nearby alley. The whole place, then, is surrounded. I quickly draw back from the window so as not to be seen by them. There is no doubt that those people are swayed by man-motion; yet their faces, instead of looking angry and vicious, are rather bright and smiling. Even so, I have already been so conditioned that I fear being seen by them; for, if seen, they might single me out as a special object of attack.[52]

These workers are not bellowing "We Want Power," yet the class struggle abides: Toomer fears a "violent mass attack." His class affiliation—or at least class position—has shifted; even though he is "personally not at odds with the strikers," he is in the company of the "inside men" of the owning class. His anxiety, it would seem, stems not only from his perception of the threat posed by the striking workers' militancy, but also from his guilt at having betrayed their cause; it is he who warns the boss of their possible attack. That their faces are in fact "bright and smiling" only increases his felt complicity in their exploitation. Displaying the continuing impact of Toomer's leftist conscience, this dream narrative suggestively links the repression of personal anxieties with the repression of insurgent social movements. The unconscious of Toomer's texts, it would appear, is "political" in a number of registers.

CHAPTER 2

The Tight Cocoon
Class, Culture, and the New Negro

Be still, be still, my precious child
I must not give you birth!
—Georgia Douglas Johnson, "Maternity" (1922)

[W]ith the Negro's emergence into self-knowledge is the discovery of the
falsity of his former illusion that the white American is actually free.
—Jean Toomer, "The Negro Emergent" (1925)

It has often been argued that Jean Toomer found his Negro identity in *Cane* only
to lose it soon thereafter. He was presumably dismayed by Horace Liveright's
decision to "feature Negro" in the publicity for *Cane*; distressed at Waldo Frank's
identifying Toomer as a Negro in his preface to *Cane*; and furious when Alain
Locke included in *The New Negro: An Interpretation* (1925) some of the sketches
and poems from *Cane* without Toomer's permission, thereby affirming Toomer's
public persona as a person of African descent at a time when Toomer was in
rapid retreat from self-identification as a black man. Some commentators have
viewed these reactions as links in a long chain of denials of African American
ancestry that would eventually result in Toomer's moving over the color line.
Others have argued that, as a member of Washington's "blue-veined" elite—and
sufficiently light-skinned to have "passed" since his youth—he had never felt
black in the first place; his post-*Cane* movement away from self-identification as
a Negro was a return to a previous norm. Still others, viewing Toomer as a racial
deconstructionist *avant la lettre*, have highlighted his increasing frustration
with friends and colleagues, black and white alike, who were proving unable to
comprehend his attempted formulation of an "American race" that would transcend inherited racial classifications altogether. Critics generally agree that the
ossifying racial dualisms of the 1920s compounded Toomer's dilemma: he was
seeking to reformulate race and evade racial binarism precisely at a time when
reinforcement of the color line was becoming a national obsession. Whether
adjudged tragic, opportunistic, or heroic, however, Toomer has been routinely

viewed as a reluctant recruit to the New Negro cultural movement of which he has been viewed, in paradoxical retrospect, as the first significant participant.[1]

I argue here that Toomer's racial self-identification during the *Cane* period was not nearly as problematic as has often been proposed. It is clear that, even before he entered into the period of intense activity that produced *Cane*, he had been attracted to the project of positing a composite "American race" that would supply an identity beyond dualism and biological essentialism. His life in Washington and various northern cities had also sheltered him from the grittier aspects of African American life. When he traveled into the Deep South in 1921 and discovered an unexpected sense of kinship with its dark-skinned peasantry, however, he was by no means wholly unprepared for the experience. Not only had his exposure to the Socialist analysis of racism furnished him with a theoretical framework within which to situate his perceptions of Georgia's peasantry. In addition, as a youth he had lived in a Negro neighborhood and attended all-black schools; as an adult, he had experienced interchanges with members of Washington's Negro intelligentsia who not only shared his interest in the sociology of race but also had ties with the left. It was primarily in correspondence with white writers and editors that Toomer stressed his chameleonlike ability to move between and among racial groups. But when he lived among African Americans—of whatever hue—Toomer did not equivocate about his membership in the group. During the *Cane* years, Toomer was a New Negro, albeit one striving to define that identity on his own terms.[2]

As with Toomer's connection with American socialism, it is important to read forward through Toomer's life and writing if we wish to ascertain with some accuracy his relationship to the New Negro Movement. Too often critics have imposed on the Toomer who wrote *Cane* the Toomer they discerned in later years—whether race traitor, proto-deconstructionist, or mystic seeking psychic wholeness. I situate Toomer's ideas about race and racial identity in the matrix of the postwar debate over the New Negro. As has been widely acknowledged, the New Negro, originally identified as a Marxist militant, gradually devolved into the culture-making hero of the New Negro Renaissance celebrated in Alain Locke's 1925 anthology; the term New Negro was a highly protean ideologeme, signaling contradictory and conflicting paradigms and programs for addressing the realities of American racism. While he is generally viewed as engaged with the less political features of the movement that would come to be known as the Harlem Renaissance, I propose that Toomer to no small degree linked his self-identification as a Negro—a *New* Negro—to his hopes for revolutionary social transformation. That this self-identification persisted for some time after the publication of *Cane* indicates the intensity with which those hopes had been held. His eventual relinquishment of this self-identification testifies not so much to the appeal of whiteness as to the intractability of American racism and the arrested dialectic of the class struggle.[3]

"The matter of race and the race problem in America": The "Mixed-Blood" Discussion Group

The full extent of Toomer's interactions with the New Negroes of Washington during the *Cane* period remains underappreciated largely because Toomer himself downplayed the importance of these ties, both at the time and in retrospect. Writing to Claude McKay from Washington in the summer of 1922, Toomer noted the "complacency" and—in a telling phrase—the "tragic consequences of spiritual abortion" of his circle of acquaintance. In letters to his mostly New York–based white male modernist friends, Toomer continually stressed the limitations of his environment. Toomer's autobiographical writings either minimize his Washington connections or to efface them entirely. The 1931 text, dubbing 1920–22 the "terrible years," gives the distinct impression that Toomer went through his period of writerly apprenticeship in near-complete intellectual isolation. Implying that he dwelled among philistines, Toomer wrote that his preoccupation with writing led "[p]eople around [to] wonde[r] what I was doing. They said things. . . . Once or twice I let fly. I got the reputation of being a very queer fellow." Although "[o]ne or two other people of my own age came in to see me," Toomer's only sustained contact was, he maintains, with his old friend Henry Kennedy ("Ken"), who "alone was with me. . . . Two or three people of my own age came in to see me. I met a sculptress, and she did a bust of me." Toomer details his research and reading—into Buddhism and other "occult" philosophies; modern literature; "the matter of race and the race problem in America"—but invites his reader to conclude that these were all solitary undertakings. For all intents and purposes, the 1931 autobiography portrays *Cane* as the outcome of white literary influences.[4]

The evidence revealing Toomer's quite substantial connections with a network of Washington, DC–based African Americans in the early 1920s offers quite a different portrait of the artist as a young man. In a January 1921 letter to Alain Locke, Toomer describes a discussion group that he has recently launched: "I have managed to hold two meetings of a group (Mary Burrill, Georgia Johnson, Miss Scott [of Howard], Mary Craft, E. C. Williams, Henry Kennedy, and myself) whose central purpose is an historical study of slavery and the Negro, emphasizing the great economic and cultural forces which have largely determined them. The aim is twofold, first, to arrive at a sound and just criticism of the actual place and condition of the mixed-blood group in this country, and, second, to formulate an ideal that will be both workable and inclusive." Noting that the group would be "cemented" by "a knowledge [and] certain fundamental facts we have in common," Toomer proclaims his leadership role ("I tried my best to throw a little fire in their hearts") and lists the current readings: T. R. R. Cobb's 1858 *An Historical Sketch of Slavery*; a book by "Wells" (most likely H. G. Wells's 1920 *The Outline of History*); and Theodore Canot's 1854 *Twenty Years of an African Slaver*. A "natural outgrowth" of the group's discussions, writes

Toomer, will be "the reading of original efforts." This group would function both as a study seminar and as a writers' workshop.[5]

This letter shows Toomer in dialogue with a multigenerational group, many of whose members were affiliated with either Howard University or Dunbar (formerly the M Street) High School: Mary Burrill, playwright and Dunbar High School drama director; Georgia Douglas Johnson, published poet and wife of Henry Lincoln Johnson, recorder of deeds; Clarissa Scott, poet and daughter of Emmett Scott, the former Booker T. Washington secretary, Howard University administrator, wartime special assistant to the secretary of war, and producer of *Birth of a Race*, the first black cinematic response to *The Birth of a Nation*; Mary Craft, granddaughter of the fugitive slaves and abolitionists Ellen and William Craft; E. [Edmund] C. Williams, Howard University librarian, former Dunbar teacher and principal, and son-in-law of Charles Chesnutt; and Ken. Drawing on some of the notable intellectual elements in Washington's Negro aristocracy, the meeting involved, significantly, more women than men.[6]

Given that most of the participants in the discussion group were of mixed-race background, one of the group's purposes was evidently to analyze the members' common status and experience. Toomer's reference to the group's being "cemented by a knowledge . . . and certain fundamental facts we have in common," as well as his call for an understanding of "the actual place and condition of the mixed-blood group in this country," implies that this group has a distinct social identity. But his declaration that the discussions would undertake a "sound and just criticism" of the "actual" status of the "mixed-blood group," with the goal of formulating an "ideal" at once "workable and inclusive," suggests an intention more interrogative than affirmative. "Workable" implies an accession to pragmatism: the "mixed-blood group" may need to have its distinct identity acknowledged. "Inclusive," however, especially in connection with "sound and just criticism," suggests that the "mixed-blood group" may need to break out of its isolation and acknowledge its oneness with the larger population possessing African ancestry.[7]

The texts Toomer proposed for study further indicate his investigative intentions. At a time when the *Crisis*, in its monthly list of suggested readings, was regularly calling attention to a wide range of books dealing with "slavery and the Negro," Toomer proposed a somewhat anomalous place to start. Wells's *The Outline of History*, while providing a grand historical overview, would be roundly drubbed by Negro reviewers for its distorted portrayal of people of African origin. Cobb's antebellum tract deploys biblical scripture and racist pseudoscience to affirm the slaveholding standpoint that "there is nothing in [the African Negro's] enslavement contrary to the law of his nature." The French sea-captain Theodore Canot's 1854 account of his slave-catching adventures contains lively descriptions of traditional African societies, but its white supremacist perspective is unqueried. Surely, if the discussion group's aim was to explore work on the cutting edge of scholarship on the Negro, this need could have been better served by any number of texts currently recommended in the *Crisis*: W. E. B. Du Bois's *The Negro* (1915) or *Darkwater* (1920); Carter Woodson's *A Century of Negro Migration* (1918); George W. Ellis's *Negro Culture in West Africa* (1914); Benjamin Brawley's *The Negro in Literature and Art in the United States* (1918); Leila Amos Pendleton's *A Narrative of the Negro* (1912); Herbert Seligmann's *The Negro Faces America* (1920).[8]

Toomer's formulation of the group's goal and agenda emphasized that the present-day status and role of the "mixed-blood group" would be explored in causal context: "an historical study of slavery and the Negro, emphasizing the great economic and cultural forces which have largely determined them." In this inquiry, the texts of Wells, Cobb and Canot presumably functioned as both secondary and primary sources, supplying not only historical information but also insight into the ideological coding of that information. Notably, both "slavery" and "the Negro" were envisioned as products of "forces." As in his 1919 *New York Call* essay "Reflections on the Race Riots"—where he had proposed that "racial differences" are both the effect and the cause of racial violence—Toomer here treats "the Negro" as coterminous with "slavery." Implied in the group's research agenda is a social constructionist approach to race based in historical materialism. The Toomer who had recently been publishing in the New York Socialist press had not relinquished his Marxist proclivities when he organized the Washington study group.

"A tiny unborn child, its head crushed in by a deliberate heel": Toomer and the Women of Washington

While Toomer would efface African American women from his autobiographical reflections on his literary apprenticeship, he in fact relied for support on a circle of women he had known since his youth—not just for emotional sustenance, but also for literary commentary, political discussion, and practical assistance in getting his work published. Jessie Redmon Fauset, literary editor of the *Crisis* from 1919 to 1926, had been Toomer's English teacher during his years at the M Street High School. Although she was based in New York while the writers' group was meeting, she maintained a correspondence with Georgia Douglas Johnson; it was to Fauset that Toomer sent a packet of his writings in early 1922. Her response—addressed to "Dear Jean"—was at once encouraging and patronizing. "It gives me a great deal of pleasure to talk to you about your work," she wrote. "I read the play and the poems and the little African folk tale. It seems to me that you have accomplished something of what you were hoping to achieve, that is, a depicting of the life of the Negro peasantry and also of the beauty, despite its pain, of our past." Remarking that she was "particularly impressed" with "Song of the Son," she asked, "Where did you get a chance to work out your technique? . . . You must have studied and practiced to achieve it." Expressing her dislike of "the modern tendency . . . toward an involving of ideas . . . a sort of immeshing [sic] the kernel of thought in envelopes of words,"

Fauset hoped "you will not fall too deeply into it"; she suggested that he read Walter Pater, as well as the French imagists in the original. But she affirmed that reading Toomer's work had "vividly . . . renewed my interest in you. When I see anybody with creative ability budding so strongly as I see you I feel as though I should like to assist in putting the world at his feet." Returning "the long poem," Fauset kept the other pieces, which she "hope[d] to publish from time to time." Aware that Toomer might be in need of financial support, she recommended that he try his hand at journalism, noting that he had "personality and no prejudicing appearances"—clear advice that he "pass" displaying quite a casual attitude toward the practice that she would treat with considerably more harshness in *Plum Bun* a few years later. Fauset closed the letter by asking Toomer to "[c]all Georgie [Georgia Douglas Johnson] and give her my love," signing off, "Sincerely, Jessie." Toomer was evidently on close personal terms with the literary editor of the premier African American journal of the day.[9]

Toomer no doubt bristled at Fauset's warning that he follow the creed of Pater and avoid experimental modernism; when Mary Burrill offered similar counsel a few months later, in reaction to his prose poem "Seventh Street," he nearly exploded. It is evident, however, that the literary editor of the *Crisis*, having known Toomer for many years, was eager to advance his writing career. It is also evident that Toomer envisioned the *Crisis* as a desirable venue for his work, since he sent Fauset a swath of writings: "The First American" (the "long poem"), "Balo" (the "play"), a number of shorter poems (among these "Banking Coal" and "Song of the Son"), and possibly the tale of Coomba and Ali from *Natalie Mann* ("the little African tale"). "Song of the Son," which appeared in the April 1922 issue of the NAACP's principal organ, was the first of *Cane*'s pieces to see publication. The poem unambiguously situates its author as a Negro and invokes the conventions of the narrative of racial return to the homeland. That Fauset should have expressed her admiration for the poem in the same letter where she suggested that he "pass" speaks volumes about the ease with which professions of racial belonging could coexist with pragmatic disavowals of Negro identity.

Although Fauset directly facilitated Toomer's becoming a published writer, among the Washington women it was Georgia Douglas Johnson who figured most prominently in his development. Apparently well-acquainted with Johnson before his December 1919 foray into the shipyard, Toomer wrote Johnson several letters seeking support for his somewhat fragile ego during his subsequent lonely attempt to break into the New York literary scene. Describing an encounter with Du Bois at the *Crisis*—where Toomer evidently had hoped for a warm reception—he shared with Johnson his disappointment at the older man's evident lack of interest in his young visitor's writerly ambitions. "I had thought he wanted to get in touch with me, even possibly to know me," complained Toomer. "Does he expect to do so by looking at my writings? . . . It will be some years before Jean Toomer the thinker, the feeler, the man in love with life in toto, passions, vices, sorrows, despairs—all of life, will be able to put half what is in him on the cool surface of a piece of paper." Toomer boasted to Johnson of having met "mostly modern poets and writers" and shared his regret that the *Liberator* editors Max Eastman and "F.D." (Floyd Dell) were not among these. He sent along drafts of poems, and proclaimed how much he had grown:

> My responses to the great and beautiful are now so keen and poignant that the feeble sensitivity of my former self seems as but faint currents in a body half alive.
>
> Among other things, I have tested for myself the salutary effects of comparative poverty and privation. I now say, for myself at least, that such things only dwarf the soul, weaken the body, dull the mind and prohibit fruitful activity. . . . I must agree with Bernard Shaw when saying that poverty is the gravest social evil.

Noting that he had stopped asking his grandfather for money, Toomer related his unsuccessful attempt to secure financial support from "a man of means . . . supposed to be kindly disposed toward men of talent. . . . What little I have done and my personality were not sufficient to convince him that a loan of $5000 would be a good investment." Johnson would presumably agree that both Du Bois and this unnamed "man of means" were seriously in error in failing to recognize Toomer's budding—if thus far unrealized—genius. Given Toomer's evident reliance on Johnson for support of all kinds, his routine put-down of her to his New York friends smacks of both hypocrisy and ingratitude.[10]

The woman who received and responded to these sophomoric missives was at once a published poet and a member of the capital city's "Negro Four Hundred." Her *The Heart of a Woman* had appeared in 1918; she was on the verge of publishing *Bronze* (1922) and would in coming years publish two more volumes of poetry and write as many as forty plays, several of these addressing the topic of lynching. After the 1925 death of her husband, the recorder of deeds Henry Lincoln Johnson, Johnson's "Saturday Nights" would soon become Washington's favored salon for Negro artists and intellectuals. Johnson also had more than incidental ties with the New York–based left. She published several poems in the *Liberator*, and it was evidently she who urged Toomer to contact Eastman and Dell. Sixteen of her poems were published in the *Crisis*; an equal number appeared in the *Messenger*. Johnson's career illustrates the difficulty of setting up absolute distinctions between Old and New Negroes.[11]

The poems contained in *Bronze* (1922)—a number of which she presumably discussed with her fellow-writers—blend conventional themes of uplift with expressions of political radicalism; drafts of these poems were her contributions to the regular meetings of the "mixed-blood" discussion group. The book's foreword reads: "This book is the child of a bitter earth-wound. . . . Yet, fully conscious of the potent agencies that silently work in their healing ministries, I know that God's sun shall one day shine upon a perfected and unhampered people." That these "potent agencies" would entail more than patient evolutionism is suggested in "To John Brown," where the speaker assures the abolitionist that "time still burgeoneth . . . the seed you spread / In terror's morning, flung with fingers red /

In blood of tyrants." At a time when conservatives fearful of the wave of postwar militancy were proposing that Harpers Ferry be the site of a monument dedicated to Heyward Shepherd—a free African American who was the first person killed by the raiders in 1859—Johnson's poem reaffirmed the legacy of radical antiracism. And at a time when Thomas Dixon's vicious portraiture of Brown as a bloodthirsty fanatic was gaining popular currency in *The Man in Gray*, Johnson's tribute stipulated that the "blood of tyrants" had to be shed if the "seed" of emancipation were to find root and bear fruit.[12]

The project of defining the peculiar status and situation of "mixed-blood" people entailed, for Johnson, a rejection of both pseudoscientific doctrines about the neurotic frailty of mulattoes and nativist proclamations of their non-belonging in the nation's body politic. In "The Octoroon"—which first appeared in the *Liberator* in August 1919—Johnson presents a pitying depiction of a speaker who, in the tradition of the tragic mulatto, bemoans the "man-wrought bars of her captivity"—a phrasing echoing William Blake's critique of the "mind-forged manacles" of dominant ideology in "London." In "Cosmopolite," by contrast, Johnson's self-confident speaker proclaims that although she is "of "alien bloods," the "product of . . . [the] interplay / Of traveled hearts," she is "[e]stranged, yet not estranged." Specially positioned as a "[s]cion of fused strength" to view "earth's frail dilemma," she concludes with an echo of Whitman: "Nor this nor that / Contains me." In "Fusion," the speaker declares that, like a grafted hybrid, she is "more gorgeous and more beautiful / Than any parent portion." Indeed, she can "trace within my warring blood / The tributary sources" which "potently commingle / And sweep / With new-born forces!" Rather than constituting a debilitating split in the self, her "warring blood" gives her added strength and enables her to "commingle" with "new-born forces" beyond the self—perhaps the revolutionary historical subjects emerging from the upsurge of 1919. Challenging the prevailing nativist trope of the "rising tide of color," which conjoined racism with anticommunism on a global scale, the metaphor of rushing waters affirms a cosmopolitanism that is at once biological and political.[13]

While Johnson's poems centering on racial hybridity voice a defiance of racist pseudoscience, *Bronze* also contains a cluster of "Motherhood" poems that feature prominently the issues of infanticide and abortion. In "Maternity," the speaker contemplates the "mezzotint" of her baby and ponders his possible death:

> Is he not thrall to prevalent conditions?
> Does not the day loom dark apace
> To weave its cordon of disgrace
> Around his lifted throat?

She laments, "Ah, did I dare / Recall the pulsing life I gave, / And fold him in the kindly grave!" While it is unclear whether the infant's "mezzotint" refers to the child's having been fathered by a white man or to its inheritance of mixed-race status from both parents, it is evident that his birth prompts not a defiant celebration of racial mingling—as in "Fusion" and "Cosmopolite"—but a recognition that, as a "babe of sorrow," he carries the mark of doom. An embodiment of the Black Madonna, the speaker projects the Pietà, the Mater Dolorosa, back onto the joyful virgin mother of the Nativity. In "Black Woman," the pregnant speaker appears determined to prevent her child—who "do[es] not know the monster-men / Inhabiting the earth"—from being born at all. "Be still, be still, my precious child," she laments. "I must not give you birth!" The threat posed by "the monster-men of earth"—of lynching if the baby is male, of rape if it is female—compels the mother to contemplate ending the child's life before it begins. In the section of the volume devoted to motherhood, the fruit of the "burgeoning seed" is less likely to produce revolution, and more likely to pay the price for being black—or "bronze"—in America.[14]

The themes of militant resistance and ambivalent maternity were taken up by other women in Toomer's literary circle in Washington. The poet and playwright Mary Burrill—who, like Fauset, knew Toomer from her years teaching and coaching drama at the M Street High School—published several pieces in the organs of the left. In December 1918 there appeared in the *Liberator* Burrill's poem "To a Black Soldier Fallen in War," in which the speaker ironically interrogates the rhetoric of patriotism, exclaiming,

> O questioning Heart, be silent,
> Allay the bitter cry—
> "Why should he thus perish?
> Why, for freedom, die?"

Published alongside a journalistic account of the police murder of an antiwar protestor, the poem contributed an African American voice to the magazine's harsh critique of war propaganda and government repression. "Aftermath," a one-act drama set in the South that appeared in the April 1919 issue, offers an unequivocal portrait of the New Negro as uncompromising militant. The protagonist, John Thornton, returns from the war to learn that his father has just been lynched for daring to challenge a plantation owner over the price of cotton. Brandishing his army pistol, he exclaims, "Ef I kin be trusted with a gun in France, I kin be trusted with one in South Car'lina." He rushes out into the "gathering darkness" to certain death, crying, "This ain't no time fu' preachers or prayers! You mean to tell me I mus' let them w'ite devils send me miles erway to suffer an' be shot up fu' the freedom of people I ain't nevah seen, while they're burnin' and killin' my folks here at home! To Hell with 'em!"[15]

While the pieces she published in the *Liberator* stressed the situation of the black soldier, Burrill examined the condition of rural African American women in "They That Sit in Darkness," a one-act play appearing in a special 1919 issue of the *Birth Control Review* devoted to Negro women. Edited by the Socialists Mary Knoblauch and Margaret Sanger and subtitled "Dedicated to Voluntary Motherhood," the magazine praised the "Soviets' care of the mother" and championed women's reproductive rights from a working-class perspective. Depicting the destructive effects of multiple pregnancies and childbearing on Malinda Jasper, a mother who dies from overwork and inadequate medical care, Burrill's play explicitly calls for poor women's access to birth control. Her choice of a title for her play suggests a connection with revolution. For the biblical phrase "They That Sit in Darkness"—derived from Jesus's call to "preach deliverance to the Slaves; to give Light to Them That Sit in Darkness"—had been taken over by W. A. Domingo and placed on the masthead of his revolutionary journal, the *Emancipator*. In its portrayal of Elizabeth Shaw, a well-intentioned white social worker who fails to grasp the desperation of Jasper's situation, the play contains an implied critique of middle-class feminism. By featuring a married woman in desperate need of contraception, moreover, the play substantially contradicts the special issue's somewhat prudish prefatory note, which links poverty and unwanted pregnancy with extramarital sexual activity: "Promiscuous sexual relationships and loose morals are an inevitable consequence of the herding of one or more families in homes of two or three rooms, whether in the South or in the North." In its unremitting emphasis on the systemic pressures on rural black women, Burrill's play portrays self-determining motherhood as integral to the project of working-class emancipation.[16]

Although there is no direct record of a relationship between Toomer and Angelina Grimké, they likely knew one another from Toomer's youth onward, since Grimké, like Burrill and Fauset, taught at the M Street High School when Toomer was a student there. Grimké was, moreover, a close friend of Georgia Douglas Johnson and a participant in her Saturday Night salons. Granddaughter of the famous white abolitionist Angelina Weld Grimké; niece of the Fifteenth Street Presbyterian Church minister Francis Grimké, who had succeeded the abolitionist Henry Highland Garnet as church pastor (and, in 1894, had officiated at the marriage of Toomer's parents); daughter of the former NAACP local chapter leader and poet Archibald Grimké: the poet, playwright and short story writer Angelina Grimké was at once a member of Washington's "Negro Four Hundred" and a feminist, political radical, and, most likely, a closeted lesbian. The correspondence in her papers indicates that she was on friendly terms with a number of prominent African American artists and intellectuals—not only Johnson but also Alain Locke, Emmett Scott, the Howard Players director Montgomery Gregory, the poet Carrie Clifford, and the sculptor Meta Vaux Warrick Fuller. Grimké was a stockholder in the *Liberator*, where she corresponded with Crystal Eastman, Max Eastman, and Robert Minor. She cultivated other ties on the left: Margaret Sanger and Mary Knoblauch of the *Birth Control Review*; the radical feminist journalist Agnes Smedley; the Communist short-story writer Gertrude Nafe; and the NAACP activist and fiction writer Lillie Buffum Chace Wyman. In December 1919 Grimké wrote to the *Messenger* in praise of its "utter fearlessness and utter courage."[17]

A dominant preoccupation in Grimké's fictional and dramatic writings, as in those of Johnson and Burrill, is the impact of racial violence on families, and especially women. Grimké's eponymous play *Rachel* treats a young woman who, learning of her father's and stepbrother's lynchings some years earlier, and witnessing directly the psychic destruction wrought by Jim Crow in children's lives, decides never to marry or bear children. "The Closing Door"—a short story appearing in the same special issue of the *Birth Control Review* as Burrill's "They That Sit in Darkness"—describes an African American woman who, learning of her brother's lynching, strangles her newborn male child rather than have him meet a similar fate. Grimké was also drawn to the representation of women who are themselves the victims of racial violence. Her short story "Goldie"—which appeared in the *Birth Control Review* in the fall of 1920—is a phantasmagoric account of a brother's return to the South, to find the bodies of his sister and her husband swinging from trees; "underneath those two terribly mutilated swinging bodies, lay a tiny unborn child, its head crushed in by a deliberate heel." Clearly haunted by the challenge of representing this grotesque version of the Holy Family, Grimké continually reworked this material in various drafts under various titles.[18]

Grimké's preoccupation with the figure of the lynched and violated African American mother was not based in invention. For Goldie's historical prototype was in fact the pregnant Mary Turner, who in 1918 had her unborn child sliced from her belly and ground underfoot as she was hanged and shot full of bullets for protesting the mob lynching of her husband. Widely disseminated even in the mainstream press as testament to the horrors of southern violence, and held up in the left and African American press as an exemplification of American racial terrorism, the story and image of Mary Turner inspired numerous artistic representations. The clubwoman and NAACP activist Carrie Clifford, a friend of Johnson and Locke, wrote an elegy titled "Little Mother (Upon the Lynching of Mary Turner)." Anne Spencer's "White Things," also based on the death of Mary Turner and her child, appeared in the *Crisis* in 1923. Meta Fuller crafted a model statue titled "Mary Turner: A Silent Protest against Mob Violence," depicting Turner as sheltering her already-born infant in a close embrace; the statue contains at its bottom the lynchers' grotesque faces and grasping hands reaching upward toward the mother and child. While these representations underplayed Turner's militancy—she in fact angrily defied and confronted her attackers—they functioned to display to the nation the brutal violation of defenseless Negro motherhood.[19]

Even as Mary Turner was being featured by some as a symbol of Jim Crow terrorism, others were renewing attempts to erect on the national mall a statue to be dubbed the Mammy Monument. A bill proposed by Mississippi U.S. senator John Williams at the behest of the Richmond, Virginia, chapter of the United Daughters of the Confederacy (UDC) requested that a site be designated for the "erection as a gift to the people of the United States [of] a monument in memory of the faithful colored mammies of the South." Just as the monument to Heyward Shepherd at Harpers Ferry—also proposed by the UDC—was intended to challenge John Brown's heroic stature among antiracists, the Mammy Monument

From the "Afro-American," Baltimore.

A COLORED ARTIST'S SUGGESTION.

"Since the Daughters of the Confederacy have obtained Sena-
torial sanction for the erection of a monument to the 'Black
Mammies' of the South," runs the commentary, "we offer the
above suggestion. It should be cast in bronze 30 feet high and
stand upon a marble shaft 20 feet square and 100 feet high. It
should also be erected on the Mall midway between the Lincoln
Memorial and Washington's Monument. The right hand of the
statue is extended for the back pay due."

Figure 1. Anonymous, "A Colored Artist's Suggestion." *Literary Digest* April 28, 1923. Satirical commentary on the so-called Mammy Monument, proposed for erection on the National Mall by the United Daughters of the Confederacy.

was locked in combat with the image of the violated Black Madonna in postwar battles over metonymy and race, region and nation. At stake was not merely the regional pride of unreconstructed Bourbons; the contestation over the figure of the black woman as ideologeme had far-reaching national implications, since the violated Black Madonna and the Mammy Monument offered diametrically opposed mediations of the relationship of laboring black women to the body politic.[20]

Reminding their audiences that the New Negro was both female and male, these black women writers and artists brought antiracist and feminist concerns to the project of postwar political radicalism. Johnson's John Brown was featured as an apocalyptic precursor to the militants of the "red summer." The publication of Burrill's "Aftermath" in the *Liberator* stressed the connections between the imperialist war overseas and the racist war at home. The appearance of "They That Sit in Darkness" in the pro-Soviet *Birth Control Review* invited readers to see parallels between black female sharecroppers and Russian female peasants: the Soviet "New Woman," freed of the constraints of compulsory motherhood, might have her analogues in a future socialist United States.

Although Washington's black women writers and artists contributed to the insurgent discourse voiced in journals of the left, their grim treatments of birthing, stillbirth, abortion, and infanticide suggested the difficulty of building a revolutionary project in the race-torn United States. The metaphor of giving birth—which delineates the process by which the contradictions within one mode of production give rise to the emergence of another—functions centrally in the writings of Marx, who famously referred to revolution as "the midwife of every old society which is pregnent with a new one." This trope appeared with some frequency in texts published in the *Liberator*. On the same page featuring Georgia Douglas Johnson's "The Octoroon," for instance, is Babette Deutsch's sonnet "Petrograd," in which the city where the Russian Revolution began is compared with a mother, "her sides . . . shaken with the weight she bore," who, having delivered "the impatient and impeded birth," now "challenges the leagued imperial earth." Claude McKay's "Exhortation: Summer, 1919" (1920) proclaims that

> [t]hrough the pregnant universe rumbles life's terrific thunder
> . . . The new birth rends the old earth and the very dead are waking
> Ghosts are turned flesh, throwing off the grave's disguise . . .
> For the big earth groans in travail for the strong new world in making.

Some texts extended the trope of revolution as birth to a Marxist retelling of the story of Christ. In "Easter," Chireton W. Rice writes,

> A young man is talking,
> He is telling the truth about Russia.
> The truth is good.
> And the people know Christ is arisen!

This equation of the workers' revolution with the Messiah would become a dominant motif of Depression-era proletarian literature, figuring in the famous finale to Mike Gold's *Jews without Money* and in Langston Hughes's greeting of the "new Christ Child of the Revolutio[n] about to be born," redeeming humanity from the cruel inequalities of capitalism symbolized in opening of the Waldorf-Astoria Hotel.[21]

Yet the often tragic portraiture of the black mother and child in works by New Negro women called into question the possibility of proletarian revolution in the United States. Where Deutsch's and McKay's portrayals of revolution as birthing featured the trope of the Nativity, texts depicting the Black Madonna often conjoined the Nativity with the Pietà. An anonymous poem published in the *Liberator* read

> I am a Negro Woman. . . .
> I have known the sorrows of Mary, Mother of Christ. . . .
> I look up from my wash-tub and watch the cloud-curdled sky. But I
>   see no beauty there, for I have also watched the blue spirals of
>   smoke curling upward from the charred body of my son.

In works of art representing the fate of Mary Turner, the hope for the birthing of a new and better world was crushed by the realities of American racism. The child was crucified even before it was born; indeed, the Mater Dolorosa was crucified, as well. While forces of reaction everywhere were heeding Winston Churchill's call to strangle the Bolshevik baby in the cradle, Mary Turner embodied the concrete form of the arrested dialectic in the postwar United States; the murders of her and her child bore implications that were simultaneously material and metaphorical. As we shall see, the tropes of birthing and infanticide, pregnancy and virginity, as well as of the Black Madonna and the Black Messiah, would figure allegorically in *Cane*'s political discourse as signifiers of both hope and despair. While Toomer would characterize Washington as a site of "spiritual abortion," there is no denying his influence by the women in the writers' group; indeed, the very metaphor by which he sought to dismiss them indicated their impact upon the terms in which he imagined life and death, possibility and constraint.[22]

It bears perhaps noting that another African American woman influenced— or, better, displayed—Toomer's racial identification during the period when he was creating *Cane*. For Toomer's principal romantic interest at the time was a dark-skinned young African American woman named Mae Wright, whom he met during the summer of 1922 at Harpers Ferry. She was considerably younger than Toomer—when they met she was sixteen, he was twenty-seven—and he appears happily to have played the role of mentor; his letters to her are replete with advice about what she should read and how she should develop. "The easy vanities and values of girlhood will pass, and in their place will come the fine depths of womanhood," he counseled. "But you will have to work and strive for them." While he lays claim to his own "unique racial and social status," he attests to his and her common identity when he refers to "we of the darker skins . . . who have Negro blood in our veins" and vituperates at the "tyranny of the Anglo-Saxon ideal." Toomer wrote affectionately of Wright to Waldo Frank and introduced them when Frank visited Washington on his and Toomer's way to South Carolina in September 1922. Toomer later commented to Frank on how his light-skinned friends—"near-whites . . . [a]s prejudiced as real whites"—had cold-shouldered Wright at a Howard-Lincoln football game: "Mae's loveliness didn't get a chance to show. Only her skin. She really seemed insignificant,—and black." Signifying not only Toomer's ability to love a woman of dark skin but also his deeply felt antipathy to intraracial racism, the relationship with Mae Wright further indicates that, in the *Cane* period, Toomer not only identified himself, but also lived, as a person of Negro descent. However he may have relegated them to the margins of his development, the women of Washington helped Toomer elucidate his identity as both a writer and a New Negro at the time when he was conceiving and creating *Cane*.[23]

"The cocoon *is* both tight and intense": Toomer as Race Man

While Toomer clearly reached out to Claude McKay at the *Liberator*, there is no evidence indicating that Toomer ever had direct contact with the Socialist and Communist New Negroes grouped around the *Messenger*, the *Crusader*, or the other black red journals emerging from the upsurge of 1919. But A. Philip Randolph taught the Economics and Sociology of the Race Problem course at the Rand School while Toomer was living in New York in the spring of 1919. Randolph was acquainted with Angelina Grimké, spoke before the Washington NAACP at the invitation of Archibald Grimké, and attended Georgia Douglas Johnson's Saturday Nights in the mid-1920s. Even if Randolph and Toomer never met face-to-face, moreover, it is evident that Toomer was familiar with the contents of the *Messenger*. Toomer's August 1919 *New York Call* article on the Washington race riot bore a marked resemblance to Randolph's class analysis of lynching in the March 1919 *Messenger*; Toomer's recollection of having viewed the shipyard bosses as "birds of prey" strongly suggests his having encountered McKay's poem of that title in the December 1919 *Messenger*. In a September 1923 letter to Frank, furthermore, Toomer notes—in reference to recent reviews of the treatment of the Negro church in *Holiday*—that "Jackson's letter is the real stuff." Toomer most likely refers here to the *Messenger*'s drama critic Wallace V. Jackson, who argued that the experience of slavery, not biology, was the basis of the "leanings in emotional expression" characteristic of African Americans. Notably, Jackson pointed up a parallel between the cultures of U.S. Negroes and Russian peasants: "[S]lavery will leave any people with such tendencies, witness the Russian serf." It would appear that Toomer followed the discussions of art and politics appearing in the principal African American magazine associated with the SPA.[24]

The likelihood that Toomer was familiar with the editors of the African Blood Brotherhood's *Crusader* is less, since the *Crusader* never attained the reputation—or the currency outside of New York—of the *Messenger*. Notably, however, there appeared in the *Crusader* of August 1921 an advertisement for the Republic Theater, of which Walter Pinchback, Toomer's uncle, was the manager: evidently the ABB had some following in Washington, DC, and Toomer's uncle—hardly a political activist—had done business with the organization. Furthermore, the *Crusader*'s steady emphasis on the international dimension of the postwar upsurge, with particular attention to developments in Asia and Africa, made it the premier radical site for commentary on the "rising tide of color" and the global antiracist alternative. The interest in the "black and brown worlds heaving upward" evinced in

Toomer's March 1923 plan for his novel suggests a familiarity with the black nationalist-turned-Communist politics of the ABB. Toomer's documented personal contacts with the left press are confined to his acquaintances on the *New York Call* and the *Liberator*; although he sought the friendship of the *Liberator* coeditor and recommended his poems to Mae Wright, he seems never actually to have met Claude McKay. Yet it is apparent that Toomer shared a number of concerns, indeed passions, with the self-described "black reds" of the postwar period.[25]

W. E. B. Du Bois was the presiding presence in the intellectual and social circles in which the young Toomer had come to maturity; the debate between Du Bois and Booker T. Washington had been widely discussed during Toomer's years at the M Street High School. Toomer's invocation of spirituals throughout *Cane*, as well as of the starkness of Georgia's red clay soil and the harshness of the labor involved in its tilling, recall the music, earth, and peasantry featured in *The Souls of Black Folks* (1903). Toomer's references to Africa in *Cane*, we shall see, suggest his acquaintance with Du Bois's foray into African history—and view of "Mother Africa" as the site of precapitalist communalism—in *The Negro* (1915). Toomer's treatment of the figures of the Black Messiah and the Black Madonna displays the influence not only of Washington women but also of Du Bois's reconfiguration of Christian religious tropes as vehicles for political commentary throughout *Darkwater*. Du Bois's politics were distinctly less radical than those expressed in the *Messenger* or the *Crusader*: the former described him as an "Old Crowd Negro," while the latter described him as "[l]ike some god standing high over the world [who] has looked down and spoken for the Negro multitude . . . [but] never spoken to them." Nonetheless, Du Bois's insistence upon linking racism with capitalism, his steady attention to the nonwhite global upsurge, and his support—at times hesitant, at times hopeful—for the fledgling Soviet Union made him a defining presence in the ideological matrix from which *Cane* emerged.[26]

Toomer did not develop a personal tie to Du Bois: the snub he received on approaching the *Crisis* editor at his New York office in 1920 appears to have been his only direct contact with the renowned scholar and civil rights leader. As the grandson of the prominent P. B. S. Pinchback, however, Toomer both knew and was known by African American race leaders based in Washington, DC. Through his grandfather's far-reaching contacts Toomer had been introduced to Linton Stephens Ingraham, the principal of Sparta Agricultural and Industrial Institute for whose position he would serve as substitute in the fall of 1921, bestowing on him the experience from which *Cane* would emerge. When he sought assistance from the YMCA leader and NAACP Washington chapter president Jesse E. Moorland in planning his and Frank's trip into the Deep South in the fall of 1922, he praised Moorland's dedication to racial uplift—"Your interest in the evolution and individual expression of the race's youth is a deep and fine act." Toomer enthused,

The shallow observations and loose thinking which have hitherto formed the bulk matter written about the Negro are now in a position to do a double injury.

They were unfortunate when public interest was at a low ebb. How much more so are they at the present time, in this decade which is witnessing a quickened interest, every man for his brother, especially every white man for his colored neighbor! This thought has often urged me in the direction of scientific statement. I'd love to write a volume whose foundations rested on a thorough training in social and biological science.

Toomer subsequently thanked Moorland for having arranged his and Frank's travel to Spartanburg, South Carolina, where "[e]verything was . . . in a nut shell: the two races in their suppressed proximity, the Main Street of the town, the better residential districts of the whites, the outlying flanks of poor-white and factory worker's homes, the Negro district, factory life encroaching upon the old agrarian community, everything."[27]

It bears noting that Toomer spoke here not as a researcher into the status of "mixed-blood" people, nor as an advocate of a new "American race," but as a knowing insider. His joking reference to the newfound interest of "every white man" in his "colored neighbor" posited unity between himself and Moorland, even if at Frank's expense. His interest in the geographical mapping of the Jim Crow political economy displayed, moreover, a conception of labor, not culture, as the principal mediation between the Negro and the land. While Moorland was an "Old Crowd Negro," Toomer apparently felt at ease in positing their common commitment to studies of the Negro based on solid "social and biological science" and in sharing with the older man the heightened understanding of the economics of racism that had emerged from his second foray into the Deep South. He spoke as his grandfather's grandson, one race man to another.[28]

By far Toomer's most significant tie with a prominent African American male writer and intellectual during the *Cane* years, however, was with Alain Locke. Toomer's autobiographical writings give Locke short shrift, focusing on his presumed sense of betrayal at Locke's appropriation of his writings for *The New Negro* but rendering scant indication of the role that Locke had previously played in his life. Because Toomer's break with Locke has figured centrally in many accounts of his eventual retreat from self-identification as a Negro, it is important to reconstruct the key features of their relationship.[29]

First approaching "Dr. Locke" deferentially in November 1919, the month before his stint at the New Jersey shipyard, Toomer renewed the contact when he returned to Washington. When he sent Locke his October 1920 *New York Call* article, "Americans and Mary Austin," Locke responded graciously, remarking that "I am much more hopeful of your future in verse writing for having seen the caliber of mind exhibited in this really good piece of prose." Soon the men had dispensed with the formalities. Toomer's evident sense that he and Locke were jointly engaged in a project of materialist cultural analysis is exemplified in a letter of August 1920 in which he reflects on a recent *Nation* article by M. H. Hedges, "The Teacher's Real Dilemma." Toomer applauds Hedges for exhibiting distress at college students' absorption in "the petty rituals of college life while the grand gestures and convulsions of the social world are passed by, unheeded." He upbraids Hedges, however, for refusing to explore the deep structural causes of student alienation and invoking instead the categories of "the pioneer . . . the utilitarian . . . [and] the Puritan." Toomer complains,

> Mr. Hedges would like to see the pioneer spirit dominant. . . . He thus reveals himself as a nineteenth century romanticist striving to interpret ideally what was and is essentially an economic and materialistic movement. If ideas of truth or even adventure were the motivating forces of Columbus, it is certain that the desire for gain populated America.
>
> . . . Of the two questions raised; why are universities sterile? and why are undergraduates stones? the first is, for Hedges, answered by indicating the utilitarian and Puritan dogmas which govern them; the second, and for us the pertinent one, is left unanswered.

Toomer concludes, "But that he voices the query would indicate the answer in general social and psychological factors rather than in strictly racial ones."[30]

Toomer himself knew something about undergraduate alienation, having studied at six institutions of higher education, most for only one semester. What preoccupied him in his critique of Hedges was not only substance but also methodology: the need for a systemic analysis of the reasons why American college students appear impervious to the world-historical events of the day. He dismissed as "romanticist" Hedges' attempt to graft an "ideal interpretation" onto "what was essentially an economic and materialistic movement"; it is telling that Toomer chose Columbus's enterprise, the founding myth of American capitalism, to illustrate his larger point about historical causality. Also significant is Toomer's comment that Hedges' discussion of undergraduate apathy—"for us the pertinent [question]"—displays the transracial nature of the problem. Implied here is his and Locke's shared understanding of how and where to distinguish causal factors that are "strictly racial" from those that are "in general social and psychological."[31]

Toomer's two letters to Locke from Sparta in the fall of 1921 reveal not only the energies gathering for *Cane* but also the importance to the younger man of Locke's friendship and influence. Writing some six weeks into his teaching, Toomer notes that "[t]here is poetry here—and drama, but the atmosphere for one in my position is almost prohibitory." Remarking on his delight in finding himself to be "a natural born teacher," he describes the "bewildered expression" on the faces of his "Old Testament (ill) taught" young students as he introduced "ideas of polytheism and deity evolution in their ancient history lessons!" He continues, "I've learned a lot. Especially from an economic, sociological standpoint. 99% of the people who write and talk about the Negro hardly know his name. Artistically, the field is virgin. I think, however, that for its real exploitation, one would have to come into it under different circumstances." The second letter notes that he leaves in a few days "both in the interest of the school (raising funds) and for purposes of my own"; that he will "be in Washington a week or so I think, and then will doubtless push on for New York [where] I am supposed to have several informal lectures arranged for me"; and that "of course I have material. Want to see you."[32]

Toomer may have been exaggerating his connections in New York; there is no evidence that he was invited to give lectures there after his sojourn in Sparta. But these letters display an easy familiarity, as well as Toomer's sense that, as sophisticated race men, he and Locke shared fundamental intellectual and political values. Both men, it appears, laughed at the backwardness of Christian fundamentalism and embraced an anthropological approach to religion; both recognized the need both for an "economic, sociological standpoint" and for artistic exploration of the "virgin field" afforded by southern Negro experience. Toomer's self-positioning within this political-cum-cultural discourse is breezily confident: presumably he will correct the errors of the "99% of the people who write and talk about the Negro [but] hardly know his name." One clear implication is that Toomer did know that name and planned to use the material he had gathered to showcase his knowledge. Another is that the man and mentor to whom Toomer wrote understands the need to integrate sociological knowledge with aesthetic expression: absent here is any rhapsodic testament to the folk's close connection to the soil, much less to the culturalist notion that artistic representation supplies the privileged route to social change. The Locke to whom Toomer wrote in 1921 bears a closer resemblance to the materialist critic of racism displayed in Locke's writings of the 1910s and early 1920s than to the celebrator of folk-based art who would publish *The New Negro* four years later.[33]

As residents of the same city, Toomer and Locke exchanged few letters once Toomer returned from Sparta in November, 1921. In an August 1922 note, however, Toomer thanks Locke, then in New York, for his commentary on "Withered Skin of Berries." "I liked your criticism," writes the younger man. "The cocoon *is* both tight and intense"—an emphasis suggesting a common understanding about the nature of mentoring. Locke continued to encourage Toomer, attempting to secure him financial support and writing to congratulate Toomer on Liveright's acceptance of *Cane* for publication. "I cannot resist the wretched pun that I hope the book will raise Cane," he quipped, noting his own plans to write a review that would "castigate Stribling, Shands and Clement Wood," three white authors who had recently published novels containing well-intentioned but problematic criticisms of U.S. racism. In July 1923 Locke offered to "try to make a small propaganda" for the book in his upcoming European visit and announced his desire to publish "Balo" in an anthology of short plays he would coedit with Montgomery Gregory. "I do so want to keep in touch with you, and more important still your work," Locke wrote. Throughout this correspondence there is no indication that Toomer in any way resented Locke's attempts to shape and promote his career. The "tight and intense . . . cocoon" of Locke's mentoring—which Toomer had purposely sought out and cultivated—was apparently welcome.[34]

"Locke tricked and misused me":
"The Negro Emergent" and *The New Negro*

Toomer's evident indebtedness to Locke before, during, and after the creation of *Cane* should be kept in mind when we peruse Toomer's 1934 account of his reaction to Locke's publication of parts of *Cane* in *The New Negro*. While critical commentary has focused on Locke's presumed hijacking of these materials and Toomer's subsequent reaction, Toomer's essay "The Negro Emergent" also figures crucially in these events, which need to be recapitulated in some detail.

Describing Toomer's 1924 return to the United States after his first visit to the Gurdjieff headquarters at Fontainebleau, the 1934 autobiography asserts,

> I was worlds removed from the literary set. . . . That I had once written a book called *Cain* seemed remote. What had happened to it I neither knew nor cared. Much less I knew of what was happening in the Negro world.
>
> Gradually, however, I began making other contacts, I began awakening with interest to the wide activities of that time. Then I discovered, among other things, that a ferment was in the Negro world also, a literary ferment, and that it was producing a new literature. I was sufficiently moved to write an article. After this I viewed the movement as a splendid thing but as something that had no special meaning for me.
>
> Time passed.
>
> I received a visit from Alain Locke. Locke said he was getting together a book of Negro material and wanted something I had written, preferably a new story or a story from "Cain." I replied that I had written no new stories of that kind and did not want "Cain" dismembered. He pressed. I thought of the article. I offered it to him. It turned out that he did not want it. My expressed attitude was—this article or nothing. I concluded that the matter was finished. Before Locke left he talked to me about Winold Reis, the artist. . . . He urged me to sit for Reis, never mentioning that he himself would use the portrait in his book. . . .
>
> Out of curiosity or vanity or something, I did sit for Reis; and, so far as I knew, that was that.
>
> But when Locke's book, *The New Negro*, came out, there was the Reis portrait, and there was a story from "Cain," and there in an introduction, were words about me which have caused as much or more misunderstanding than Waldo Frank's![*sic*]
>
> However, there was, and is, among others, this great difference between Frank and Locke. Frank helped me at a time when I most needed help. I will never forget it. Locke tricked and misused me.[35]

This account is inaccurate—indeed, disingenuous—on a number of counts. Toomer's antipathy here to Locke's "dismembering" of *Cane* flies in the face of Toomer's own practice, which had been to publish the separate parts of his text, even after he conceived of them as a book, in as many venues as possible. In addition, his statement that Locke's anthology contained "the Reis portrait" and "a story from 'Cane'" conflates the two versions of the anthology: the shorter one appearing in the *Survey Graphic* in March 1925, in which the poem "Song of the Son"—Toomer's sole contribution—appeared, and the book-length one appearing in December 1925, which contained, in addition to this poem, the stories "Carma" and "Fern" and the poem "Georgia Dusk," as well as Reis's portrait of Toomer. While this inaccuracy might be attributed to Toomer's blurred memory nearly a decade later, it occludes the fact that "The Negro Emergent" was in fact written *in response to* the March 1925 magazine version of Locke's project. As Toomer wrote in an unpublished draft of the essay, "The recent Negro number of the *Survey Graphic* may be taken as convenient evidence of a two-fold fact, the fact that the Negro is in the process of discovering himself, and of being discovered. . . . The Negro who is discovering himself . . . has been called the New Negro." In penning his essay, Toomer was injecting himself into current debates over the definition of the New Negro. He may have already spent some time with the Gurdjieffians in Fontainebleau, but his stance was hardly—yet—that of an outsider. How might we interpret Toomer's faulty memories of 1934?[36]

Although Toomer's autobiographical account does not discuss "The Negro Emergent," that essay can help answer this question. There are numerous indications that "The Negro Emergent" is written as a reply to Locke's March 1925 preface. His statement that the Negro is currently emerging from "a crust, a false personality, a compound of beliefs, habits, attitudes, and emotional reactions superimposed upon him by external circumstances" resembles Locke's claim that, until recently, "The Negro has been more of a formula than a human being," and that the Negro's "shadow . . . has been more real to him than his personality." His closing proposition that, through the act of artistic creation, the Negro will "at once create himself and contribute his value to America" accords with Locke's observation that the Negro "now becomes a conscious contributor and participant in American civilization," having attained "a significant and satisfying new phase of group development, and with it a spiritual Coming of Age."[37]

But Toomer's "The Negro Emergent" differs from Locke's March 1925 prefatory essay in some crucial respects. Locke passes over economic exploitation and racial violence as causes of the Great Migration, arguing instead that its participants should be viewed as pioneers, comparable to those who "push[ed] back the western frontier in the first half of the nineteenth century." While Locke observes that the migrants' transition from South to North can be compared with the movement from the Middle Ages into modernity, he recasts the Marxist modes of production narrative into one of metonymic nationalist progress: the Negro, in becoming an urban proletarian, establishes his credentials as an American. Toomer, by contrast, asserts that the Negro "could not generously partake of America" because "he felt himself the least of aliens, though he knew himself in essence to be native." Where Locke evades the discourse of "100% American" nativism, Toomer addresses it directly: the Negro's hoped-for "contribution" to

the nation will not go uncontested. Where Locke argues that Negro art and literature testified to "an imagination that has never broken kinship with nature,"
Toomer notes that the Negro's agrarian roots should not be subjected to "poetic
exaggeration." The Negro "could not love the soil when those above him tried to
force his face into it—and then allowed him no real possession." Where Locke's
analysis occludes the Negro's exploitation as a producer of profit for the owner
of the land, Toomer features labor as the principal link between man and nature,
folk and soil, peasant and land.[38]

Where Locke dismisses Marxist and other radical influences as "quixotic,"
moreover, Toomer insists upon a class analysis of the basis of racial division:

> [W]ith the Negro's emergence into self-knowledge is the discovery of the falsity
> of his former illusion that the white American is actually free. Because the white
> man is not racially oppressed, the Negro has tended to picture him as existing
> in a state of perfect freedom and happiness. Economically, all sorts of avenues
> and opportunities are imagined to be open to him, so that, if he but wishes
> and works for it, the fruits of the earth will come into his possession. . . . There
> has been a strong tendency to think of the white man as being psychologically
> free: he can think, feel, and do just what he pleases. It is assumed, among other
> things, that the white man *voluntarily* oppresses the Negro, that he freely hates
> him, that white mobs are acting from free will when they lynch a Negro. . . . It is
> now being realized, however, that the mass of whites, save in the single instance
> of racial oppression, are as bound and determined as the mass of blacks, and
> that their transcendence demands something more than the mere possession
> of a white skin, or of a white psychology.

By contrast with his 1919 article on the race riots, Toomer has toned down his
language; he speaks now of "transcendence" rather than of class struggle leading
to a "socialized reality." Nonetheless, this formulation echoes key assertions in the
earlier piece. White workers ("the mass of whites") are "bound and determined"
by the same forces that oppress blacks; they act not out of "free will" but out of
the illusion that "white psychology" and "white skin" constitute some kind of
objective benefit. Indeed, Toomer here implicitly challenges not just Locke's anti-
Marxist formulation but also Du Bois's assertion that "the discovery of personal
whiteness among the world's peoples" has not only justified "the exploitation of
the darker peoples" but also made it advantageous for the "middle class and . . .
the laborers" to support the capitalists. For Toomer, by contrast, the New Negro's
"emergence" necessitates the growth of class consciousness: "self-knowledge"
hinges on discarding the "illusion that the white American is actually free," which
in turn hinges on a grasp of the real relations of production shaping the social
totality. Situating Toomer at—or at least toward—the left end of the spectrum
of current debates over the identity of the New Negro, this formulation places
him at odds with most of the analyses that would dominate the discourse of the
Harlem Renaissance.[39]

In "The Negro Emergent," Toomer is wearing two hats: he is at once the confident metonymic nationalist, proclaiming the Negro's rootedness in the soil of the South and capacity to stand for the nation, and the left-leaning sociological realist, ever aware of the economics of sharecropping and the hypocrisies of American democracy. In both these roles, however, the author of the essay—although he does not write in the first person as a "Negro"—would seem to be drawing on personal experience when he writes about "the Negro's emergence into self-knowledge." Indeed, in an early draft of the essay he criticizes African American intraracial racism, noting that "the split within the Negro group due to difference of color and economic preferences [is] often stimulated by the white group," resulting in "disdain and contempt on the part of those of lighter color and better position" and "distrust and jealousy on the part of the others." In the margin, he jotted, "Economic powers." These are not the words of a man seeking to contest the reality of existing racial categories, much less disavow his own membership in the broad category, "the Negro." Indeed, he actively seeks to promote both racial solidarity and awareness of the grounding of racism in capitalism.[40]

Locke's reasons for rejecting "The Negro Emergent" are not known. While the essay is not openly Marxist, its insistently sociological and economic emphasis—of which Locke might have approved a few years before—may have put him off. As Locke undertook the book-length version of the anthology, he excluded some of the harder-hitting commentaries on race and racism in the United States that had appeared in the March 1925 issue of the *Survey Graphic*; evidently, too, he asked a number of contributors to tone down their submissions when they revised them for the later version. Toomer's proposed contribution to the anthology could have fallen under this editorial ax—particularly since Locke had in March 1925 featured Toomer as belonging to a cluster of young Negro writers who possessed an "instinctive gift for the folk-spirit" and a desire to "[be] racial . . . purely for the sake of art." Among these, Locke wrote, Toomer was distinctive for giving "a lilt and an ecstasy to the American modernists." This portrait of Toomer as the lyrical enshriner of folk culture was reinforced by Locke's decision to include, in the anthology a version of *The New Negro*, William Stanley Braithwaite's "The Negro in American Literature," which ends with the assertion that "*Cane* is a book of gold and bronze, of dusk and flame, of ecstasy and pain, and Jean Toomer is a bright morning star of a new day of the race in literature." The abidingly sociologically minded Toomer of "The Negro Emergent" did not fit in with the portraits offered by Locke and Braithwaite. But if Locke's motivations cannot be known, Toomer's—at least as recorded in the 1934 autobiography—are more mysterious still. Since Toomer wrote "The Negro Emergent" in response to the *Survey Graphic* special issue on the New Negro, edited by Locke, this means that not only had he seen "Song of the Son" in the magazine version, but he also had not objected to its inclusion. Indeed, he may well have approved its publication. If, after turning down "The Negro Emergent," Locke went ahead and pilfered additional texts from *Cane* for the book version of

The New Negro, Toomer would justifiably have been miffed—but not because this was the first time he had seen any of the pieces of *Cane* appear in an anthology by and about New Negro artists and writers published by Locke.[41]

In his 1934 retrospective account, Toomer states that he was dismayed on the book publication of *The New Negro* to see not only "the Reis portrait" and "a story from *Cane*," but also, "in an introduction . . . words about me which have caused as much or more misunderstanding than Waldo Frank's!" What were these words? In the book version, Locke retitled his discussion of the emerging generation of Negro writers, "Youth Speaks," as "Negro Youth Speaks," and he expanded his earlier commentary on the significance of *Cane*: "And so not merely for modernity of style, but for vital originality of substance, the young Negro writers dig deep into the racy peasant undersoil of the race life. Jean Toomer writes: 'Georgia opened me. And it may well be said that I received my initial impulse to an individual art from my experience there. For no other section of the country has so stirred me. There one finds soil, soil in the sense the Russians know it,—the soil every art and literature that is to live must be imbedded in.'"[42]

Toomer's stated discomfiture at Locke's formulation is susceptible to a range of interpretations. If what he recalls in the 1934 autobiography is in fact the distress that he experienced on reading Locke's book-length anthology, this may have resulted from Locke's conversion of Toomer's distinctly regionalist statement—he designated Georgia as a "section of the country"—into the racialist (and tauto-logical) claim that the "racy peasant undersoil of the race life" was the source of the "vital originality of substance" in *Cane*. Locke's move—congruent with the way he used the organic trope throughout the anthology to signal a link between folk, soil, region, and nation—recruited Toomer's text to exemplify the romantic racialism against which Toomer had explicitly warned in "The Negro Emergent." Toomer's parallel between his project and that of "the Russians," moreover—reflecting a transnationalist conception of the connection between "soil" and "art and literature," as well as a continuing enthusiasm for the part of the globe where the hammer and sickle now prevailed—became lost in Locke's essentialized treatment of Toomer's creative practice. Toomer's distress at Locke's formulation might have sprung from his resentment at Locke's imposition of his own largely depoliticized project for Negro art on Toomer's work.[43]

If we scrutinize Locke's words about Toomer in "Negro Youth Speaks," how-ever, we note that more than half of them are drawn from Toomer himself—in particular, from Toomer's own publicity sketch for *Cane*. As we see in the next chapter, Toomer composed this sketch in response to a request from his publisher, Horace Liveright. While Toomer refused to comply fully with Liveright's desire to "feature Negro" as regards his own racial heritage, he described the contents of part 1 of *Cane* as "simple tales of peasant sorrow" and concluded with the proposition that his book should be read as "black vaudeville . . . black super-vaudeville out of the South." The latter description can be read as a clever masking of Toomer's intentions in *Cane*, but it is also open to racist caricature—as was in fact shown in its being carried over into a number of the most derogating reviews of *Cane* that appeared in the mainstream press. We may speculate that Toomer's presumed anger at Locke's "words about me" may have been directed not so much at Locke for generating "misunderstanding" about the author of *Cane* as at himself for having acceded to the very "exoticism" that he proclaimed to disdain. If Toomer did experience discomfiture encountering Locke's book-length anthology soon after its publication, this may have resulted from the cognitive dissonance arising from his own participation in the public presentation of *Cane*. Culturalism and political radicalism offered significantly different grounds for defining the term New Negro, which was emerging as an increasingly contested ideologeme as the postwar tide of antiracist militancy receded and Jim Crow reasserted its supremacy. Debates over the identity of the New Negro were fought out within Toomer as well as in the world at large; in his 1934 narrative, however, he would repress the memory of this internal conflict, displacing it onto Locke's presumed bad faith.[44]

"We know this restaurant is all right for us to eat at": Toomer during and after *Cane*

It would appear that the Jean Toomer who recalled his 1925 encounter with Locke from the standpoint of 1934 was simply lying: he had passed over the color line and was eager to disavow his connections with the New Negro Movement. As we approach the issue of Toomer's increasingly tangled relationship to his Negro ancestry, however, it is important to recognize that he did not isolate himself from the New Negro Movement in the period surrounding—and for some time following—the publication of *Cane*. He evinced interest in publishing "Kabnis" in a special "Negro issue" of *Broom*, in which he hoped to be "well represented." Writing to Sherwood Anderson in December 1922 regarding the "resistance to my stuff" on the part of "the mass of Negroes who are too instinctive to be anything but themselves," he expressed his interest in bringing out "a magazine, American . . . that would consciously hoist, and perhaps at first a trifle over emphasize a Negroid ideal." When Claude Barnett of the Associated Negro Press, curious about the blend of racial themes and experimental form in *Cane*, inquired about the racial identity of its author, Toomer replied that while the "style and finish" of his text bespoke his involvement with "the entire body of contemporary literature," he was "body and soul . . . Negroid." He declared, "I am the grandson of the late P B S Pinchback. From this fact it is clear that your contention is sustained. I have 'peeped behind the veil.'" While evidently viewing his work as stylistically distinctive—even unique—among contemporary African American writers, Toomer expressed no reluctance at identifying the author of *Cane* as a Negro—indeed, one proud of his distinguished ancestry.[45]

Toomer's actions on arriving in New York indicate his readiness to live among African Americans and, at least for a time, his easy self-identification as a Negro.

Figure 2. "To Harold Jackman." Auto-
graphed photograph of Jean Toomer,
undated, Countee Cullen-Harold
Jackman Memorial Collection, Atlanta
University Center, Robert W. Woodruff
Library

As he planned his move, Toomer originally contemplated staying at the Hotel
Theresa in Harlem. After he moved out of the apartment of Gorham Munson and
his wife, where he did not want to outstay his welcome, Toomer's first apartment,
on Gay Street, was in one of the few African American enclaves in Greenwich Village. Although Toomer primarily interacted with white modernists after moving
to New York, he maintained friendly contact with Locke, Charles Johnson, and
other figures associated with the New Negro Movement; a photograph of Toomer
inscribed with the words "To Harold Jackman," a figure prominent in Harlem
Renaissance circles, suggests his cordial relations with the uptown artistic crowd.
In his memoir of the 1920s modernist scene, Munson recalled that Toomer was a
friend of Alain Locke: "I saw Alain Locke with him several times. He was a friend
of Charles S. Johnson, editor of *Opportunity*, who later became, I think, president
of Fisk. At one time Jean arranged for me to lunch with Johnson. We met at a little
restaurant on lower 6th Avenue [about] which Jean told me in advance, 'We know
this restaurant is all right for us to eat at.'" Not only does this account suggest that
Toomer's 1934 account exaggerated his alienation from Locke; it also indicates
that Toomer spoke in solidarity with darker-skinner African Americans forced to
contend with northern Jim Crow. Munson further notes that, as Toomer became
involved in the Gurdjieff movement, he was "the proud leader of [a] group in
Harlem which was 100 percent Negro." Toomer's romantic involvement in the late
1920s with an African American woman he knew through the movement—the
Harlem Renaissance writer Dorothy Peterson—suggests that, at least when he
was in New York, he was making no attempt at racial "passing."[46]

Equally relevant to our inquiry is the fact that, after moving from Washington, DC, to New York in the summer of 1923, Toomer remained willing to self-identify not only as a Negro but also as a "Negro writer." When Locke approached him in August 1923 about contributing a play to the anthology *Plays of Negro Life* that he anticipating editing with Montgomery Gregory, Toomer offered "Balo." Invited in May 1924 by *Nomad* editor Albert Rosenthal to edit a special issue on Negro writers, Toomer declined politely, expressing interest—"I would like to do a Negro number for you"—but noting that "unfortunately the thing is not possible" for logistical reasons. But he had recently accepted an invitation from Ernestine Rose of the 135th Street branch of the New York Public Library to speak on the subject of Negro literature. In 1925, "Georgia Dusk" appeared in a cluster of poems by and about African Americans in *May Days: An Anthology of Verse from the Masses-Liberator*, edited by the leftist poet Geneviève Taggard and published by Boni and Liveright. As late as 1927 Toomer agreed to publish a group of seven poems from *Cane* in Countée Cullen's anthology *Caroling Dusk*, subtitled *An Anthology of Verse by Negro Poets*. For all his later stated antipathy to Locke, moreover, in 1927 Toomer allowed five poems from *Cane* to be republished in Locke's pamphlet anthology, *Four Negro Poets*. Toomer's turning down Charles Johnson's invitation to attend the March 1924 Civic Club dinner that would usher in the Harlem Renaissance has often been cited as evidence of Toomer's having decided, within a few months of the publication of *Cane*, to disavow any connection with the label "Negro writer." But matters are not so simple. Toomer appeared in *Who's Who in Colored America* as late as 1927—not incidentally, perhaps, the last year when his name also was listed on the masthead of the *New Masses*. His 1929 essay "Race Problems in Modern Society" did not present itself as authored by an African American, but its forthright discussion of race and class, as we have seen, suggested an intimate acquaintance with the workings of racist ideology. Just as Toomer did not readily relinquish his identification with class-based radicalism, he did not readily abandon his connections with the New Negro Movement.[47]

Toomer's relationship with the New Negro literary movement did indeed become increasingly tenuous. As he became more deeply involved in the Gurdjieff movement and its Harlem acolytes dropped away, Toomer moved further into the white world; on arriving in Chicago to lead the Gurdjieff work in late 1926, he effectively began to live as a white man. His abiding reputation as the author of *Cane*, he complained, constrained his opportunities to publish other work. In 1929 French publishers turned down his recent work after seeing a review of *Cane* that "called me a black poet, grouping me with Walrond and McKay." Toomer observed, "This strange coincidence, the fact of *Cane* once again coming upon me and forcing me to again realize the difficulty caused by my being associated with Negro" renewed his awareness of "the real difficulties involved in managing this organism named Toomer." When in 1930 James Weldon Johnson requested permission to publish parts of *Cane* in *The Book of American Negro Poetry*, Toomer famously refused:

I do not see things in terms of Negro, Anglo-Saxon, Jewish, or so on. As for me personally, I see myself an American, simply an American. As regards art I particularly hold this view. Accordingly, I must withdraw from all things which emphasize or tend to emphasize racial or cultural divisions, I must align myself with things which stress the experiences, forms, and spirit we have in common. . . . I recognize . . . that the Negro art movement has had some valuable results. It is, however, for those who have and who will benefit by it. It is not for me.

In response to Nancy Cunard's 1932 invitation to contribute to her anthology *Negro*, he wrote, "Though I am interested in, and deeply value the Negro, I am not a Negro." His résumé would routinely omit the *Crisis* as the first venue in which his imaginative writings had been published, just as his *New York Call* writings would also be effaced.[48]

But while Toomer's letters to Johnson and Cunard are widely cited as proof of his abandoning his identity as a Negro writer, it bears noting that Toomer continued selectively to allow his work to appear in anthologies and magazines featuring Negro writers. In 1929 "Fern," "Georgia Dusk," and "Song of the Son" appeared in V. F. Calverton's *Anthology of American Negro Literature*, which purported "to represent what the Negro in America has achieved in the art of literary forms"; the book was explicitly a gathering of texts by, and not just about, African Americans. In 1932 an untitled poem by Toomer appeared in the "As the Eagle Soars" column in the *Crisis*—not in itself a proclamation of identity as a Negro author, since non-Negro writers occasionally contributed to the NAACP magazine, but hardly a means of evading such a designation. In 1941 four pieces from *Cane*—"Blood-Burning Moon," "Avey," "Song of the Son," and "Georgia Dusk"—appeared in Sterling Brown's *Negro Caravan: Writings by American Negroes*. The proposition that, once he became involved in the Gurdjieff work, Toomer cut all ties with his identity as the author of *Cane*—and hence as a "Negro writer—is disproven by the historical record.[49]

"My earth-life was liberated from the pot of myself": Toomer's Retreat

Even as Toomer sporadically acknowledged a continuing affinity with the "literary ferment . . . in the Negro world," however, he was making increasingly strong denials of Negro ancestry in his personal life. In his 1931 certificate of marriage to Margery Latimer, Toomer is designated as "white," and "Nina Reichback" as the name of his mother. That the effort to pass as a white couple exploded in his and his wife's faces seems only to have increased his attempts to mask his racial identity. In the *Baltimore Afro-American* he declared in 1934, "I would not consider it libelous to anyone to refer to me as a colored man, but I have not lived as one, nor do I really know whether there is any colored blood in me or not." As we see in chapter 4, in versions of his autobiography composed from 1934 onward, Toomer would sporadically assert that his grandfather Pinchback had been a white man passing as black in order to advance his career in Reconstruction-era Louisiana; Toomer at times also stated that his mulatto grandmother, Emily Hethorn Pinchback, was white. His deconstructive approach to race had largely devolved into a denial of the African strain in his ancestry. And yet, when he registered for the draft in 1942, Toomer once again self-identified as a Negro. He was nothing if not inconsistent.[50]

As Toomer rewrote his own racial history, he recomposed the narrative of his experiences in the Deep South, effectively deracializing the Georgia of 1921. In one variant, Toomer wrote that he had gone south because a man came by and invited him to take the teaching job "out of the blue"; apparently Pinchback's ties with Linton Stephens Ingraham, the principal of the Sparta Agricultural and Industrial Institute, were no longer relevant. Toomer described his social interactions with a colorless folk: "I had seen and met with people of all kinds. I had never before met with a folk. I had never before lived in the midst of a people gathered together by a group-spirit. . . . They worked and loved and hated and got into trouble and felt a great weight on them." These "folk," defined by their "group-spirit" and simple emotions, are unsituated in history or geography; the source of the "great weight on them" is left unspecified. Their propensity to "get into trouble" (an eerie replication of the phrase often used to justify lynching) takes shape as an unfortunate accompaniment to their elemental existence. The relationship of the folk to the land, moreover, is an emanation of a near-biological essence: "Here the earth seemed part of the people, and the people part of the earth, and they worked upon each other and upon me, so that my earth-life was liberated from the pot of myself. The roots of my earth-life went down and found hold in this red soil, and the soil became a shining ground." While Toomer makes mention of "red soil," nothing in the text identifies the site of his liberation from "the pot of myself" as Georgia—much less of its moment as the aftermath of the Great War and the "red summer" of 1919. Indeed, where Toomer had once criticized exoticized descriptions of "soilness" for papering over the social contradictions that "would not allow the Negro possession" of the land, here he goes beyond Locke's tracing of writerly inspiration to the "racy peasant undersoil of the race life." Toomer now equates "soil" with "earth," proposing a hyper-material relationship between the land and its inhabitants that is bereft of any mention of labor. Indeed, even region and nation are now left out of the signifying chain connecting the soil, the folk, and the artist: the occlusion of both class and race has stripped the chain of any extension into broader social experience.[51]

That Toomer experienced a good deal of discomfort—indeed, suffering—from his repression of his African heritage is manifested in dreams he recorded when undergoing Jungian psychoanalysis, beginning in late 1949. Apparently forthright with his analyst about what he called his "strange white-Negro difficulty," Toomer detailed several dreams in which he experienced confusion and alienation resulting from his ability—and frequently his decision—to pass without notice from black to white, or indeed from white to black. In one dream, for instance, he finds himself in the South traveling in a Jim Crow car:

> With the Negro section actually in view, I do not feel I belong in it. . . . Among
> black people my relative whiteness and other different qualities would make
> me as conspicuous as would my relative darkness and different qualities among
> white people. Nor do I want to place myself within the limitations and implica-
> tions of Jim Crow. . . . On the other hand, I know and feel that neither do I quite
> belong in the white section. I know, further, that were the white people to know
> the racial facts, they would definitely feel I did not belong in the white section.

After several sudden shifts of scene, all involving anxieties about racial identity,
he concludes with an interpretive statement:

> There is part of me that is . . . a weakly inferior colored boy, who feels sick and
> hurt by my position, but accepts it without outward protest or fight. . . . That
> colored boy has never changed much or grown up. . . . Another boy has grown
> up. He has pushed the colored boy into the background, so as to get him out of
> sight, out of life. . . . But sometimes [the colored boy] cannot be kept back. Then
> the discrepancy between the two becomes marked, the conflict active, acute. . . .
> This touchy part shall be admitted to full membership in the psyche of the pres-
> ent individual. With God's help we shall redeem that colored boy. . . . He shall
> be included and transformed for his sake but not his sake alone; for my sake,
> but not for my sake only. He shall be transformed for the sake of colored people
> and white people also, for since it was largely the influence of white people that
> brought him into being, he is theirs too. He is me, he is mine. He is also ours.[52]

Whatever one thinks of Toomer's various racial evasions in the public sphere,
one cannot fail to register the poignancy of the "active, acute . . . conflict" that
accompanied him into late middle age. The "colored boy" who had been pushed
aside for so long insisted upon claiming "full membership"—upon being "included
and transformed [and] redeemed"—in the psyche of the older man. That the aging
Toomer at the same time had disturbing dreams about his class partisanship is
not incidental: the angry workers outside the factory also demanded reentry into
the consciousness of a writer who had once, as both a New Negro and a socialist,
fervently advocated for the cause of oppressed and exploited humanity.

"One solid stake of oak": "Balo"

While Toomer's deconstruction of race eventually devolved into a pattern of
routine—if not entirely consistent—racial denial, this process was, as we have
seen, an extended one; the Toomer of later years simply cannot be read back
into the Toomer who produced *Cane*. Both his light-skinned appearance and his
awareness of the arbitrariness of racial designations led him to believe that the
nation—and the world—would be greatly improved if the notion of race were
to evaporate. But the author of *Cane* was deeply implicated in the debates of his
day over the definition and representation of the New Negro. For a time, Toomer
believed that the abolition of capitalism would entail the abolition of not just rac-

ism but race. His social constructionist approach to defining "the Negro" was at once economic, cultural, ideological, and historical: when he wrote *Cane,* Toomer was less interested in abolishing the category of race than in understanding how it had come into being, how it affected thought, emotion, and action, and how it served the interests of those in power, past and present.

Early manifestations of Toomer's divided impulses in portraying southern Negro life—toward a class-based analysis of racial division on the one hand, toward a folk-ish culturalism on the other—are displayed in "Balo," a one-act play that Toomer wrote soon after returning from Sparta. Toomer included "Balo" in the packet of texts he sent to Fauset at the *Crisis* in the spring of 1922; evidently she turned it down. In a July 1923 letter to Toomer, however, Locke wrote that he and Montgomery Gregory were "getting together a volume of race plays or rather Plays of Negro Life. (I prefer this way of putting it.) We will include Balo—if you can not give us something more mature—either in the same vein or a satirical vein. Both are needed. The great lack as I see it is in these two fields of the poetic-folk-play and the satire." Although he viewed "Balo" as "somewhat sketchy," Toomer agreed to submit the play. His 1921 memorandum book suggests that even while he was in Sparta he was wishing to explore "[t]he question: is the impulse behind the Negro's shouting to be found in true religious fervor, or does it arise from the repression of the emotional nature? Write a play centering around this conflict: outside pressure for race solidarity and seclusion contending with an inner impulse to embrace humanity." Staged in the 1923–24 season of the Howard Players, "Balo" appeared in Alain Locke and Montgomery Gregory's 1927 anthology, *Plays of Negro Life.*[53]

The implication of Locke's letter is that "Balo" qualifies only as a "poetic-folk-play" and possesses no satiric edge. But Toomer's one-act drama contains—at least up until its ending—a strong critique of the basis of religious false consciousness in capitalist social relations of production. The lengthy stage directions situate the relationship between the black farmer Will Lee and his white neighbor Jennings in a Marxist framework. Little separates the two families, notes Toomer, other than the "one solid stake of oak" serving as the "dividing line" between their properties. "[B]ut for the tradition of prejudice and the coercion of a rural public opinion," remarks Toomer, the "poor-white family . . . would . . . be on terms of a frank friendship with their colored neighbors, a friendship growing out of a similarity of occupations and consequent problems. As it is there is an understanding and bond between them little known or suspected by northern people." The Jenningses, we learn, occupy the old manor house, while the Lees inhabit a cabin in the former slave quarters; Jim Crow requires hierarchy, even among the oppressed. But both the Lees and the Jenningses have "resisted the temptation to invest in automobiles and player-pianos, saved their money, and so, this season, though their cotton crop failed with the rest, they have a nest egg laid away."[54]

Nonetheless, both families have been hard-hit by recession, deflation, the boll weevil, and the stranglehold of monopolist transportation costs; as the opening dialogue reveals, they have been reduced to barter. Will Lee remarks, "Money ain't t' be made when syrup can be bought fer what it takes t' haul th' cane, an' get it ground an' biled. An' corn at fifty cents a bushel." The eighty gallons of cane syrup that Will Lee's sons Balo and Tom have just stayed up all night to produce cannot figure as a commodity, for they have no exchange value. While super-abundant—they are "more'n we can use"—these gallons of syrup have only use value and will accordingly be shared with Will Lee's neighbor, on the understand-ing that at some point Jennings will mend Will Lee's ax or perform some other favor. The law of value does not mediate their exchange of goods and services: while commonly beleaguered by the market that determines the value of their produce, they practice barter in a local economy that is cooperative, even com-munistic. Cane, rather than possessing "deep-rooted" prophetic powers—as would be proclaimed in the epigraph to *Cane*—serves as a reminder of the dom-ination of small farmers by monopoly capitalism.[55]

While this primer on capitalist economic realities is confined to the stage di-rections, it frames the opening conversation between Will Lee and his younger son, Balo. Will Lee obsessively views the incursions of the boll weevil as pun-ishment for the sins of humanity: he chastises his sons for falling asleep while reading the Bible. To the audience, however, it is clear that the hard labor that Tom and Balo have performed all night, not their sinfulness, is what has made them drop off. Will Lee's preoccupation with the realm of spirit and inattention to the realm of the body—"Susan, whar is that there theology book? Mus' be studyin.' Can't afford t' waste no time when I's in th' service of th' Lord"—wearies his wife and his sons, who must take up his share of the work while he reads. Will Lee is not a wholly unsympathetic character, but the audience is invited to view his harsh parenting and fervent religiosity as displaced reactions to his straitened material circumstances. The Toomer who, in a letter to Locke from Sparta, referred to the need for "an economic, sociological standpoint" on rural black experience is evidently in command, perhaps writing with Marx at his elbow: labor occupies a central role in the play's initial presentation of the characters' mutual relations.[56]

This critical portraiture of Will Lee frames the audience's initial response to the blind former slave Uncle Ned. With a "far-away, other-worldly expression such as might have characterized a saint of old" on his aged face, Uncle Ned is even more convinced than Will Lee that the weevil is punishment from God. Scolding the rural folk who gather in Will Lee's house to play cards, he declares, "[I]n every weevil I see th' fingers of th' Lord. . . . Reckon you farmers better drap down on your knees an' pray, an' pray ter th' Lord fer ter free you from yo' sins." Yet the audience has not viewed any sinfulness among the people he addresses; although boisterous in their card-playing, they treat one another with generosity, affection and respect. Their "frolic" after a week of hard labor in the shadow of monopoly capital hardly signals the devil's work.[57]

Balo's mysticism, which dominates the last half of the play, invites a contradic-tory response. Awakening from his nap, Balo reads from the Book of Matthew a passage that proclaims death and destruction for those who do not follow the way of Jesus; he chants,

> An the floods came, an' the winds blew,
> O Lord, have mercy, Lord, O Lord
> Have Mercy on a soul what sins,
> O Lord on a darky sinner's soul.

While he evidently concurs with Will Lee and Uncle Ned about the readiness of the Lord to punish "darky sinners," Balo is aware that not all sinners are Negroes. As Jennings reports, he saw Balo "a while back . . . actin' like he was crazy" and repeating, "White folks ain't no more'n niggers when they gets ter heaven, white folks ain't no more'n niggers when they gets ter heaven." Balo's vision of heaven is prompted by a yearning for the abolition of Jim Crow: his God is at once authoritarian and egalitarian. When Balo begins to sing, the play's exploration of the query Toomer set himself—"Is the impulse behind the Negro's shouting to be found in true religious fervor, or does it arise from the repression of the emotional nature?"—takes center stage. Balo's words about Saul on the road to Damascus— "Th' voice that spoke t'Saul when he was born again"—signals that Balo feels he has been "saved": "Jesus, Jesus, I've found Jesus." But the next spiritual—"Steal away, steal away to Jesus, / . . . steal away home, / I ain't got long to stay here"— possesses a dual signification. As Toomer, a student of "slavery and the Negro," well knew—and as Du Bois had pointed out in his chapter on the spirituals in *The Souls of Black Folks*—"Steal Away" not only reflected a yearning to escape "over Jordan" but also was a coded signal among slaves planning to escape from a bondage very much in this world.[58]

As the card players abandon their game and join the chorus, however, the play's closing tableau dissolves its earlier tension between folk lyricism and satiric critique, the Bible and *The German Ideology*. Balo throws himself into the arms of Uncle Ned—who, according to the stage directions, "encircles him in love"; the card players "file out, heads lowered, in sheepishness and guilt." While Uncle Ned's beliefs about boll weevils and sin have been satirized earlier in the play, his closing embrace of Balo precludes ironic interpretation. Indeed, it suggests the humanity of a folk Christianity that supersedes the harshly judgmental doctrines embraced by Will Lee. The neighbors have still not been shown to have any objective basis for feeling guilt. But their status as rural laborers enmeshed in the social relations of capitalism has been trumped by their representation as black folk in danger of losing connection with their cultural roots. Jennings—along with the class analysis of race and racism associated with his role—is notably absent in the final scene. The culturalist turn embodied in the play's ending sutures over the critique of political economy with which the play began; the conventions of the folk play preempt "Balo"'s hesitant attempt at satiric commentary.[59]

Toomer would not retreat from the contradictions embedded in the project of "Balo" when he turned to the writing of *Cane*.

CHAPTER 3

The Experiment in America
Sectional Art and Literary Nationalism

The soil stands ready to be turned.
—Waldo Frank, *Our America*

Russia must be very stimulating just about now. But somehow I do not
envy you your trip. The Experiment here in America has an almost
complete hold upon my interests and imagination.
—Jean Toomer to Claude McKay, 23 July 1922

Jean Toomer's mid-1922 letter to Claude McKay—written soon before the poet
would travel to the USSR, where he was to participate in the Fourth World Congress of the Comintern—testifies not just to Toomer's attraction to current developments in the Soviet Union but also to his increasing fascination with what
he called the "American Experiment"—the literary nationalist-cum-modernist
movement that was going forward under the banner of Young America and largely
identified with the critic and novelist Waldo Frank. Although Toomer's period
of maximum involvement with the Young Americans (1922–24) followed upon
his earlier passions—his interest in socialism emerged as early as 1916, while his
active intellectual engagement with Washington's New Negroes began in 1920—
it would be a mistake to view this temporal phasing-in of his involvements as
indicative of a corresponding phasing-out. The fact that the African American
Marxist McKay was the addressee in Toomer's letter demonstrates the continuity
between and among Toomer's various commitments, all of which emerged from
the matrix of post–World War I radicalism and its denouement.

Because of the preponderant influence of Frank on Toomer during the gesta-
tion and creation of *Cane*, the contradictions informing the project of Young
America figure crucially in any historically situated consideration of Toomer's
1923 masterwork. Even as it promised that U.S. society could be defined by the
"good nationalism" of cultural pluralism rather than the "bad nationalism" of
"100% Americanism," Young America's rhetorical panache was compatible with
a quietist culturalism; its democratic progressivism could coexist with a racist
paternalism. Indeed, Toomer was to find that the place of race in the signifying chain linking folk, soil, region, and nation was by no means clear. Toomer's

personal relationship with Frank became fraught with an ambivalence that was all the more conflicted for being unacknowledged; the cognitive dissonance that would emerge in his remembered conflict with Alain Locke was writ large in his friendship with Waldo Frank.

"In a dying world, creation is revolution": Waldo Frank's America

Literary history has not been kind to Waldo Frank; his name is known mainly to specialists in American modernism, and most of his books have been out of print for years. But when Toomer sought and secured his sponsorship, Frank was one of the preeminent voices on the modernist literary scene. He had been associated with the *Seven Arts* and the *Dial* and was currently well connected with the "little magazine" movement; his novels were hailed for their avant-garde experimentalism; he was invited to lecture at the Rand School about art and politics. His 1919 critical study *Our America* had been greeted as the manifesto of a new direction in art and literature. Giving a radical turn to Van Wyck Brooks's psychoanalytic thesis that U.S. cultural history had been dominated by the conjoined legacies of puritans and pioneers, Frank highlighted the connections between psychological repression and capitalist class rule. The American Revolution "marked the triumph of the capitalistic state"; industrial modernity, producing the "extraverted man," was symbolized by the Machine, a "sucking monster, which as it sucked swelled larger and so sucked more." Democracy was a lie: "Labor in this country is cheated of its own resurgence by the common myth that any workman may reach the employer's class." The control of the nation's educational and publishing apparatus had been displayed in the recent firings of antiwar professors, dispelling "the myths of American free thought and American free speech."[1]

In sympathy with the political left, Frank claimed Marx as a "Jew [who gave] . . . form, substance, the passion of organic hope . . . [to the] social Revolution stir[ing] on its long and bloody course." The recent war signaled a "dying" world—embodied in "the Capitalist and his slave-orders, the European snob, the belated Colonial, the suppressed lover of blood"—even as "in the East where the Old World had gone down, the new World had risen." But culture was to be the key means to social transformation. The United States was "a turmoiled giant, [with] tied . . . tongue," waiting to be "lift[ed] into self-knowledge." The coming revolution required artists and writers to engage in "spiritual pioneering." There was a native usable past on which to draw: the gritty populism of Carl Sandburg and Edgar Lee Masters; the "buried cultures," Mexican and Indian, of the Southwest; the democratic universalism of Walt Whitman, in the "Word" of whose "Vision" was "a perfect sea, and in the sea a world, and in the world all men." What was now needed were "revolutionists" who were "cultural leaders" and "cultural leaders" who were "revolutionists." The radical essayist Randolph Bourne had condemned the mentality of the wartime "herd"; his critique of Anglo-Saxon bias in "Trans-National America" had pointed the way toward a "fusion" of politics and art. Although the *Liberator* group carried promise, the "soldier" who would be "the bringer of a new religion [and] the maker of multitudes" is "still not numerous, not articulate." The United States, with its history of expanding frontiers, lacked the store of "potential energy" that had enabled the "peasant and proletarian peoples of Europe" to rise up in "the kinetic energy of revolt"; the "impulse of New America is still unfused . . . [and] cannot [yet] prevail against the entrenchment of the Old." But writers and artists could cause the needed rupture: "In a dying world, creation is revolution."[2]

Frank's prose was animated by metaphors drawn from both science and politics. Tropes accenting the opposition of heat with cold, light with darkness, kinetic with potential energy, conveyed the contradictory forces operative in U.S. life. Whitman, he asserted, "underst[ood] how far the fire must burn down to make luminous the whole." The growing frustration of writers during the war was "a simmering pot of water over a heightening fire, without outlet. Each molecule of our social substance became more agitant, became the carrier of greater force." Drawing on leftist poetic conventions associating revolution with both fire and dawn, Frank wrote, "[I]n the scattered corners of the great Darkness, many men light many fitful fires. When once they meet, a flame will blaze across the sky." He quoted from Sandburg's "The Prairie":

> I speak of new cities and new people.
> I tell you the past is a bucket of ashes. . . .
> I am a brother of the cornhuskers who say at sundown:
> To-morrow is a day.

Frank also drew on the Marxist trope of parturition: when Sandburg's middle generation emerged from the "clamped dominion of Puritan and Machine," their call, a "frail outset of the flesh," was a "birth-cry." While the universities, controlled by the "moneyed classes," were "incubators of reaction," leftist writers and artists "bring their mastering love, their power of succinct analysis, to the nascent revolution"; John Reed "covers the battlefields of Europe watching for the birth he knows is due."[3]

Frank's dominant imagistic pattern connecting the artist to the nation drew on the *combinatoire* of terms comprising the organic trope. "Because [industrialism] cannot satisfy but a tithe of the humans whose suffrage it requires . . . [it] holds the seed of its own dissolution," he wrote. Rootless, "the average New Yorker is caught in a Machine [and] is whirled along . . . dizzy . . . and helpless. . . . [H]e must face to-morrow without that seed of dream, by which it might be rendered fecund." More often, however, botanical imagery functioned symbolically to limn the ideologeme of metonymic nationalism by linking seed with soil, soil with folk, folk with region, and region with nation. While Sandburg's generation could not harvest what it had planted, the coming generation of revolutionary writers "make loam for the growing prairie. The materialism of the middle-generation falls back to the despair that gave it birth. . . . It burned down the stubble of ancient harvests: it cleared the field for the new planting. The soil stands ready to be turned." Frank was calling not for a return to the soil but instead for a recognition of the potential future buried in the depths of the present, waiting to be brought to life.[4]

While clearly intended to offer a counter-discourse to the nativism of "100% Americanism," Frank's program was not without its shortcomings. The doctrine of "fusion," coupled with Frank's rejection of bourgeois notions of individual development, made his fiction tend toward a plotless lyricism, as was noted by grumpy reviewers of his early novels. Even the unanimistic short-story cycle *City Block* (1922)—which Toomer would view as Frank's stellar embodiment of "spherical form"—ends up homogenizing the characters' personalities and superseding their conflicts. Frank's project of subjecting an entire society to psychoanalysis ran the risk of creating stereotypes that mechanically—and at times racially—map out the zones of ego psychology. In his critical writing, moreover, Frank's antipathy to the Machine, although drawing on Marx's notion of capital as vampire, verged on a formalistic rejection of industrial modernity as such, while his doctrine of "fusion" threatened to suture the very contradictions it was meant to confront and remedy. His insistent use of naturalistic metaphors to describe historical processes at times carried the suggestion that those processes were themselves natural. Presumably constituting an alternative to the rhetoric of the nativists (for whom seed and plant growth signified, in connection with non-Anglo-Saxons immigrants, not belonging, but invasion), his tropes could end up fetishizing forces beyond human intervention. The call upon purposive historical actors to "turn the soil" is undermined by the proposition that the seeds they plant are "eternal." The hyper-materiality routinely accompanying Frank's use of the organic trope suggests a larger unresolved contradiction between the roles of immanence and agency in transforming U.S. cultural and political life.[5]

Frank's nationalism blended loyalty with opposition, quietism with rebellion. Of particular importance to Toomer would be the limitations—as well as the temptations—of its tendency to absorb historical critique into a spatialized pluralism. Frank's project of recovering the "buried cultures" of the Southwest ended up oddly inverting the discourse of manifest destiny. Even as it condemned the historical process by which "we walk a land that is a place of death . . . [while] [b]eneath our feet, lie buried the remains of a human world," his "we" was resolutely white. Meanwhile, people of African descent were entirely absent from Frank's historical survey. While he declared that "[s]lavery was merely the most ugly mark of the ugly spirit of the times," his narrative focused on conflict internal to Lincoln, not on the past and ongoing struggles of the enslaved and their descendants. Frank's view of the cultures of the nation's dark-skinned peoples as either "buried" or nonexistent suggested his acceptance of the view, widespread among the Socialist left, of these people as "non-historical." His psychoanalytic approach to the nation as a whole only further relegated its darker inhabitants, past and present, to the cellar of the nation's collective psyche. While cultural renewal would entail national self-scrutiny and purgation, the principal benefi- ciaries of this therapy need not unduly fear the return of the repressed.[6]

Our America, invoking the contested status of the ideologeme "America," dis- played the contradictory features of the metonymic nationalism emerging from the crucible of 1919. In his acknowledgment of the nation's expansionist past and capitalist present, Frank was substantially to the left of the currently hegemonic regionalist discourse: John Dewey's call for localism as the antidote to an oppressive homogeneity, Frederick Jackson Turner's contention that sectionalism constituted a force for "moderation" in American political life. Although these projects embraced an essentially federalist accession to states' rights and a dehistoricized notion of regional "genius," Frank acknowledged the temporal roots of intersectional conflict and linked these with the development of class conflict, alienation, and exploita- tion. His view of New York as the vanguard of coming cultural and political change expressed not merely a sectional bias but a view of the metropole as the formative ground of a revolutionary culture with national reach. Nonetheless, the program called for in *Our America* was—like the racialized program for which Locke would issue a call in 1925—unmistakably culturalist; its vanguard consisted of writers and artists, not the anonymous toilers comprised in the "turmoiled giant" of labor. Moreover, Frank's imagined redeemed republic bore little connection to the world revolution "in the East where the Old World had gone down, [and] the new World had risen." While McKay worked his way to the other side of the globe to examine the Soviet "experiment" and witness the gathering of the nascent Comintern, Frank lamented the nation's lack of peasant or proletarian traditions and focused instead on the fulfillment of its stated pluralistic ethos. In the Thermidorian repression following the upsurge of 1919, this would prove no small task; but it was hardly a route to the "socialized reality" for which the young Jean Toomer was issuing a summons even as *Our America* was appearing in the bookstores.[7]

"Her eyes still focus on the unfused metals of the melting-pot": "Americans and Mary Austin"

Although Toomer enjoyed relatively little success in his attempts to enter in the New York literary scene during the lonely months after he left the shipyard in the early winter of 1920, his meeting with Waldo Frank in June 1920 would prove life-changing. Toomer's subsequent reading of *Our America* inspired "Americans and Mary Austin," his first published piece of cultural criticism, which appeared in the *New York Call* in October 1920. Taking issue with a recent *Nation* article by Mary Austin, "New York: Dictator of American Criticism," Toomer lambasted the popular Western novelist for her charge that New York–based Jews had taken over the nation's cultural apparatus and were "dictating" their views to everyone else. Austin—who purported to advocate on behalf of both Native American culture and, more broadly, writers from the Midwest and the West—had charged that the New York cabal could not appreciate "the general movement of non–New York American writers to absorb into their work the aboriginal, top layer of literary humus through which characteristically national American literature, if we are ever to have it, must take root." Austin professed her pluralism—"there is nothing un-American in being a Jew"—but wondered, "Can the Jew, with his profound complex of election, his need of sensuous satisfaction qualifying his every expression of personal life, and his short pendulum-swing between mystical orthodoxy and a sterile, ethical culture—can he become the commentator, the arbiter, of American art and American thinking?" At stake in Austin's nativist polemic was the issue of metonymic nationalism: which writers could, by virtue of their regional or ethnic/demographic identification, claim to stand for the nation as a whole?[8]

Toomer's riposte was searing. He concedes Austin's point that it is vitally important to explore the relationship between Indian cultures and the broader U.S. culture: "This omission places a handicap on every effort at a true interpretation and understanding of what is comprehensively American." But he notes Austin's bypassing of the wretched conditions faced by the Japanese in Austin's own California and analogizes her view toward Jews with the "attitude [of the average Southern white] toward the Negro: 'No, th' nigger ain't un-American, so far as that goes: a good nigger's all right. An' he's damn useful pickin' cotton. But let him keep away from them polls. I ain't going to have no nigger legislatin' for me.'" Toomer opines that "New York and the New Yorkers are dictators of American criticism for the same reason that Moscow and the Bolsheviki are dictators of the present course of Russia, namely, that they are doing the job better than any others are now capable of doing it." Austin's "nominally valid protest against the one-sided development of the American intellect," he concludes, "degenerates into a force misdirected against the intellect vested in a single race; although it purports to desire 'the inevitable amalgamation and consequent cultural unity,' Miss Austin's article has given cause for old race consciousness. . . . [H]er eyes still focus on the unfused metals of the melting-pot."[9]

Austin's failure to set forth the terms in which "national ideals," "a national type," and "a national culture" might be formulated gives Toomer the opportunity to air his own developing conception of an "American race" transcending racial categories. "Though we are some distance from a realization of the race to be known as the American, yet in general contour and aspirations it is visible to those who see," he writes. "It is certain that it will be a composite one, including within itself, in complementing harmony, all races. . . . The splendid fire [of the grandeur of its destiny] will eventually coalesce what straggling tendencies to antagonism and disruption may still be hanging over from the former individual race consciousnesses." While racial amalgamation is the nightmare of the "narrow and prejudiced," there is "tremendous good" in the "certainty" of "nature's elements," where "rests the seed of the true American, the evolved spiritual pioneer of humanity." From this source, he concludes, "will a continent of Walt Whitmans evolve, universal in their sympathies and godlike of soul."[10]

Toomer's sharp response to Austin—a liberal who wrote for the *Nation* and taught at the Rand School—indicates his awareness that "rising tide of color" nativists like Gertrude Atherton and Lothrop Stoddard were not the only enemy: bigotry also prevailed among putative cultural pluralists. His sardonic quotation of the words of the "average Southerner" links Austin's anti-Semitism with the white supremacy and economic exploitation of Jim Crow, recalling the argument of "Reflections on the Race Riots" published in the *New York Call* the previous year. Toomer's comparison of "New York and the New Yorkers" with "Moscow and the Bolsheviki" not only analogizes "the New Yorkers" with the leaders of the Russian Revolution (a bit of a stretch) but also supports the New Yorkers' claim to speak for the nation. By linking Moscow, the political capital of the new proletarian state, with New York, the cultural capital of the United States, Toomer's claim is not only geographical and cultural but historical and political: with the New Yorkers at the helm, the United States may be heading toward a socialist future. Indeed, his claim recalls Lenin's description of New York as the quintessential example of the assimilation of nationalities through capitalism, where the eradication of national differences would become one of the driving forces to turn capitalism into socialism: "What happens in large, international scope in New York occurs in every big city and in every factory." In its enshrinement of Whitman and its call for "spiritual pioneer[ing]," Toomer's article is evidently inspired by *Our America*. Toomer's version of metonymic nationalism is, however, more explicitly anti-racist—and certainly more explicitly revolutionary—than Frank's. Indeed, Toomer supplies the link to the world revolution almost completely absent in Frank's text.[11]

At the same time, Toomer's argument is contained within the limits of Frank's nationalist counter-discourse. Toomer's all-embracing conception of the "seed of the true American" effectively refutes Austin's nativist view of the rootless Jew. But his insistence that the "true American's" implantation is an "evolved" process possessing "certainty" (both "true American" and "evolved" are repeated in the course of the 1,800-word essay)—displays his reliance on tropes drawn from botany and biology to describes processes that are fundamentally social— indeed, that require purposive social action of the type undertaken by "the Bolsheviki." The "fire" that will "coalesce [the] straggling tendencies to antagonism and disruption [that] may still be hanging over from the former individual race consciousness" is not, it seems, the fire of revolution. Instead, this fire will efface contradiction by conjoining all those "unfused metals of the melting-pot" that

Austin views with dismay. The contested nature of "America" in current debates is at once recognized and sloughed over.[12]

Even as the ideas and tropes informing Toomer's riposte to Austin reflect Frank's marked influence, Toomer's argument presages future conflicts with his soon-to-be mentor. Toomer clearly deplores Austin's anti-Semitism, equating it with the crudest Jim Crow racism. But he agrees with her argument that the "omission" of the "cultural resources of the Indian . . . places a handicap on every effort at a true interpretation and understanding of what is comprehensively American." His clear implication is that *any* race-based "omission" from a program for a national literature and art substantially diminishes that program's claim to representative status—a shortcoming that Toomer would immediately interrogate when his contact with Frank was renewed a year and a half later. Furthermore, Toomer's acute awareness of the need to overcome the economic exploitation and cultural marginalization of existing groups defined by race or ethnicity is presumably compensated by his utopian forecast of a future America in which the "old race consciousness" will have been superseded, apparently through racial amalgamation. The very different types of language in which these propositions are represented, however, signal his recognition of a gulf between the world of the present—where "th' nigger ain't un-American," in fact is "damn useful pickin' cotton" if he "keep[s] away from them polls"—and that of the future, whose denizens are described rhapsodically as "godlike of soul." The former linguistic usage suggests the author's acquaintance at close hand with the language of bigotry and identifies him as, most likely, a Negro. The latter suggests his kinship with a realm of beauty from which race has been abolished. How the two will connect—other than through "evolution"—is not revealed, nor is Frank's program seen to show the way.

"Keep yourself warm underneath, in the soil, where the throb is": Toomer, Frank, and Metonymic Nationalism

Toomer sent "Americans and Mary Austin" to Frank—as he did to Locke—in the fall of 1920; Frank responded graciously but distantly, remarking, "I doubt if the frowsy-minded Mary Austin deserved such intelligent destruction." It was only when Toomer wrote again to Frank in March 1922, shyly requesting, "I wonder if you wouldn't like to read a few of my things?" that their relationship took shape. In this outreach, Toomer gently chastised Frank—"I missed your not including [*sic*] the Negro in *Our America*"—but complimented his handling of the interracial relationship between two female characters in Frank's third novel, *Rahab*. Toomer introduced himself as having expertise in racial matters—"I spend a disproportionate time in Negro study"—and went on to note that he was himself of racially mixed background. Not too subtly suggesting his credentials as a protégé who might prove useful to Frank in the project of expanding the compass of *Our America*, Toomer described himself as containing "at least six blood minglings" and having "lived between the two worlds, now dipping into the Negro, now into the white. The texts that he sent for Frank's perusal—the play *Natalie Mann*, the closet drama "Kabnis," the poem "The First American," and several of the poems and sketches that would appear in *Cane*—testified to the aspiring writer's acquaintance with a world not familiar to Frank, as well as his ease in different genres. He was at once a New Negro and a ready recruit to Young America.[13]

The two men quickly moved to the stage of friendship, addressing one another as "Brother" and sharing observations and plans pertaining to their common literary program. Both men benefited from the friendship. Frank gave Toomer extensive commentary on his manuscripts, mixing enthusiastic encomiums with incisive critique; he helped edit, assemble, and order the jumble of texts—the "still unorganized mosaic"—that would eventually be *Cane*, playing Pound to Toomer's Eliot. Moreover, he supplied contacts with magazine editors and introductions to writers and critics of the avant-garde, arranged for the publication of *Cane* with Horace Liveright, and wrote a foreword giving Toomer's text the stamp of modernist approval. Toomer acknowledged Frank's impact on his project, writing to their mutual friend Gorham Munson, "I cannot *will* out of Waldo. With the exception of Sherwood Anderson some years ago (and to a less extent, Frost and Sandburg), Waldo is the only modern writer who has immediately influenced me." Toomer, for his part, attempted to gain an African American audience for Frank's work by promoting *City Block* among his Washington acquaintances. At Frank's request, he accompanied the older writer on a trip to the Deep South to gain background for Frank's lynching novel, *Holiday*, in the process enabling the deeply tanned Frank to travel as a Negro and gain direct exposure to Jim Crow. Toomer advised Frank regarding *Holiday*'s use of African American language and edited the final draft. He favorably reviewed Munson's *Waldo Frank: A Study* for the little magazine *S4N*. While the relationship would end in mutual bitterness, for a time it constituted one of the most productive interracial literary friendships in U.S. cultural history to date.[14]

The term "America" figures explicitly in the two writers' assertions about their shared mission. In his welcome to Toomer, Frank declared, "O if there is one thing I have learned, living in America . . . it is that the artist must have the greater wisdom of fighting for himself, of knowing that only so can the time come when the American world will be a place in which he can live." Toomer thanked Frank effusively for admitting him to the fold—"You have definitely linked me to the purpose and vision of what is best in creative America"—and soon spoke of their connection as a partnership. "How our mother, this America of ours, needs us, dear brother," he wrote from Washington's Meridian Hill, as he observed statues of Joan of Arc and Dante and pondered the absence of a comparable tribute to Whitman. Referring to the circulation of *City Block* among his capital-city ac-

Figure 3. Jean Toomer and Waldo Frank in South Carolina, fall
1922. Series 3, Family Papers, Jean Toomer, Photographs, Yale
Collection of American Literature, Beinecke Rare Book and
Manuscript Library

quaintances, he enthused, "I cannot think of myself as being separated from you
in the dual task of creating an American literature, and of developing a public,
however large or small, capable of responding to our creations."[15]

A soil-soaked nationalism underlay Toomer's often hyper-material use of the organic trope in letters to Frank and other modernists about the creation of a pluralist
U.S. culture. At times the trope was distinctly racialized, as when Toomer described
Frank's potential local readership: "[Although] the path to both of us is blocked by
rigid moral conventionalism, underneath, the soil is good rich brown, and should
yield splendidly to our plowing." Describing the Washington streets in springtime,
Toomer wrote, "Budding above the stems of streets and pavements, [the faces of
Negroes] are deep clusters of macadam-flowers." More often, however, Toomer
deployed the trope to depict the link between aesthetic creation and nurturing soil.
Proposing that he, Frank, and Munson edit a new magazine embodying the goals
of Young America, the increasingly self-confident Toomer declared, "Damn but I
would like to see a triumvirate of you, Munson, and myself. [Munson] has *roots* (is
he not coming up through *you*?) and *feelings*." Toomer reiterated this motif in a letter
to Munson about his book on Frank: "[Y]our approach, too, shows you coming up,
unfolding from your own soil. You are organic. You have roots." To Jane Heap, the
editor of the *Little Review*, Toomer enthused that the magazine "is itself germinal.

It needs no anterior functioning to explain it. It is the fulfillment of its own seed. It seems not to move, yet it does move. It is vibrant within itself, as all balanced life is." Writing to Lola Ridge about the New Orleans–based *Double Dealer*, Toomer praised the magazine's mission of bringing modernism to the South, "its pruning of what is false and imitative in art . . . its struggle to sink roots into deep American soil. . . . I should love to see the D-D both plant and harvest." While Toomer was obviously currying favor with his newfound modernist acquaintances—and papering over his criticisms—it bears noting that he consistently deployed the *combinatoire* of seed, soil, root, plant, fruit, and harvest to describe, and insert himself within, the project of creating a nationally based modern literature.[16]

Toomer also consistently described his own literary production by means of botanical imagery. Toomer originally envisioned *Cane* as a tripartite text, each section of which would be designated by a botanical header. "I think that I shall call it CANE," he wrote to the *Double Dealer* editor John McClure in mid-1922, "[h]aving as sub-heads Cane Stalks and Choroluses [*sic*] (Karintha, Fern, etc and two longer pieces), Leaves (poems), and Leaf Traciers [*sic*] in Washington." His text in progress, he wrote to Frank, was "a leaf that will unfold, fade, die, fall, decay, and nourish me." His friend had supplied the soil in which *Cane* was growing to fruition: "I've got to get Cane planted, and sink deep into you before it can come off." When the book appeared, "the soil" of "Kabnis" was dedicated to his friend and mentor, to whom he had written, "You not only understand CANE; you are in it, specifically here and there, mystically because of the spiritual bond that is between us." Having effected—with Frank's help—a merging of poetry and prose in the final version of *Cane*, Toomer reflected to Munson, "I see the importance of form. The tree as a symbol comes to mind. A tree in summer. Trunk, branches: structure. Leaves: the fillers-out, one might almost say the padding. The sap is carried in the trunk etc. From it the leaves get their sustenance, and from their arrangement comes their meaning."[17]

For both Frank and Toomer, metaphors associating the planting of seeds and the bearing of fruit often carried distinctly sexualized, even androgynous, overtones. In his first commentary on Toomer's work, Frank noted of *Natalie Mann* that, while the play's "vision" was "mothered and fathered of true temperament, [passion], [and] intellectually well-midwifed," the form was "not yet there." By contrast, "Kabnis," while yet an "only partly formulated organism," contained "the embryon of an expression which America has not had even the faintest inkling of, and which America demands." He urged his young friend to "nourish" this newly formed life "with the best of yourself." Noting that "the so-called literary and artistic milieus are indeed strewn with excrement and decay . . . but so are the fallow fields," Frank advised, "Keep yourself warm underneath, in the soil, where the throb is . . . and use every decent means in your reason to protect yourself from a too early pushing to the surface. . . . You must preserve for yourself the freedom, the quiet, and the peace in which the spirit may turmoil and seethe and ecstasy to birth." The author here is at once father, mother, and midwife of his text, as well as the embryo nestled in the womb/soil of the nation.[18]

Toomer responded to Frank in kind. Noting his dissatisfaction with a current project of his own—most likely "Withered Skin of Berries"—he wrote, "The skeleton is knit by the . . . dry cartilage of the two races. But what are bones! The flesh and blood and spirit are my own. It is struggling, of course, to an impartial birth. My recompense is its creation." "Kabnis," he wrote as *Cane* neared completion, "took a year to grow in me." Comparing Frank's work with that appearing in Munson's new avant-garde magazine *Secession,* Toomer praised his mentor's "richer, purer, more sheer poetry, [which] seems eternal against the impression of their transience." He added, "Nor do I feel in them the travail which promises greater births." As he offered Frank detailed advice about how best to capture the nuances of black speech, as well as to convey black-white interactions in the South, he noted that emerging "beauty" of *Holiday* "comes with blood and soil and warmth . . . [T]he soil is close to [the characters] . . . It breathes." He concluded, "[A]ny number of scenes . . . have the heaving pulsebeats of arteries. . . . You have released this thick beauty from yourself. . . . You are budding to poetry my brother."[19]

The sometimes dizzying metaphors conjoining literary creation with parturition and plant growth that Toomer developed through his correspondence with Frank converge in the complex trope framing Toomer's famous description of the creation of *Cane* in his December 1922 letter to Sherwood Anderson:

> Just before I went down to Georgia I read Winesburg, Ohio. And while there, living in a cabin whose floorboards permitted the soil to come up between them, listening to the old folk melodies that Negro women sang at sun-down, the Triumph of the Egg came to me. The beauty, and the full sense of life that these books contain are natural elements, like the rain and sunshine, of my own sprouting. My seed was planted in the cane- and cotton-fields, and in the souls of black and white people in the small southern town. My seed was planted in *myself* down there. Roots have grown and strengthened. They have extended out. I spring up in Washington.

Toomer here proposes himself as exhibit A, displaying the genesis of art in the nurturing soil of a folkish nation. Writing to a white man, he takes care to distance himself from a specifically racialized portrayal of that folk; he stipulates that his "seed was planted . . . in the souls of black and white people in the small southern town." His primary inspiration by the "old folk melodies [sung by] Negro women at sundown" locates his text not only in Anderson's earlier efforts to depict black characters—as in "Out of Nowhere into Nothing," in *The Triumph of the Egg*— but also in Toomer's own experience with black culture, which lends particular legitimacy to the birthing of *Cane*. His description of writerly parthenogenesis reinforces his text's claim to authenticity; his comparison of writerly inspiration to a plant whose root system extends from the Deep South to the nation's capital reinforces his text's claim to embed the national in the sectional. If Toomer's prose creaks somewhat under the weight of its hyper-material metaphors, this strain results from the considerable effort required to place Negro folk songs at one end of the metonymic chain extending from folk—black folk in particular—to nation. But his determination to assert the existence of this chain—and to place himself in it as a vital link—is evident.[20]

"I want great substance, great power": Frank, Munson, and the Literature of Technological Modernity

Even as Toomer was drawn to the project outlined in *Our America*, this project was undergoing change. By the time Toomer and Frank became friends in the spring of 1922, Frank was acknowledging that the revolutionary cultural movement he had proclaimed in 1919 had not come into being. "When I wrote Our America I thought I was heralding a fact, not prophesying," he wrote. "I was at least time-dimensionally wrong. We must still persevere alone." He was also relinquishing some of his more radical propositions. In a May 1922 review of current literary trends titled "The Major Issue," Frank lamented the preoccupation with "psychology" and "documentary material" in current fiction; there were, he believed, only "a few true creators, capturers of organic form—which is another term for life—from the hinterlands at which mankind kindles its fires and forges its tomorrows." Rather than naming these writers and expanding on their contributions, though, as he had done in *Our America*, Frank now focused on the barrenness of the notion of "realism"—"as senseless a term as has ever been picked up from a junk shop"—for its pretension to adequate representation. Frank's rationale was largely epistemological. Because "our standard of reality is an accumulating, gyrating and disappearing flux of subjective contributions," he averred, any "program-making" for linking art with reality must "start from a recognition of the extra-intellectual nature of creation." He wrote, "Let the novelist think that he is primarily concerned with socialism, housing problems, psychoanalysis and the like. If he is an artist, his thinking will be but a detail of his work; and if he is not an artist his work will be but a negligible detail of his thinking." Where three years before, in *Our America*, Frank had praised Randolph Bourne for his "fusion" of art and politics, here he stressed their essential separation.[21]

Toomer praised Frank's review as "a much-needed shaft in the right direction" and expressed his agreement with Frank's statement that "'every artist that has lived in the world is a realist insofar as he himself is real and as his material, determined by himself and the world, must be real.' A dream is real; a dray is real." While applauding his newfound mentor's critique of conventional realism, however, Toomer seemed to have downplayed his differences with Frank's antipathy to "program-making" and embrace of subjectivity as the key to "organic form." After all, Frank's stance ran directly counter to Toomer's own earlier critique of Richard Aldington, in which Toomer had written that—contrary to the prominent imagist's contention that "the old cant of a poet's 'message' is now completely discredited"—"'messages' are now as always measured by their merit. . . . [A] fine message beautifully expressed, or a strong message vigorously expressed, will be accepted and appreciated now as much as in any former time." In fact, in his letter Toomer singled out for praise the very aspect of Frank's aesthetic theory that Frank himself—in a text otherwise dedicated to an attack on the notion of "realism"—had termed "realist." Toomer's continuing reluctance to voice—perhaps even to formulate—his misgivings about Frank's positioning within the culture wars would emerge a few months later in a commentary on a recent criticism of Frank by the writer and critic Kenneth Burke. Toomer defended Frank's fiction from Burke's charge that it lacked coherence and complained that Burke "completely passes the aesthetic of your language." He remarked, however, that "Burke's questioning of the structural significance of CB [*City Block*] is his best taken point. Just this, with the serious critics, will dog you." Despite his expressed admiration of his mentor's critical and creative work, Toomer, as he became more confident of his own creative abilities, registered a growing uneasiness with the idealist mimetic theory underlying Frank's oeuvre.[22]

Throughout the latter part of 1922, Toomer was also widening his modernist lens and becoming increasingly attracted to the group of writers clustered around *Secession* and *Broom*. Where Frank was essentially allergic to the advanced technology of industrial modernity, viewing it as the source of "mechanical civilization," the proponents of an alternative version of the avant-garde held up the machine as a means to emancipation from weary cultural and literary conventions. Drawing on both prewar European futurism and the explosion of a machine-based discourse in postrevolutionary Russia, the U.S.-based proponents of an art that embraced the machine—sometimes dubbed "skyscraper primitives"—were broadly cosmopolitan in outlook. Gorham Munson's *Secession*—a magazine that made its debut in 1922 while Toomer was immersed in the creation of *Cane*—was premised, as its title suggested, on the notion that expatriation was not the only option available to the writer reacting against the "aesthetic sterility of the present directions of American letters." Munson declared, "The young American can now function in his home milieu. If he doesn't like it, he has another and less distorting alternative than revolt into exile: he can secede." Munson's machine aesthetic laid claim to a variant on U.S. nationalism that invoked the notion of civil war: those writers dissatisfied with the literary status quo could and should stand their ground, rather than abandon the terrain to magazines fearful of the avant-garde. Claiming to have been "in every power-house in the city, years before I dragged myself to the Corcoran Gallery of Art"—indeed, to have been drawn to "such things as motorcycle motors, dynamos, and generators" from childhood onward—Toomer applauded Munson's "acceptance of the machine, the attitude (the only healthy, the *only* art attitude) which uses modern forms, and not the hurt caused by them, as the basis of literature." In correspondence with Lola Ridge, Toomer praised *Broom* in comparable terms, noting approvingly the magazine's promotion of a "national culture" that overcomes the "sterile, abortive condition" of "the artist's separation from and denial of what is salient and positive in his country, its forms and people." He continued, "The machine, its motion, mass, and precision is at last significant not because of the pain it inflicts upon sensitive maladjusted spirits, but for the reason that its elements are the starting-points of creative form. . . . *Broom*, as no other, has served the purposes of transition (revolution!) and liberation."[23]

Even as he aligned himself with *Secession* and *Broom*, however, Toomer was aware of the shortcomings of an avant-garde project that confined its embrace of the machine to formal experimentation. After approving Munson's "acceptance of the machine," Toomer continued:

> There's something lacking in your program. Take the machine: you get form, you get simplification, you get at least the basis for strangeness, you get abstractness. . . . A toy model of a machine would give you these. Whats lacking in the toy? Power, friend. Power! . . . A weak machine is ready for the scrap heap. Whatever its design, what significance is there to a machine if it will not do work? What to a poem or a sketch or a novel if they will not do their work. . . . [T]he dualism of form and substance is largely specious. . . . Great design cannot rise from puny matter. I want great design . . . great substance, great power.

Notably, Toomer designated "work" and "power"—terms possessing both physical and political resonance—as the key features lacking in Munson's program. We are reminded of Toomer's claim, in his *New York Call* essay on Mary Austin, that "Moscow and the Bolsheviki . . . are doing the job better than any others are now capable of doing it," as well as his *Cane*-era journal meditation about the need for "the workers [to] bellow, 'We Want Power!'" Indeed, his critique of Munson's formalism suggests an affinity with Lenin's 1920 declaration that "communism is Soviet power plus the electrification of the whole country"; electrical power could not be disjoined from workers' power. Toomer's differences with both Frank and Munson were inseparable from his continuing demand for "extra-artistic consciousness" in works of art and literature; this "extra-artistic consciousness," in turn, was inseparable from Toomer's continuing commitment to a leftist politics and practice.[24]

That Toomer envisioned his own synthesis of the organic and the mechanical as a potential carrier of "great power" is indicated in his correspondence with both Munson and Ridge. Extending the intricate organic metaphor comparing his text with a tree in his March 19, 1923, letter to Munson, Toomer continued, "This symbol is wanting, of course, because a tree is stationary, because it has no progressions, no dynamic movements. A machine has these, but a machine is all form, it has no leaves. Its very abstraction is now the death of it. Perhaps it is the purpose of our age is to fecundate it? But its flower, unlike growing things, will bud within the human spirit." The political implications of an art aiming to "fecundate . . . the machine" were developed in Toomer's description to Ridge of the envisioned contribution of "Kabnis"—forthcoming in *Broom*—to the project of the magazine: "The aesthetic of the machine, the artistic acceptance of what is undeniably dominant in our age, the artist creatively adopting himself to angular, to dynamic, to mass forms, the artist creating from the stuff he has at hand,— these things have life and vitality and vision in them. . . . And I think my own contribution will curiously blend the rhythm of peasant[r]y with the rhythm of machines. A syncopation, a slow jazz, a sharp intense motion, subtilized, fused to a terse lyricism." Toomer's proposed fecundation of the machine would entail drawing together in a single text not only the different "rhythms" of the country and the city but also the differentiated modes of production based on peasant and industrial labor. The "terse lyricism" drawing on the "angular, . . . dynamic, . . . mass forms" of modernity would derive from its engagement with the historical forces shaping the emergence of the present and the future from the past.[25]

These forces were, moreover, not limited to the boundaries of the nation; this project would transcend the limitations of sectional art. Although Toomer characteristically stressed what was "American" in the tasks facing his contemporaries and himself, he continued to describe the challenge of the day in transnational terms. Writing to Rex Fuller of the Poetry Society of South Carolina in early 1923, Toomer predicted that "[a] great literature will spring (is springing) from [the South]. A literature, sectional, in that its source is a complete experience of the immediate environment. A literature national in all else, and the best of it, universal." In the plans for his next project—sketched in a letter to Margaret Naumberg in the summer of 1923 and expanded in some fragmentary notes titled "General Ideas and States to Be Developed"—Toomer contemplated a bildungsroman allegorically conjoining the regional and the national with a larger "universal." The text's narrative arc—seemingly a counter to that of *Cane*—would take the protagonist from North to South to North: "Beginning with a New York of scattered, brilliant surfaces, of up-rooted industrialism, business, machines, thoughts, art,—of these things stray, futile, neurotic, tortured, clogging a deep spiritual heave,—external movement converges to an inner intensity that shoots the central character to the soil of Georgia, and plants him there." The organic trope prevails in the sketch: "For months [the protagonist] is submerged and germinal" before returning to the city. Yet he is also "a generator, making his own qualitative energy," and "a transformer, turning the crude energy of his material world into stuff of higher, rarer potency": the discourse of futurism describes the energies driving the hero's geographical transit. New York "takes what is native to America and lifts it to a station half-way between the provincial and the true cosmopolitan, arrests it mid-way between earth and heaven. It is the factory of internationalism, but not yet the school of universal man." Aiming at the "racial unification of America," the text would lead to "a perception that is satisfied with nothing less than essentialized MAN"; its "art-form" would be "inclusive: American, extra-American, European. Universal? I hope so."[26]

Indicating that Toomer did not need to visit Gurdjieff in Fontainebleau to discover his mystical vein, these notes demonstrate that, for Toomer, the notion of the "universal" enabling transcendence of the national was taking on an increasingly cosmic tinge; there is no mention of the "brown and black worlds heaving upward" in a movement toward "the proletariat or world upheaval." Nonetheless, his designation of New York as the "factory of internationalism" suggests a continuing adherence to the Leninist conception of the U.S. metropole as a site resembling a factory under whose roof national differences are dissolved. These notes and summaries suggest that, even in the wake of *Cane*, Toomer did not conceive of the "experiment in America" as the necessary end point of the metonymic chain linking the peasantry of the Deep South with a broad notion of human liberation. "Our America" would have to lead beyond America in order to emancipate those dwelling within the borders of the United States.

"The invasion into this womb of the ferment seed": Frank's Foreword to *Cane*

Toomer's continuing commitment to an antiracist internationalism is important when we consider the vexed question of his eventual break with Frank. Frank's famous foreword to *Cane*, which is often seen as occasioning the rupture between the two men, needs to be quoted at length:

> Reading this book, I had a vision of a land, heretofore sunk in the mists of muteness, suddenly rising up into the eminence of song. . . . This book *is* the South. . . . A poet has arisen . . . who writes, not as a Southerner, not as a rebel against Southerners, not as Negro, not as apologist or priest or critic: who writes as a *poet*. . . . He has made songs and lovely stories of his land . . . not of its yesterday, but of its immediate life.
>
> The gifted Negro has been too often thwarted from becoming a poet because his world was forever forcing him to recollect that he was a Negro. The artist must lose such lesser identities in the great well of life. . . . The whole will and mind of the creator must go below the surfaces of race. And this has been an almost impossible condition for the American Negro to achieve, forced every moment of his life into a specific and superficial plane of consciousness. . . .
>
> For Toomer, the Southland is not a problem to be solved; it is a field of loveliness to be sung; the Georgia Negro is not a downtrodden soul to be uplifted; he is material for gorgeous painting: the segregated self-conscious brown belt of Washington is not a topic to be discussed and exposed; it is a subject of beauty and of drama, worthy of creation in literary form.
>
> How typical is *Cane* of the South's still virgin soil and of its pressing seeds! Part One is the primitive and evanescent black world of Georgia. Part Two is

the threshing and suffering brown world of Washington, lifted by opportunity and contact into the anguish of self-conscious struggle. Part Three is Georgia again . . . the invasion into this black womb of the ferment seed: the neurotic, educated, spiritually stirring Negro. As a broad form this is superb, and the very looseness and unexpected waves of the book's parts make *Cane* still more *South*, still more of an aesthetic equivalent of the land.

. . . The notes of [Toomer's] counterpoint are particular, the themes are of intimate connection with us Americans. But the result is that abstract and absolute thing called Art.[27]

Toomer's immediate response to Frank's manuscript version of the foreword was, to all appearances, one of heartfelt gratitude: "The one thing I was uneasy about in a foreword was this: that in doing the necessary cataloguing and naming etc the very elements which the book does *not* possess would get plastered across its first pages. . . . The facts for a curious public to toss about, are there. But your point of view is so overwhelmingly that of Art that the divisions and parcellings do not obtrude." In particular, he thanked Frank for describing *Cane* as "an aesthetic equivalent of the land" and the emerging writer himself as "a force, personal [and] artistic." In his 1931 autobiography, however, Toomer would write that, when he read Frank's foreword to *Cane*, he had felt wounded by Frank's insisting upon identifying the book's author as a Negro:

Well, I asked myself, why should the reader know? Why should any thing be incorporated into a foreword to *this* book? Why should Waldo Frank or any other be my spokesman in this matter? All of this was true enough, and I was more or less reconciled to letting the preface stand as it was, inasmuch as it was so splendid that I could not take issue with it on this after all minor point, inasmuch as my need to have the book published was so great, but my suspicions as to Waldo Frank's lack of understanding of, or failure to accept, my actuality, became active again.

As I found out later from several sources, my doubts were warranted. I have been told that Frank, after seeing myself and my family, after hearing my statement, not of words or visions but of facts, returned to New York and told people of the Negro writer who was emerging into the world of American literature. In any event, it was thus through Frank's agency that an erroneous picture of me was put in the minds of certain people in New York before my book came out. Thus was started a misunderstanding in the very world, namely the literary art world, in which I expected to be really understood. I knew none of this at the time. . . .

Coupling this 1931 recollection of Toomer's frustration with Frank with his 1934 retrospective account of his anger at Locke, scholars have often concluded that both reactions were rooted in the same cause. In one interpretation, Toomer was grasping the tragic difficulty of persuading even his closest literary allies, white and black, of his avant-garde position on race. In another interpretation, he was beginning the retreat from acknowledgment of his African American heritage that would culminate in his passing over the color line. Both variants assume, however, that the later autobiographical accounts contain accurate representations of Toomer's original responses.[28]

Frank had offered contradictory formulations in his foreword to *Cane*, at once asserting the racial identity of the text's author and declaring that this identity was superseded by the imperatives of "Art." But there is reason to take with several grains of salt Toomer's later insistence that he had been distressed by Frank's designation of *Cane*'s author as a Negro, which presumably reflected Frank's "lack of understanding of, or failure to accept, my actuality." In early 1923, when arranging for Toomer to take part in a "series of recitals" involving modernist poets and musicians, Frank had encouraged Toomer to "do your Negro stuff. . . . It will of course be necessary . . . to feature something special like that, as by yourself you arent a drawing card—AS YET." Toomer replied, "Sure, feature Negro." Later thanking Frank for the foreword, Toomer granted "the necessary cataloguing and naming" and acknowledged that "the facts for a curious public to toss about are all there." His original fear—which had been allayed, he claimed, by Frank's text—had been the "obtru[sion] of "divisions and parcellings" that might result from this "cataloguing and naming." These communications suggest that, at least in 1923, Toomer was by no means upset by Frank's allusions to the racial heritage of the author of *Cane*. Mentioning the foreword in a January 1924 letter to Montgomery Gregory, indeed, Toomer noted, "[T]he introduction is good. It is a statement of a general truth. It gives the only attitude that will yield art from Negro material. It furnishes a fine lead-up to *Cane*, and posits the point of view from which the book may truly [be] appreciated."[29]

Toomer's participation in the publicity for *Cane* further documents his collusion in the marketing of *Cane* as the work of a Negro writer. Horace Liveright aggressively sought to advertise *Cane* as black-authored, writing to Toomer, "I feel that right at the very start there should be a definite note sounded about your colored blood. To my mind this is the real human interest value of your story and I don't see why you should dodge it." Toomer replied:

> My racial composition and my position in the world are realities which I alone may determine. . . . As a B and L author, I make the distinction between my fundamental position and the position which your publicity department may wish to establish for me in order that *Cane* reach as large a public as possible,—in this connection, I have told you, I have told Messrs. Tobey and Schneider to make use of whatever racial factors you wish. Feature Negro if you wish, but do not expect me to feature it in advertisements for you. For myself, I have sufficiently featured Negro in *Cane*. Whatever statements I give will inevitably come from a synthetic human and art point of view; not from a racial one. As regards my sketch-life—it was not my intention or promise to give a completed statement of my life. It was my intention to give briefly those facts which I consider to be of importance, and then to allow your publicity department or the writers on the various papers and magazines to build up whatever copy seemed most suited

to their purposes. I expect, therefore, that you so use it. With this reservation: that in any copy not used for specific advertising purposes the essentials of my sketch be adhered to. I mean, for instance, that in copies of *Cane* sent out to reviewers (these are not advertisements)—that any pamphlets included in these copies should follow the essential lines of my sketch. All this may seem over-subtle and over-refined to you, but I assure you that it isnt.

Rudolph Byrd and Henry Louis Gates Jr. voice the mainstream critical opinion when they propose that Toomer "refused to cooperate" with Liveright in publicizing the book. But although the opening salvo of Toomer's reply displays his irritation, the rest strongly suggests that Toomer was attempting to have his cake and eat it, too. The "advertising" and "publicity" for his book could "feature Negro" if this copy was composed by someone on Liveright's staff; any "pamphlets" accompanying copies of the book sent to reviewers, however, were to adhere to Toomer's own largely deracialized autobiographical sketch and textual commentary. Toomer apparently did not feel that this position was "over-subtle and over-refined," but it may have created considerable confusion for his publisher.[30]

Toomer's sketch for Liveright, furthermore, teased the reader about the identity of the author of *Cane*, as well as about the generic identity of the text. While Toomer portrayed his upbringing in race-neutral terms and omitted all mention of his participation in the artistic circles of Washington's Negro intelligentsia, he acknowledged the genesis of *Cane* in the author's encounter with "rich, dark-skinned black life" in the Deep South. This assertion suggestively referenced an experience unavailable to someone not permitted entry into the world "behind the veil." Toomer's description of *Cane*—which was reproduced both in his authorial sketch and on the inside flap of the dust jacket—also indirectly "featured Negro":

This book is a vaudeville out of the South. Its acts are poems, sketches, short stories, and one long drama. The curtain rises (Part One) upon the folk life of southern Negroes. Their simple tragedies, their wistfulness, and their crude joy in life become articulate in prose and poems. The color of Georgia soil is in them. And the old folk songs are ever heard as overtones.

Part Two is the more complex and modern brown life of Washington. Jazz rhythms all but supplant the folk tunes—one simple narrative weaves its plaintive way, and is almost lost amid the complications of the city.

Part Three (a single drama), Georgia again. But this is not a brief tale of peasant sorrow. It is a moving and sustained tragedy of spiritual suffering. For here a nervous and dynamic northern sensitivity comes to grips with the crude beauty and ugliness of the South, and a northern intelligence battles with the southern Negro waywardness, oppression, and superstition of southern Negro life.

There can be no cumulative and consistent movement, and of course no central plot to such a book. It is sheer vaudeville. But if it be accepted as a unit of spiritual experience, then one can find in *Cane* a beginning, a progression, a complication, and an end. It is too complex a volume to find its parallel in the

Negro musical comedies so popular on Broadway. *Cane* is black vaudeville. It is black super-vaudeville out of the South.[31]

It has been proposed that Toomer's designation of *Cane* as "black super-vaudeville" was his publisher's invention. To be sure, the advertisement that appeared in *Publishers' Weekly* in July 1923 contains a closing sentence that could hardly have been penned by the author: "This book is vaudeville out of the South. Its acts are sketches, short stories, one long drama and a few poems. Through them all one feels the primitive rhythm of the Negro soul." Toomer evidently omitted this last statement—most likely written by someone in the Boni and Liveright publicity department, perhaps Liveright himself—from the sketch he wished to be distributed to reviewers and included on the dust jacket of *Cane*. But there is no question that Toomer played a key role in composing the longer version of the sketch, in which "vaudeville out of the South" was changed to "black super-vaudeville out of the South." Different versions of the sketch exist among his papers, all carrying notations and revisions in Toomer's hand. The text contains, moreover, a number of terms and expressions occurring elsewhere in Toomer's writings, such as the description of the North as "complex" and the references to the "beauty and ugliness," "waywardness," and "superstition" of the South. Toomer's principal concern was to supply the reviewers and readers of *Cane* with guidelines for understanding the book as both a work of modernist experimentalism and an engagement with the full range of African American life. Toomer was clearly reluctant to fetishize his text as an essentialist expression of a fixed Negro identity; indeed, his insistence upon the book's avant-garde features—its lack of a "central plot" or "cumulative or consistent movement"—is integral to his claim that it is impossible to designate a single experience as *the* Negro experience. But his description of the ways in which *Cane* itself "features Negro" strongly suggests that only a Negro could have authored the text. As in the case of Toomer's 1934 repudiation of Locke's having published portions of *Cane* in *The New Negro*, his retrospective 1931 account of Frank's role in promoting his text tells us far more about Toomer's racial attitudes in the early 1930s than about the attitudes and emotions animating the man who had written *Cane* nearly a decade before.[32]

"Temperamental variations which so delight the experienced reader": Toomer on *Holiday*

Although Toomer may not have resented Frank's identification of *Cane*'s author as a Negro when *Cane* first appeared, his critical comments on *Holiday*, Frank's lynching novel, suggest that he was coming to view Frank's notions about race, as well as the antirealist thrust of Frank's prose, with increasing skepticism. Toomer's letters to Frank indicate that he offered nothing but effusive praise when he read the novel in draft in late 1922. Upon the simultaneous publication of their works by Liveright in September 1923, Toomer professed writerly solidarity: "Well old soldier it looks as if Holiday and Cane are going over. Not best sellers—hell no— but the sort of selling and notice that really counts." In a review published the next month in the *Dial*, however, Toomer offered a not-so-gently barbed critique. Asserting that "Frank is too subtle for an arbitrary portioning of repression, in a block, to the whites of the South . . . [or for] a rigid symbolizing of the blacks as expression," he retracted the compliment almost immediately. "[I]n this novel the blacks generally represent a full life," observed Toomer, "while the whites stand for a denial of it." Noting that the novel's "subjective design" makes "whatever local or racial truth or untruth the work may contain . . . a purely secondary fac- tor," Toomer asserted that the novel's characters are "purely Frankian in origin." Toomer was now turning against Frank the proposition—articulated in "The Major Issue"—that "our standard of reality is an accumulating, gyrating and disap- pearing flux of subjective contributions." Apparently Frank's "subjective design" had entailed a disregard for authentic representation, leading him to reproduce Freudian racial binaries that, Toomer adjudged, contain more "racial untruth" than "racial truth." Although Toomer concluded that "as an art form [*Holiday*] is clean, superb," this testimony to the powers of art—or Art—clashed with the realist premises undergirding Toomer's critique. Notably, the accuracy of Frank's mimesis with regard to race was what had aroused Toomer's ire.[33]

Toomer reiterated this judgment of Frank's propensity for racial stereotyping in "The South in Literature," his anonymously authored comparative review essay on *Holiday* and *Cane* that he had written with the intention of having it published in the *New York Call*. Toomer asserts that the two texts contribute to the "matura- tion of a sectional art" by focusing on the South, which "has a peasantry, rooted in the soil, such as neither the North nor the West possesses," but "the expression of which the general cultural body stands in sore need of." The essay then drops its bombshell. Since "the juxtaposition of the white and black races is so typical of Southern life," Toomer continues, "it is of real interest to know that the authors of these books are personally expressive of this racial contrast. For Waldo Frank is of white, while Jean Toomer is of Negro descent." While Toomer proposes that the texts' authors, as "artists . . . are not thus concerned with a limiting of life to rival claims," he asserts that "[i]nevitably racial difference has its function in pure litera- ture." Indeed, it is the "temperamental variations which so delight the experienced reader" that supply the basis for distinguishing between the two texts. The Toomer who presumably resented Frank's designation of him as a Negro writer here deploys this racial identity to undermine Frank's claim to legitimacy.[34]

Toomer contrasts the two books in a double-edged discourse. Referring to the stark contrast between "whitetown" and "niggertown" in Frank's Nazareth as "typically Southern," Toomer outlines Frank's conceptions of the two populations. In *Holiday*, "[t]he cabins and the black peasantry of niggertown are ingrown products of the soil. Negroes are as firmly rooted as the pine trees are. Like these trees, black men sprout to life with movement circumscribed." The inhabitants of "whitetown," by contrast, are "compressed and restricted" by conventional limitations"; when aroused in a religious frenzy, they form a mob and lynch an innocent man. "Anyone at all familiar with the South," writes Toomer, "will recognize this scene and plot and these materials as typical of it." In his discussion of *Cane*, Toomer stresses the Negro author's grounding of racial violence in the southern political economy. The Middle Georgia setting of part 1 is described as "a symphony of red soil, pine trees, canebrakes and cotton fields, swamps, saw-mills, old Negro cabins, and hills and valleys saturate with the blood and toil, the songs and sufferings of the slave regime." Noting that the section "ends in a lynching," Toomer laconically remarks, "Readers of these two books will find it of interest to compare the temperamental approach to this theme with the approach to the similar one in *Holiday*." Describing part 2 of *Cane*, Toomer stresses that "life becomes more conscious, more restless and stirring, and hence more complex," with characters displaying "spiritual growth and psychological subtlety." Discussing "Kabnis," Toomer cites Gorham Munson's judgment that the text, for all its "ramif[ying] deeply into the soil and into life . . . reaches up to a stunted broken intellectualism [and] is not simply a thick concentration of Southern Negro life. . . . [It is] an American equivalent to a Russian drama by Maxim Gorki or Anton Chekhov. . . . Its production should be undertaken by an American equivalent to the Moscow Art Theatre, which unhappily does yet not exist." This quotation from Munson is somewhat self-serving; Toomer ached to have "Kabnis" put onto the stage. But the reference to the Soviet theater also suggests that, despite his July 1922 statement to McKay that he found "the Experiment in America" more exciting than what was going on in the Soviet Union, he hardly viewed them as separate projects. Indeed, he wishes *Cane* to be compared with the traditions of Russian realism and proletarianism.[35]

Toomer ends the essay by reiterating his opening assertion that *Holiday* and *Cane* jointly contribute to "our [American] sectional art"; he quotes Frank's praise of *Cane* as embodying "that abstract and absolute thing called Art." Toomer's own commentaries on the two texts strongly suggest, however, that *Holiday* displays Frank's inability to move beyond fairly crude racial binaries. Frank, when first proposing their trip south, had specified that he wanted to visit "some small town with a typical division of white and black folk." Toomer's insistent reference to the "typicality" of *Holiday* carries the implication that this "typicality" is a feature not so much of the social reality being depicted as of the consciousness, the "subjective design," of the white man doing the depicting. In his discussion of *Cane*, by contrast, the word "typical" never appears; instead, Toomer emphasizes the economic, sociological, and psychological intricacy of the text's portraiture of African American life in both the rural South and the urban North. For all his insistence that in both *Cane* and *Holiday* "one finds the South," and that "because of their sheer literary achievement one finds here the South as a significant contributor to our sectional art," it would appear that "sectional art" is an ideologeme open to considerable contestation.[36]

Toomer's insistence upon viewing *Cane* as an example of sectional art in "The South in Literature" may have been tailored in part to conform to the outlook of the SPA's *New York Call*, which by 1923 had abandoned its earlier revolutionary élan and embraced a left-liberal American nationalism. Nonetheless, the essay illuminates crucial features of Toomer's outlook soon after the publication of *Cane*. It reveals that Toomer was by no means reluctant to identify himself as a Negro writer and in fact viewed this racial identity as central to his creation of *Cane*. His assertion that Frank's outlook is "typical" of a white social experience suggests, moreover, that a white writer is far more likely to engage in simplified notions of race—indeed, "divisions and parcellings"—than is one of Negro descent. Crucially, then, Toomer's critical assessment of Frank consists not in Frank's having designated Toomer a Negro writer—as he would state in the 1931 autobiography—but in Frank's limited understanding of what being a Negro is all about.

Toomer's comments on *Holiday* in both the *Dial* review and "The South in Literature" invite us to rescrutinize Toomer's retrospective account of his reactions to Frank's foreword to *Cane*. Not only should we query Toomer's assertion that he had been offended by Frank's identifying him as a Negro writer; we may question whether Toomer did in fact view everything else about the foreword to be "splendid." Toomer no doubt appreciated Frank's praise of *Cane* as "Art." But the foreword's generalizations about Negro life—its "primitive" quality, its shrouding in "mists of muteness," its previous consignment to the "plane of the specific and superficial"—may have stuck in the craw of the young man who had recently studied "slavery and the Negro" with the Washington, DC, study group and discussed the sociology of race with the pre–*New Negro* Locke. Frank's generalizations about *Cane* itself—that the text's dominant tone is one of "loveliness" and "beauty"; that it treats a land where lynching is commonplace as "not a problem to be solved"; that Washington's segregation is "not a topic to be discussed and exposed"; that "immediate life" is shown in isolation from "yesterday"—all these assertions significantly underplay *Cane*'s serious engagement with history and political economy. Indeed, despite his praise for *Cane* as "Art," Frank's insistence that *Cane* "*is* the South" divests the text of its status as an artistic mediation of its subject matter: in its invocation of "immediate life," the text itself becomes "immediate."

We may especially wonder what Toomer thought of Frank's allusion to Kabnis's trip to Georgia as an "invasion into this black womb of the ferment seed." While Toomer had written to Locke from Sparta of the "virgin territory" the South supplied for creative artists, this conventional trope was different in both degree and kind from Frank's description of an authorial seed engaging in something approximating a physical assault on a woman. In reference to a book largely preoccupied with the sexual exploitation of black women, Frank's phrasing is, to say the least, ill-chosen. It contrasts dramatically, moreover, with Toomer's own deployment of the seed metaphor to signify a connection between geography and creativity—as in his letter to Sherwood Anderson in which he compared planting a seed in the soil with planting a seed within himself. Toomer's metaphor is overwrought, to be sure; but insofar as it invokes sexuality, it links the creative process not with rape but with parthenogenesis.

The truth about Toomer's initial reaction to reading Frank's foreword to *Cane* may never be known; given Toomer's deep indebtedness to—and genuine affection for—Frank, no doubt his feelings were complicated. But both the *Dial* review of *Holiday* and "The South in Literature" indicate that, by the time Toomer had helped Frank edit his lynching novel and had himself completed *Cane*, their friendship had entered a problematic phase. Various critics have speculated that the trip the two men took to South Carolina in the early fall of 1922 gave Toomer the opportunity to see his mentor up close and to reassess his character. Until that time, after all, Frank and Toomer had only two face-to-face meetings; their passionate attestations to brotherhood had developed entirely from their written correspondence. Although Toomer and Frank were more deeply enmeshed than ever in criticizing and editing one another's work when they returned from Spartanburg, Toomer was now perusing what Frank had carried away from the trip and was putting into the drafts of *Holiday*. Moreover, Toomer had renewed his own acquaintance with what he called the "bite and crudity of pure Negro-white southern life" in his correspondence with Jesse Moorland. As we shall see, a number of short stories that Toomer produced in the late fall of 1922 signaled a marked shift—away from lyrical nostalgia, toward a grittier engagement with politics, economics, and violence—distinguishing them from the texts produced in the spring and summer of that year. As Toomer was taking to new levels his consideration of the constraints of black life under Jim Crow, he was being newly exposed to Frank's simplistic approach to racially inflected character portrayal.[37]

My purpose in tracking Toomer's increasingly troubled relationship with Frank has not been to subject Waldo Frank—whose racial attitudes were in fact considerably more advanced than those of most of his white contemporaries—to an anachronistic political litmus test. Nor has it been to claim that Jean Toomer was exempt from the social forces shaping the outlook of his friend and mentor. Both men emerged from the crucible of 1919; both entertained hopes for a revolutionary transformation of U.S. society; both were deeply pained at the apparent arresting of the historical dialectic. Toomer at first willingly—indeed, exuberantly—embraced much of Frank's nationalist program for cultural renewal; Frank, in turn, extended to the younger man a genuine and warm invitation to participate in, and contribute to, the project of Young America. But Toomer's relationship with Frank became laced with an ambivalence that cannot be attributed primarily, as is often thought, to Frank's "outing" Toomer as a Negro writer in the foreword to *Cane*. Rather, this ambivalence stemmed from Toomer's growing perception of Frank's entrapment within reductive racial binaries—a deficiency enhanced by Frank's embrace of a subjectivist aesthetic theory that negated the necessity of querying the adequacy of those binaries as descriptors of social reality. That Frank would write a novel in which both of these shortcomings were prominently displayed shook Toomer's confidence in his mentor and friend. But the fact that Toomer had encouraged and flattered Frank throughout the composition of *Holiday*—indeed, had colluded in Frank's creation of dialogue and description representing the South, and had pronounced the novel, upon completion, "quite perfect as it stands"—compounded the cognitive dissonance experienced by the younger writer. Just as Frank was "in" *Cane*, Toomer was "in" *Holiday*. Pressures were building within the author of *Cane*—all the more stressful, we may imagine, for being unacknowledged.[38]

"A river . . . spattered with blood": Race and Nation in "Withered Skin of Berries"

Toomer's short story, "Withered Skin of Berries," composed in the late spring and early summer of 1922, displays Toomer's engagement with the project of Young America when he was midway through the composition of the poems and prose pieces that would soon be gathered as *Cane*. When Toomer wrote to Frank in July 1922 that he had been staying in Harpers Ferry and working on a "long piece" that "made use of the . . . opportunity for a vivid symbolism" supplied by its setting, he was evidently referring to this tale. Unpublished in Toomer's lifetime, the story would probably not be of much scholarly interest had it not been authored by the creator of *Cane*. Composed during the first phase of his connection with Frank, however, "Withered Skin of Berries" displays not only the distinctly New Negro point of view that Toomer brought to the formulation of an oppositional "our America" but also the international standpoint from which he understood the necessity for emancipation from racism. Its image-driven narration embodies Toomer's aspiration on the one hand to create "the image saturated in its own lyricism," on the other to convey "extra-artistic consciousness" through complex artistic forms. Even the story's shortcomings (its overwrought symbolism, its truncated narrative resolution) can be read as testimonies to Toomer's inability to think his way through and past the objective barriers to revolutionary social transformation—the arrested historical dialectic—that he increasingly perceived at the time of the tale's composition. A symptomatic reading of this tale proves a useful point of entry into an analysis of *Cane*.[39]

The plot of "Withered Skin of Berries" revolves around the love choices of Vera, a sexually and emotionally repressed young woman who, light-skinned enough to "pass," works as a typist in a segregated government office in the nation's capital. One suitor, her coworker Carl, is white, passionless, and racist; another suitor, Art Bond, is black, sensual, and beset by internalized racism; a more successful contender for her heart and body is David Teyy, a man of mixed racial heritage, a poet, a radical, and a lover—evidently a projection of Toomer's idealized vision of himself—who challenges her to overcome her knotted internal state. Place figures crucially throughout the story, which moves from the sterile offices and marble monuments of the District of Columbia to various history-laden settings along the Potomac, especially the Great Falls downriver from Harpers Ferry. The penultimate scene near the falls features David recalling the hanging of John Brown and the sacrificial spattering of blood on the rushing river as he, Carl, and Vera stand by a massive boulder associated with an Indian named Tiacomus. The denouement shifts abruptly back to a description of Vera in her office; presumably she has been unable to respond to David's call to live a life untrammeled by convention. The narration is framed by a repeated paragraph that—thematically recalling Sherwood Anderson's lonesome grotesques and structurally invoking Frank's conception of spherical form—describes Vera as an unattainable object of fantasy for both black men and white men, who can "only in retrospective kisses . . . know the looseness of her lips . . . pale withered skin of berries." Only on its surface the story of a love quadrangle, the story is essentially an allegory of national destiny: Vera is a symbol of the nation, and her suitors map out the choices, positive and negative, open to U.S. society in the aftermath of the "red summer" of 1919. The story's Freudian and Marxist discourses are mutually supportive: the necessity of overcoming psychological repression—at once emotional and sexual—is linked with the necessity of engaging in, or at least identifying with, antiracist class struggle.[40]

The buildings in the nation's capital convey a critique of white supremacist "100% Americanism." In the company—at different times—of both Art and David, Vera rides by the Masonic Temple; Art, in her eyes, is "impersonalized . . . in the shadow . . . of its great bulk," but David points out that she too lives in its shadow. Vera and Carl drive past Negro laborers who are "working on the basin of an artificial lake that was to spread its smooth glass surface before Lincoln's Memorial"; notably, "[t]he shadow of their emancipator stir[s] them to neither bitterness nor awe." Washington, DC, readers of the story in 1922 would have recognized Toomer's oblique references to recent and current events. The Masonic Temple had been the site of white supremacist gatherings; the Lincoln Memorial had been dedicated in May 1922 before a segregated audience, to the particular chagrin of Washington's "blue-veined aristocracy." The Negro press was full of acerbic commentary on the politics of monuments: Toomer's readers would have been aware of the efforts of the United Daughters of the Confederacy to promote the construction of the Mammy Monument on the nation's mall, as well as of the proposal to dedicate a memorial boulder to Heyward Shepherd at Harpers Ferry. Wilsonian-era segregation had brought Jim Crow to the nation's capital. As Toomer wrote in early 1922 to Angelina Grimké's friend Lillie Buffum Chace Wyman, the "effort to cement the white race by the use of a propaganda of color hatred," while enjoying "in reality . . . only partial . . . success," had "developed

[into] . . . a nation-wide system of segregation," leading "many . . . to accept this fact as evidence of a white solidarity of hate," as well as to "stimulate in the colored group a reciprocal sentiment of prejudice."[41]

The federal office buildings embody the effects of segregation on whites and blacks alike: "[G]rey gastronomic structures, innocuously coated with bile. They pollute the breath of Washington. . . . Routine segregates niggers. Black life is more soluble in lump. White life, pitiably agitated to superiority, is more palatable." The body politic metaphor at once reveals that blacks and whites commonly make up the nation and displays the unease produced by denial of this fact. One of Vera's coworkers, sure of her ability to spot Negroes attempting to "pass," declares that "nigger blood will out. . . . You cant fool all of the people all of the time. I wonder if they know that saying of Lincoln's?" Yet these white workers, bound to mindless labor at their clattering typewriters, are themselves fooled by a tawdry American dream. They are "Young girls who work all month to imitate leisure-class flappers. . . . Widows of improvident men who had been somebody in their day. Boys who have left school. Men dreaming of marriage and bungalows in Chevy Chase." The young man who had fled from the shipyard had not forgotten its lessons about the alienation of labor.[42]

Vera's different suitors limn the consequences of segregation for both its victims and its supposed beneficiaries. Her "almost perfect white" coworker Carl wholeheartedly embraces the doctrines of racial supremacy, male superiority, and imperialist domination; in his "pioneer aggressiveness," Carl is the "average American" of whom Toomer had contemptuously written in "Americans and Mary Austin." Ignoring the "clustered shanties—poor white homes"—by the roadside, Carl complains that "America, now the war is over, don't give a young fellow with push and brains and energy half a chance." He cites Vanderbilt, Carnegie, and Rockefeller as his role models and tells Vera of his plans to make money in the "virginal" Argentine. "I'll feel superior to those greasers—all Americans do," he crows. "And thats the reason why we're running things." But Carl's racism lacks conviction: asked by Vera, "Why do you hate niggers?" he replies, "Hang if I know. Dont you?" His money-lust, moreover, cannot compensate for his lost connection with the soil: he was a "field man," he confesses, before his father became an oil-trading entrepreneur. In his characterization of Carl, Toomer undertakes a portrait of Waldo Frank's repressed and extraverted "pioneer" from the standpoint of a class-conscious New Negro. Insofar as Vera "passes" in Carl's company, however—she declares that she is of "Spanish" descent—she is absorbed into his racist worldview. She thinks of Argentina's "pampa grass" as a "great stationary sea" inhabited by "untamed Indians. . . . Stealthy marauding savages"; she is complicit in his imperial aspirations.[43]

Carl's assumption of superiority is further undermined by the haunting memory of his college friendship in Wisconsin with a "dark" fellow student who turns out to have been the redoubtable David Teyy. By the falls that "conjur[e] the sense of an impending lightning," he recalls to Vera David's words during a nocturnal canoeing trip:

> "Carl," he said, his eyes were gleaming, "the wonder and mystery of it. . . . Dead leaves of northern Europe, Carl, have decayed for roots tangled here in America. Roots thrusting up a stark fresh life. Thats you. Multi-colored leaves, tropic, temperate, have decayed for me. We meet where a race has died for both of us. Only a few years ago, forests and fields, this lake, Mendota, heard the corn and hunting songs of a vanished people. They have resolved their individualism to the common stream. . . . Deep River spreads over Mendota . . ." He closed his hand over mine. Me, a football man, holding hands with a man on the lake.

Carl's heterosexual Nordicism is patently fragile: he yearns to be immersed in the "common stream" conjoining African American ("Deep River") and Indian ("Mendota") cultures. David's invocation of the organic trope to represent his and Carl's lineages in different climates and continents indicates that, in repressing his attraction to his "dark" friend, Carl is rejecting the promise embodied in "our America," whose "buried cultures," reemerging as "roots thrusting upward," would reconnect him with his past identity as a "field man" were he only to seize the opportunity.[44]

If Carl's racial irrationalism signals the false benefits of white supremacy, Art's inarticulate passions signal the destructive effects of internalized racism. Envious of his rivals' cars, ill at ease in his "black" skin, jealous and worshipful of David Teyy—whom he terms a "genius, and the poet of Washington"—the southern-born Art becomes tongue-tied and can express his love for Vera only through his body. When Vera recoils from Art's sexual approach as a "black wedge of hot red life" and gasps, "Black nigger beast," her words return him to slavery: "Art swung loose, and as if a lash had cut him, groaned. . . . Shrinking on a slave-block black man groan!" Vera's reaction at once "bonds" Art and reveals her own fear of acknowledging her African heritage; displaying the connection between sexual repression and racial denial, her lips are pale and withered because they have suppressed the flow of blood.[45]

Yet just as Carl confesses to be at heart a "field man," Art tells Vera that he is an "inland man" and—shifting from incoherence into a rhapsodic linguistic mode—lyrically recalls the activities of the "syrup-man":

> He comes to boil the cane when the harvest is through . . . . Men are seated around. . . . They tell tales, gossip about the white folks, and about moonshine licker. The [syrup-man's] face is lit by the glow. He is the ju-ju man. . . . Your soul rises with the smoke and songs above the pine-trees. Once mine rose up, and instead of travelling about the heavens, looked down. I saw my body there, seated with the other men. As I looked, it seemed to dissolve, and melt with the others that were dissolving too. They were a stream. They flowed up-stream from Africa and way up to a height where the light was so bright I could hardly see, burst into a multi-colored spraying fountain.

Souls rising in pine smoke, juju men, storytellers clustered around the kettle of boiling cane, the David Georgia–esque "syrup-man": Art's "out-of-body" experience issues from the imagination that is simultaneously creating *Cane*. Affirming the communality of African survivals in black folk culture, Art's vision of the "multi-colored spraying fountain" recalls the "common stream" described by David to Carl. The imagery of water flowing "upstream from Africa" suggests the common origins of the world's peoples; the descriptions of Carl and Art as, respectively, "field man" and "inland man," rather than white and black, designate not genetic pools or national boundaries, but unmapped locations, as sources of identity.[46]

Both the "field man" and the "inland man" are foils to David Teyy, the philosopher, poet, and man of "multi-colored leaves" who haunts, attracts, and gains carnal knowledge of the woman his rivals desire. Driving in Carl's car past cherry trees in bloom, with the "white marble splotches" of Arlington Cemetery visible across the "muddy . . . seaweed-streaked" Potomac on which a tug "draw[s] a canal barge from miles in the interior," Vera free-associates from her visual impressions to thoughts of David. Seeing by the trees a "group of Japanese, hats off . . . reverently lost in race memories of reed lutes," Vera feels "an unprecedented nostalgia, a promise of awakening"; this leads to the "unbidden" memory of a poetic fragment: "[F]ar-off trees / whose gloom is rounded like the hives of bees / All humming peace to soldiers who have gone." Authored, we soon learn, by David, the poem not only pays tribute to the soldiers lost in the recent war—contrasting with Carl's selfish reaction to the postwar recession—but also connects Vera's "promise of awakening," initially prompted by the sight of people of another race, with the reality of wartime carnage. This linkage is reinforced—for the reader, if not for Vera—by her and Carl's arrival at a point along the Potomac where "a hydro-plane was humming high above the War College," an image affording further contrast between the peaceful "humming" imagined in David's tribute to the dead and the "humming" of wartime planes strategically deployed by the military masters housed in their headquarters by the river. Among the "white marble splotches of Virginia's hills" across the river, after all, is the Tomb of the Unknown Soldier, dedicated in a massive display of patriotism less than a year before. Vera may experience her "awakening" as an unfocused desire for oneness, but the reader intuits that her association with David will required her to come to grips with some harsh realities about both the nation and the world.[47]

Subsequently in David's company, Vera hears him chant another poem:

> Court-house tower,
> Bell-buoy of the Whites,
> Charting the white-man's channel,
> Bobs on the agitated crests of pines
> And sends its mellow monotone,
> Satirically sweet,

To guide the drift of barges. .
Black barges . . .

African Guardian of Souls,
Drunk with rum,
Feasting on a strange cassava,
Yielding to new words and a weak palabra
Of a white-faced sardonic God.

Recalling the "canal barge from miles in the interior" that Vera saw when driving with Carl, the poem links the exploitation of black labor with the legal powers of the state and the legitimating role of Christianity. It also rearticulates—and politicizes—the water imagery informing the memories of Carl and Art. No "common streams" and "multi-colored spraying fountains" here: in the zone ruled by the "court-house tower," African survivals—in the person of the "guardian of souls" turned Christian minister—"yield" to the bidding of a deity who assists in guiding the "black barges" that bear goods down the "white-man's channel." David's poetic practice recalls Toomer's stipulation, in his essay on Aldington, that an image can at once be "clear-cut" and "convey a rousing message."[48]

David's powers of critique would appear to derive not only from his acknowledged kinship with "buried cultures"—Negro spirituals, Indian hunting chants—but also from his secure location within modernity, signaled by his intimacy with automotive machinery. When David picks up Vera to drive to the falls, she senses that "[s]omething from David Teyy ran down the steering-gear, down the brakes and clutches, and gave flesh and blood life to the car. Vera was curled, as if she was in the dark enclosure of a womb. She could drive on forever. Covered by life that flowed up the blue veins of the city. Up Sixteenth Street. David was a red blood center flowing down. She sucked his blood. Go on forever with David flowing down." Although linked with the "multi-colored leaves" of the natural world, David is not a primitive but a member of the avant-garde; indeed, he has mastered a high-powered vehicle similar to those used during the bloody 1919 riot by armed African American residents who drove around Washington defending their neighborhoods from the invading racists. Phallic propulsion is associated with the liquids coursing through the car that David deftly drives through the neighborhood inhabited by the city's light-skinned elite. Unambiguously masculine, David also figures androgynously as a mother figure, providing Vera with a nurturing womb. Under the control of this confident—indeed, futuristic—New Negro, the machine is in harmony with both history and nature; indeed, he has "fecundat[ed] the machine." But while his arterial blood—flowing in the opposite direction from that of the élite proud of their blue veins—brings Vera the oxygen she needs, her sucking action is at once infantilized and vampiric. The nation needs the energy that the New Negro can supply: but whether she will be nurtured by him, or drain his blood, remains open to question. Will a new nation be birthed from David's metaphoric womb? Or will it be stillborn?[49]

While the action of the story entails a good deal of automotive movement in the Washington metropolitan area, it is the Great Falls of the Potomac that supply the story with its principal geographical-cum-historical reference point, as well as whatever narrative climax is possible within the constraints of the text's image-driven form. When Vera visits the falls in the company of the white supremacist Carl, she sits "Indian fashion" by Tiacomus's boulder, "responding, perhaps, to some folk persuasion of the place." But she sees the river merely as "churning to a cream foam against mud-colored rocks . . . carrying the brown burden of a wasted sediment . . . John Brown's body . . . from Harper's Ferry to the Chesapeake and the sea." Even though the river symbolically displays the social construction of race—the "cream foam" of whiteness is created through its "churning . . . against mud-colored rocks" signaling its racialized other—Vera views the river's "brown sediment," and, by extension, herself, as something "wasted," a "burden." She sees herself as the dross left at the bottom of the melting pot; she has internalized the nativism of Mary Austin. When Vera is passing over the color line with the white supremacist Carl, "John Brown's body" is merely a fragmented phrase from a forgotten anthem.[50]

When Vera visits the point along the Potomac in David's company, by contrast, she beholds a "[m]obile river, scintillant beneath the moon" and is propelled into a confrontation with the history—past and recent—that she has repressed: "Open ocean for brown sediment of the river. Tide in, send your tang. Resistant ripples. Wave in, send your waves. Wash back. John Brown's body rumbles in the sea. . . . Lights twinkle on the wharves of Seventh Street. Wash red blood. Search-lights play on Lincoln Memorial and the Monument. Wash red blood. Blue blood clots in the veins of Washington. Wash red blood. John Brown's body." Vera initially feels desperate, thinking, "Oh God, I dangle" as she recalls the words of "Deep River": "I want to cross over into the camp ground." But she comes to realize that "[b]eneath the scum I am a river": the words of the spiritual have gained new meaning. She intuits that her allegiance to her "blue blood" is what "clots" the city's veins; "red blood" is needed to "wash" the city clean. She must learn the lesson of Georgia Douglas Johnson's "Fusion": that she is a compound of "tributary sources" that "potently commingle / And sweep / With new born forces!" The Lincoln Memorial and the Washington Monument are subjected to "search-lights"; their integrity is suspect, as is their status as representative monuments. But the lights that "twinkle" on the wharves of Seventh Street—which farther north supplied the hub of the 1919 race riot—signal that this thoroughfare, the longest street in the city, at its southern-most point connects, via the tidal basin, with the Chesapeake Bay, the ocean, and the rest of the world. The passage suggests not only Toomer's accord with Frank's praise of Whitman's democratic universalism—the poet's vision of "a perfect sea, and in the sea a world, and in the world all men"—but also the felt need to contest contemporaneous racist doctrines of the "rising tide of color." The "artificial lake" under construction before the Lincoln Memorial has a "smooth glass surface," reflecting the false peace following the postwar repression; in contrast, the Potomac is in constant motion. The "resistant ripples" in the tidal basin are caused by the interaction between the Potomac's descending waters and the ever-moving ocean; the false peace of official nationalist doctrine is belied by the continuing resistance of the dispossessed, the rising tide of global anti-capitalism.[51]

Conjoining Freud with Marx, David challenges Vera's tendency to "make of love a sort of sublimated postponement," one that "holds little or no solution for the outside world." He adds, "Perhaps in a better day. . . . Especially is this true of the two worlds you dangle over. . . . The western world demands of us that we not escape." The "outside world," the "two worlds" of Vera's background, and the "western world" commonly demand that Vera come to terms with her racial and sexual identities: clearly her crisis in identity, her inability to be "true," has global implications. But Vera fails to respond to David's challenge: when they have sexual intercourse, she experiences David as a "sharp wedge . . . cleaving," with lips "tast[ing] of copper and blood"; afterward she lies "a limp, damp thing, like a young bird fallen from its nest." In the story's penultimate scene where he confronts Vera and Carl by the falls, David "stampede[s] these pale ghost people":

> "Know you, people, that you sit beside the boulder where Tiacomus made love. Made love, do you understand me? Know you, people, that you are above a river, spattered with blood, John Brown's blood. With blood, do you understand me? White red blood. Black red blood. Know you, people, that you are beneath the stars of wonder, of reverence, of mystery. Know you that you are boulders of love, rivers spattered with blood, stars of wonder and mystery. Roll river. Flow river. Roll river. Flow river. River, river, roll. Roll!"

David then goes on to chant one of his poems:

> The river was empty, flowing to the sea,
> From Harper's Ferry to the Chesapeake and the sea—
> . . . They hung John Brown . .
> . . .
> John Brown's body, rumbles in the river,
> John Brown's body, thunders down the falls—
> . . . Roll river roll!

The passage by the falls ends: "The boulder seemed cleft by a clap of thunder. As if the falls had risen and were thundering its fragments away." In its explicit allusion to the raid on Harpers Ferry, David's speech recalls Brown's famous final written words, on the day of his hanging, that "the crimes of this guilty land will never be purged away but with blood."[52]

David's closing poem clearly intends to carry a "rousing message." His invocation of the spiritual "Roll, Jordan, Roll!," contrasting with the quietism of "Deep River," invites the reader to supply the next line: "No more driver's whip for me!" David's assertion that Tiacomus "made love" by the falls implicitly contrasts his and Vera's aborted relationship with the presumably superior emotional state of the nation's aboriginal people; Tiacomus's boulder memorializes a lost society from which much remains to be learned. Given the story's satirical commentary on whitewashed monuments—as well as its historical placement amidst current controversies over the Mammy Monument on the national mall and the Faithful Slave Memorial honoring Heyward Shepherd at Harpers Ferry—David's homage brings Frank's "buried cultures" into the present. If any historical figure metonymically signifies the meaning and heritage of the region, it is neither a dead president, nor an iconic faithful servant, but Tiacomus. Through David Teyy, Tiacomus lives in the present: he is redeemed from identification with a "non-historical people." Indeed, the thunderbolt that breaks his boulder in two may allude obliquely to Claude McKay's revolutionary prophecy in "Exhortation: Summer, 1919": "Through the pregnant universe rumbles life's terrific thunder, / And Earth's bowels quake with terror." As he authored "Withered Skin of Berries," Toomer may already have been imagining his novel about the upward heaving of the nonwhite world.[53]

The signal feature of David's closing speech, however, is its synthesis of the trope of blood with that of the river of history through the connecting figure of John Brown, who not only called for the use of force in combatting slavery but also declared his personal dedication to this task: "[I]f it is deemed necessary that I should forfeit my life for the furtherance of the ends of justice, and mingle my blood further with the blood of my children and with the blood of millions in this slave country whose rights are disregarded by wicked, cruel, and unjust enactments, I say let it be done." The story's earlier reference to Seventh Street, the "bloodfield" of the 1919 race riot, links past to present: Brown's prophecy about the necessary spilling of blood in the fight for equality continues to resonate in the thundering falls. David's proclamation that "white red blood" and "black red blood" have merged in the river of history not only refutes the "mongrelization" discourse of contemporaneous scientific racism but also recalls the multiracial character of the Harpers Ferry raiders, whose blood was indeed commonly "spattered" where the Shenandoah River merges with the Potomac. Indeed, the words "black red blood" echo the contemporaneous use of the term "black reds" to describe the African American Communists emerging from the crucible of 1919. But, as Toomer well knew, both African Americans and political radicals of all racial backgrounds were the targets of state-sponsored and vigilante violence in the wake of the Great War, the most recent "mingling" of bloods in the river of history. The brooding presence of Brown in the history-saturated landscape of the Potomac Falls displays the need for renewed abolitionist commitment—and, perhaps, renewed civil war, this time under the banner of a multiracial "red" politics.[54]

While David's speech takes place in a distinct region with a distinct history, his meaning is hardly sectional; the choice facing Vera is the choice facing the nation. As the story's many references to the world beyond the United States suggest, moreover, this choice occurs in a global context. Art's vision of the bodies of men "flow[ing] up-stream from Africa and . . . burst[ing] into a multi-colored spraying fountain," along with Carl's memory of his conversation with David about their origins on different continents, reminds the reader of the pre-Columbian situation of humanity. Vera's intuitive connection with non-white peoples (her appreciation of the Japanese tourists viewing the cherry blossoms, her sensitivity of the "folk-persuasion" of the woods by Tiacomus's boulder) indicates her—and by extension the nation's—unexplored capacity for broader human identification. But Toomer suggests the limitations of a universalism confined to culture and consciousness. The utopian imaginings of Art and Carl as, respectively, "inland" man and "field" man, cannot find expression in their restricted—and restricting—social identi-ties. Vera's accession to racial passing leads her to embrace Carl's vision of the inhabitants of the Argentine as "marauding savages" and of the pampa grass as a "stationary sea." She senses, in David's presence, the need not only to accept her own mixed heritage but also to recognize, in the public sphere, the links conjoin-ing Washington's white marble monuments, the recent rebellion along Seventh Street, and "resistant ripples" of incipient international revolt. But she cannot bear the burden of this knowledge; clinging to her "blue-veined" heritage, she prefers the still waters of a quiescent nationalism to the rising tide of global revolution. David, by contrast, both sees and heralds the connections among the "black barges" along the Potomac, the dead soldiers in Arlington National Cemetery, the raid on Harpers Ferry, and the continuing pressures of the "outside world."

Read as a Freudian Marxist allegorical commentary on postwar political possibilities, the image-driven plot of "Withered Skin of Berries" conjoins vari-ous modes of repression—sexual and racial, psychological and political. The tale's abrupt finale invites interpretation as a symptomatic commentary both on Toomer's failed hopes for revolutionary change in the aftermath of 1919 and on his awareness of the limited role that cultural production can play in creating historical change. For, after the apparently supernatural bolt of lightning splits Tiacomus's boulder, the text's reversion to Vera's office suggests that the arrested movement of the narrative enacts the arrested dialectic of history. The "red sum-mer" did not, as Toomer had devoutly hoped in "Reflections on the Race Riots," result in the "substitution of a socialized reality" for the race-torn capitalism of the United States. Instead, the Carls of the nation evolved into its Babbitts, while its Arts remained subjected to the bondage, both internal and external, of Jim Crow. In this context, David's odd surname, Teyy, suggests the defeat—or at least the deferral—of revolution: it has not "yet" arrived. The closing portrait of the still-"passing" Vera clattering her typewriter keys in the bile-encrusted federal office building reveals that the nation has rejected the revolutionary courtship—and ignored the revolutionary poetry—of David Teyy. It has abjured its multiracial inheritance; it has not been "true" to itself. The narrative's deployment of spheri-cal form only superficially fuses beginning with ending; no imaginable narrative resolution can suture over the text's disappointment with the failed generation of a new world. Registering the inability of its poet-hero to arouse Vera from her lassitude—to inject life and blood into her withered lips—the story displays the limitations of Frank's assertion that "in a dying world, creation is revolution"; something more than the recitation of poetry by the falls of history is needed to arouse the nation to action. Indeed, the story suggests the limitations of the nation itself as the site of revolutionary social change: both poetry and nationalism are called into question at the ending of the tale.

To propose that Toomer's tale pushes against the limits of the political and formal doctrines advocated by Waldo Frank is not to assert that it contains an explicit critique of Young America. Indeed, the text's reliance on key tropes and themes drawn from *Our America* marks it as an intended contribution to the literary nationalist project. When Toomer authored the story in the late spring of 1922, he was riding the crest of his wave of enthusiasm for the program of his newfound mentor and friend. What the story reveals, however, is that Toomer's conception of the place of "the Negro" in an expanded version of *Our America* entailed much more than an additive contribution to the liberal notion of "e pluribus unum." Drawing "the Negro" into "our America" would require recognition of the central roles played by slavery, abolition, and continuing antiracist rebellion in the nation's past and present. Sectional art must be true to history; it cannot afford to view the past as, in Sandburg's words, a "bucket of ashes." It must also be true to the geography of the globe: if the project of Young America is to include "the Negro," this Negro must be the New Negro who is a citizen of both the nation and the world.

CHAPTER 4

All the Dead Generations
Jean Toomer's Dark Sister

The tradition of all the dead generations weighs like a nightmare on the
brain of the living.
—Karl Marx, *The Eighteenth Brumaire of Louis Bonaparte*

I hoped that you
Would help me tap the second stream
And reverse my steps, the ages
I have walked away
Seeking I knew not what.

You did not fail me.
To the second station I did not arise,
Hearing the strange accents
Of our native language
While those around me
Call me dead.

Dead to the first,
I live to the second.
And when I die where now I live,
And all these people call me dead,
Do you, dark sister,
Not forsake me.
—Jean Toomer, "Be with Me"

At some point in the 1930s, Jean Toomer wrote a poem titled "Be with Me" that
ends with the plea, "Do you, dark sister, / Not forsake me." The poem's address to
this "dark sister" can be interpreted as a reference to the phases of transcendence
set forth in the doctrines of George Gurdjieff. The poem can also be interpreted
as an articulation of Toomer's inner conflicts in the wake of his passing over
the color line: the speaker, regretting having "walked away / Seeking I knew
not what," finds himself strangely suspended between life and death. What will
be considered here is another, more specific and literal reading—namely, that
Toomer did indeed have a "dark sister" (more precisely, a half-sister) to whom
the unpublished poem pays oblique tribute. Her name was Mamie Toomer; she

was the youngest of the four daughters of Nathan Toomer, Jean Toomer's father, by his first marriage to an enslaved woman of mixed ancestry named Harriet. The history revolving around Mamie draws in a number of other family members: Amanda America Dickson Toomer, Nathan Toomer's second wife and the heiress of a huge fortune; David Dickson, Amanda's wealthy planter father; Julia Lewis, Amanda's mother; Charles Dickson, Amanda's younger son (and thus Jean Toomer's stepbrother); and Charles Dickson's wife, Kate Holsey Dickson, daughter of the prominent Colored Methodist Episcopal Church churchman, Lucius Holsey. The distinct possibility that Toomer pieced together significant parts of the family puzzle around the time of his stay in Sparta, Georgia, in the fall of 1921 invites speculation about the extent to which this knowledge inspired—or forced itself into—the outpouring of creativity that would result in *Cane*.[1]

Two methodological points are in order. First, as indicated by my provisional language in the preceding paragraph ("possibility," "invites speculation"), the inferences and conclusions set forth in this chapter remain tentative. Most studies of Toomer that draw on his family history feature his relationships with four important figures: Nathan Toomer; Nina Pinchback Toomer, Jean Toomer's mother and Nathan Toomer's third wife; Jean Toomer's maternal grandmother, Emily Hethorn Pinchback; and, above all, Jean Toomer's maternal grandfather, Pinckney Benton Stewart Pinchback, who had briefly served as governor of Louisiana at the end of Reconstruction and, after moving to Washington, DC, in the early 1890s, figured as a prominent presence among the capital city's African American elite. While there has been considerable debate over what these relationships meant and how they might figure in a reading of *Cane*, the scholarship revolving around these figures has been able to draw on a documentary foundation consisting of more or less verifiable information. By contrast, the case for concluding that Toomer discovered various skeletons in the Toomer/Dickson family closets is based largely on triangulation among various texts; there is, so to speak, no smoking gun definitively establishing Toomer's knowledge of all the different strands of family history described here. My reading of *Natalie Mann* at the end of this chapter should, however, indicate that Toomer's creative processes entailed grappling with some painful family secrets. Part 2 of this book proposes that *Cane* cannot be fully understood without attention to Toomer's felt need at once to express and repress a very personal history that hurt.

Second, I am cognizant that this foray into Toomer's family history complicates the notions of repression—and of the political unconscious—guiding this book. Heretofore the focus has been on the public historical forces shaping Toomer's consciousness: the arrested dialectic of revolution and the various ideologemes to which this foreclosure gave rise. The political unconscious is, in this broadly social register, a collective unconscious, if individually registered in and through Toomer's personal experiences. Aspects of Toomer's biography—his occluded experience with the Palmer Raids and the 1919 Washington race riot, his ambivalent relationships with Alain Locke and Waldo Frank—have been analyzed primarily in connection with practices and discourses articulated in the public sphere. The following inquiry into Toomer's buried feelings surrounding the story of his "dark sister" shifts our focus toward distinctly private matters: indeed, Freud's classic "family romance"—in which a child imagines for himself an idealized family very different his own—plays a central role. But while Freud will make distinctive claims on our attention, these will not trump the claims of Marx; the symptomatic readings of Toomer's texts yielded by both psychoanalysis and historical materialism will prove to be mutually reinforcing. For the causal dynamics driving the story of the Toomers, Dicksons, and Pinchbacks are deeply embedded in the specificities of time and place: indeed, the tale of Toomer's "dark sister" epitomizes the tangled relations of race, class, and gender that shaped the lives of propertied elites, white and black, in the Jim Crow South. Toomer's personal trauma is inseparable from the larger historical nightmare of slavery and its aftermath; Marx's famous comment about the weight of tradition bears a multivalent relation to Toomer's life and work.[2]

This examination of familial matters also illuminates the issue of Toomer's complicated racial self-identification by indicating its inseparability from his class identity. I have been arguing that the Toomer who authored *Cane* did not shun identification as a Negro, even as he simultaneously sought to limn the contours of a world in which race would no longer exist: critics who read back into the Toomer of the early 1920s and the racially evasive Toomer of later years blur the lenses through which we should understand the author and read the work. Nonetheless, those who have detected an aura of secrecy in the various authorial presences projected in *Cane* are not wrong: the text's hints of concealed knowledge continually tease the reader with the sense that more is going on than meets the eye. Where a number of commentaries on *Cane* propose that its buried secret is the South's hidden history of miscegenation, however, I propose that the political unconscious of the text is the site of a repressed history that is, while grounded in the political economy of slavery and Jim Crow, intensely personal. The text's Gothicism stems not so much from a generalized awareness of the interracial sexual mingling unmentionable in the Deep South as from the rattling of various unquiet ghosts inhabiting Toomer's own family dungeon. Toomer felt compelled at once to voice and to deny the anxieties aroused by his awareness of his family's checkered past, a past that implicated him, willy-nilly, in a history of exploitation that was unacceptable to his sense of himself as a New Negro entertaining hopes for world revolution.[3]

"I was born into a world of panic": Toomer's "Blue-Veined" Youth

As in his recollections of his activities as a socialist, a New Negro, and a literary nationalist, Toomer's accounts of his family differ dramatically in the various versions of his autobiography. The 1931 text, written at the height of his involvement with the Gurdjieffian movement, offers a largely guilt-free description of his family's insertion in the class relations prevailing among Washington, DC's African American elite. His grandfather, Toomer observes, had "ideals and aims for his children" that were "similar to those of most ruling-class Americans of his time." The larger society into which Toomer was born consisted of an "aristocracy, such as perhaps never will exist again in America—midway between the white and Negro world." The 1934 text, also from the Gurdjieff years, contains a similar description: "In the Washington of those days—and those days have gone now—there was a flowering of a natural but transient aristocracy, thrown up by the, for them, creative conditions of the post-war period. These people, whose racial strains were mixed and for the most part unknown, happened to find themselves in the colored group. They had a personal refinement, a certain inward culture and beauty, a warmth of feeling such as I have seldom encountered elsewhere or again." Toomer's characterization of Washington's light-skinned upper class as a "natural" aristocracy, possessing "personal refinement" and "inward culture and beauty," as well as his assertion that his peers from this group were "my kind," indicate a more than casual elitism. Unmentioned in both accounts—which also give short shrift to Toomer's early exposure to socialism and his experience in the shipyard—are the sources of the wealth enabling these aristocrats to enjoy the good life. The autobiographical voice heard here acknowledges his membership in a mixed-race group but insists upon its having been unaffected by the racism of the larger society. He is far from self-identifying as a Negro, let alone a New Negro. Indeed, he has carefully tailored his self-portrait to appeal to the liberal—but not too liberal—racial attitudes of the largely upper-middle-class white acolytes of the Movement for a Higher Consciousness.[4]

"Book X," written in 1935, sketches Toomer's class background in more defensive terms:

> We were, I suppose, of the upper middle class. But class, in this divisional sense, seemed to have no hold on my family. Class, in the sense of quality, certainly did—and then and ever since I have had rather strong feelings about it, feeling myself rightly placed in the company of others of corresponding quality, feeling out of place and prejudiced against spiritual coarseness or vulgarity. I have always felt myself to be at once a natural democrat and a natural aristocrat. But as for class in the class-conscious sense—no, it did not exist in my home, nor have I acquired it since.

Stepping back from his earlier claim to have come from "ruling-class" origins, Toomer here notches the Pinchbacks down to "upper middle class" status. While still preening himself on being a "natural aristocrat," averse to "spiritual coarseness or vulgarity," he now asserts his family's lack of snobbery. Written when Toomer had stepped back from the Gurdjieffian movement and was attempting to come to terms with his abandonment of the shipyard workers some fifteen years before, this text acknowledges the proletarian discourse current in the mid-1930s even as it denies its relevance to Toomer's personal history.[5]

"Incredible Journey," begun in the late 1930s, gives a starkly different shape to the world into which Toomer was born, stressing the social upheavals surrounding the safe haven in which he had spent his privileged childhood. "Just as I, today, am directly or indirectly involved in every major struggle of my time," he writes, "so were my parents involved in much the same kind of major struggles back in 1894. They may have tried to live, as most of us are prone to do, a private life in a private world. . . . But regardless of their wishes the larger world caught them up—they were made dependent upon the shifts of fortune and misfortune common to the great body of their countrymen." Discussing the historical circumstances surrounding the moment of his birth, Toomer calls attention to the vast gulf separating the elite from the masses: "The very morning I was born, some million and more stunted malnourished children, less fortunate than I was to be, arose early and went to work to slave, as adults did, in mills and other factories of profit, returning after a long gruelling day to fling themselves down on makeshift beds, used up, utterly exhausted." The wealth of the owners was premised, moreover, on the poverty of the producers:

The fundamental economy of the nation, including the economy of the predominantly agricultural states, continued to shift from an agrarian to an industrial base. Industry expanded, agriculture shrunk [sic] in importance. Industrialists displaced planters and farmers as power-possessing men. Machine-owners prospered; land-owners were squeezed.

The mass of the w p [white people?] bent their backs to new masters. The mass of the c p [colored people?] did the same. Chattle [sic] slavery had been abolished by law, but wage slavery increased.

Finance, ever more increasingly centralized in N. Y., was becoming n [national?] and international. America had been a borrowing nation; now she was well on her way to becoming a lending nation. Wall Street, in the minds of the people, was becoming . . . a symbol of despotic remote control. . . .

More and more machines were being used in farming, to some advantage, to some disadvantage. The machine was not then, and is not now, an unmixed blessing. In some cases, no doubt, progress was made. In other cases the soil itself was as shocked by machinery [and] the new methods of cultivation as were the men, who found that they must scrape up enough cash to buy machines if they were to keep pace with a rapidly changing world. The need to purchase farm machinery was another factor causing the farmer to raise cash crops. And just at this time crop prices were falling.

Toomer concludes, "The dispossessed did not take it lying down. They arose to contest. In every field the shifts of power occasioned strife."[6]

It is not simply abstract economic forces that produce social upheaval, contends the Toomer of "Incredible Journey." The class struggle has conscious agents among possessors and dispossessed alike.

I was born into a world of panic.

Grover Cleveland was in the White House. He, and the men of government, and the men of affairs all over the country had a financial panic on their hands and a headache in their heads that bromoseltzer would not alleviate. The early hours of the very morning of my birth the President may have had a nightmare, compounded of flat money, legal tender, Silver Law, treasury deficits, gold reserve, government bonds, labor strikes and riot, Coxey's army. . . . and from this fantastic and horrible nightmare to be awakened in cold sweat by a dream that blood-and-power thirsty socialistic revolutionaries had marched on Washington and were breaking into the White House to set up a replica of the Paris Commune.

Toomer adds that his grandfather Pinchback, hearing the news of the impending march of the unemployed on the nation's capital, would have been "all serious. . . . For, he, then, was among the 'haves,' and the haves then as now were sufficiently upset by any demonstration of solidity and power on the part of the 'have-nots.'" In this retrospective account, Toomer appears to have rethought his earlier contention that there had been no "class consciousness" in his family. Indeed, Pinchback is identified with a ruling class characterized not by personal refinement but by the exploitation of labor and the repression of resistance.[7]

Patently drawing on the vocabulary of Marxist class analysis, "Incredible Journey" emphasizes the commonalty of the fates of people caught up in the economic and political crises produced by the shift into industrial modernity. Toomer characterizes the postbellum social relations of production as "wage-slavery"; registers the impact of the rise of finance capital on all sectors of the nation's economy; and describes the violent struggles that resulted from increasing class polarization. The delight with which he imagines Grover Cleveland having nightmares about a possible variant on the Paris Commune in the nation's capital—on the day of Toomer's birth, no less—suggests that the radical who had written about the need for a "socialized reality" in the *New York Call* some two decades previously had hardly disappeared. Also noteworthy is Toomer's survey of the effects of mechanized agriculture on the land, which is viewed as the site of production for profit, not of rhapsody over the folk and the soil. Toomer here acknowledges the exploitation of land and labor as the source of wealth; "aristocracy" is a social relation, rather than inner essence.

Oddly, however, even though he mentions that both white and "colored" workers bent their backs to the post–Civil War industrial regime, there is no mention in "Incredible Journey" of the racial terror visited on black labor that was surely a signal feature of the mid-1890s. In Toomer's references to Pinchback and other members of his family in this final version of the autobiography, moreover, there appear only the faintest allusions to the Pinchbacks' racial ancestry. For years Toomer had been hedging on his family's background in his various autobiographies. While he acknowledged that the Pinchbacks moved among an elite consisting of "mixed . . . racial strains," he offered contradictory accounts of the mixture of "bloods" in his own family. In "On Being an American" (1934), Toomer speculated about Pinchback's background: "I would judge that the admixture of dark blood or bloods, whatever they were, occurred in his mother's line two or more generations before her. It is probable, then, that his mother herself did not know. Whatever she believed had reached her by hearsay. Certainly what reached him was hearsay." In this account, Toomer effaced the lineage of his mixed-race maternal grandmother, Emily Hethorn Pinchback, describing her as "a white woman of English-French stock." In "Book X" (1935), Toomer asserted that Pinchback's racial identity could not in fact be known, by him or anyone else. "It would be interesting if we knew what P himself believed about his racial heredity," wrote Toomer. "Did he believe he had some Negro blood? I do not know. What I do know is this—his belief or disbelief would have no necessary relation to the fact—and this holds true as regards his Scotch-Welsh-German and other bloods as well." Indeed, Toomer went so far as to propose that Pinchback opportunistically passed as Negro during Reconstruction in order to further his political career. "What had served him would not serve me, and I could not be bound one way or the other by his role," concluded Toomer. "What he had claimed for his purposes, I would unclaim for my purposes, if need be." A few years later, in "Incredible Journey," Toomer more forthrightly acknowledged Pinchback's claim to Negro ancestry, even identity, noting that, when the question arose regarding where his grandson should attend elementary school, the old man would not send the child to a white school: "No, that will not do. It might look as if he were going back on his race and wanting to be white." What Toomer stressed in this portraiture, however, was that, for his grandfather, being identified as a Negro was a matter of choice, not of necessity. Pinchback was above all else "a member of the upper class, the governing class, the aristocracy"; Negro and white visitors to the house alike "look[ed] up to him [as] the leader, the governor."[8]

While Toomer evidently had Marx on the mind as he limned the portrait of his maternal grandfather in the mid-to-late 1930s, it does not take much perspicacity to realize that a Freudian ax is being ground at the same time. Nathan Toomer was absent from the life of his son; Pinchback was the dominant—and domineering—male figure in Jean Toomer's youth and young adulthood. As surrogate father, Pinchback clearly aroused strong emotions—many of them hostile—in his grandson, whose unfocused ambitions and peripatetic behavior in turn aroused strong emotions in the older man. Having referred to himself as a "prodigal son" in his 1923 authorial sketch for Liveright, Toomer struggled in his subsequent autobiographical writings with his Oedipal ambivalence in relation to his grandfather, an ambivalence that endured for many years after Pinchback's death. Toomer's description of his grandfather as a member of the "ruling class," solidly leagued with the "haves" against the "have-nots," enabled

Figure 4. P. B. S. Pinchback (Jean Toomer's maternal grandfather). "Gov. Pinchback," Library of Congress Prints and Photographs Division, Brady-Handy Photograph Collection

Toomer to express his continuing radical affinities; at the same time, his emphasis on Pinchback's racial identity as a matter of performance stripped away some of the older man's status as a battler against lynch violence and segregation from Reconstruction onward. Toomer's otherwise class-conscious commentary on his family history in "Incredible Journey" is vitiated by its failure to register the impact of Jim Crow on all segments of society, from bottom to top.[9]

"An unheroic sort of tragedy":
In Search of Nathan Toomer

In biographical approaches to Toomer's writings, it is generally acknowledged that his lack of contact with his father was a determining absence, leaving a psychic wound from which the abandoned son never fully healed. Toomer claimed to have seen his father only once, when he was a small child and his father accosted him and his mother on the street. "My total information or misinformation about him," Toomer wrote in "Incredible Journey," "scant though it was (hardly sufficient for me to draw the picture of a shell of a man, a shell without a kernel) was enough to serve my purposes throughout most of my life." Nathan Toomer died in 1906, when his son was eleven; he remained, Toomer wrote "a sort of mystery" to his wondering son. Toomer may not, however, have been as ignorant of his father's life as he later let on.[10]

The marriage of Nathan Toomer and Nina Pinchback, Jean Toomer's mother, was short-lived. Meeting at the Pinchbacks' Bacon Street housewarming reception in December 1893, the fifty-two-year-old Nathan and the twenty-eight-year-old Nina married in March 1894; nine months later Nathan Eugene Pinchback Toomer, their only child, was born. Although Nathan Toomer gave Nina some $12,000 with which to purchase a house in Washington, DC, he did not buy adequate furnishings for it; absent from Washington for increasingly long periods even before his son was born, he failed to support Nina, whose father did not come forward to finance the second household. Nina was unwilling to follow Nathan's bidding and move to Georgia, where—according to his assertions in their divorce proceedings—he "possessed a good comfortable and commodious home fully furnished and equipped, all ready and in perfect order for her to step into and assume charge and control of as mistress of the same." Instead, Nina moved back to her parents' home with her son in 1898 and was granted a divorce in 1899. Her petition for alimony noted that Nathan Toomer had told her that he owned two plantations around Sparta, Georgia, and had recently acquired some $60,000 or $70,000 "as a result of transactions in stocks." Nina reassumed her maiden name; Nathan Eugene Pinchback Toomer—later Jean Toomer—became Eugene Pinchback. "Nathan P. Toomer sounded too much like Nathan Toomer," Toomer later recalled. "It was a constant reminder of what they wanted to forget." Because Nathan Toomer refused to pay alimony, moreover, he was threatened with arrest should he appear in the District of Columbia; the name of Nathan Toomer was never mentioned in the Pinchback house while the son was growing up. When Toomer's mother died in 1909—after a second marriage to an insurance salesman named Archibald Combes, whom Toomer apparently detested—"[w]hatever my mother [had learned] of Nathan Toomer's early history," Toomer wrote regretfully, "she took into her grave."[11]

Nathan Toomer, it turns out, continually asked after the "dear darling" and "Little Colonel" in letters to his Washington business acquaintance Whitefield McKinlay, who was also a close friend of the Pinchback family and frequently saw the growing child. Eugene/Jean, however, never knew of his father's continuing concern; for all practical purposes the child had been left to be reared by a fond but authoritarian grandfather who had helped to send the child's father into exile, along with a doting but passive grandmother and a neglectful mother. In a version of the family romance in which the grandfather took on the role of the father, and the actual father the role of the fantasized ideal parent, Toomer wove a romantic web around the image of Nathan Toomer, portraying him as "semi-feudal, aristocratic, unrelated to the urges of the mass of people seeking equal rights and privileges under a theoretical if not actual democracy." The only possessions Toomer inherited from his father were "some beautiful silk handkerchiefs, a set of small diamond shirt studs, and a slender ebony cane with a gold head," along with two portraits. One of these

> showed his complexion [to be] fair. As I recall him in life his color was more swarthy. He had a fine head on his broad shoulders, well-modeled features, soft greying hair. His face was unlined and rather youthful looking, clean shaven except for a trim grey mustache which bore no resemblance to the "handlebars" that were fashionable in those days. His lips and chin were not particularly strong, not noticeably weak. His eyes, generously spaced apart, were level-looking, quick with feeling. The one time I saw him he had a brooding expression, a rather extraordinary expression. It came from deep within him and seemed to reach towards something far away. As I reflect on that expression now, a feeling comes to me that among his many puzzling features he may have had a streak of genius in him—a streak that, never finding its proper occupation, disturbed his inner life and sometimes came to the surface in a mood of creative brooding.
>
> I search my memory of his picture. I search my memory of his face as I saw it in life. I search in vain for visual signs of the deceits and weaknesses that undoubtedly were there.

Toomer's own self-concept doubtless colors his perception of his father's "genius." Yet his memory of his single encounter with Nathan Toomer combines with his interpretation of his picture to produce a portrait at once admiring and apologetic. The class judgments resulting in a harsh portrait of the grandfather are considerably softened in the depiction of the father.[12]

Toomer elaborated on the "semi-feudal" features of Nathan Toomer's class position:

> I know nothing of him or of his ways that would deny or even modify the assertion that most of his life, though not without charm and the capacity to captivate men as well as women on first acquaintance, was, to put it harshly, a life of utter parasitism. Nor was he a cultured parasite. Cultured parasites, though parasites, do take in the best of books, music, and the arts and philosophies generally. . . . Not so Nathan Toomer. He was too busy with his own emotions to read of the emotions of others. He was too entangled in his own schemes to have time or inclination for studied philosophy. Life as he found it, present life, first-hand life was his vice and his avocation. This might have been all to the good had he been more of an artist in life, less of a bungler. As it was, an unheroic sort of tragedy seemed to have dogged him from beginning to end. Those whom he loved he left injured. Those whom he touched, with few exceptions, sooner or later turned from him. And in the end he himself died, prematurely, self-destroyed.
>
> As far as I know he had but one enduring affection, and this was for the South.

It is difficult to separate what Toomer is offering as fictionalized speculation from what he is proposing as fact. But there is a clear contradiction between Toomer's statement that he knew practically nothing about his father and his assertions that Nathan Toomer "left injured . . . those whom he loved" and that "those whom he touched, with few exceptions, sooner or later turned from him." Toomer also offers no basis for his conclusion that his father's "one enduring affection" was "for the South."[13]

As with the racial background of the Pinchbacks, Toomer gives widely varying accounts of Nathan Toomer's ancestry in different versions of his autobiography. In the 1934 manuscript, he wrote that Nathan Toomer was "of English-Dutch-Spanish stock. I gather that he lived in the South as a white man." He queried—in language closely replicating his contemplation of his grandfather's ancestry and identity—"Did he have Negro blood? It is possible." This assertion is contradicted in "Incredible Journey," however, by Toomer's admission that, during his childhood, the knowledge that his father was "colored" constituted Toomer's "weak spot. I was vulnerable through him." In another draft of "Incredible Journey," Toomer wrote that, in 1913, when he was eighteen years old, he summoned up the courage to query his grandfather about his father. Pinchback at this time told him that Nathan Toomer, the son of a Georgia planter, had a broad acquaintance in "the region of Georgia bounded by Augusta and Macon . . . [and] was known to have some colored blood. Nonetheless, he lived amongst both white and colored people. The rigid division of white and Negro did not apply in his case." According to the last version of Toomer's autobiography, then, he had known at least since his teenaged years, and probably considerably before, that his father was of mixed racial background. During the 1913 conversation recalled in "Incredible Journey," moreover, Toomer learned that Nathan Toomer had inherited from his plantation-owning white father "considerable land and a fair amount of cash money" but had "run through" the legacy and "begun borrowing." This "borrowing" had apparently extended from Middle Georgia to Washington, DC: referring to McKinlay, an astute businessman as well as a friend of the family, Pinchback chuckled, "Your father, boy, was a sharp one. He was sharp enough to touch Whitefield McKinlay for a sizeable sum of money." Toomer learned as far back as 1913 that Nathan Toomer's "creative brooding" had not prevented him from feathering his financial nest.[14]

Writing some twenty-five years after this conversation, Toomer created an imaginary scenario in which Pinchback vigorously opposed Nina's defiant decision to marry the recently arrived Nathan Toomer:

> Nothing she could possibly *say* about Toomer would change the *facts. He* said that he knew *the facts* about Toomer and that in opposing the marriage he was doing it, not for himself, but for her, for her own good. . . .
>   Having seen with his own eyes things in Toomer he did not like, he had made inquiries around town. What he learned was not to Toomer's credit. . . . He was . . . a persuasive and therefore dangerous fraud. . . . The more he learned the more Pinchback was convinced that Toomer's pockets were as empty as his character. . . . "That fraud from Georgia [was] a charlatan, a bluff."
>   For all I know to the contrary, Pinchback may have gone further. By some

means or another he may have obtained information, or misinformation, about Toomer's past, particularly about his previous two marriages, damaging information. [original emphasis]

Besides speculating that Pinchback, when investigating the background of his daughter's suitor, discovered "damaging information," this account adds further information about Nathan Toomer's past that presumably Pinchback had not conveyed to his grandson in the 1913 conversation, namely, that Toomer's father had been married twice before he wed Toomer's mother.[15]

When and how, we might wonder, did Toomer begin to intuit that information about Nathan Toomer's "previous two marriages" had been at the core of Pinchback's distrust of his daughter's future husband? In one draft of "Incredible Journey," Toomer proposes that it was not until after the deaths of both his grandparents—that is, sometime after Emily Hethorn Pinchback's death in 1927, but before he began research for the final version of his autobiography in the late 1930s—that he obtained documents attesting to the marriage registration of his own parents. Noting that at the time of his document search he had "a vague memory of having heard that [Nathan Toomer] had been married before," Toomer claims that he wrote to the Department of Vital Statistics in Washington, DC, and learned that his father, in registering for his marriage to Nina, acknowledged that he had been married two times previously. Toomer also asserted that Nathan and Nina had described themselves as "colored" in their marriage registration. He wrote, "By now I understood enough about them and about their circumstances to understand why [they put themselves down as colored]. The surprise would have been had I found that they had put themselves down as white." As elsewhere in "Incredible Journey," this statement contradicts Toomer's repeated assertions in his mid-1930s autobiographies that it was impossible to ascertain whether or not any or all of his forebears, on either side of his family, were of Negro ancestry. Although he still insists, somewhat implausibly, that his mother and father, like Pinchback, chose freely in claiming "colored" identity, now he presents himself as unruffled by this news. He goes on to write, indeed, that what surprised him more was that Nathan Toomer described himself not as a "planter" but as a "farmer": while Nathan Toomer might have "worked on the land . . . possibly as a boy, or a young man . . . by the time of his third marriage [he] had been off the land many a year." What Toomer found hard to believe in the marriage registration was the fact that, on the verge of marrying the daughter of P. B. S. Pinchback, Nathan Toomer chose to describe himself in such "modest" terms."[16]

Toomer's confused and confusing accounts of what he knew and when he knew it shed considerable light on why he was never able to complete his autobiography. There are simply too many contradictions not only within the different versions of his narrative but even among different drafts of the same version. Clearly a key cause of these contradictions was his tangled response to what he was to call his "white-Negro difficulty" when he underwent psychoanalysis in the years after he abandoned the attempt to write his life story. The hesitant, prevaricating Toomer of the autobiographies contrasts sharply with the Toomer of the era of *Cane*, who had written to Mae Wright of the "Negro blood in our veins," boasted to Claude Barnett that his Pinchback lineage had enable him to "peep behind the veil," and forthrightly acknowledged the Negro identity of the author of *Cane* in "The South in Literature."

But I want to back up for a moment to examine more closely a claim that will prove important in my analysis of Toomer's *Cane*-era writings. This is Toomer's statement that at the time of his writing to the Department of Vital Statistics for his parents' marriage license—presumably sometime after 1927, the year of his grandmother's death—he had only a "vague memory" of having heard that his father had been previously married. The clear implication here is that, when he visited Sparta in 1921, and subsequently returned home to begin work on *Cane*, he had no knowledge of the particulars of his father's marital history—that this history became known to him only many years later. Yet, if we are to believe that Toomer discussed his father with Pinchback as early as 1912 or 1913—an assertion repeated in various drafts of "Incredible Journey"—then it would appear that the Jean Toomer who arrived in Middle Georgia in 1921 to take up his responsibilities as substitute principal at the Sparta Agricultural and Industrial Institute was aware of at least several things. He knew that he was entering his father's home turf; that his father, a man of mixed racial background, had moved between the white and black worlds; and that his father had lost money in dealings with a Sparta businessman.

That this background information was crucially supplemented when Toomer was in Sparta is indicated in a draft of "Incredible Journey" that has thus far escaped scholarly notice. It is widely acknowledged that Toomer heard mention of Nathan Toomer when he visited a barbershop during his 1921 stay in Sparta and was informed that a man of the same surname had visited the barbershop many years before. According to the version of their conversation routinely referenced by scholars, the barber recalled that a man named Nathan Toomer "had business, and he was paying attention to ___. The man mentioned a woman's name that I have since forgotten. I asked about the woman and was told she was a great beauty, the illegitimate daughter of a wealthy white man, herself now having considerable money in her own right. Did Toomer want to marry this woman? I asked. Seemed so, said the man, Did they get married? I asked. No, said the man." Another man in the shop then broached the subject of Nathan Toomer's finances, noting that the white man with whom he had been doing business in Sparta "took all of his money away." Evidently recalling Nathan Toomer's treatment of "Old Mac," Toomer wrote, "So! If this were true, and if what my grandfather had said was true, my father, it seemed, could not only fleece but be fleeced." Inquiring whether Nathan Toomer had been regarded as white or colored, Toomer was told that the visitor had stayed at the white hotel while he "payed [*sic*] attention to a colored woman." The conversation was terminated, however, by an interruption "a propos of nothing": "Then a third man said one of those things that are never said in the South, yet sometimes are said: The white boss of this town is called a nigger behind his back by his enemies. They say he has some Negro blood. What do you make of that? No one wanted to make anything of that. Not a single word was spoken thereafter. Every man in the shop felt that too much had been said as it was."[17]

While this version of the Sparta barbershop incident has been taken as definitive of Toomer's inquiries into his father's past, another version, contained in the handwritten manuscript of "Incredible Journey," offers a significantly different account of Toomer's thoughts as his hair was being cut. "My curiosity burned me," he wrote. "Here was my chance, perhaps the one chance I'd ever have, to get some information about my hidden father from those who may have seen him as he lived in the South." In this variant, the barber did not deny that Nathan Toomer married the heiress, but simply noted that "[s]he had money and a plantation." Toomer then wondered, "Who was the woman? What her name? If they married, any children? What had become of them? When was all of this? What year? Could it have been after my mother divorced him? I had a feeling it must have been before. Perhaps the woman mentioned was one of the three [*sic*] married by Nathan Toomer before his marriage to Nina Pinchback." At this point, the third man in the barbershop made his comment about the "white boss of this town," and the conversation ceased. But there had occurred to Toomer a series of questions that he wished, but did not dare, to ask. "Burn[ing] [with] curiosity," he engaged in far-ranging speculations about his father's past marriages, wondering in particular whether he, Jean Toomer, might have had a mulatto heiress stepmother and half-siblings. According to this account of the barbershop incident, then, not only was Toomer fully cognizant—*before* he arrived in Sparta—that Nathan Toomer had had business dealings in Hancock County and been previously married. He also was prepared further to connect the dots about his father's past.[18]

"Incredible Journey" takes us no further, however; according to all the drafts, the trail at this point grew cold. His father's earlier life remained a mystery, Toomer writes, and he was left wondering, "Through what moulds of life in Georgia, through what fires in himself, had Nathan Toomer passed to become fashioned into the man who arrived in Washington, D. C., in 1893? And why did he come to Washington? What had he been up against? What had he come through? What had he overcome?" The only other information Toomer presumably gleaned about his father during his Georgia stay was from some Augusta acquaintances who informed him that Nathan Toomer had died there in 1906, "a heartbroken man, baffled, bewildered, stunned, sometimes all but paralyzed by the seemingly uncaused reversals of [his] life." Toomer leaves the reader also somewhat baffled and bewildered: how can Toomer be so certain that his father had experienced such trauma, when he yields up no particulars? How did he know that "[t]hose whom [Nathan Toomer] loved he left injured" or that "[t]hose whom he touched, with few exceptions, sooner or later turned from him"?[19]

But was the trail in fact so cold? Did the dots remain unconnected?

"The wealthiest colored woman in the world": Nathan Toomer and Amanda America Dickson

Although it might be argued that the second version of the barbershop visit is no more reliable than the first, I propose here that it brings us at least closer to the threshold of the truth. Once one knows who Nathan Toomer's second wife was, it becomes difficult—indeed, well-nigh impossible—to imagine that the son could not remember the name of the woman his father had courted or did not attempt to learn more about what his father had "been up against . . . come through . . . and overcome" in the South. For this second wife, Amanda America Dickson Toomer, was a figure of considerable notoriety—not just local but national—at the time of her marriage to Nathan Toomer in July 1892. Born in 1849, Amanda Dickson was the daughter of David Dickson—in 1860 adjudged the wealthiest planter in Hancock County—and Julia Lewis, his slave and concubine, with whom he lived openly for many years, to the consternation of his white neighbors. Raped at the age of thirteen by David Dickson, who pulled her up onto his horse and spirited her away, Lewis never forgave him, according to family lore; she subsequently "ruled David Dickson with an iron hand," had the keys to the plantation, and controlled everything, even handling monetary transactions with local merchants. Amanda, once weaned, was taken away from her mother; as a child she slept in the bedroom of her white grandmother—and owner—David Dickson's mother, Elizabeth Dickson. Amanda was raised in an atmosphere of physical and emotional comfort; her first husband, Charles Eubanks, was a white Civil War veteran (and David Dickson's nephew, hence her own first cousin) by whom she had two sons, Charles and Julian. In 1871 Amanda returned to David Dickson's house to live, along with her two sons; between 1876 and 1878 she attended college in Atlanta. David Dickson publicly treated both Amanda and her sons with respect, insisting that any guests who came to dinner sit at the same table as Amanda and his grandsons. Soon after his grandsons came to live with him, Dickson took them to New Orleans and "had them declared white"; when they later opted to marry Negro women, both had to obtain legal permission—that is, be re-declared Negro—in order to do so.[20]

Although David Dickson eventually married a white woman, Clara Harris, in 1871, she predeceased him by twelve years without having borne children. When he died in 1885, David Dickson left the vast bulk of his estate, worth over $400,000, to Amanda, "free and clear and exempt from the marital rights, power, control or custody of any husband she may have"—and to her children upon her death. Amanda moved to Augusta after settlement of the will; when she died in 1893, the obituaries in white newspapers described her variously as "the wealthiest colored woman in the world," "the wealthiest Negro in the United States," and—according to the *New York Times*—"the wealthiest colored woman alive." That her middle

Figure 5. Amanda America Dickson in mourning attire for her father, David Dickson. She was the second wife of Jean Toomer's father, Nathan Toomer, and the mother of Charles Dickson. By permission of the Amanda America Dickson Estate

name was "America"—presumably given her by her father—only compounds the ironies surrounding her at once anomalous and strangely typical situation.[21]

The fight over the Dickson will—which took place in the Hancock County courthouse in Sparta's central square—was one of the most vigorously contested in the history of the Georgia courts. Indeed, it gained national prominence and was reported in newspapers as far north as Cleveland. The lawyers for David Dickson's white relatives argued their case vehemently, proclaiming that "the future of the Anglo-Saxon [and] the traditions of the past" were at stake. But the courts decided, at both the circuit and the state levels, that Amanda's property rights must prevail. As the Georgia historian Jonathan Bryant has pointed out, the property rights of southern landowners had to be treated as absolute, since "any relaxation of property owners' rights weakened planters' authority over their workers"—white as well as black sharecroppers. But "if property rights are to be absolute, then such rights must be protected for every person: the white man who chooses to devise his property and the black woman who is to receive it." Developments in late-nineteenth-century legal practice throughout the United States further affected the outcome of the Dickson will case. For with the rise of powerful corporations, the Constitution was increasingly converted "into a new bill of rights designed to protect American business." As a consequence, "courts at all levels protected private property rights at the expense of state interests." Lawyers for the white Dicksons were invoking a "public interest" argument when they spoke of preserving the Anglo-Saxon past and future. But the public interest represented by time-honored traditions of white supremacy was countered by the superior present-day private interest of individual property rights. Amanda America Dickson, the daughter of a raped field slave, was the beneficiary of laws that were enabling the postbellum robber barons to amass and safeguard their wealth.[22]

Amanda America Dickson, cognizant of the value of good neighborly relations, sweetened the pie for her white neighbors by forgiving a number of debts to the Dickson estate. She expressed her gratitude to the legal system that had safeguarded her fortune by using an additional portion of her inheritance to build an elegant new courthouse—complete with an impressive tower—on Sparta's town square. The legal system that preserved her right to inherit her father's property did nothing, however, to extend the civil rights or improve the livelihoods of the overwhelming majority of Georgia's black folk. As a slave master, Dickson had not only engaged in scientific soil conservation but also had done motion studies to increase the productivity of his cotton pickers, "increas[ing] a slave's daily average to 300 pounds, with 700 for the best pickers." As a post–Civil War plantation owner, he had become renowned for the Dickson Compound, an effective fertilizer sold widely in the South. He had further expanded his wealth by adopting a system of tenancy that allowed tenants one-third of the crop but required them to receive two-thirds of their wages as share-wages, to be spent at the plantation store, with the rest set aside as disaster insurance. That Dickson's workers were not altogether content with this arrangement was signaled by two gin burnings on his plantations, one in 1870 and one in 1884. Dickson's advocates believed, however, that his scientific approach to both labor and the land promised a "counter-revolution" in the New South, one that would reinstitute "diversity of condition and distinction of class based upon a landed proprietorship" as "the light and life of society." While Dickson evidently had loved—after his fashion—his mixed-race daughter and her children, he had been a pillar of white supremacy in the amassing of his great fortune.[23]

The absolutization of property rights signaled by the Dickson will case deprived his white relatives of what they considered their rightful inheritance, but it did nothing to change existing patterns of land ownership or labor exploitation. If anything, it contributed to the extension of debt peonage and the reduction of more and more black farmers to sharecropper status. "Ironically, in the same year as the Dickson decision," writes Bryant, "the Georgia legislature began the process of black disenfranchisement by passing the first cumulative poll tax." By 1900, blacks constituted 47 percent of the population but owned only 4 percent of the land. In the Black Belt, 60 percent of all farms were operated by blacks, but of these 90 percent were cash share tenants. As possessor of extensive landholdings in Hancock County, Amanda America Dickson drew the bulk of her current income from the labor of sharecroppers, tenant farmers, and debt peons; the capital she inherited from her father had its origin in slave labor subjected to a regime of maximum profit extraction. When Toomer described the social relations of production in the postbellum rural South in "Incredible Journey," he was delineating the source not of Pinchback's wealth—which had derived from political wheeling and dealing and commerce rather than from landowning—but of the wealth to which Nathan Toomer had gained access through his second marriage.[24]

Soon after winning her lawsuit, Dickson moved in 1886 to Augusta, where she purchased a mansion on Telfair Street in an exclusive part of town. In 1891, she met Nathan Toomer, a fifty-year-old widower with four daughters, the youngest of whom, Mamie, was only twelve years old; in July 1892, eleven months after his first wife, Harriet, died, Nathan Toomer and Amanda Dickson were married. Notice of the wedding appeared on the third page of the *New York Times*. Upon her death in June 1893, the bulk of Amanda Dickson Toomer's estate went to her sons; although Nathan did not receive any significant acreage—precluding any description of himself as a "planter"—Nathan was willed the contents of her house and a relatively small sum of money. Not one to let the grass grow under his marital feet, Nathan Toomer would soon turn up in Washington, where he quickly courted and married the daughter of the prominent Pinchback; money he had inherited from his second wife presumably helped Nathan Toomer purchase for $12,000 in cash the Washington house he presented to his new bride. Nathan Toomer continued to be tied to the Dickson estate, however; the principal business that carried him back to Georgia, forming the basis of Nina's charge of desertion, was his suit against Julia Lewis and Charles and Julian Dickson over their seizure of household goods that Amanda had willed to him. It is probable that Nathan Toomer held off furnishing the nearly empty Washington house where Nina and young Nathan Eugene were living because he hoped to regain his property from the Telfair Street house in Augusta, Georgia—the "comfortable and commodious house, fully furnished and equipped, all ready and in perfect order . . . to step into," of which Nina expressed no interest in being the "mistress . . . [in] charge and control."[25]

"If they married, any children?":
Mamie Toomer as Little Sister

Less than a year after Amanda and Nathan's marriage, her twenty-three-year-old son, Charles Dickson—who had been married at the age of seventeen to eighteen-year-old Kate Holsey—manifested an intense infatuation with Nathan's youngest daughter, Mamie, then fourteen years old. Charles, by all reports an arrogant, self-indulgent wastrel, almost succeeded in kidnapping Mamie from the

Baltimore convent where, in March 1893, Amanda and Nathan had placed her to keep her out of her stepbrother's reach. The plot was foiled when, two months later, Nathan and Amanda rushed northward to intervene. But Amanda, always of frail constitution, collapsed when, on the way home, their first-class Pullman car was detached from the rest of the train in Columbia, South Carolina, and left in the railroad yard in the broiling June sun. She died within hours of returning to Augusta after a twenty-four-hour delay; she was forty-three years old. Nathan had seen his youngest daughter nearly abducted and violated by his formerly white stepson, who evidently viewed the sexual possession of the adolescent Mamie as his right, his *droit du seigneur,* just as his grandfather had viewed the thirteen-year-old Julia Lewis as personal property. The recently twice-widowed Nathan Toomer had also been deprived of the fruits of his second marriage to "the wealthiest colored woman in the world" by the sexual rapacity of his stepson. His dogged pursuit of his inheritance in Georgia destroyed his third marriage and alienated him permanently from his only son. As in a Gothic novel, the wealth of David Dickson proved not a boon but a curse, poisoning the lives of those who laid claim to it.[26]

In "Incredible Journey," Toomer tantalizes the reader with his speculations about his father's marital past:

Figure 6. Charles Dickson, younger son of Amanda America Dickson and Charles Eubanks, and his wife, Kate Holsey Dickson. By permission of the Amanda America Dickson Estate

He loved women. He married. At what time in his life? What happened? Did she die? Were they divorced? If so, on what grounds? Were there any children?

He married again. When? Where? At what time in his life? What happened to this second marriage?

He had been married twice before he met and married the woman who was to be my mother.

He implies that these questions occurred to him only after he obtained the documentary information about Nathan Toomer's previous marriages on the marriage license that he obtained before writing "Incredible Journey." It is probable, however, that Jean Toomer had learned a good deal about his father, his stepmother, and their unhappily conjoined stepfamilies by the time he began gestating and imagining *Cane*. The tantalizing references to "the facts" and "damaging information" dropped in "Incredible Journey" seem like sly hints more than expressions of genuine mystification.[27]

Had Toomer been seeking information about his father when in Hancock County in 1921, the trail would not have been entirely cold, even if there was nothing more to be learned in the barbershop. Kate Holsey Dickson—who had sued Charles Dickson for divorce in March 1893 and obtained the divorce in 1900—was by 1921 long gone to Atlanta, where she had moved to take care of her eminent churchman father, Lucius Holsey. But Toomer could readily have learned that Julian Dickson, then living in Beaufort, South Carolina, was in 1920 still one of the wealthiest property owners in Hancock County, with 1,994 acres in land and total property worth more than $20,000. Julia Lewis, Julian and Charles's mother—and coconspirator in the plot to deprive Nathan Toomer of the furnishings of Amanda's house—had continued to live in Sparta until her death in 1913, eight years before Toomer's visit; her house, where gambling and other illegal activities took place, had acquired notoriety. Toomer would also have found it easy to identify the man who had tried to get Nathan Toomer's money thirty years before as William Hix Burwell, Sparta's most prominent businessman and politician. In 1900 Burwell had attempted to build a new textile factory on the site of "Factory Town"; in 1902 he purchased the new Sparta Telephone Company, located across the central square from the courthouse. As Speaker of the Georgia House of Representatives, he had the reputation of being a "windbag politician"; during the Great War he organized a patriotic rally in front of the courthouse at which he lambasted the Populist Tom Watson as a man who had "turned his hand against the Red Cross and the YMCA." A street in the center of Sparta was named after Burwell; the Burwell family mansion was the largest house in town; Burwell was almost certainly the "boss of the town" referred to in the gossip that Toomer overheard during his barbershop visit. The son who admired his father's ability to stay in the white hotel and engage in commercial transactions with white businessmen could surely have connected the dots.[28]

When in Middle Georgia, moreover, Toomer spent several weekends in nearby Augusta, where he visited with the Negro elite, a tightly knit group whose older generation had been well acquainted with their famous neighbor Amanda America Dickson Toomer. Her Telfair Street house was still one of the finest in town; her memorial headstone, reading "TOOMER," was—and still is—one of the largest in the city's historic Negro cemetery. Augusta was, furthermore, the location of the Paine Institute, which had been founded in 1882 by Lucius Holsey, the father of Charles Dickson's wife, Kate. The Paine Institute—despite its reputation for intraracial color prejudice and political conservatism—was the premier postwar institution of Negro higher education in Middle Georgia; both Charles Dickson and Kate Holsey had been students there, as had many members of Augusta's "blue-veined social circles." Dickson, Holsey, and Toomer would have been familiar names in the company in which Toomer moved during his weekend visits. In "Incredible Journey," Toomer mentions only that he stayed in Augusta on his way home from Sparta and was told by his hosts that Nathan Toomer years ago "left these parts and went to Washington. The next we knew we heard he had married, married the daughter of Governor Pinchback. Then in no time at all, here he was back in Augusta." Queried about the manner of Nathan's death, Toomer's host replied that he had "died of a broken heart." Since Nathan Toomer had never lived in Augusta until he arrived there as the husband of Amanda, however, and since his return to the city was precipitated by his attempts to recover his part of her estate, it defies plausibility that Toomer's hosts would not have mentioned that they were acquainted with Nathan as first the husband, then the broken-hearted widower, of the wealthiest woman of color ever to have lived in Augusta.[29]

Toomer's Washington, DC, connections could also have supplied him with information about his father's "travails," either before or after the 1921 trip south. The very fact that "Col. Tumer" had been invited to the 1893 Bacon Street housewarming at which he met Nina Pinchback indicates that his fame had preceded him. No matter how guarded Nathan Toomer may have tried to be about his past, it is unlikely that the influential P. B. S. Pinchback—himself a native of Middle Georgia and no stranger to Georgia politics and gossip—would have allowed any "facts" or "damaging information" about his daughter's paramour to remain vague and unsubstantiated. The world of Washington's "Negro Four Hundred"—the "tight cocoon" that would both nurture and smother the young Jean Toomer—was small (if not as small as that in Augusta). Francis Grimké—uncle of the writer and M Street English teacher Angelina Grimké—had officiated at the marriage of Nathan Toomer and Nina Pinchback. Charles Dickson had been a childhood friend of Henry Lincoln Johnson, the husband of Georgia Douglas Johnson. For several years after he was banned from Washington, moreover, Nathan Toomer kept in regular contact with Pinchback's crony "Old Mac," who handled several of the exiled man's business affairs, including the attempted collection of the sizeable debt owed to Nathan Toomer by William Hix Burwell. McKinlay regularly relayed information about the young Jean to his curious father. In letters he wrote to McKinlay from Sparta, Nathan Toomer was voluble on the subject of Charles and Julian Dickson, writing disgustedly of their alcoholism and philandering—Charles had become the father of an extralegal second family—and expressing sympathy with the plight of Charles's wife, Kate ("Caty") Holsey Dickson. "Old Mac," who would live in Washington until his death in 1941, was a repository of gossip and information; the young Toomer could have learned a good deal about his father from this old family friend.[30]

In short, if Toomer wished to gain more information about the history surrounding his absent father—whether in Sparta, Augusta, or Washington, DC—all he needed to do was ask. How, we might now inquire, might Toomer have processed this information at different points in his life? Despite his residual Marxist leanings, the middle-aged Quaker who was effectively living as a white man when he authored "Incredible Journey" clearly would have had an overriding interest in shrouding certain features of his past. But the young man who had written *Cane* after eliciting information about Nathan Toomer from Pinchback and visiting the Sparta barbershop would have been preoccupied with quite a different set of concerns. In particular, Toomer's inheritance of the remaining value of the Twelfth Street house could have given rise to a good deal of race- and class-based guilt. For the "turning of the worm" that Toomer experienced on abandoning the New Jersey shipyard had been significantly facilitated by his receiving from Pinchback in early 1920 the windfall sum of money that enabled him to stay in New York for several more months. This money, Toomer knew, came from the sale of his mother's house in Washington—the house that Nathan Toomer had bought with $12,000 in cash in 1894. If he had come to know the source of his father's wealth in the estate of David Dickson, this means that the young man who had been attempting to meet up with the "labor movement," and who had been writing about exploitation, racism, and imperialist war for the *New York Call*, had only to follow the money. The funds enabling Toomer to escape the fate of the working class had been extracted from the labor of sharecroppers, and before them slaves, on Dickson's Georgia plantations. The tradition of all the dead generations that weighed like a nightmare on Toomer's brain consisted of rapacious sexual practices on the one hand and the congealed labor of bonded Africans on the other.

Toomer's awareness of his family's history would also have produced further complications in the family romance that he had constructed around the figures of his father and his grandfather. For the story of Mamie and Charles signaled a direct familial connection with the violent legacy of slavery and Jim Crow, in particular the rape of women of African descent by white men of power and wealth. The story of the nearly white (indeed, once officially white) Charles Dickson's attempted ravishing of his adolescent mixed-race stepsister—Toomer's own "dark" half-sister—would not have sat easily with the young man who had been reading the feminist poetry and plays composed by the women writers in his Washington study group. Squirming under the discipline exerted by the authoritarian Pinchback, who had forbidden the mention of Toomer's father's name—indeed had changed the grandson's name to efface all traces of the father—Toomer was eager to surround his absent father with an aura of romance. His "real" father would fulfill the function of the imagined ideal parent, in contrast with the oppressive regime of the grandfather, playing here the role of the "real" father. "Incredible Journey" suggests, too, that Toomer felt some filial pride in Nathan Toomer's skill in moving in and out of the white world, courting wealthy women, perhaps even fleecing "Old Mac" as he had himself been fleeced by Burwell. In this narrative, Nathan Toomer could be portrayed as at once a victim of Pinchback's domination and a victor over the restrictions of Jim Crow.[31]

But there was a limit to both Pinchback's nefariousness and Nathan Toomer's heroism. Pinchback, for all his domineering behavior in the household, had nonetheless played an important public role in dismantling slavery and resisting Jim Crow; he was anything but complicit in the regime that had produced the fortune of David Dickson. Toomer's father, by contrast, had been, Toomer admitted, a "parasite"—"not even a cultured parasite"—who largely made his way through life by cheating (or being cheated) in business transactions and marrying wealthy women. In his pursuit of a comfortable berth with Amanda America Dickson, Nathan Toomer had been "too busy with his own emotions to read the emotions of others," thereby exposing his youngest daughter to the danger posed by her predatory stepbrother. Toomer's desired identification with the absent father would thus have been substantially impeded by his awareness of the tragic outcome of Nathan Toomer's second marriage for the women in his life—not only for Mamie Toomer, Kate Holsey Dickson, and Amanda Dickson Toomer, but also for Nina Pinchback Toomer, who had been dragged into a third marriage fated to ruin from the outset. And indeed for Jean Toomer himself, who had been deprived of a father by the machinations of the adult world. In the context of patriarchal Jim Crow, Toomer's family romance was from the outset tainted; there was no good father who could step in to take the place of the bad one.[32]

Of the various victims of the unthinking selfishness of the men in the Dickson-Toomer narrative, children stood out, particularly the girls: Julia Lewis and her step-granddaughter Mamie Toomer. Like her half-brother who would be born in 1894, Mamie Toomer was a wholly innocent victim of adult transgressions. Although she was born in 1879 and would have been fifteen years older than Toomer, in his imagination his "dark sister" remained frozen in time as a pubescent maiden in need of adult brotherly protection. Toomer would defend his little sister; he would be the good brother; he would protect black womanhood from seduction and rape. He would do better than his father. And he would expiate his guilt at having received property derived from bonded black labor.

"Where'd the money come from?":
Class Consciousness in *Natalie Mann*

The most compelling evidence that Toomer was by the early 1920s aware of his family's buried history is contained in the cracks and interstices of *Cane*, especially the "Kabnis" section. But some provocative indications of Toomer's being haunted by the skeletons in the Toomer-Pinchback closet are contained in *Natalie Mann*, a play Toomer authored early in 1922. Set among the mulatto elite of Washington, DC, the play addresses a number of the concerns preoccupying Toomer in the early 1920s: Socialism, the New Negro Movement, the project of Young America. But the play's emphasis on the centrality of sexual revolution to social revolution suggests not only Toomer's interest in feminism but also his thoughts and feelings surrounding the fate of his "dark sister." The central action of the play revolves around the relationship between Natalie Mann, a brilliant young pianist who initially lacks self-confidence, and Nathan Merilh, a Toomer-esque artist and mentor figure—more than faintly resembling David Teyy of "Withered Skin of Berries"—who functions as what the *dramatis personae* designates as Natalie's "instrument of development." By proclaiming her alliance with the radical and bohemian Nathan, Natalie repudiates the regime of her conservative parents, who embody "blue-veined" arrogance in its most philistine form. Nathan, while from a wealthy background, and apparently known to the older generation characters from his childhood onward, aligns himself with both the African American working class—as exemplified by Tome Mangrow, a bootlegger, and Etty Beal, a dancer at the Black Bear cabaret—and New York's mainly white cultural left. A secondary thread of the plot involves a public school teacher named Mertis Newbolt and her lover, a friend of Nathan's named Therman Law. Some years previously Mertis had given birth out of wedlock, a circumstance propelling her into activism around "the wrongs suffered by my people" but into silence as regards feminism. When Mertis becomes pregnant, this time by Therman, she is fired from her teaching job—largely at the incitement of Natalie's mother, Mrs. Mann—and subsequently dies from a botched abortion. A third strand of the plot—actually more a character study than a separate thread of action—deals with the conflicted situation of Mary Carson, a middle-aged sculptor who straddles the worlds of New Negro creative artistry and Old Negro cultural aridity.[33]

Having read the play, Frank wrote to Toomer that its "central drama . . . is smothered by the form of the other stuff, the teaparties, the talk of the incidental." The play is, to be sure, long on talk and short on action; although Toomer evidently had various George Bernard Shaw plays in mind when he composed *Natalie Mann*, he was an imperfect imitator of his favorite dramatist. But *Natalie Mann* contains a few expressionistic scenes where a distinctly modernist reworking of folk art takes center stage: Natalie's announcement of her feminist transformation through the telling of an African folktale; Nathan's entertainment of his New York circle with a performance of "Karintha," here presented as his composition; and Nathan and Etty's two avant-garde dances, the second of which supplies the play's finale. The closing stage directions read, "Beginning as a medley of national, racial folk tunes, [the music] spirals into a music that is individual and triumphant. At the very crest of creation, something inside of Merilh gives away." As his "limp form" lies prostrate—perhaps fatally—from exhaustion, Natalie exchanges a look of solidarity with Etty and declares to the older women looking on, "What are you weeping for, you silly women, who see him only a man?" Set in a Seventh Street cabaret with the U.S. flag hanging overhead, the play's dramatic conclusion starkly counterposes the "our America" of sexual freedom, class transgression, and New Negro racial pride with the "their America" of sexual repression, social hierarchy, and Old Negro shame at the cultural legacy of the folk. While Frank was essentially correct in his judgment that the play lacks dynamism, *Natalie Mann* nonetheless exhibits the young Toomer attempting to draw under the rubric of a vaguely socialist-cum-feminist politics his interest in the New Negro as cultural vanguard of Young America.[34]

Toomer's critique of "blue-veined" Washington's stultifying pursuit of white-encoded respectability—as well its preservation of the racial hierarchy that it presumes to have transcended—comes out most sharply in his portrayal of Mary Carson and her circle, which includes the puritanical Mrs. Mann, the mindless Mrs. Hart, and assorted other petty and quarrelsome members of the black bourgeoisie who exhibit contempt for both the rural peasantry and the urban proletariat. Based on a sculptor of Toomer's acquaintance—May Howard Johnson, who had in fact done a bust of the young Toomer—Mary Carson is aware of the barriers faced by women of color who aspire to the arts, but she proclaims her antifeminism, urging Natalie to "[g]et married. Any man will do." She attacks Nathan as "a socialist and a bolshevist and an analysist and a freakist and I dont know what all." Her argument for the irrelevance of political radicalism to African Americans is premised on an odd blend of racial essentialism and intraracial snobbery:

> [T]he world is drifting into an almost complete materialization of thought, and chaos. This newest fad, psychoanalysis, says that everything is sex, physical sex. . . . And then there are the socialists. Who are they? Materialists, materialists bent on a crude material conquest of the world. They would disrupt the home. But they are strong. Physically strong, and the idols they hold up to the masses are calculated to capture their credulity. Who wouldnt be a socialist if he was offered, gratis, an equal share of the world's wealth? But anyhow, all these forces are tending towards materialism. Now the colored people are by nature spiritual. They actually see ghosts. Let the scientific ignoramuses who will, call that superstition. They know how to cast spells and control unseen forces. They are the coming people. We are a section of them. We are an intelligent section. Therefore it is our duty to combat materialism with our own God-given spiritual weapons. We must consecrate ourselves to that cause.

Mertis Newbolt objects that "there are more immediate problems which we ought to clear up first, Lynching and Jim-crowism, for example"; Therman Law chimes in, "Besides, how are you going to combat this materialism that you speak of unless you go for its concrete manifestations?" To these radical young New Negroes, Carson blandly reasserts her idealist premise: "Thought, Mr. Law, is the ruling power of the world. Beautiful thoughts will supplant evil ones. They will reshape the whole contour of the world." In Carson's worldview, racial essentialism, philosophical idealism, red-baiting, and antifeminism are mutually reinforcing. Nathan tells Natalie that "in a more happy society" Carson would be "spending [her] energies" in a far more productive way. This vague gesture toward socialism recalls David Teyy's statement to Vera, in "Withered Skin of Berries," that "perhaps in a better day" personal love will be something other than an escape from "the outside world." Carson has made her choice, however; in the play's final cabaret scene, she turns her back on her upper-class companions but still sits on their side of the stage, across from the radicals and their working-class friends.[35]

Nathan Merilh, Toomer's Washington Pygmalion, sets forth an alternative view of the role of art in social transformation. An aspiring playwright committed to authoring dramas based on Negro folk music, Nathan has been alienated from his wealthy father, whom he describes as a man who was "no more than an animated shadow around the house" but who "bulldozed the world . . . in exchange for bread and butter, demand[ed] obedience, killed my mother, and then became sentimental over it." The relationship between father and son ended when the former refused to "financ[e] a little theatre. He thought only of money and profits; I, only of art." Friends with the iconoclastic Therman Law, Nathan also reaches out across class lines to Tome Mangrow, who is initially hostile to Nathan as the scion of a family that has "got their dirty money beating ignorant colored folks out of insurance, and swindling them when they were slaving to buy a home." Tome challenges, "Aint he wearing the clothes his old man gave him? Where'd the money come from? Aint he had easy times and nose-bags always full? . . . Aint he got clean sheets and a soft bed to tuck into tonight?" Nathan replies:

> I have been fortunate in wealth, Mr. Mangrow, but still more fortunate in disposition, energy, and point of view. You think that money has made them possible, but you are mistaken. My family's money, my family's position, have been almost maliciously hostile to them. I have had to fight through. Money would have made me like my father. Education would have made me believe as all the upper classes do. My sole obligation would have been to preserve, to increase, what an all-wise God in His unfailing charity and beneficence had given me. Those who didnt have, werent supposed to have. Else He'd have given it to them. Duty to myself and to my God who never failed to look after all His children. And you? You would have been one of those divinely destined to achieve your recompense in another world. . . . You may not have intellectually understood a single word I've said. It does not matter. A conviction has found a lodging in your heart that will not hereafter allow a single questioning as to my motives.

Nathan's arrogance is barely, if at all, ironized; the admixture in his creator of the "natural aristocrat" and the "natural democrat" evidently spilled over into his creation. Nonetheless, Toomer conveys through this interchange a critique not only of the basis of wealth in exploitation but also of the role of education and religion in perpetuating hierarchical social relations. Indeed, Nathan observes that unless "our accumulations of knowledge, wealth, and institutions" can be "direct[ed] toward the welfare of a universal mankind," they will "bury . . . all of us, by the uncontrolled destructive agencies that are inherent in them all." Although Nathan avoids the language of class struggle, there is a distinct continuity between the hero of *Natalie Mann* and the author of "Reflections on the Race Riots," who had written of the "controlled" press and educational apparatus and advocated the transition to a "socialized reality."[36]

"There was an African princess":
Feminism, the New Negro, and Young America

Natalie Mann conveys a somewhat contradictory doctrine about the connections among art, tradition, and social change. In conversation with Natalie, Nathan condemns the "anemia of American Negro art," noting that its emphasis on the lack of "opportunity and circumstance" among Negroes, while appealing to the "democratic dogma," ends up "mak[ing] one sympathetic to the point where he is inhibited from touching the vital elements that inhere in social evil and oppression." He favors an art that unabashedly draws its energies from the folk. In his Washington apartment, African figures—including a "reproduction of the African Guardian of the Souls"—dominate the décor. But the portrait of an unnamed "powerful black man" hangs alongside one of Tolstoy, while between is a "remarkable idealization which might easily be a composite of the other two." Toomer supplies a comparable blend of classical, folk, and popular, European and U.S., in the music performed throughout the play. Natalie, in the opening scene, adeptly plays the final movement of Beethoven's "Moonlight Sonata." In Nathan's apartment, she and he strum mandolins and guitars and sing "Deep River," "Roll, Jordan, Roll!," and "Steal Away." The two scenes set in the Black Bear cabaret, prominently featuring the blues singer and dancer Etty Beal, suggest the expanding cultural influence of Memphis's Beale Street in the nation's capital.

Even as he distinctly valorizes African and African American art and culture, Nathan envisions these as part of a larger pluralist program. Describing to Natalie the members of the "International or Cosmopolitan Club" whom he has invited to meet at their New York apartment, he joyfully exclaims, "They had something like that at the university; but as I was never invited, I dont exactly know. I was too much like the real thing for them I suppose. . . . Yep, young America shall gather under this roof tonight. Jews and Germans and Irish and Russian and Latin, God Almighty's Anglo-Saxon, and Niggers! Wheee!" But when this microcosm of "young America" arrives, Nathan scores his guests for their limitations. He criticizes Ben Kaufmann—who, with his Jewish name, may stand in for the "dictators of American criticism" whom Toomer had defended in his 1920 *New York Call* article on Mary Austin—for leaving the Negro out of his "catalogue"; Toomer was evidently preparing for his coming confrontation with Waldo Frank about the omission of the Negro from *Our America*. Nathan also criticizes Kaufmann for embracing a "part-philosophy [that] excludes . . . all but aesthetic values"—also an interesting remark for its early critique of the limitations of Frank's program. Galt, evidently the socialist in the group—he "wont include [Nathan's] revolted bourgeois and intellectuals in the proletariat"—"cant see any but economic." Greta, apparently the Freudian, "cant see any but sex." Brown, presumably an African American—"he see[s] [Nathan] as inimical to the race"—"cant see any but racial." Nathan, it appears, transcends the limitations of "formula" by means of his "inclusive . . . philosophy," which alone offers "young America" the means to realize its potential. Notably, however, their club is named the "International or Cosmopolitan Club"—terms carrying a distinctly Marxist overtone in the wake of the Russian Revolution. Nathan is hardly a member of the Communist Third International; but his efforts to win "young America" to a global outlook, combined with his critique of the "destructive agencies" inherent in the dominant capitalist U.S. culture, indicate the need to move beyond a quietist cultural nationalism.[37]

Missing from the concerns addressed by Nathan's guests is feminism; Greta's preoccupation with the "originat[ion] [of] fundamental art impulses . . . in sex" is the closest approximation. Natalie, however, sees clear connections between individual liberation from restrictions of gender and the larger project of social transformation: she has grasped the lesson that Vera, of "Withered Skin of Berries," will never learn. Responding to one of Nathan's lengthy monologues about her need to emancipate herself, Natalie asserts, "I think that you have just stated the case of the creative soul with more precision and strength than I have ever before heard it. Bernard Shaw (*Merilh gives her a sharp glance*) puts it graphically, 'This is the true joy in life: the being used for a purpose recognized by yourself as a mighty one; the being thoroughly worn out before you are thrown on the scrap-heap; the being a force of nature, instead of a feverish, selfish little cold of ailments and grievances.'" Declaring that she loves Nathan—"It is you who do not know what that means"—Natalie explains herself by means of a folk parable:

> There was an African princess, and her name was Coomba. Her father, king of many towns, enslaved the man she loved and sent him to the west-coast, to a pirate slave-ship. Coomba followed through the forests. She sold herself that she might accompany her lover to the other shore. Reaching America, they worked side by side in the fields by day. They planted rice and cotton. They harvested cotton and rice. They cut the trees and cleared the ground. They were the real pioneers. And when night came, their wretched cabin was a love abode. Coomba was well-formed and beautiful. Ali, as straight as a phallic pole. One day, in her

sight, Ali was killed. Before night-fall, Coomba had been cruelly violated. The
story tells of how, that night, America heard the first folk-song.

Natalie then draws a personal lesson from her tale: "I love with the passion of
that woman. My love is the need of working with you day by day. Of planting
and harvesting. Of clearing ground. Of seeing the sunset in your eyes at night.
You said a little while ago that something in me was swollen. You implied that it
should be reduced to the relative and normal. Follow that thought and you will
see that the straight line to creation runs directly through you. I am a woman,
as conscious of her immediate needs as you are of her far-off ones. I will not be
denied." The stage directions specify, "*She takes him in an embrace that will admit
of no qualification.*"[38]

Although Natalie has proclaimed to Nathan that "the straight line of creation
runs directly through you," she seems to have read Shaw's *Man and Superman*
(the source of the "true joy in life" quotation) without his guidance. She is also an
adept critic of *Our America* in her own right. Evidently conversant with Frank's
notion that the standard narrative of U.S. history needs to be revised to accom-
modate immigrant experiences and "buried cultures," she does Frank one better.
She retells the story of the new world garden, here featuring people of African
heritage as the "real pioneers" who are not only the nation's first ground clearers,
planters, and harvesters, but also the originators of its "first folk song." But Natalie's tale of New Negro pioneering is inseparable from its tragic underside. Ali is
murdered—presumably lynched and dispossessed of his "phallic pole"—while
Coomba is raped; it is out of her violation that, nightingale-style, the nation's first
folk song is born. Natalie's account thus corrects Frank's as regards both race and
gender; where he had confined his critique of manifest destiny to the "burying" of
native cultures, and had elided gender oppression with the puritanical suppression
of sex impulses, Natalie's brings lynch violence and rape to the fore, connecting
them with the disciplinary enforcement of slave labor. Her narrative of the history that hurts implicitly corrects Nathan's culturalist relation to Africa: while his
inclusion of an African figurine in the décor of his Washington apartment may
signal a romantic Afrocentricity, she cagily notes that Ali was sold into slavery by
an African chief, indeed Coomba's father. Even as it testifies to the Americanness
of Negro folk music, Natalie's tale cautions against a view of history that would
ignore the role of exploitation and violence—indeed, rape and lynching—in the
making of "our America."[39]

Natalie's narration of the tale of Coomba and Ali prepares the way for the next
set performance in *Natalie Mann*, namely, Nathan's reading of "Karintha" before
the gathering in the New York apartment. This scene supplies one of the play's
dramatic high points; in performance, with lowered lights and musical accompaniment, it would demonstrate what "young America" has missed by excluding
the Negro from its conception of national art. While clearly embodying Nathan's
program for grounding experimental art forms in folk material, the story's ac-

count of a young woman's act of infanticide is linked thematically with Natalie's preceding tale of Ali's murder and Coomba's rape, as well as with the news of Mertis's death by abortion soon to come. Pursued by men who would "ripen a growing thing too soon"—who ignore the women their own age and "could not count the time to pass until she would be old enough to mate"—Karintha displays the extent to which slavery-era patterns of sexual exploitation continue to shape interactions between women and men in the Jim Crow South. The fact that the smoke rising from the body of her burning baby inspires "someone" to create a folk song indicates, as in the tale of Coomba and Ali, that the culture of the Negro peasantry has emerged from the effort to wrest compensatory beauty from systemic oppression.[40]

But "Karintha"—which will soon reappear as the opening sketch of *Cane*—is not the finale of *Natalie Mann*. As the play approaches its dramatic conclusion, Natalie's feminism extends from her assertion of sexuality and her identification with Negro folk traditions to her rebellious solidarity with a woman whose transgression of domestic norms has led to unwanted pregnancy, abortion, and death. After Mertis dies, her brother John Newbolt—apparently more upset by the manner than the fact of his sister's death—excoriates Therman: "You should be taken to the first lamp-post and strung up.... You killer.... Why couldnt you have taken a rat? Why did you have to take a respectable girl?" Natalie sharply upbraids John for "speaking as if 'rat' and 'respectable' could divide the essential fact of Woman. As if a violation of one would not also violate the other. As if 'whore' and 'sister' bifurcated the insistency of sex. The one, sterile and pure; the other, fruitful, but impure. What wild oats nonsense.... What sort of duty do you call it that so restricts a daughter's needs that she must become a mother under conditions that convince her of its sin?" Alluding to the polarization of "whore" and "sister" in terms similar to those used by Du Bois in "The Damnation of Women," Natalie defies her brother's sexual categorization of black women: "respectable" male Old Negroes are as capable as white supremacists of deploying the discourse of lynching when defending their women against male invaders. Natalie's inquiry into the connections among sexual repression, religious authoritarianism, and the banning of birth control suggests the extent to which Toomer had absorbed the concerns of the African American women with whom he had been exchanging creative writings for more than two years. The deaths of both Mertis and her fetus, coupled with Karintha's infanticide, suggest the impossibility of the female New Negro's figuring as a Black Madonna as long as African American communities replicate the destructive sexual morality of the dominant culture. Nathan's having been dubbed a "Bolshevist" by Mary Carson, moreover—as well as his founding of the "Cosmopolitan" Club—links him, and by extension Natalie, with the very different sexual practices in the Soviet Union, where abortion was legalized in 1920. Sexual and social revolution are, the play suggests, inseparable.[41]

Although Toomer is clearly invested in the character of Nathan Merilh, it is significant that the play is titled after its central female figure and ends with the tableau of Natalie and Etty exchanging a glance of feminist mutuality over the collapsed body of their "instrument of achievement," who has played out his Shavian role. That the drama's final dance takes place in a Seventh Street cabaret that has been festooned with U.S. flags sends a clear visual message to the audience: the cultural leadership of "young America" is being transferred to two young New Negro women artists who embody urban modernity: they are history-making people. They are, moreover, making history in a sphere completely separate from the home. Domesticity must be negated if women—and men—are to be free.

"Cant you see her?": The Ghost of Mamie Toomer

The feminist perspective embodied in *Natalie Mann*, which marks the play as distinctive in Toomer's oeuvre, suggests that Toomer was grappling with a very personal history that hurts as he created the drama's principal characters and events. Yet he had to mask this history, even as it erupted upward, pressing for representation; the text's play on names offers some insight into the workings of its political unconscious. Toomer once commented that he delighted in wordplay, especially with names; displayed extensively in *Cane*, this proclivity is anticipated in *Natalie Mann*. Some of Toomer's play with surnames is broadly thematic. Mertis, for instance, encounters the "new bolts" of Victorian morality by which the Washington Negro elite, freed from slavery, have re-enchained themselves; Therman is confined by the "laws" that constrain his radical politics. "Man" crops up in "Ther-man Law" and "Tome Man-grow," as well as in the family name—Mann—of the play's protagonist and her family members. Therman Law is being prevented from being the man he wishes to be, rather than "the[i]r man." Tome Mangrow enables the play's male protagonist to "grow" into the democratic "man" that he claims to be. The surname "Mann" reflects ironically on the situation facing Natalie's antifeminist and cruelly judgmental mother: while destroying Mertis's independence as a self-supporting teacher, she is herself simply "Mrs. Mann," with no given name. The surname also challenges Natalie to be her own "natal man": her final dismissal of the Old Negroes for seeing Nathan as "but a man" suggests her having attained a vision of personhood beyond gender.[42]

Other names of the play's dramatis personae invite decoding in particular relation to the playwright's life; here the psychological plot thickens. Tome Mangrow's given name clearly enough suggests "Toomer." It was only with his ascension to adulthood that Toomer (renamed "Eugene Pinchback" after his parents' divorce) had shed the surname "Pinchback," insisted upon by his grandfather, and reverted to the name of the father. The fact that Nathan Merilh's growth toward "manhood" is facilitated by his friendship with a working-class bootlegger named "Tome" enacts Toomer's rebellion against Pinchback's domination; Toomer's decision to name his male protagonist "Nathan" constitutes a further act of defiance. Moreover, Nathan Merilh's complete alienation from his father—who is portrayed as brutal to his wife, exploitative of the black working class, and hostile to his son's democratic impulses and artistic aspirations—suggestively conveys Toomer's resentment of his grandfather, here assigned the role of the bad father in the family romance. That Pinchback died soon before Toomer began work on *Natalie Mann* indicates the cathartic role that writing the drama may have played in enabling Toomer to come to terms with his mixed feelings toward the dominant male presence in his youth and early manhood.

The presence of Pinchback in the background of *Natalie Mann* is fairly easy to discern. But the drama's intricate wordplay with its characters' names suggests that Toomer also had in mind the family history of the Toomers and Dicksons. "Nathan" is present in the names of not only the male protagonist but also the female lead: "Nathan" and "Natalie," after all, begin with the same first three letters. (It bears noting, too, that Natalie, Etty, and Therman all give Nathan the peculiar nickname "Han"—"Nate" would be a more likely shortening of his name—thereby highlighting the portion of the name—Nat—that he and Natalie share.) Further anagrammatical examination reveals that the first and middle names of Nathan Toomer's second wife and Jean Toomer's stepmother—Amanda America Dickson—are encoded in the names of the play's characters. The first syllables of Nathan's and Natalie's last names—Merilh and Mann—conjoined with a prefatory "a," result in "Aman-" and "Ameri-." A similar patterning underlies the names of Mer-tis and Ther-man: again, if one adds the prefatory "a" to the relevant syllables, one gets "Amer" and "Aman."[43]

Why might Toomer have been engaging in this wordplay? There are several possibilities. The presence of both Amanda America and Nathan in the names of the play's two principal characters may signal a critical reflection on the bourgeois institution of marriage, in which Toomer's father and his second wife were entrapped. Natalie and Nathan cohabit on equal terms, rarely discuss money or property, and have no plan for marriage, which Natalie describes as a "sepulcher." By contrast, the marriage of Amanda America and Nathan, which was all about property and possession, resulted in unmitigated disaster for all involved. The allusion to Amanda America in the names of another pair of lovers, Mertis and Therman, further points to the poisoning power of great wealth. As radical New Negroes, these characters challenge Mary Carson's state of willful denial about the realities of debt peonage and lynch violence—the social practices that had sustained Amanda's fortune. Yet the veiled presence of Amanda America in the names of this tragic young couple may suggest the need for would-be New Negroes to repudiate fully the continuing presence of plantation-based capital in the lives of urban African Americans. The play's final words—Natalie's bold challenge to the sheltered women who "see [Nathan] only a man"—may signal Toomer's comment on the necessity for this tie to be severed if the liberated self, female or male, is to be truly "a man," and not "Aman." At the same time, Toomer, aware of the constraints on women of color even when they possessed great wealth, may have wished to acknowledge the common destiny conjoining Amanda America—herself a victim of manipulation by men of varying degrees of wealth and power—with Mertis and Therman.

Still another woman, however, lurks in the wings of *Natalie Mann*. For the dramatic showcasing of "Karintha" at the play's midpoint suggests the haunting presence of the figure of Mamie Toomer. Charles Dickson, first encountering Mamie when she was twelve, could not "coun[t] the time to pass" before Mamie would be "old enough to mate"; nor could he restrict himself to his wife Kate Holsey Dickson, the "grown-up girl" who should have occupied his attention. In attempting to snatch up his adolescent stepsister and carry her away, Charles was patently rehearsing the behavior of his white grandfather, David Dickson, in relation to his black grandmother, Julia Lewis. Preoccupied with his "dark sister'"s near-violation by her nearly white stepbrother some three decades before, Toomer was cognizant of the role played in these events by the "wayward" Nathan Toomer who, in his self-absorbed search for wealth and gentlemanly comfort, had created the vulnerable situation into which his youngest daughter was thrust. Hence Nathan's embedded presence in the name "Karintha," which contains nearly all the letters in the name "Nathan."

But the son, Jean Toomer, who was also named "Nathan," rescues the sister, Mamie, from her—their—rapacious stepbrother and neglectful father. Toomer frees Mamie from her fate as a mere pawn in the contestation between Nathan Toomer and Charles Dickson by assigning a degree of agency to her fictional analogue. If men are bent on "ripen[ing] her too soon," at least she will extract some monetary benefit from the transaction; when impregnated, she will refuse to become a mother. She will not, like Mertis, die from entrusting to the hands of others the task of aborting the life she carries; she will carry the child to term and dispose of it in her own way. Toomer will save his little sister by enshrining her in art. "Cant you see her?": the symbolic act of creating "Karintha" sutures over the pain of history by memorializing the dusky child-woman through a performance that compels the attention of all involved. Amanda America and Nathan—the father and stepmother who failed to protect Toomer's "dark sister"—are embedded in the names of the young man and woman who chant the memorial to Mamie. That Toomer was unable directly to address the tangled past of the Dicksons and the Toomers is demonstrated in his elaborate work-play; that this past cried out for recognition and acknowledgement is equally evident. In *Natalie Mann*, Nathan Eugene Pinchback Toomer exerted control, however provisionally, over the family history that weighed like a nightmare on his brain.

This history would continue to haunt Toomer as he immersed himself in the writing of *Cane*.

PART II

CHAPTER 5

In the Land of Cotton
"Kabnis"

The crisis consists precisely in the fact that the old is dying and the new cannot be born; in this interregnum, a great variety of morbid symptoms appear.
—Antonio Gramsci, *Prison Notebooks*

"[K]indly remember youre in th land of cotton—hell of a land. Th white folks get th boll; th niggers get th stalk. An dont you dare touch th boll, or even look at it. They'll swing y sho."
—Jean Toomer, *Cane*

In the publicity sketch accompanying Liveright's advertisement for *Cane*, Jean Toomer wrote that "there can be no cumulative and consistent movement, and of course no central plot to such a book. It is sheer vaudeville. But if it be accepted as a unit of spiritual experience, then one can find in *Cane* a beginning, a progression, a complication, and an end." While this description apparently describes the sequential structure of *Cane*, starting with "Karintha" and ending with "Kabnis," Toomer's December 1922 comment to Waldo Frank suggests a quite different conception of his text's organizing scheme:

> From three angles, CANE's design is a circle. Aesthetically, from simple forms to complex ones, and back to simple forms. Regionally, from the South up into the North, and back into the South again. Or, from the North down into the South, and then a return North. From the point of view of the spiritual entity behind the work, the curve really starts with Bona and Paul (awakening), plunges into Kabnis, emerges in Karintha etc swings upward into Theatre and Box Seat, and ends (pauses) in Harvest Song.
> Phew!

Frequently noted in analyses attempting to probe the structure of Toomer's text, the spatialized mapping supplied in the letter to Frank offers a more complicated—if contradictory—description of the "spiritual entity" ordering *Cane*'s component parts than that given in the publicity sketch. South-North-South and North-South-North are, after all, hardly congruent schemes, even if they both designate the primacy of spherical form; the description of the texts gathered in part 1 and "Kabnis" as less "complex" than those in part 2 is equally puzzling. Toomer's "Phew!" may suggest exhaustion at his own dizzying attempts to chart his text's formal coherence rather than satisfaction at having done so successfully.[1]

If somewhat puzzling as a description of the structure of *Cane*, Toomer's stipulation that his book "really starts with Bona and Paul" and "ends (pauses) in Harvest Song" supplies a useful point of departure for considering the text from a biographical point of view. For Toomer's description of his text's circular "design" roughly recapitulates the order of its composition. The earliest written short story that would end up in the published text was "Bona and Paul." "Kabnis" was written next. Toomer then composed most of the sketches and poems located toward the beginnings of both parts 1 and 2 in the published book; among the texts he sent to Frank for criticism in April 1922 were "Becky," "Carma," "Evening Song," "Seventh Street," Beehive," and "Avey." "Esther," "Blood-Burning Moon," "Theater," and "Box Seat" were composed in the fall of 1922 after the trip to Spartanburg with Frank, as were "Prayer" and "Harvest Song." Toomer's description of the text as beginning with "Bona and Paul" and ending with "Harvest Song" thus correlates roughly with the order in which much of the text was brought into being. Starting our examination of *Cane* with an analysis of "Kabnis" enables us to read forward through the process of the text's production.[2]

Presumably based on "Georgia Night," a now-lost story that Toomer sent to the *Liberator* from Sparta in late November 1921, "Kabnis" was drafted at white heat on his return to Washington to care for his dying grandfather. Although Toomer revised the text substantially when he returned to it in the late fall of 1922, and he would carve away portions for publication in *Broom* in 1923, he wished the text to retain its impression of rawness. "I'm adding things here and there," he wrote to Frank. "Bringing things into relief and fusing them. But I am not re-creating. The bulk of the old Kabnis will still be there. And the dialogue basis of the old form. To essentially change that would be to re-create, and in this case thats not what I want to do. I want Kabnis to remain an immediate record of my first contact with Southern life." As an "immediate record," "Kabnis" was to register the Real prior to textuality, even as it sought to represent the terms in which the Real might be comprehended—and confronted.[3]

Mediation and Immediacy

It is necessary to pause here for a brief excursus into the ways in which the terms "mediation" and "immediacy" function in the following analysis of *Cane*. "Mediation" signifies the dialectical process establishing connections between and among categories of experience and thought inhabiting different ontological registers. Rather than simply juxtaposing two fundamentally unconnected terms, mediation brings out an internal relation between the two that yields, in turn, a fuller understanding of the reality in which these entities and processes are enmeshed. Through negation and sublation, mediation enables a continuing sequence of further mediations, each supplying a more comprehensive understanding of the relation of the particular to the general, the part to the whole. In the Hegelian-Marxist tradition extending through Lukács and beyond, mediation is a highly valorized term, providing both a safeguard against mechanical models of causality and a privileged access to totality. By contrast, the presumed opposite of mediation, "immediacy," entails the reified substitution of stasis for process and of fragment for whole, reinforcing what Lukács referred to as the "contemplative attitude" that begets both surface understanding and political paralysis.[4]

The correlation of mediation with totality will prove central to key features of my reading of *Cane*—from its figuration of the different moments of capital to its formal refraction of the arrested dialectic of history. But a blanket valorization of mediation over immediacy cannot account for the range of ways in which ideologemes function in the text, at once representing and cloaking social realities. For the Lukácsian formulation implicitly asserts that hegemonic social relations are legitimated only by means of arguments based in the fragmented and static realm of immediacy, that is, reification. Immediacy is thus irretrievably anchored in the realm of ideology, while mediation provides access to, if not the realm of "Truth," at least increasingly accurate approximations of truth. As István Mészáros argues, however, capitalism has created a *combinatoire* of institutions and practices—from wage labor to the nuclear family to the world market—that constitute what he calls "second-order mediations." Although failing to resolve the antagonisms at the core of capitalism, these second-order mediations—C. J. Arthur calls them "alien mediations"—supply plausible connections between and among the ideas and institutions that order social life. Albeit ideologically saturated, these second-order mediations are not merely the phantoms of false consciousness; their appearance corresponds to an essence that is, while distorted and distorting, also real. The challenge, then—at once epistemological and political—consists not in attempting to recover the first-order mediations of a golden age before alienation, but in constructing alternative second-order mediations that will contest existing paradigms and prepare the way for revolutionary social transformation. In this formulation, mediation is in itself neither emancipatory nor constraining, but simply a means of establishing connections possessing greater or lesser explanatory power. Transposed to the project of literary representation, this more neutral approach to mediation directs attention to the procedures by which symbolic action embodies core beliefs and assumptions. As we shall see, *Cane* is in many places dominated by the ideologeme of metonymic nationalism and its accompanying doctrine of sectional art; the text's heavy reliance on the organic trope as a means of elucidating the relationship of African American folk to the land is especially pronounced in the texts Toomer composed during the spring and summer of 1922, when his Sparta memories had receded somewhat and he had settled back into life in Washington, DC. Even in these texts, however,

competing conceptions of various ideologemes—from the New Negro to Georgia
to the Machine—contest the doctrines inherited from Young America. Mediation
entails a continual struggle over contesting explanatory paradigms, a continual
process of de-mediation and re-mediation.[5]

Conversely, "immediacy" need not always signify reification. To be sure, the
assertion in Waldo Frank's foreword that Toomer "has made songs and lovely
stories of his land . . . not of its yesterday, but of its immediate life" exemplified
just such a notion of dehistoricized immediacy. Especially in "Kabnis," however,
Toomer's attempt to create "an immediate record of my first contact with Southern life" entails not effacing but confronting the "yesterday" shaping "immediate
life." For here the history that hurts—gestured toward in barely veiled allusions
to recent notorious instances of lynching and debt peonage that would have been
recognized by many of the text's original readers in 1923—is more naked, more
visible, more *im*-mediate, than elsewhere in *Cane*. In "Kabnis," Toomer clearly
indicates the embedded causality of racial violence in the political economy of
Jim Crow. His representation is by no means un-mediated, for he proposes that
labor—super-exploited labor—is what principally mediates between African
Americans and the soil. At the same time, he portrays the traumatized effects of
a traumatizing social order in Kabnis's anguished requirement that a "split-gut
song" be heard over the chorus of "golden words." Just as Hegel maintains that
immediacy is never entirely banished from the dialectic, but is carried over, at
least in traces, into new mediations through the processes of negation and sublation, Toomer insistently brings us back to the history that hurts. If this analysis
of *Cane* is to capture fully the text's insertion into its moment and conditions of
production, then, some familiar meanings associated with "mediation" and "immediacy" will have to be held in suspension. The racialized realities of capitalism
by which Toomer was confronted—in more than trace amounts—impose this
necessity on both him and us.[6]

"THINK OF IT!": The Killings
of Walter Smalley and Mary Turner

When Toomer journeyed to Sparta in late September 1921—a year when more
lynchings occurred throughout the South than in any previous year other than
1909—his familiarity with the left and Negro press, as well as his ongoing participation in the discussion group on "slavery and the Negro," would have made
him well acquainted with the reputation of the state he was entering. Although
race riots had convulsed urban centers in several states, and the 1919 massacre
of some scores—possibly hundreds—of sharecroppers in Elaine, Arkansas, had
made headlines across the country, Toomer probably knew that Georgia, the
heart of the "American Congo," held the national record for rural lynchings. The
New York Call, where Toomer had published his two commentaries on racism

and war in the spring and summer of 1919, reported that Georgia had led the nation in the number of lynchings during the previous year. The NAACP's 1919 survey, *Thirty Years of Lynching in the United States*, reported that of all regions in the deep South, Georgia had the largest number of lynchings (386) in the years 1889–1918; updated NAACP 1921 statistics indicated that the trend still held, with 429 total recorded lynchings in Georgia. Had he investigated Middle Georgia's recent history, Toomer would have discovered that the area within a fifty-mile radius of Sparta had been plagued with an especially large number of lynchings. In three successive days in October 1919 alone, five black men were killed by white mobs in four unrelated incidents; one man, in a lynching advertised in advance in the press as a "wake," was burned alive before a crowd of over one thousand. Although Hancock County had the reputation for being a "good county," according to the local historian Forrest Shivers, adjoining counties more than made up the deficit. "Georgia" was a metonymy for racial violence.[7]

A month before Toomer arrived in Sparta, the Middle Georgia press was rife with accounts of—and apologias for—atrocity. On August 15, the front page of the *Augusta Chronicle* featured a story about a North Carolina lynching—"Tarheels Lynch Negro for Attack on White Girl"—in which fifteen hundred to two thousand people had participated and over one thousand bullets had been fired into the victim's body. Two days later, the paper recounted that a South Carolina mob had entered the Richmond County jail in Augusta, Georgia, without resistance from the sheriff; they had seized two black men charged with having killed a white man from Columbia, South Carolina. Both men were taken from the jail and lynched; the *Chronicle* praised the sheriff for "doing the correct thing . . . to avoid unnecessary bloodshed." Advocacy of states' rights did not preclude cross-border vigilante activity when the occasion required.[8]

"Kabnis" most likely alludes to a lynching that occurred in Augusta—the urban center closest to Sparta—on August 18, 1921, soon before Toomer arrived. In conversation with Kabnis and Halsey, the itinerant preacher Layman claims to have "[s]een um shoot an cut a man t pieces who had died the night befo. Yassur. An they didn't stop when they found he was dead—jes went on ahackin at him anyway" (88). Layman's account apparently refers to an incident in which Walter Smalley, a chauffeur, was accused by a wagon works foreman, Benjamin Hightower, of having stolen the lugs and bolts from a car wheel that Smalley's employer had asked him to take to Hightower for repair. Smalley retorted by calling Hightower a liar; Hightower, according to the *Augusta Chronicle*, "gave the boy a good licking." Later that day Smalley presumably "ran amuck," killing Hightower and a local policeman before being shot by a mob. Deprived of its live victim, the mob that night broke into the hospital morgue where Smalley's body was kept, seized the corpse, and burned it along a rural road. The Augusta City Council passed a resolution to the effect that "there is no race riot in Augusta; there has been no race riot in Augusta; that there has been a white man's riot in part and that the city council of Augusta, and if needs be the citizens here, should offer any amount of reward and any amount of endeavor to bring to punishment the men implicated in the theft and burning of the negro Smalley's body." There is no record of any further action having been taken.[9]

Toomer probably learned of these and similar local incidents either when he arrived in Sparta or during his weekend visits to Augusta in the fall of 1921. Layman focuses at greater length, however, on two instances of racial violence that had gained national notoriety. Layman relates to a frightened Kabnis the death of a woman named Mame Lamkins: "She was in th family-way, Mame Lamkins was. They killed her in th street, an some white man seein th risin in her stomach as she lay there soppy in her blood like any cow, took an ripped her belly open, an the kid fell out. It was living, but a nigger baby aint supposed t live. So he jabbed his knife in it an stuck it t a tree. An then they all went away" (90). Layman's account differs only slightly from NAACP investigator Walter White's account of the May 1918 killing of Mary Turner near Valdosta, Georgia:

> At the time she was lynched, Mary Turner was in her eighth month of pregnancy. The delicate state of her health . . . may be imagined, but this fact had no effect on the tender feelings of the mob. Her ankles were tied together and she was hung to the tree, head downward. Gasoline and oil from the automobiles were thrown on her clothing and while she writhed in agony and the mob howled in glee, a match was applied and her clothes were burned from her person. When this had been done and while she was yet alive, a knife, evidently one such as is used in splitting hogs, was taken and the woman's abdomen was cut open, the unborn babe falling from her womb to the ground. The infant, prematurely born, gave two feeble cries and then its head was crushed by a member of the mob with his heel. Hundreds of bullets were then fired into the body of the woman, now mercifully dead, and the work was over.

Layman's is the documentary voice of history: his account would have resonated with anyone familiar with the NAACP's widely disseminated official account of the Turner killings.[10]

The lynching of Mary Turner and her unborn baby was one in a series of eleven killings following the death of Hampton Smith, a plantation owner who, according to the *Crisis*, had practiced debt peonage, acquiring his laborers by "going into the courts and whenever a Negro was convicted and was unable to pay his fine or was sentenced to serve a period in the chain gang, Smith would secure his release and put him to work out his fine on his (Smith's) plantation." He was murdered by Sidney Johnson, a debt peon who had quarreled with Smith over unpaid work. Mary Turner's husband, Hayes Turner, who also worked for Smith, had served a term on the chain gang for threatening Smith after the plantation owner had beaten and sexually threatened Mary Turner. After Smith's death, rumors circulated that his murder had been planned during a group meeting at the Turner house, and the killings began. Will Head and Will Thompson were seized and lynched; over seven hundred bullets were fired into their bodies. Hayes Turner was arrested and mysteriously taken from the sheriff on a country road by forty masked men; after his lynching, his body was allowed to hang for two days, and a Sunday afternoon crowd of several hundred came to gape before it was cut down by convict labor and buried at the foot of the lynching tree. Another man, Eugene Rice—who had no connection with the Smith murder—was lynched in a spot called "the old Camp Ground." A week later, three bodies of unidentified black men were taken from the nearby Little River, though the corpses soon disappeared. Then Mary Turner was killed; then three more men, Chime Riley, Simon Schuman, and, finally, Sidney Johnson. In all, eleven people—twelve if one counts the Turners' unborn child—were murdered in the rampage following the death of Hampton Smith.[11]

The *Savannah Morning News*, like most of the local Georgia newspapers, blamed Mary Turner for her own death:

> Death Dealt to Man and Wife
>   Hays [*sic*] and Mary Turner Lynched by Mob Near Barney
>   Result of Smith Tragedy
>   Assassination of Smith Planned in Turner House
>   While talking of the lynching of her husband to-day Mary Turner further enraged the community and a mob took possession of her, hanged her to a tree and riddled her body with bullets.

While Mary Turner would be memorialized in most artworks as a gentle Black Madonna, she appears to have defied the murderous mob. Like Walter Smalley, she had refused to accede quietly to the ethics of living Jim Crow.[12]

Toomer was clearly acquainted with the 1918 death of Mary Turner well before his trip to Sparta. The Valdosta-area killings had been recounted in both the *Crisis* and *Thirty Years of Lynching*. The particularly heart-wrenching murder of Mary Turner and her child had been featured in poems and stories; it had been widely denounced in the black and liberal-to-left press as the epitome of southern barbarism. In their July 1919 editorial, "The Hun in America," Randolph and Owen of the *Messenger* had fulminated, "In Georgia, the abdomen of a woman, upon the eve of bearing a child, was ripped open, the form emptied upon the ground, while American HUNS buried their heels in its brains. THINK OF IT!" Occurring while U.S. soldiers—some of them African American—were fighting to make the world safe for democracy overseas, the death of Mary Turner was a grim reminder of the war at home. Indeed, one of the small changes that Toomer made in his retelling of the Turner murders—he shows the baby being impaled to a tree rather than ground underfoot—reinforces the notion that the U.S. South is peopled by "Huns" of its own. Besides invoking the trope of the lynching tree, Toomer's alteration of the historical record connects Turner's death with the image, widely disseminated in governmental wartime propaganda, of Germans

as bayonet-wielding baby killers. Toomer's depiction of the death of Mame Lamkins not only anchors fiction in history but suggests a connection between the
violence of the Jim Crow South and the brutality of imperialist war.[13]

"We just threw 'em off":
The Jasper County "Death Farm"

Although the death of Mary Turner, occurring in southern Georgia toward the
end of the war, was widely viewed as the epitome of Jim Crow barbarism, in
"Kabnis" Toomer evinced awareness of a more recent set of killings that featured
still more prominently the centrality of economic exploitation to lynch violence—
namely, the killing of eleven debt peons on the notorious John S. Williams "death
farm" near Monticello in Jasper County, only thirty miles northwest of Sparta,
less than a year before Toomer's visit. This massacre is referred to directly when,
in response to Kabnis's hopeful query that "Things are better now though since
that stir about those peonage cases, arent they?" Layman remarks that the effect
of the cases was like "th brick thrown in th hornets nest" that "just stirs up the
hornets to sting." To Kabnis's desperate plea, "[C]ant something be done?" Layman answers, "Sho. Yassur. An done first rate an well. Jes like Sam Raymon done
it" (87). Layman elaborates:

> Th white folks (reckon I oughnt tell it) had jes knocked two others like you kill
> a cow—brained um with an ax, when they caught Sam Raymon by a stream.
> They was about t do fer him when he up an says, "White folks, I gotter die, I
> knows that. But wont y let me die in my own way?" Some was fer gettin after
> him, but th boss held um back and says, "Jes so longs th nigger dies—" And
> Sam fell down ont his knees an prayed, "O Lord, Ise comin to y," and he up an
> jumps int th stream. (88)

While twenty-first-century readers of *Cane* may be confused by this account—it
is not entirely clear whether Halsey views Sam Raymon's jump into the stream as
the act of a victim or that of a trickster—many of Toomer's 1923 readers, especially
African Americans, would have caught the text's historical allusion. In February
1921, a series of bodies of drowned black men—most of them chained together in
pairs and weighted down with bags of rocks—were found in the Yellow, Alcovy,
and South Rivers. The corpses were identified as those of former workers on the
Williams farm, where investigators from the office of Federal District Attorney
Hooper Alexander suspected several earlier murders to have occurred and had
recently been attempting to conduct an investigation into debt peonage. Williams
denied involvement in any and all killings, but his black foreman, Clyde Manning,
confessed to having carried out a string of murders under threat of death from
Williams, who feared that the men would reveal to the investigators their conditions of servitude. "The boss said he wanted to get rid of them negroes and that
if I didn't make 'em disappear, he'd kill me," testified Manning. The first killings

took place on the Williams farm. "Another one of Mr. Williams' trusty negroes put in a little work—he killed one suspicious negro by braining him with an ax," said Manning. "I knocked four negroes in the head with an ax [in] one week and buried them in the pasture back of Mr. Williams' house." Then several men were drowned in nearby rivers:

> "I don't know how many negroes there are in the river, but I helped Mr. Williams drown six. . . . We took the other five to the river at night, after getting them out of their houses, and chained 'em down with rocks and threw 'em in.
> "Yes, sir, they all cried and begged—and some of 'em asked to be knocked in the head before being thrown in, but Mr. Johnny wouldn't do it and wouldn't let me do it. We just threw 'em off and rode on back to the plantation."

One man, Harry Price, was loaded down with rocks but allowed to drown himself. "Harry Price, he got out," Manning testified in the trial, "and says, 'Don't throw me over, I'll get over,' and he says, 'Lord have mercy,' and he went over." In all, eleven men were murdered by Williams and Manning between February 24 and March 8: Charlie Chisholm, Johnny Greene, Willie Givens, Fletcher Smith, Lindsay Peterson, Willie Preston, Harry Price, "Big John" Manning (no relation of Clyde Manning), Johnnie Williams (no relation, needless to say, of John S. Williams), a man known only as "Little Bit," and—in a cruel irony—a man named John Brown. Although there is no evidence that any of the murdered workers on the Williams farm had approached federal investigators with their stories, the Monticello area was under surveillance; Williams was not taking any chances.[14]

The *Atlanta Constitution* followed the story in lurid detail. After children out fishing and swimming started to find corpses in rivers, hundreds watched the sheriff and his deputies drag the Alcovy River for more bodies. When an African American congregation of several hundred held a prayer service on the banks of the Alcovy, Williams's sons, attempting to divert attention from their father's crimes, spread the rumor that race war was impending; several score white residents, fearing an uprising, temporarily fled from their homes. In April, viewers packed the Covington courtroom in Newton County where Williams was tried for murder. Williams was convicted of murder and sentenced to life in prison—the only southern white to be convicted of killing a black man, it would turn out, between Reconstruction and 1966. In a July 1922 second trial, Manning was given twenty years on the chain gang, a ruling tantamount to a death sentence; he in fact died on the gang soon thereafter, of unspecified causes that can be reasonably guessed. Williams became a prison "trusty" and, in a weird twist of fate, was killed trying to prevent a prison break.[15]

The Williams case brought national attention to the phenomenon of debt peonage, occasioning shocked commentary in mainstream newspapers and journals; the *Literary Digest*, which summarized the press coverage of important events, recorded accounts in a dozen newspapers around the country. Angelina Grimké's clipping and saving a March 1921 Associated Press article about the "death farm"

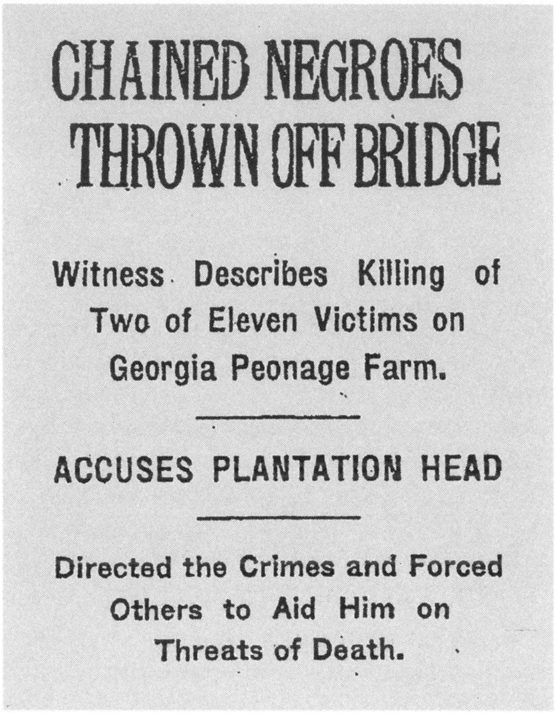

CHAINED NEGROES
THROWN OFF BRIDGE

Witness Describes Killing of Two of Eleven Victims on Georgia Peonage Farm.

ACCUSES PLANTATION HEAD

Directed the Crimes and Forced Others to Aid Him on Threats of Death.

Figure 7. "Chained Negroes Thrown Off Bridge." *New York Times*, April 7, 1921. Newspaper headline reflecting the national publicity surrounding the John S. Williams "death farm" in Jasper County, Georgia.

indicates that the story was most likely noted by Toomer's colleagues in the Washington, DC, study group on "slavery and the Negro." While the early stages of the investigation and trial were blacked out in the small-town southern press, after the verdict various local papers, including the *Sparta Ishmaelite*, praised the presumed even-handedness of Georgia's system of justice. Georgia governor Hugh Dorsey responded in April 1921 to the scandal by publishing *The Negro in Georgia*, a pamphlet detailing 135 instances of peonage, brutality, and murder; Dorsey called for penalties against counties where officials had "failed in their duty" to prevent lynchings. Although the NAACP expressed relief at Williams's sentence and congratulated Dorsey for his courageous stand, the left press offered scathing denunciations of both the court's sentence—Williams was convicted of murder, but not of debt peonage—and Dorsey's belated, and largely pragmatic, reaction. The *Crusader* editors predicted that "when the excitement has died down and the rest of the country forgets about Williams and his eleven Negro victims—forgets about Williams and the peonage system which made his crimes possible and which have created and are creating other Williamses just as vicious and just as murderous as the one now behind bars—when the country forgets, why anything can happen—in Georgia." In the *Liberator*, Esau Jones cynically noted that Williams was being scapegoated because he had gone "too far." He "ought to have shown better judgment in the time and quantity of his killings.

To clear the good name of Georgia he must be sent up." Kabnis might hope that the exposé of the "peonage cases" would improve conditions in Georgia, but his creator—who had dubbed the first version of Kabnis's experiences "Georgia Night"—knew better. By reproducing in Sam Raymon's words an almost exact replica of Charlie Price's final interchange with Clyde Manning, indeed, Toomer further ironizes his protagonist's naiveté: any reader familiar with the course of the Manning-Williams trial would have known that the "death farm" murders had if anything solidified the terroristic hold of debt peonage over labor in the Deep South. The Dyer Anti-Lynching Bill was being held up in the U.S. Senate; it would be defeated in the year of *Cane*'s publication, and federal antilynching legislation would not be passed for another forty-five years.[16]

Evidently haunted by both the death of Mary Turner and the infamous Jasper County killings, Toomer signaled his awareness that the institution of debt peonage was the root cause of both white repression and black resistance. When Kabnis hopefully observes that the South is not "half the terror" pictured in "northern exaggeration," Halsey reminds him, "[K]indly remember youre in th land of cotton—hell of a land. Th white folks get th boll; th niggers get th stalk. An dont you dare touch th boll, or even look at it. They'll swing y sho" (87). Williams, Smith, and other plantation owners could go to the nearest city jail and—at a price far lower than had been paid for a laborer under slavery—bail out a black man who had been arrested for "vagrancy" or some other petty "crime." This worker could be kept indebted for months, often years, locked in at night and laboring under conditions that one historian has dubbed "worse than slavery." Dorsey's warning that landowners should change their practices if they did not wish to drive away their workers, as well as the *Atlanta Constitution*'s caution that white Georgians should not "kil[l] the goose that laid the golden egg," indicated a conflict among ruling elites about how best to control the labor supply. This conflict was exacerbated by the bottoming-out of the cotton market in 1921, which led to plantation owners withholding payments and refusing loans to their tenants while compelling them to remain on the land.[17]

The Macon-based Guardians of Liberty were outraged by Dorsey's pamphlet, declaring that "no living man will stand by while a villain defiles his mother. Georgia—our mother—is being defiled before the world." Arguably, however, Dorsey and the editors of the *Atlanta Constitution* were thinking of the long-term interests of Georgia's ruling elite when they chastised those farmers engaged in the crudest methods of coercion. Hooper Alexander's investigations into debt peonage were spurred by the national government's recognition of the need to stem the hemorrhaging of labor to the North. (After the Valdosta massacre, the *Crisis* reported, "[m]ore than 500 Negroes left the vicinity . . . leaving hundreds of untilled acres behind them.") But racial violence—whether doled out in individual portions or erupting in massacres—was a necessary enforcer of labor discipline; rather than a barbaric holdover from a precapitalist mode of production, it constituted an integral feature of the modern plantation of the New South. The black and radical press of the day framed the political economy of debt peonage in a variety of ways. While the phrase "new slavery" designated debt peonage as a betrayal of the promise of Emancipation codified in the U.S. Constitution, the phrase "American Congo" linked Jim Crow with colonial racism. Comparisons of the South's sharecropping workforce with Russian serfs, moreover, not only discovered a historical analogy between the United States and the Eurasian continent but also forecast revolution as the possible antidote to southern oppression. As the British journalist Stephen Graham opined—somewhat apocalyptically—in his account of his travels through Georgia in *The Soul of John Brown*, "Russian serfs and military slaves and wage slaves and Negroes are finding an accord," supplying "the foundation for a grand proletarian revolutionary movement throughout the world." The day might be approaching, he wrote, when the white "lynching crowd" and the "Negro mob" would make common cause against "those who should have administered the law . . . the Pilate governors."[18]

As he journeyed to Sparta in the fall of 1921, however, Toomer would have been aware that scattered rural acts of resistance to Jim Crow were trivial in comparison with the recent resurgence of the Ku Klux Klan, which had been detailed in the Negro press in the weeks before his departure. Spurred in part by D. W. Griffith's *The Birth of a Nation*, whose immensely popular screening in 1915 jumpstarted the revival of the Klan, the white supremacist organization had grown rapidly after the war. Its new headquarters were located in Stone Mountain, on the outskirts of Atlanta and less than eighty miles from Sparta; in 1925 Du Bois would designate Georgia as the "Invisible Empire State." The Klan was hosting open meetings of thousands of robed members in Atlanta in the early 1920s; in February 1921, according to the *Sparta Ishmaelite*, it even initiated an organizing drive in Hancock County. By October 1921—the midpoint of Toomer's Georgia sojourn—national Klan membership had risen, a local newspaper reported, to 126,000. Although some of this gain occurred in northern cities where the Klan specialized in campaigns against immigrants, trade unionism, and sexual immorality, the central site of the Klan's terrorist activity remained the Deep South; by the mid-1920s, Georgia ranked eighth nationally in Klan membership, but second in the South. Klan warnings to potentially rebellious tenants and sharecroppers, often scribbled on notes attached to rocks and thrown into houses, were frequent. The term "rivering" came to designate one of the Klan's favored means of murder: the deaths of Charlie Price and the other Jasper County debt peons were signified by a neologism in the Southern lexicon.[19]

That Toomer had Klan terrorism on his mind during his stay in Sparta is suggested by an unsettling—and barely legible—handwritten poem among his papers. Although it is undated, we can speculate that it was authored during or soon after his Georgia visit:

> "I'm not looking beyond myself tonight, sister."
> mob up dusty cornfield flares white-hooded riders

and a white aproned horse robes and hoods black robes with
white sashes long white capes with red linings bright blue
tow-soaked [?] cross "everybody sets on their knees a [?]
before Jesus Christ"
nigras burr-headed nigra mongrelization
red clay roads raw hillsides

Anticipating key images of "Banking Coal," the references to fires and hooded robes are embedded in the words of a traumatized observer-listener barely able to register the sights and sounds of a nighttime Klan raid in the making. Hardly a poem, the text exemplifies the role of terrorism in preventing the making of poetry. Its immediacy testifies not so much to a reified consciousness as to the repressive racism that "thingifies" its targets as "burr-headed nigras."[20]

Recent Georgia history supplied Toomer with more than sufficient material to limn the violence and exploitation of Jim Crow; in "Kabnis," history is a present, not an absent, cause. It bears noting, however, that during his sojourn in Sparta Toomer may have learned of a local act of resistance that—albeit in the more distant past—exemplified a quite different response to the violent exploitation of the Deep South. For in January 1863 Sparta had been the site of an aborted revolt on the part of some forty enslaved African Americans who were accused of planning to "fire" the town and run off to join the forces of the Union Army. The plot was foiled before it could be put into practice; two of its four ringleaders were severely punished; the other two were hanged. One of these—known as the mastermind of the operation—was named John Cain. While there is no evidence that Toomer knew of this occurrence, some of the descendants of its participants would have been living in Sparta at the time of his visit. Toomer's habit of frequently spelling his book's title as "Cain" in his correspondence and autobiographies has routinely been interpreted as an allusion to the biblical Cain, suggesting that his book had become a racialized curse that he was forced to bear. It is possible, however, that he titled the book "Cane" in part to signal the continuing potentiality for resistance to oppression. Sempter might not currently figure as the site of rebellion; but Sparta had done so in the past, and might again in time to come, were more John Cains to rise up against the conditions of their bondage.[21]

"The goddam nightmare that's burned int my soul": The Poetry of Trauma

A feature of "Kabnis" that continually tantalizes readers is the nature and extent of the creator's identification with his artist-hero. To what degree is Kabnis an autobiographical projection? To what degree is he a fictional character, subject to ironic distancing? Toomer's own comments are ambiguous. On the one hand, upon completing *Cane* Toomer declared to Frank that "Kabnis is me" and wrote to Kenneth Macgowan that "Kabnis" was "really the story of my own real or imaginary experiences in Georgia"—a formulation that, while obscuring as much as it reveals, implies that Kabnis shared at least some "experiences" with his creator. That Toomer himself may have encountered some frightening situations in Sparta in the fall of 1921 is indicated in his comment to Frank, when they were planning their trip into the Deep South a year later, that "[m]y actual experience down there will interest you. I barely avoided a serious time." Pressed by Frank to supply as "authentic" a site as possible for their destination, Toomer wrote, somewhat mysteriously, that he would have "suggested [Georgia] in the first place were it not for the fact that certain conditions there (in Sparta, and which I shall tell you about when I see you) make it not the best place in the world at this time." Kabnis's terror at dwelling in a place where "they lynch and burn men" may reflect anxieties and fears experienced in the Deep South by Toomer himself. Kabnis's conjunction of "lynchers and business men," moreover—and his grouping of them with "that cockroach Hanby" (83)—indicate his creator's understanding of the connections among economics, education, and vigilante violence in maintaining the status quo.[22]

On the other hand, Toomer's retrospective comments on *Cane*, which largely stress his protagonist's defeat, suggest his distance from his fictional creation. After asserting his kinship with Kabnis, Toomer went on to remark to Macgowan that "[t]he central figure reacts with a certain intensity to the beauty and ugliness of Southern life. His energy, dispersed and unchannelled, cannot push him through its crude mass. Hence the mass, with friction and heat and sparks, crushes him." In "The South in Literature," Toomer offered a similar assessment of Kabnis:

> The elemental pulse of a peasant people, together with the impalpable fog of white dominance and its implications which the raw sensibility of Ralph Kabnis (the protagonist) spreads over the entire countryside, are too strong and oppressive for his depleted energies to successfully grapple with. Hence Kabnis progresses downward from rejection and defiance to a passive acceptance of them. Such acquiescence, in a man potentially capable of directing life, signifies frustration and defeat. This drama is then the tragedy of a talented Negro whose forces have been dissipated, whose remaining strength is unequal to the task of winning a clear way through life.

Although Toomer clearly empathizes with Kabnis's terror, the creator of Kabnis gives little indication here of identifying with his character's "tragedy." "Kabnis is me" is thus both true and untrue.[23]

Toomer's investing his protagonist with a personalized set of neuroses helps to establish ironic distance. In the opening scene, Kabnis masturbates, throttles a chicken for being "an "egg-laying bitch" (82), and curses the white father who made him a bastard: one need not be fully versed in Freud to see that the fictional character is undergoing psychoanalysis in the hands of his creator. But the fear and anger that Kabnis displaces onto the hen clearly derive from the pervasive atmosphere of racial terrorism; individual psychological repression is inseparable from ritualized societal repression. "Fantastically plastered with red Georgia mud" (91) after his flight from Halsey's house, Kabnis is filled with fear that a lyncher may hide behind every tree; his castration anxieties have other than Oedipal origins. His paralysis is compounded by the "acquiescence" of men like Layman and Halsey, who—although a preacher and a middle-class artisan, respectively—exemplify the "elemental pulse of a peasant people" unable to dissipate the "fog of white dominance." When Kabnis abandons the world of words for the world of physical labor, he has not joined the ranks of an insurgent proletariat but has instead acceded—"progress[ed] downward"—to the "passive acceptance" prevailing among Sempter's African American population. Mr. Ramsay's ax, whose repair Kabnis so badly fumbles, may, for all he knows, have been used to murder men like Sam Raymon's fellow-workers; Halsey's kowtowing to Ramsey and repairing the ax for free indicate the wheelwright's fear of resisting the status quo. "Through Ramsay, the whole white South weighs down upon [Kabnis]" (100): Ramsay embodies not the "white South" of the workers who defended the black trade unionist at Bogalusa but the "white South" of Valdosta, Elaine, and Monticello; its "weight" is the principal source of the nightmares occupying Kabnis's brain. In Middle Georgia, opposition to rural black super-exploitation has resulted not in the growth of mass resistance but in mass murder and infanticide; John Cain has not found a modern incarnation.[24]

The tropes informing "Kabnis" indicate the extent to which Kabnis's "raw sensibility" is shaped—indeed overwhelmed—by the "raw hillsides" of Jim Crow violence. The spirituals sung at dusk, rising like "tallow flames" (96), have their genesis in the flames that have consumed black bodies and "burn [the] soul" of the poet as well. The winds that blow dust through the cracks of Kabnis's cabin are "vagrant poets" (81); even poets, it seems, can be charged with the crime that results in imprisonment, debt peonage, and possible death. Kabnis's dilemma as an artist, many critics have observed, stems from his desire to "become th face of the South . . . th lips of its soul," even as he feels reduced to "an atom of dust in agony on a Georgia hillside" (83). Drawn to the hills "heaving with folk-songs," he yearns to "shape words that are "beautiful an golden an have a taste that makes them fine t roll over with y tongue" (109–10). To represent the world inhabited by Mame Lamkins and Sam Raymon, however, he feels compelled to produce "[m]isshapen, split-gut, tortured twisted words" fed by the "[godam nightmare] thats burned int my soul . . . an wont stay still unless I feed it" (110). While Toomer and Frank would exchange letters laden with metaphors joyously comparing writing with childbirth, Kabnis feels himself gestating a monstrous progeny, one he imagines subjected to the same fate as Mame Lamkins's baby. His use of the term "split-gut" to describe the antithesis to "golden words" is telling: as aspiring creator of an art commensurate with the realities of the South, he identifies with the mother whose belly has been cut open. And he also identifies with her murdered progeny: in a paroxysm of despair at "this whole

damn bloated purple country . . . going down t hell in a holy avalanche of words,"
he wishes "t God some lynchin white man ud stick his knife through [my soul] an
pin it to a tree" (110). "Things are so immediate in Georgia" (84): the inability of
poetic language celebrating the folk to suture the violence of the South experienced
by its peasantry is starkly displayed in Kabnis's creative paralysis; the text's crisis in
symbolic action is both thematized and enacted. Rebirth in the realm of art cannot
occur so long as actual babies are daggered to Georgia's lynching trees. Labor, not
culture, supplies the principal mediating connection between the Negro and the
Invisible Empire state.[25]

"Cant hold them, can you?":
Kabnis, Lewis, and the New Negro

But the hero-as artist (or would-be artist) is not the only protagonist—or stand-in
for the author—present in "Kabnis"; also challenged with the task of dissipat-
ing "the fog of white dominance" is Lewis. The somewhat mysterious northern
outsider who at once invites respect and arouses anxiety among Sempter's black
citizenry by his continual probing into local instances of racial violence, Lewis
figures as both double and antithesis to Kabnis. Although the two men "oddly
resemble one another"—and Kabnis, on first meeting Lewis, feels the impulse to
"rush into his arms and call him 'Brother'—they are starkly differentiated: Lewis
is, the narrator comments, "what a stronger Kabnis might have been" (95–96).
That these contrasting personalities embody more than idiosyncratic differences
is signaled by the wordplay contained in their combined names. If we recall the
kind of anagrammatical combinations Toomer effected with the names of the
dramatis personae of *Natalie Mann*, especially the interwoven names of Nathan
Toomer and Amanda America Dickson, we realize that Kabnis and Lewis, conjoined, yield up what "New bla[c]k is." The expressionist drama of "Kabnis" largely
revolves around the choice the reader/viewer is invited to make between these
counterposed aspects of a single self; this single self is, in turn, a composite—if
internally conflicted—New Negro.[26]

Toomer evidently intended the two men to function as a thematically contrasting pair. In the Liveright publicity sketch, Toomer's description of Kabnis as a
"northern sensitivity at grips with the crude beauty and ugliness of the South"
is set against the depiction of Lewis as a "northern intelligence battling with the
oppression and superstition, with the waywardness of southern Negro life." That
Toomer viewed Lewis as the stronger of the two is suggested in his comment to
the *Broom* editor Lola Ridge that "Lewis, in point of origin, is as authentic as
Kabnis. For I myself am frankly the source of both of them. Lewis has the sense
of direction and the intelligent grip of things that Kabnis lacks. Whereas Kabnis
has the emotion that I could not possibly give to Lewis without bringing Lewis
into the foreground more than I care to in this instance. . . . Perhaps I only want

him to be a suggestion, a unique outline, an imperfect incarnation of possibilities, particularly, a projection of Kabnis' possibilities." Toomer's view of both men as extensions of himself indicates that terror was not his only experience of the Deep South: he also occupied the positions of interlocutor, investigator, and dispassionate observer.[27]

Indeed, invested with the magnetic aura surrounding such valorized protagonists as David Teyy and Nathan Merilh, Lewis at times threatens to eclipse Kabnis entirely. Where Kabnis, with his thin hair and "lemon face" (81) evidently lacks sexual appeal, the "copper-colored" Lewis mesmerizes the young Carrie Kate Holsey with his "Christ-eyes" and masculine presence (95, 101). Where Kabnis fears that potential lynchers lurk behind every sweet-gum tree, the intrepid Lewis refuses to be frightened by the message attached to the rock thrown through Halsey's window: "You northern nigger, its time fer y t leave. Git along now" (90). Where Kabnis bends to Hanby's will, this local avatar of Booker T. Washington shrinks from confronting the stranger from the North. Where Kabnis repudiates any connection with Father John, the former slave inhabiting Halsey's cellar, Lewis embraces the old man as "the symbol, flesh, and spirit of the past," even as he rejects the folk superstition, voiced by "old Blodson," that "[w]eevils and wars are the pests that God sends against the sinful" (107, 99). The binary oppositions constituting the doubling of Kabnis and Lewis would seem to be indisputably loaded in Lewis's favor.[28]

Lewis's superior position in this schematic doubling is associated to no small degree with his identity as a man of action. While his particular mission in coming to Sparta—his monthlong "contract with [him]self"—is not specified, his interest in Layman's account of Mame Lamkins's death ("Noted what I said th other day, an that weren fer notin down," grumbles the preacher) suggests that he may be an investigator of reported incidents of lynching or debt peonage. As a reader of the *Crisis*—to which he would soon submit both "Banking Coal" and "Song of the Son"—Toomer was familiar with the activities of such NAACP field investigators as James Weldon Johnson and Walter White. The former had investigated the 1918 Valdosta lynchings, including that of Mary Turner; the latter had carried out over thirty-six investigations into lynchings and eight investigations into race riots by June 1922, his investigation into the Elaine massacre being the most life threatening of these experiences. Lewis's figuring as the target of the threatening message alludes to the kinds of warnings NAACP investigators routinely received. Where Toomer, in his *Cane*-era journal, reflected self-critically on his own weakness as a writer isolated from the social struggles of his day, Lewis exemplifies an involved engagement with the harsh realities of the postwar world. He is the New Negro as political activist; his counterposition with Kabnis may in part reflect Toomer's own regret, after "the worm had turned," that he had not stuck more steadfastly to the radical activist path.[29]

Besides directing attention to Kabnis's comparative cowardice in confronting Jim Crow, Lewis poses a challenge to Kabnis's internalized racism. Where Kabnis is deeply ambivalent about his mixed racial heritage—alternatively laying proud claim to his "Southern blue-bloo[d] . . . ancestry" (107) and referring to himself as "what sin is" as a member of the "bastard race that's roamin round th country" (115)—Lewis acknowledges his hybrid ancestry with ease. In their first meeting, Kabnis is described as "a promise of soil-soaked beauty; uprooted, thinning out. Suspended a few feet above the soil whose touch would resurrect him" (96). Lewis subsequently goads Kabnis: "Cant hold them, can you? Master; slave. Soil; and the overarching heavens. Dusk; dawn. They fight and bastardize you. The sun tint of your cheeks, flame of the great season's multi-colored leaves, tarnished, burned. Split, shredded; easily burned. No use . . ." (107). As deployed by Lewis, the organic trope offers a means of both diagnosing Kabnis's dilemma and redeeming him from its effects. Kabnis can be "split, shredded, easily burned"; until he accepts the "sun tint" and "flame" of his own complexion, he will be of no use to himself or others. By contrast, Lewis—like David Teyy a man of "multi-colored leaves"—is rooted in the soil because he accepts his multiracial heritage. Lewis is at once an unabashed New Negro and an embodiment of Toomer's new American race.

But even as the Kabnis-Lewis doubling invites decoding by means of binary oppositions favoring the northern activist as the bearer of redemption, Lewis's declaration contains contradictions of its own. Lewis may be a tribune of the South's oppressed masses, but when he views the revelers in Halsey's basement he is overwhelmed by the "pain and beauty of the South" (106). For all his apparent commitment to ferreting out the truth, Lewis flees when confronted by it. The redemptive quality that Lewis shares with David Teyy and Nathan Merilh has limited potency, it would appear, when transposed from the Black Bear cabaret or the Potomac's Great Falls to Middle Georgia. Moreover, the hyper-material imagery through which Lewis diagnoses Kabnis's psychic malady blurs the distinction between oppositions that are part of nature and antagonisms that are part of history. Soil and sky, dusk and dawn form naturally counterposed elements of space and time. Master and slave, however, inhabit a dialectic constituted by social and historical forces. Lewis's metonymic preoccupation with roots and soil as spatial markers of regional and racial belonging bypasses the fact that the land—where the master dominates, not merely contrasts with, the slave—consists of demarcated private property. To propose, as Lewis does, that Kabnis needs to accept all dualisms, natural and social, in a Whitmanesque spirit of embracing multitudes, carries the implication that Kabnis's "bastardization" is a product of natural differences, when it is the result of the historical rape of black women by the white men who own the land. That Kabnis is "suspended" above the soil, too, suggests that, as metaphorical lynchee, he hangs from a tree: Lewis's call for acceptance of his mixed-race ancestry cannot encompass the extent of his anguish.[30]

Although he is apparently an antilynching activist, in this confrontation with Kabnis, Lewis strikes an oddly culturalist posture, one that would propose to suture social contradictions by linguistic means. Lewis's allusions to fire presumably signal Kabnis's need to acknowledge the "sun-tint" in his cheeks and to fuse an identity that has been "split, shredded, easily burned." But Lewis's speech invokes other images in the text carrying quite different implications: of women split open and riddled with bullets, of men hacked to pieces and set on fire. Lewis's advice that Kabnis embrace the "flame" of his mixed-race ancestry as equivalent to the ripened leaves of autumn carries its own negation. The organic trope, even when voiced by a redemptive hero, cannot contain the contradictions that it sets out to resolve; Lewis's "golden words" are at odds with Kabnis's "split" situation. The text's formal contradictions on the level of symbolic action play out the contradictions informing the binary opposition between art and action in the ideologeme of the New Negro.

"New bla[c]k is . . .": "Kabnis" displays the impossibility of completing this sentence. There is no unitary essence to the New Negro because there is no clear path to a better world. *Pace* Locke, the writer cannot simply dig into the "racy soil of the race life" to discover who he is; *pace* Frank, creation is not revolution. Neither a politics of identity nor an aesthetic of pluralism can contest the state power embodied in the courthouse and the violence embodied in Ramsey's ax. The dialectic of history has been arrested by forces that have brought the New Negro into existence but blocked forward movement.

"Burn, bear black children":
The New Negro as Mater Dolorosa

While Kabnis and Lewis bear the joint burden of articulating the challenges facing the male New Negro in the Jim Crow South, the text's many references to black women—especially in connection with their labor as mothers or nurses—complicate the identity of the New Negro by elaborating on the trope of the Black Madonna. The text's play on "Deep River"—which appears on the first page and reappears two more times—links Jim Crow violence with the tragedy of African American motherhood:

> White-man's land.
> Niggers, sing.
> Burn, bear black children
> Till poor rivers bring
> Rest, and sweet glory
> In Camp Ground. (81, 85, 103)

In the original spiritual, "Deep River" signifies "my home . . . over Jordan"; the singer yearns "to cross over into camp ground." In the Georgia of the 1921 "death farm," however, the river of spiritual transcendence has been superseded by "rivering." One of the victims in the Valdosta massacre, moreover, had been lynched at a site named the "old Camp Ground." In a series of imperatives answering the hegemonic needs of the "white men" who own the land, both songs and children are the products of the labor of black women, here designated as "niggers." While the text reserves the definition of the New Negro for its heroic (or would-be heroic) male characters, its female characters—and female presences—limn the contours of the social reality that the New Negro must address and transform. The themes and tropes emphasized in the writings of Toomer's largely female-based Washington circle—rape, infanticide, aborted birth—circulate throughout the gendered subtext of "Kabnis."[31]

With the exception of Carrie Kate Halsey, women characters do not figure centrally in the action of "Kabnis": the only other females (besides the hen that Kabnis throttles in the opening scene) are Cora and Stella, the mixed-race women who participate in the party in Halsey's basement in the narrative's penultimate scene. Their names ironically recalling shepherdesses in the pastoral tradition, these two characters are linked with conventional discourses figuring women as earth mothers. Halsey recalls his past love for Stella when "th moon is thick an I hear dogs up th valley barkin an some old woman fetches out her song, an th winds seem like th Lord made them fer t fetch an carry th smell o pine an cane" (108). On the morning after their night of sex for sale, the two women are described in the stage directions as "two princesses in Africa going through the early-morning ablutions of their pagan prayers" (112). It will take more than a narratorial proclamation, however, to extend the metonymic chain from Africa to America via Georgia. For it emerges that the mixed-race ancestry of both Cora and Stella is the product of rape. As Stella recalls of her father, "A white man took m mother an it broke th old man's heart" (107). Their revels in Halsey's basement lack "good-time spirit": as Lewis sits by Father John, "merg[ing] with his source and let[ting] the pain and beauty of the South meet him there," the presence of the white rapist is pervasive: "White faces, pain-pollen, settle downward through a cane-sweet mist and touch the ovaries of yellow flowers. Cotton-bolls bloom, droop. Black roots twist in a parched red soil beneath a blazing sky" (106). The flowers' ovaries are invaded by whiteness; the organic trope supplies no transcendence. Nor does the imagery connecting fire with the tallow candles of folk inspiration: it is when Halsey reaches out for Cora, and she first "struggles," then "settles, spurting like a pine-knot fire," that Lewis feels "the glowing within him subsid[e]." The "too intense . . . pain" of the inhabitants of the cellar—of the "southern town"—is what sends him "plung[ing] through the work-shop and out into the night" (110–11). For all his chastening of Kabnis for not accepting the "fire in his cheeks," Lewis "cant hold" the history of sexual violation embodied in Stella and the fire-spurting Cora.

More central to the female presence in "Kabnis" are two interpolated passages of narration. In the text's opening scene, Toomer invokes the most famous lullaby in Western literature:

> The half-moon is a white child that sleeps upon the tree-tops of the forest. White winds croon its sleep-song:

rock a-by baby . .
Black mother sways, holding a white child on her bosom.
when the bough bends . .
Her breath hums through pine-cones.
cradle will fall . .
Teat moon-children at your breasts,
down will come baby . .
Black mother. (82)

Inverting the image of the faithful servant to be enshrined in the Mammy Monument," Toomer suggests a terrifying narrative. For the "black mother"—here serving as wet-nurse to a "white child" who presumably has first access to the milk the mother's own child would otherwise drink—threatens to kill the baby entrusted to her care. The hand that rocks the cradle threatens revenge against those who rule the world. The power relations embedded in this scenario are underlined when, a few moments later, Kabnis imagines that the "court-house tower . . . dull silver in the moonlight" is a "[w]hite child that sleeps on the top of pines"; he then envisions himself being "yanked beneath that tower" while "white minds, with indolent assumption, juggle justice and a nigger" (83). What began as a lyrical description of the white moon in the embrace of dark pines has metamorphosed into a panicked vision of state-sanctioned racial violence, undertaken by the white child now grown into an adult.[32]

Besides referencing the lurid implications embedded within "Rock-a-bye Baby," Toomer may have been alluding to some recent reworkings of the text. In 1918 the vaudeville singer and blackface actor Al Jolson had popularized a version titled "Rock-a-Bye Your Baby with a Dixie Melody":

Rock-a-bye your baby with a Dixie melody
When you croon, croon a tune from the heart of Dixie
Just place my cradle, mammy mine
Right on the Mason Dixon line
And swing it from Virginia
To Tennessee with all the love that's in ya.
"Weep No More, My Lady"—sing that song again, for me
Sing "Old Black Joe" just as though you had me on your knee
A million baby kisses I'd deliver
If you would only sing that Swanee River
Rock-a-bye your rock-a-bye baby with a Dixie melody.[33]

The speaker who demands the lullaby—half-man, half-baby, it would seem—evinces no anxiety that the mammy will let his cradle fall. Indeed, singing of Florida's Swanee River all the while, she will make Jim Crow—the "heart of Dixie"—the culture of the nation as a whole: although the cradle is placed on the Mason-Dixon Line, it swings not between north and south but ever-farther South. If Toomer is alluding to Jolson's song, widely heard on the radio in the period when *Cane* was being cre-ated, the irony is searing. And if we bear in mind that the "Mammy Monument" was intended not for a southern state capital, but the nation's mall, the irony is more devastating still. Jim Crow is not restricted to the Deep South: it as an American as the nation's capital. As Kabnis rails, "This whole damn bloated purple country . . . [is] goin t hell in a holy avalanche of words" (110).

Toomer's allusion to the famous nursery rhyme from *Mother Goose* may also have been spurred by Lola Ridge's poem "Lullaby," which appeared in *The Ghetto and Other Poems* in 1918. The poem recounts the horrific murder of a black baby during the 1917 East St. Louis race riot by a mob of white women who sang the lullaby as they "flung a living colored baby into the heart of a blazing fire":

> Rock-a-by baby, woolly and brown . . .
> (There's a shout at the door, an' a big red light . . .)
> Lil' coon baby, mammy is down . . .
> Hans that hold yuh are steady an' white . . .
> . . .
> Rock-a-by baby—higher an' higher!
> Mammy is sleepin' an' daddy's run lame . . .
> (Soun' may yuh sleep in yo' cradle o' fire!)
> Rock-a-by baby, hushed in the flame . . .

Ridge based her portrayal of the violence in East St. Louis on the reportage of Du Bois and Martha Gruening, who had investigated the riot and published their findings—including the mob's singing of "Rock-a-Bye Baby"—in the *Crisis*. The overlap between Toomer's "Burn, bear black children" and the fire imagery in Ridge's poem supplies a grim historical subtext in which fire was anything but metaphorical—and anything but a harbinger of proletarian revolution. While re-versing the races of the women and children—in "Kabnis," it is the black mother/nurse who threatens to kill the white child in her care—Toomer's invocation of Ridge's poem emphasizes the warping role played by racial antipathy in American life. No domestic space, no mother-child relation, is, it would seem, sacrosanct.[34]

Finally, Toomer's delineation of the treacherous nurse in the interpolated "Rock-a-bye baby" poem may draw on still another source. His choice of the unusual surname "Lamkins" for his fictional version of Mary Turner brings to mind the seventeenth-century English ballad "Lamkins," which was widely per-formed throughout the early twentieth-century South by people of both African and English heritage. The ballad tells the blood-curdling tale of the murder of the wife and baby son of a wealthy landowner by Lamkins, a skilled mason whom the landowner cheated out of pay earned in building the lord's mansion. Lam-kins acts in league with the baby's wet-nurse, who is weary of feeding the baby on command and resentful of her mistress's life of luxury. When the landowner is away, the nurse lets Lamkins into the house; piercing the baby's heart with a pin, the nurse and Lamkins trick the mother into coming downstairs in the dark when she hears the child's cries. The nurse refuses to bring a basin for the flowing blood, declaring,

> There need nae bason, Lamkin,
> lat it run through the floor;
> What better is the heart's blood
> o the rich than o the poor?

As the baby bleeds to death, the mother pleads in vain for her own life (in some versions of the ballad she offers her other child, a girl, as a substitute victim). The husband arrives home and finds the blood-soaked bodies of mother and baby; Lamkins is burned in a furnace and the nurse is hanged. A harsh tale of exploitation and revenge, "Bo Lamkins" links the historical circumstances surrounding the deaths of the Turner family—including rebellion against unpaid labor and retaliatory violence by both oppressed and oppressors—with comparable class relations in European feudalism. The Jim Crow South is at once premodern and all too modern.[35]

We cannot know whether or not Toomer intended his readers to hear an echo of "Bo Lamkins" in his renaming of Mary Turner. But there are a number of noteworthy parallels between the two narratives. In both accounts, the baby is murdered with a pin or a knife; the nurse and Lamkins are executed by burning and hanging—deaths conjoined in the killing of Mary Turner. A nickname for "Mary," moreover, is "Mame." Similarly, we cannot know whether Toomer intended his readers to pick up on allusions to Ridge's "Lullaby" or Al Jolson's recent Jim-Crowing of "Rock-a-Bye Baby." Once we become aware of these echoes, however, it is difficult to unhear them: as he composed "Kabnis," Toomer was preoccupied with not only the violence of the Jim Crow South but also the cultural media through which this violence was either legitimated or condemned. At stake, too, was a struggle over metonymy: Toomer's insistent allusions to Georgia's violated black women contested the white supremacist claim, in connection with the revelations surrounding the "death farm," that "Georgia—our mother—is being defiled before the world."

The second passage in "Kabnis" featuring the metaphorical presence of the black mother appears at the beginning of section 5, which narrates the descent into the Hole: "Night, soft belly of a pregnant Negress, throbs evenly against the torso of the South. Night throbs a womb song to the South. Cane- and cotton-fields, pine forests, cypress swamps, sawmills, and factories are fecund at her touch. Night's womb-song sets them singing. Night winds are the breathing of the unborn child whose calm throbbing in the belly of a Negress sets them somnolently singing. Hear their song" (103). As with the earlier lullaby, the passage suggests, on a first reading, a densely lyrical equation of the black mother with the earth. But closer scrutiny reveals that the woman's womb signifies not the soil—as might be expected from a trope linking birthing and fruition—but the night. Moreover, the means of production that become "fecund at her touch" are sites not of Nature but of political economy: the fields and forests that yield the crops and lumber that are in turn processed in the mills and factories. That this passage is immediately followed by a reiteration of Toomer's ironic revision of "Deep River"—which begins with the phrase "White-man's land"—recalls who owns the land and its bounty. "Hear [the winds'] song": the poem's command to women to "burn, bear black children" reminds us that, when a "Negress" like Mame Lamkins defies the owners in the land of cotton, the death of the unborn child will precede its birthing. Where the British journalist Stephen Graham had hoped for multiracial solidarity between rank-and-file white lynchers and Christlike black lynchees, united in their common opposition to the Pontius Pilates representing the owning class, Toomer proposes a far less optimistic fate for the Black Messiah. Indeed, the Black Madonna is the Mater Dolorosa: she will not bear her child, let alone see it come to maturity.

It has been argued that the figure of the Black Madonna is a dehistoricizing presence in *Cane*, but the opposite is closer to the truth: she signals the presence of the Real. The murder of Mary Turner and her baby was a raw and recent public memory; controversy about the proposed construction of the Mammy Monument flared during the time when Toomer was writing *Cane*. The text's persistent if subliminal emphasis on the figure of the violated—and at times vengeful—black woman suggests that Toomer had absorbed significant lessons about both female oppression and female resistance from the women in the Washington writers' group. We will recall, too, that some of these women—Burrill, Grimké, Johnson—had significant contacts with the left; their representations of situations and problems specific to African American women appeared in magazines concerned with U.S. working-class movements and international anticolonial insurgencies. In these magazines, the trope of pregnancy and birthing frequently functioned to signify social revolution: the mother's womb constituted the site of the new society developing within the old social order; the moment of delivery the insurrection; the baby the new society. Toomer's preoccupation with images of full wombs and dead babies throughout "Kabnis" suggests the conjoining of metaphor with material causality: the murdered infant is the aborted future, while the racialized act of murder is the reason for its abortion. That the failure to bring to term, birth, and nurture the hoped-for child is linked with fire reinforces the connection between racial violence and the quashing of revolutionary aspirations in the wake of 1919: the flame of revolution—the "one grand flare" kept alive in the embers of "Banking Coal"—has its Jim Crow counterpart in the command to "burn, bear black children."[36]

"Want th whole family history?": Toomer's Family Romance

Toomer's letter to Frank about the circular structure of *Cane* conveys the sense of satisfaction he experienced on completing his text. But this statement needs to be set alongside his admission, some ten months later, that *Cane* had been "born in an agony of internal tightness, conflict, and chaos," and in particular that "I had labored to write Kabnis. . . . The book as a whole was somehow distilled from the most terrible strain I have ever known." This "terrible strain," I suggest, derived to no small degree from the way in which the creation of the text—especially "Kabnis"—called on Toomer to make connections between his scattered knowledge of family history and the realities of Jim Crow revealed during his Sparta sojourn. Investigation of these connections sheds new light on Toomer's enigmatic admission, "Kabnis is me."[37]

In conversation with Lewis, Kabnis evinces a teasing evasiveness regarding his background. First boasting that his Georgia ancestors were "Southern bluebloods" and that he is descended from a "family of ORATORS," Kabnis then refuses to elaborate. "I'm Ralph Kabnis," he declares. "Aint that enough fo y? Want th whole family history? Its none of your goddam business, anyway. Keep off me" (106–7). Scholars reading *Cane* in connection with Toomer's biography have generally concluded that Kabnis's hostile assertions reflect Toomer's ambivalence toward P. B. S. Pinchback, whose reputation for eloquence as a Reconstruction-era political figure qualified him as an "orator" even as his light skin qualified him as a "blue blood." Pinchback is, arguably, present in "Kabnis"; he can be glimpsed in the portrait of Halsey's white great-grandfather, who is pictured as "a bearded man. Black hair, thick and curly, intensifies the pallor of the high forehead. The eyes are daring. The nose, sharp and regular. The poise suggests a tendency to adventure checked by the necessities of absolute command" (85). This description resembles Toomer's remarking, in "On Being an American," on a photograph of his grandfather showing "a sturdy fearless man of prominent forehead, bold dark eyes, a black beard, forceful personality" (see fig. 4, chapter 4). Looking down from the wall of Halsey's parlor, this possible surrogate of Toomer's powerful maternal grandfather sees Kabnis cringing at the thought of racial violence and pleading, "But they wouldnt touch a gentleman—fellows, men like us three here." Layman's reply—"Nigger's a nigger down this way, Professor" (87)—contains a hard-nosed realism that Pinchback, a seasoned participant in the Civil War, Reconstruction and its bloody aftermath, would have wryly acknowledged.[38]

If Pinchback looks down from the wall in Halsey's parlor, however, his presence signals not so much Toomer's continuing need to flagellate himself in front of his grandfather as his desire to rewrite the family history in such a way that the domineering grandfather is divested of his power to do anything more than look on as a narrative featuring other key figures unfolds. For Sparta/Sempter was a geographical site associated, for *Cane*'s author, more with the name "Toomer" than with the name "Pinchback." The "silver tower" of the courthouse—which prompts Kabnis's terrified vision of being "yanked beneath the tower" where "white minds . . . juggle justice and a nigger"—was built with funds supplied by Amanda America Dickson after she won her legal case against the relatives of

David Dickson's deceased wife. As David Teyy's poem about the "black barges" in "Withered Skin of Berries" indicates, Toomer was fully cognizant of the role played by the justice system in controlling the black labor at the foundation of the plantation system. By displaying Kabnis's fear of being subjected, as a Negro, to the vagaries of Georgia's courts, Toomer indicated his emotional identification with the victims, rather than the beneficiaries, of Jim Crow. Moreover, it was most probably because Amanda America Dickson had inherited the wealth symbolized by the Sparta courthouse that Nathan Toomer had courted her, beginning the fateful sequence of events that would result in her death and send him seeking a bride in Washington, DC—and eventually abandoning his new wife and small son as he sought to recover the Georgia estate due to him as widower of his former wife. In this sequence of events, Pinchback had played a key role by renaming the grandson and prohibiting mention of the name of the father; but he was by no means the only, or most important, player.

The names of other characters appearing in "Kabnis" have both public resonance and a specific connection to Toomer's family history. While there was in fact a mixed-race family in Hancock County named "Halsey," giving plausibility to the text's portrayal of the family of Sempter's wheelwright, Toomer's choice of this surname also enabled him to frame a critique of the Christian conservatism associated with the name "Holsey." Lucius Holsey—founder of Sparta's Ebenezer Colored Methodist Episcopal (CME) Church, as well as of Augusta's Paine Institute—was renowned for his connection with both Bourbon accommodationism and intraracial racism. In his autobiography, he had written of having "no complaint against American slavery. It was a blessing in disguise to me and to many. It has made the negro race what it could not have been in its native land." On the Sunday when Kabnis visits Halsey, hysterical singing emanates from Ebenezer Church next door, suggesting the church's role in containing and sublimating the mass trauma of southern oppression and violence. At the same time, Ebenezer Church followed the "brown bag" rule, excluding dark-skinned aspiring parishioners from its fold. Fred Halsey's criticisms of the racism at the unnamed school he attended in Augusta are explicitly aimed at Paine Institute. It was a "pussy Sunday-school," he tells Lewis, where "[i]f you was nearly white, they liked y," but "[i]f you was black, they didn't" (108). That the light-skinned Halsey has rejected the opportunity of inclusion in the high-toned CME fold, choosing instead the life of an artisan laborer consorting with Sempter's rank and file, speaks volumes about intraracial color prejudice. We are reminded of Toomer's assertion, in a draft of "The Negro Emergent," that "economic powers" were generating "the split within the Negro group due to difference of color and economic preferences," resulting in "disdain and contempt on the part of those of lighter color and better position." Toomer's representation of both the church and the college linked to Lucius Holsey afforded him the opportunity to critique the forces within the African American community that were sustaining rather than opposing Jim Crow.[39]

But Toomer may have had another, more personal, motivation in choosing the name "Holsey" for Sempter's wheelwright and his little sister. For Kate Holsey, the daughter of Lucius Holsey, was also the wife of Charles Dickson, the would-be abductor of his young stepsister (and Toomer's half-sister), Mamie (Mary) Toomer; it was "Caty" Holsey whose fate aroused the pity of Nathan Toomer in his letters from Sparta to Whitefield McKinlay. While the historical Kate Holsey, after her divorce from Charles Dickson, returned to the house of her father and cared for him until his death in 1920, in Toomer's text, Carrie Kate Halsey proves true to a different calling. She devotes herself to the aged former slave Father John—illiterate, dark-skinned "like a bust in black walnut" (104), and incisively aware of the role of the church in perpetuating "the fog of white dominance." Toomer's allusion to Kate Holsey in his naming of Carrie Kate Halsey not only rescues her historical prototype from the humiliation she endured as the wife of the licentious Charles Dickson, it also liberates her from the accommodationist legacy of her father. Toomer's imagined renarration "carries" Kate to a better world, one where she belongs to a family aligned with those who worked as slaves and sharecroppers rather than with those who lived parasitically off the fruits of their labors.

More crucially, Toomer's fictional portrayal of Fred Halsey's younger sister enables him to save his own "dark sister" from the clutches of her rapacious stepbrother. Even before Carrie Kate appears in the flesh, the reader has been introduced to a family photograph—set alongside a clock that has stopped—revealing the Halseys' mixed genetic heritage. Two of the children are, we are told, quite dark-skinned, taking after their "rich brown" father. Fred and his sister, taking after their "practically white" mother, are light in complexion: "[Fred's] face was an olive white, and his hair luxuriant and dark and wavy. . . . [T]he girl, quite young, is like Fred" (85–86). When Carrie Kate first enters Halsey's workshop, her physical resemblance to her brother is stressed: "Black bangs curl over the forehead of her oval-olive face. Her expression is dazed, but on provocation it can melt into a wistful smile. Adolescent. She is easily the sister of Fred Halsey" (101). The reader assumes that the "quite young" girl in the photograph is Carrie Kate.

There is a problem, however: the photograph was taken, we are told, some thirty years before. Fred Halsey, evidently a middle-aged man when "Kabnis" takes place, can plausibly have been the youth in the photograph taken three decades previously. But the adolescent Carrie Kate who brings lunch to the men working in the wheelwright's shop—in what is approximately 1921, the year of Toomer's visit and also of "death farm" killings alluded to by Layman—can hardly have appeared in a photograph taken in 1891. Perhaps the girl in the photograph is not Carrie Kate, but an absent older sister. The repeated insistence that Fred resembles both the sister in the photograph and Carrie Kate, however, in addition to the fact that no other sister is ever alluded to, strongly inclines the reader to conclude that Carrie Kate and the "quite young" sister in the photograph are one and the same person.

Carrie Kate Halsey could not have been alive thirty years before. But Mamie Toomer most surely was. Born in 1879, Mamie Toomer would have been "quite young" in 1891—the very year when Nathan and Amanda met and Charles Dickson would have encountered his then-twelve-year-old stepsister, thereby setting in motion the sequence of events that resulted in Amanda's death, Nathan's remarriage, and Toomer's birth—indeed, in Kabnis/Toomer's presence in Sempter/Sparta thirty years later. Frozen in her youth for three decades (the clock, notably, has stopped), Mamie Toomer awaits her reawakening in *Cane* by the kiss of the good half-brother who—addressing her as "child," "baby," "little sweetheart," and "dear little sweet sister" (114–15)—will undo the evil wrought by the bad stepbrother. As in his redemptive renaming of Kate Holsey, Toomer rewrites the family history in accordance with a plot more to his liking.

While Toomer had a significant personal investment in retelling the stories of Mamie Toomer and Kate Holsey, this renarration had a public dimension as well. For Kabnis's affectionate references to Carrie Kate as his "little sister" echo the use of that term in D. W. Griffith's *The Birth of a Nation*, where it is heard in connection with Flora Cameron, the young white girl who, rather than succumb to the lust of the former slave Gus, throws herself off a cliff. It is in presumed retaliation for this attempted crime, embodying the travesties of Reconstruction, that the heroic Ku Klux Klan, coming to the rescue of southern civilization, creates the conditions in which the post-Reconstruction "nation" can be "born." But in Toomer's family history—as indeed throughout the history of the South—it had been young women of African descent like Julia Lewis and Mamie Toomer, not white girls like Griffith's Flora, who had been subjected to routine sexual violation. As he rewrites the history of the Dicksons and Toomers by preserving Carrie Kate from the advances of a near-white adult stepbrother, Toomer simultaneously challenges the mass-cultural racist convention associating female sexual innocence with whiteness; his enshrinement of his own "dark sister" enables him to advocate on behalf of other dark-skinned and mixed-race young women as well. And, indeed, to call for the birth of a very different kind of nation.[40]

"Sleepy windows of the southern town": "Kabnis" and Closure

At the very end of "Kabnis," we emerge from the Georgia night of racial violence and repressed family secrets into the light of common day. Lewis has disappeared; the blind prophet Father John has finally spoken; Kabnis has descended into the basement of history and endured his dark night of the soul. If the Liveright publicity sketch supplies at least a partial key to the structure of the published text, Toomer's finale was intended to enable the reader to view *Cane* as "a unit of spiritual experience" possessing "a beginning, a progression, a complication, and an end." The closing scene in "Kabnis" rounds off various themes and tropes that have structured the text to this point and—as many interpretations of the text suggest—can be read as an affirmation of possible forward movement. "Sin. . . . Sin. . . . Sin. . . . Th sin whats fixed. . . . upon th white folks—. . . . f tellin Jesus— lies. O th sin th white folks 'mitted when they made th Bible lie": Father John's words refute Kabnis's disabling notion, voiced in his opening monologue, that as a bastard he is an embodiment of sin (115). Indeed, as various commentators have noted, the old man's pronouncement helps to turn the "sin ba[c]k" ("Kabnis" spelled backwards) to where it came from, namely, the white supremacist invoca- tions of the Old Testament as the basis for African enslavement. The enclosure of Father John and Carrie K. in a halo-like circle of light can be counterposed to the authoritarian and hypocritical versions of Christianity controlling the Ebenezer congregation; like the ending of "Balo," this finale can be read as an endorsement of a restorative folk spirituality. Carrie K., moreover, is said to be in a state of "nascent maternity" (114): since it is clear that her brothers, real and surrogate, have protected her from anything resembling physical contact with a man, her "pregnancy" will result in the virgin birth of a symbolic messiah. "Jesus come" (116): the Black Madonna, until now the subject of infanticide or the object of predation, will finally be able to deliver and nurture the fruit of her womb. The women of *Cane* are, it seems, redeemed, making possible the birth of a nation beyond race and racism.[41]

The final paragraph of "Kabnis"—and that of *Cane*—can be read as drawing together the tropes of botanical organicism and temporal cycles with the themes of rebirth and achieved artistry: "Outside, the sun arises from its cradle in the tree- tops of the forest. Shadows of pines are dreams the sun shakes from its eyes. The sun arises. Gold-glowing child, it steps into the sky and sends a birth-song slanting down gray streets and sleepy windows of the southern town" (116). While dusk and night have dominated the text's portrayals of the South, the sun no longer sets but rises: the nightmare of history has passed. Indeed, the sun becomes the son of the South; the baby, no longer identified as either white or black, just as a baby, is safe, and trees function as cradles rather than sites of lynching. Kabnis's frustrated search for "golden words" ends with the "gold-glowing child" that utters a "birth-song": the text's final two words—"southern town"—affirm the project of metonymic nationalism by proclaiming the emergence of a sectional art. The "birth-song" heralds the "birth of a nation," an "our America" finally inclusive of the nation's diversity: culture will put back into motion the arrested dialectic of political and social history. Even Kabnis's apparent obliviousness to both the sunrise and the halo of light encircling Carrie Kate and Father John need not be viewed as a negation of the text's optimistic message. The bucket of dead coals that he drags up the cellar steps can signify not his loss of inspiration, but his triumph over the "nightmare . . . burned into [his] soul." Indeed, Toomer may be seen as gesturing here toward the passage from Carl Sandburg's "The Prairie" that Frank had highlighted in *Our America*: "I speak of new cities and new people. /

I tell you the past is a bucket of ashes. / I am a brother of the cornhuskers who say at sundown: To-morrow is a day." Rather than signaling Kabnis's inability to confront his African ancestry and its connection with slavery, the bucket of ashes suggests his ability to dispense with the painful residue of the past. Georgia, where they burn and lynch men and women and pin babies to trees, has, in this interpretation, been claimed for spiritual pioneering.[42]

Although the ending of *Cane* is susceptible to such an affirmative, indeed celebratory, interpretation, the finale equally invites an ironic reading. Carrie K. and Father John remain in the basement where, Kabnis notes, "they used t throw th old worn-out slaves" (113); the folk Christianity embraced by the young girl and the old man is part of a "buried culture" that will remain buried. Carrie Kate's "nascent maternity" is, in this reading, merely metaphorical; the preservation of her chastity may satisfy the needs of the brother of Mamie Toomer, but—sequestered in her brother's basement and bound to the past—she is one more Black Madonna who will not give birth. Moreover, while Father John's long-awaited words of wisdom may not warrant Kabnis's cynical response that the former slave is "an old fakir," throughout "Kabnis"—indeed, throughout *Cane*—it has been repeatedly suggested that "white folks" have "made the Bible lie": the blind prophet's pronouncement conveys no startling insight of use to those subjected to the rigors of present-day Jim Crow. Indeed, Kabnis's bitter accusation that Father John "died way back there in the sixties" (113) may even refer to John Cain, who was hanged in 1863 for attempting to lead an abortive slave revolt: no comparably courageous leader has since emerged. Toomer's comment on Carrie Kate and Father John in a January 1924 letter to the Howard Players director Montgomery Gregory is telling. After thanking Gregory for his defense of *Cane*'s portraiture of Negro women, Toomer noted that Gregory had "caught one of the main implication[s] of Kabnis," namely, that "Father John, the past, the past unless it articulates in the present, is mute. Carrie Kate, love and sympathy,—love and sympathy powerless unless coupled with knowledge and the means whereby. Etc." Toomer suggests the limited reach of folk authenticity in the absence of a transformative praxis grounded in modernity. The resolution proposed in the folk play "Balo" is not possible in the expressionist drama "Kabnis," where the potentially redemptive characters have been rendered "mute" and "powerless" by their confinement within an arrested historical dialectic.[43]

In the context of an ironic reading, the themes and tropes alluded to in the text's final paragraph take on an evasive, indeed apologetic, quality. Earlier in "Kabnis," treetops were murderous nurses, cradling the monstrous offspring of the courthouse tower, and Mame Lamkins's baby was daggered to a tree: golden words may substitute for, but they cannot negate, the "split-gut song" erupting throughout the preceding text. Kabnis himself has failed to create an art that would represent "the face of the South"; it is the sun, rather than any human agent, that delivers the closing birth song. Although the image of fire-as-sun closes the text, the fire trope makes its penultimate appearance in the bucket of ashes that Kabnis bears up the cellar stairs. This burden may as readily signify Kabnis's loss of contact with the "tallow-flame" of the folk, and his final disconnection from the "flame" in his own cheeks, as it may convey his triumph over fear in a land where "men are lynched and burned." Even if the text obliquely alludes to Frank's featured quotation from Sandburg's "The Prairie," it may do so skeptically. Midwestern cornhuskers are able to repudiate the past—to view history as a "bucket of ashes"—as they follow the course of manifest destiny. African Americans confined by the political economy of Jim Crow are far less able to unburden themselves of the past and play the role of pioneers in a revitalized "our America."

Toomer continued revising "Kabnis" until he sent the manuscript off to Liveright. While the nature and extent of these revisions can only be guessed, he left a few suggestive indications. In an early version of "Kabnis," one apparently containing more dialogue and less narration than the published text, Toomer gave Father John—tongue-tied and nearly mute in the published text—a more substantial role. Frank, advising Toomer about possible revisions to his closet drama, commented that "the speech of the Ancient at the end" entails "a sudden drop into particulars failing to take along . . . the general atmosphere you had built about his relationship with Kabnis." Toomer granted Frank's criticism of the old man's garrulousness, remarking that "[t]hose Ancients have a peculiar attraction for me. I am very apt to let them say too much." It is tempting to speculate about the content of the "particulars" to which Frank objected; a lifetime spent in the Invisible Empire state surely qualified Father John to present a detailed catalogue. He might have expanded on his critique of organized Christianity; he might have supplemented Layman's comments on peonage cases and lynching; he might even have testified to the hanging of John Cain fifty-eight years before. Indeed, it is not difficult to imagine that the "particulars" of which Frank complained would have contained a historically specific account of slavery and Jim Crow. Toomer, eager to retain the respect of his modernist mentor and to get *Cane* into print, may have sacrificed an interesting excursus into the sociological impulse that animated his Sparta-era letters to Alain Locke.[44]

As he prepared the shortened version of "Kabnis" that would appear in *Broom*, Toomer appears to have considered omitting various lyrical passages uttered by the narratorial voice. After viewing one revision of the text, *Broom* editor Lola Ridge complained, "[Y]ou have cut some beautiful bits of description in your story . . . you have cut in the wrong places here and there. I feel sure that I am not unskilled—that I did not dream the beauty in this story + when you begin, 'night, soft belly of a pregnant Negress'—was there not much more? I hope you will put the poetry *back*." Toomer replied, "What you say about the new Kabnis touches—and pains me. You are right about the 'night, soft belly of a pregnant Negress' figure. I altered with a view to my ending. And I lost. I have already replaced the essentials of the first version. Hope I haven't lost in this way all through. Don't think I have."

Toomer evidently at one point felt that the "pregnant Negress" passage—along with other "beautiful bits of description" appearing "all through" the text—contradicted its ending and needed to be eliminated. While he apparently restored the lyrical passages that Ridge missed when reading his first revision, it would appear that his initial conception of the ending of "Kabnis" did not readily accord with this material. One is thus led to wonder whether "Kabnis" originally ended with the image of Kabnis trudging up the stairs carrying the burned-out coals, and whether the final paragraph depicting the rising sun might not have been added when he reinstated the "beautiful bits of description."[45]

A comment about his compositional process that Toomer dropped into an October 1922 letter to Frank may illuminate Toomer's decision making about the ending of his text. He wrote, "Sunday I finished rewriting, or rather, re-creating a piece: the one whose situation Lola R liked; whose realization she didnt. (Neither did I.)" A key aspect of this "re-creation" was an altered finale: "And near the end, while trying to somehow make it fit the old patern [sic] I suddenly became conscious of what I had done, of the emotional as well as the intellectual implications. And I finished with a flare of poetry. (The former ended on a sterile, aloof, disillusioned note.) This makes me feel fine!" While the text in question here was probably "Bona and Paul," this statement applies more generally to Toomer's compositional process: he was not only capable of dramatically altering his endings but also fully aware of the "emotional and intellectual implications" of such changes. A "flare of poetry" would produce an impact diametrically opposed, both emotionally and intellectually, to a "sterile, aloof, disillusioned note." But he also suggested that his proclivity—the "old pattern"—was for a skeptical rather than an affirmative effect: optimism was not part of his habitual outlook.[46]

There is no way of knowing whether Toomer altered the ending of "Kabnis"— and thus of *Cane* as a whole—as an afterthought. But it is arguable that the "flare of poetry" embodied in the text's closing image is not consistent with much of the preceding text. The "gold-glowing child" that utters its "birth-song" arises from the same cradle in the treetops that had carried the monstrous offspring of the court-house tower. The "gray dust streets and sleepy windows of the southern town" supply a peaceful surface beneath which, in Halsey's cellar, remain both the memory of slavery and the continuing oppression of Jim Crow. Indeed, the movement from underground to aboveground suggests a denial of the economic, social, and psychological repression on which the social order of the "southern town" relies—an order reinforced, as Toomer neared completion of his manuscript, by the Mammy Monument controversy and the impending failure of the Dyer Bill. The town's ability to stand for a region that will in turn stand for the nation—its promised embodiment of sectional art—is haloed in ideological haze; metonymic nationalism is affirmed only through an obliteration of the historical record.

Rather than proposing a forthrightly ironic reading of the finale to "Kabnis," however, we may find it more fruitful to link the text's closing suspension between the poles of antinomy to the arrested historical dialectic by which Toomer felt himself confronted. The grim testimony in "Kabnis" to the pervasiveness of racial violence suggests the continuing fate of those who resist—or are even suspected of resisting—the regime of "lynchers and business men." Toomer's shamed awareness of the connections between his own family history and the regimes of slavery and post-Reconstruction Jim Crow could only reinforce the sense of paralysis attributed to his fictional creation. The artist-hero's evident identification with the victims of Jim Crow violence, as well as his inability to devise a "split-gut song" that can do justice to the Real, indicate Toomer's own profound ambivalence about the ability of art—even an art striving to make good the promise of "our America"—to remedy the crises of the larger social realm. An added "flare of poetry" cannot compensate for the loss of the "grand flare" of revolution.

CHAPTER 6

Georgia on His Mind
Part 1 of Cane

> However long a series of periodical reproductions and preceding
> accumulations the capital functioning today may have passed through, it
> always preserves its original virginity.
> —Karl Marx, chapter 24, *Capital*

> Give virgin lips to cornfield concubines
> —Jean Toomer, "Georgia Dusk"

Jean Toomer wrote most of the poems and sketches in part 1 of *Cane* during the six months following his completion of the first draft of "Kabnis" in January 1922. He undertook the fall 1922 trip to South Carolina in the company of Waldo Frank in part because, as he wrote to his friend in July 1922, "the impulse which sprang from Sparta, Georgia last fall has just about fulfilled and spent itself." The two prose texts in part 1 that he composed on returning from Spartanburg—"Esther" and "Blood-Burning Moon"—display a significant shift, both stylistic and thematic, from the earlier poems and tales. Almost all the short pieces in *Cane* that have been most frequently anthologized were composed during the months following Toomer's direct engagement with the Real of the Jim Crow South that was first represented in "Kabnis." *Cane*'s abiding reputation as a literary work conveying golden melancholy and lyrical nostalgia—epitomized in the contemporaneous praise of Waldo Frank and William Stanley Braithwaite and reiterated in many critical commentaries to this day—rests largely on such incantatory poems as "Georgia Dusk" and "Song of the Son" and such imagistically saturated stories as "Karintha," "Carma," and "Fern." Read alongside Toomer's exuberant letters to his modernist acquaintances about Georgia's soil-soaked folk—as well as his often-quoted autobiographical reminiscence of "the folk-songs and spirituals" that he first heard in the "strangely rich and beautiful . . . valley of 'Cane,' with smoke-wreaths during the day and mist at night"—these texts have largely determined the course of *Cane*'s canonical career.[1]

My sequential mapping of the composition of *Cane* leads me to quite a different assessment of the portrayal of the rural South in the text's opening section. I argue here that many of the texts in part 1 display Toomer's continuing attempt to incorporate Sempter/Sparta into the program for sectional art that had failed to achieve effective expression in "Kabnis." While "things are so immediate" in the Georgia that traumatizes Toomer's artist-hero, in part 1 the word "Georgia" figures prominently among the symbolic acts that link the soil and the folk through the ideologeme of metonymic nationalism. "Georgia Dusk" features a "genius of the South" embodied in a chanting collective of lumber workers; David Georgia distributes free syrup in "Becky" and presides over the kettle of boiling cane at the beginning of "Blood-Burning Moon"; the mystically minded narrator in "Carma" views the eponymous protagonist's wagon as a "Georgia chariot"; the identity-seeking tourist in "Fern" repeatedly names Georgia as the site where "vision" is to be had. Such references to Georgia propose that the folk culture located on the Dixie Pike is a vital spiritual link in the chain connecting region with nation and affirming the belonging of African Americans in an expanded version of "our America." Routinely deploying the "golden words" of which Kabnis was so distrustful, these texts propose second-order mediations between people and the land that abandon the "raw hillside" of Jim Crow violence and assert the pastoral belonging of the folk on the soil they till. Throughout much of part 1 of *Cane*, Kabnis's "split-gut song" is silenced.[2]

But nothing in *Cane* is simple: even in the short lyrics and sketches redolent of romantic nostalgia, the repression of the history that hurts is incomplete. Tropes of failed parturition and consuming fire contest the hyper-materiality of the dominant organic trope; the self-consciously spectatorial narrator falters in his attempts to imagine Georgia's women as embodiments of the earth; Georgia emerges as the site of racist murder in "Portrait in Georgia" and "Blood-Burning Moon." Toomer's preoccupation with his "dark sister" is less pronounced in part 1 than in "Kabnis." But Mamie Toomer continues to haunt "Karintha"; while oblique references to Toomer's own life story in "Esther" and "Blood-Burning Moon" signal his abiding absorption with the links between private and public history. As the opening section of *Cane* approaches its violent finale, the text's strategies of metonymic nationalist mediation come under increasing pressure from alternative hypotheses for imagining the connection between region and nation. The "Invisible Empire state" erupts from the political unconscious of the text.

Central to the emerging comprehension of the social totality toward the end of part 1 of *Cane* is the gradual intrusion of the temporality of capital. The poetic/narratorial voice heard in a number of the lyrics and portraits has been preoccupied with images and instances of refused motherhood or recovered virginity as means of transcending the despoilment of Georgia's women. But these women's objectified status ramifies beyond their gendered condition to the alienated situation more generally facing the peasantry of the Deep South. The text's sporadic attempts at lyrical transcendence of the hurting history endured by black female bodies cannot efface the origin of their exploitation—as sites of both production and reproduction—in the imperatives of the plantation economy. As the Real increasingly comes to the fore in the closing poems and sketches of part 1, moreover, the abiding presence of congealed dead labor in constant capital compels the reader's attention. What Marx called the "original virginity" of the different means of production successively used up in the making of commodities, whether agricultural or industrial, retains its immediacy. In particular, the cotton boll—even as it undergoes the multiple mediations involved in its transfer from the southern soil to the world market—remains present as a marker of the surplus value exacted under conditions of extreme duress. The text's re-encounter with historical process toward the end of part 1 entails a reencounter with the social relations of production shaping experience and consciousness in the Deep South.

"Smoke is on the hills": Georgia's Political Economy

Since the *combinatoire* of images comprising the organic trope—seeds and fruit, soil and roots—figures so centrally throughout *Cane*, it is useful to examine the actual referents of these entities in the political economy of early 1920s Georgia. Toomer's retrospective descriptions of his Sparta experiences in his correspondence and autobiographies recount only part of what he saw—and understood. At both the University of Wisconsin and the University of Massachusetts, Toomer had intended to study agronomy. His 1921–22 letters to Locke and Moorland displayed an intense interest in the sociology of the Jim Crow South. In "Incredible Journey," Toomer's observations about the economic history of agriculture revealed that, nearly two decades after composing *Cane*, he retained much of the historical materialist perspective that had guided his original interest in the political economy of the Jim Crow South. The idealist in Toomer rhapsodized over Georgia's earth and soil, absorbing the second nature produced by human use into a first nature prior to human agency; the materialist remained alert to the land as always already the site of private ownership, production for profit, and super-exploited labor.[3]

   Cotton was in crisis when Toomer arrived in Sparta in the fall of 1921. The record levels reached by cotton prices during the war had encouraged farmers to devote most of their acreage to cotton planting even after the arrival of the boll weevil. Starting in 1920, however, Georgia's cotton crop was decimated; the area around Sparta was among the hardest hit in the entire state. In 1919, 19,789 bales of cotton were produced in Hancock County, selling at 40 cents a pound; in 1920, 11,685 bales were produced, selling at 16 cents a pound; in 1921, a mere 1,509 bales were produced, selling at 17 cents a pound. In 1922, the price went up to 23 cents, but only 710 bales were harvested. The 1921 cotton depression drove down the value of labor, compounding the outmigration of the previous decade and precipitating the remaining sharecroppers and tenant farmers into conditions of increasing economic dependency and—as the killings on the Monticello "death farm" revealed—still harsher conditions of debt peonage.[4]

   Such was the situation in cotton farming and labor markets that Toomer encountered when he arrived to serve as substitute principal of the Sparta Agricultural and Industrial Institute. During the summer and fall of 1921, the *Sparta Ishmaelite* was full of advice to farmers about diversifying crops, using anti-weevil poisons, and hoarding existing cotton stocks until the price should rise again. When he returned from his fund-raising trip to Boston—the reason for his having hired Toomer—the school's principal, L. S. Ingraham, loyally proclaimed that southerners were "enjoying much better times here in the South than are the people of the North." But he worried that "there is danger of many going hungry" and "plead[ed] with his white and colored friends here and everywhere to plant more grain in the next crop." Cotton was no longer—and never again would be—the mainstay of the Hancock County economy.[5]

A second site of labor central to Sparta's economy was the lumber industry. Throughout Middle Georgia in the early 1920s, the mills were principally of the variety dubbed peckerwood—that is, mills using relatively inexpensive movable machinery that operated near small stands of forest for short periods of time and then relocated when the lumber had been removed. This "cut-and-get-out" approach to natural resources left behind a patchwork landscape, with denuded former forest lands adjacent to still-yielding stands of pine forest. The loggers and planers hired to chop down and process the shrinking forests were drawn from the local farming population, black and white. While the lumber industry provided intermittent employment to many tenant and sharecropping families, this modest source of income came under threat in 1921, when the market for lumber shrank and the industry entered a temporary depression. The *Sparta Ishmaelite* reported the closing of several local lumber companies in the months preceding Toomer's visit, producing layoffs among a workforce already strapped by the collapse of the cotton market. In Bogalusa, Louisiana, it had been lowered wages in the lumber industry that, in 1919, sparked the militant union movement that gave rise to the possibility that "Bogalusa" might emerge as the symbol of a new age of multiracial labor activism. In 1921, however, the sound of a Middle Georgia sawmill, and the sight of smoke rising from its heaped-up detritus, signaled not a future of improved working conditions and steady employment, but the final phase of a development that would soon strip the land of its woods and leave much of its population more impoverished than ever.[6]

Finally, there is the matter of cane—"oracular, deep-rooted cane." From Toomer's title and epigraph, as well as from the omnipresence of cane fields, canebrakes, and cane stoves in the text, one might conclude that cane was essential to the economy of Sparta. But there were in the 1920s no large-scale stands of sorghum cane in Georgia equivalent to the immense sugar cane plantations then existing in Louisiana and Texas and developing in Florida. Sorghum cane figured primarily in Middle Georgia's subsistence economy, furnishing animal feed and syrup and molasses for home use: the average inhabitant consumed four gallons of homegrown and home-ground cane syrup per year. Some farmers marketed their surplus: the *Atlanta Constitution* routinely carried ads for various-sized containers of syrup. As Toomer indicated in "Balo," however, during the depression of the early 1920s the price of sorghum cane syrup had fallen so low, and shipping costs had become so high, that it was not economically viable for farmers to get their product to market. In the Hancock County of 1921, cane syrup was a superabundant use-value, possessing limited nutritional value for a population threatened by pellagra and, indeed, starvation. The bartering and sharing of cane syrup and molasses could not compensate for the harshness of the markets associated with cotton and lumber.[7]

Toomer's Sparta-era pocket notebook records that one evening he sat on a log, whittling a stalk of cane, and thinking to himself, "I am not a failure. Not yet." That stalk of cane, symbolically encompassing prophetic meanings, would constitute Toomer's bid for fame. But it would also contain and manage the contradiction between cane's embodiment of use-value and communalism on the one hand, of private property and exploited labor on the other. Moreover, its homonym, "Cain," would evoke the biblical curse on the son of Adam and Eve that had been used to legitimate chattel slavery, as well as the name of the leader of Hancock County's 1863 rebellion against the "peculiar institution." Cane would conceal as much as it would reveal.[8]

"Dusky cane-lipped throngs":
Lyrics of Labor and the Land

"Reapers," the opening lyric in *Cane*, was drafted while Toomer was in Georgia. The partially illegible version in Toomer's notebook reads thus:

> Black workmen with the sound of steel on stone
> Are sharpening scythes they swing them through the reeds
> Mules pulling a mowing machine fill ___
> A rat with belly close to ground
> A ___ machine.

Noteworthy in this early draft is the absence of the speaker as observer, who in the published poem emphasizes his distance from the workers in the field:

> I see them place the hones
> In their hip-pockets as a thing that's done. . . .
> I see the blade,
> Blood-stained, continue cutting weeds and shade.

Conjoined with this contemplative stance, the published poem's title, central image, and central action invite interpretation along the lines of pastoral allegory: powerless to hold back the scythe of Father Time, the poet beholds the contrast between the controlled, semiautonomous motions of the reapers, utilizing a centuries-old technology associated with peasant labor, and the violent death of the field rat caught under the horse-drawn mower. This contrast juxtaposes the manual laborers' harmonious relation to the land with the brutality of the mechanized Grim Reaper of modernity, with the fate of the rat signaling what will happen to the reapers themselves when the "blood-stained blade" of the machine comes to dominate the field of their activity.

Even as the poem gestures toward pastoral conventions counterposing nature and the machine, however, the speaker's detached stance can be read not as that of a Wordsworthian romantic absorbing the song of a solitary reaper, but as that of a student of agronomy who sees that it takes several reapers to do the work of one machine. We should recall that the young man who observed these men at work with their scythes and mowers was not only an enthusiast for futurism and a professed lover of machines but also a fervent supporter of the fledgling Soviet Union, where industrial mechanization promised—once the present struggle for survival had passed—to benefit laborers on the land and in the factories alike. Drafted in the depths of the Jim Crow South, where African American laborers had no choice but to conform to what Toomer would call the "peasant-adjustment rhythm" of life in "The South in Literature," the poem looks not backward to a happy preindustrial age—what would that be, if not slavery and Jim Crow?—but forward toward the different futures potentially embedded in the present. The reapers are clearing the land for new planting: will the "turning of the soil" result in a bumper crop of new forms of art and consciousness for "our America," as Waldo Frank was hoping, or in a diminished harvest of arrested expectations?[9]

"Cotton Song" also features the activity of black laborers, here preparing the ginned and baled cotton for transport. At first glance—or listening, for the poem features what the poet hears, not what he sees—the poem apparently portrays the muscled workers loading cotton as a spiritualized folk, and the cotton itself as a means of transcending alienated labor. The laborer dominating the poem's beginning and ending proclaims, "Cant blame God if we don't roll"; he views the cotton he heaves as a means to heavenly redemption. "Cotton bales are the fleecy way / Weary sinner's bare feet trod," he chants, as he urges his coworker, "Come, brother, roll, roll!" His echo of "Roll, Jordan, Roll!" invites the reader to fill in the next words: "My sins so heavy I can't get along. Ah! / Roll, Jordan, Roll!" There are, however, two voices in the poem, not one. The mystical baler's companion wants compensation in the here and now—he twice declares, "'We aint agwine t wait until th Judgment Day!'"—and experiences not the ethereal fleeciness but the earthly weight of the cotton that he heaves: "'Nassur, nassur, / Hump. / Eoho, eoho, roll away!'" (9). For him, "rolling" signifies not the wages of sin but work for wages. The part of "Roll, Jordan, Roll" that he may be thinking of is "Done wid driber's dribin,' / Roll, Jordan, Roll! / Done wid Massa's hollerin.'" In their status as workers, the folk are thus not unitary. For some members of the southern black proletariat, religious idealism reinforces the "peasant-adjustment rhythm" of life; for others, awareness of exploitation entails consciousness of historical necessity. While in "Reapers" the spectatorial stance of the poet precludes entry into the consciousness of any of the scythe-bearing workers, in "Cotton Song" he overhears a debate about what is to be done between proletarians whose labor mediates the passage of cotton from the field to the market.[10]

The "dusky cane-lipped throngs" encountered in "Georgia Dusk," by contrast, experience no such internal debates over the meaning of their labor. These work-ers returning home through the swamp after a day's labor in the sawmill figure as emanations of the natural landscape ("the chorus of the cane") and bearers of a spiri-tuality at once Christian ("Carol[ing] their vespers to the skies") and Afrocentric ("race memories of king and caravan / High priests, an ostrich, and a juju-man"). Apparently unaware of their status as bearers of culture, they "ma[ke] folk-songs from soul sounds"; through them, "some genius of the South" ventriloquizes a communal consciousness reflecting an unalienated connection to the soil (13). Chosen by Alain Locke for inclusion in *The New Negro* book edition—and since then widely anthologized, often alongside "Song of the Son"—"Georgia Dusk" has routinely been treated as a distillation of Toomer's lyrical achievement in *Cane*.[11]

The poem corrects a wholly romanticized view of black labor in relation to the soil: the landscape has been denuded by the lumber mill, and the factory whistle determines the workers' relation to time. If Toomer read the *Sparta Ishmaelite* during his 1921 visit, however, he would have known that the local peckerwood mill, having used up much of Hancock County's pine forest, would soon close; that the seasonal sawmill workers were experiencing shortened hours and re-duced take-home pay; and that, in their alternate capacity as sharecroppers and tenant farmers, the real-life prototypes of his singers at dusk would have had scant access to whatever "bumper" crop might be wrung from the drought- and weevil-beset soil of the land they tilled but did not own. Instead of featuring the labor conditions signaled by the factory whistle, however, Toomer's persona opts for discourses of premodernity: the description of the setting sun as a "tourna-ment for flashing gold" suggests the era of European feudalism, while the African heritage of the black workers is portrayed as an ahistorical brew of Egyptian (the "pyramidal sawdust pile") and sub-Saharan ("juju man") cultures. This heritage is, moreover, portrayed as classless, even though the "caravan" of the "king," as well as the pyramids, would have been sites of enslaved labor. The designation of this folkish tableau as "*Georgia* Dusk" contains a bid for viewing African American "buried culture" as paradigmatic of a region of the South—and, by metonymic extension, of the nation. In order to construct this signifying chain, however, the poem occludes the workers' status as wage laborers engaged in the destruction of their own means of livelihood, portraying them instead as a nearly prelinguistic collective whose "voices rise" through an animistic "chorus of the cane." For all the authenticity of their connection with precapitalist ancestral cultures, these chanting millworkers emerge as "non-historical people."[12]

But the alien second-order mediations of capital—the regimentation of wage labor by the time clock, the workers' impending unemployment, the naturaliza-tion of the market—cannot be dispelled, even though they may be sutured over. Intruding on this bucolic tableau is a disturbing note of violence. The sky "passively darkens for night's barbeque": while presumably a "feast of moon and men and barking hounds"—that is, a nighttime hunting expedition—this "orgy for some

genius of the South" involves "blood-hot eyes and cane-lipped scented mouth."
At a time when lynchings were routinely described as "barbeques," this portrait of
men with "blood-hot eyes" against a "passively dark[ening] . . . sky" suggests the
poem's struggle to appropriate and defuse the discourse of violent racial repression. "Georgia Dusk" is not a portrait of an actual lynching; an early draft shows
that Toomer had in mind a nighttime possum hunt by blacks, not a manhunt by
whites. But the deployment of images ordinarily associated with lynching indicates
an eruption of the bloody record limned in Hugh Dorsey's *The Negro in Georgia*
on the folkish landscape limned in "Georgia Dusk." In this context, the persona's
interpretation of the millworkers' chant as a call to "give virgin lips to cornfield
concubines" instances a further "heaving upward" from the political unconscious
of the text. For the word "concubine" suggests not simply sexual activity outside
of marriage, but the inferior social position of a woman whose sexual favors are
the exclusive possession of the man of high status and wealth who finances her
upkeep: it signifies the dominated position of many African American women in
the southern plantation system, during slavery and beyond. Reading into the millworkers' chant a utopian reversal of the deflowering of Negro women by powerful
white men, the speaker in "Georgia Dusk" obliquely expresses as wish fulfillment
what will emerge as explicit rebellion in "Blood-Burning Moon."[13]

"Song of the Son"—selected by Locke for inclusion in both versions of *The New
Negro*, and the most frequently anthologized text drawn from *Cane*—is routinely
read as the author's simultaneous celebration of his rediscovered African American identity and his recognition of the coming dissolution of preindustrial folk
culture in the crucible of modernity. In its imagistic and thematic compression,
the poem contains a near-complete catalog of the organic trope's *combinatoire*,
including soil, land, sun, tree, grass, pines, seed, and fruit; indeed, only "root" is
needed to round out the roster. The clustering, alliteration, and repetition of these
and other monosyllabic words—son, soul, smoke, song, slaves—create an incantatory effect: land and soil, by the light of the setting sun, pour forth their soul
through the smoke of burning sawdust and the song of "Negro slaves"; the son,
hearing the soulful song, carries away the last fruit of an old tree; once ingested,
the fruit's seed becomes a song, and the son himself becomes a singing tree that
interprets and preserves the soul of a vanishing people. The organic trope here
signifies not only the identity of the folk with the region but also the embedding
of the poet in the folk and of their song in the poet. Along with the "birth-song"
featured at the end of "Kabnis," "Song of the Son" plays a crucial role in suturing
the text as a whole, conjoining New Negro culturalism with Young American
metonymic nationalism.[14]

But the very beauty of "Song of the Sun" raises important questions about the
seductive power of "golden words"; Kabnis, we may imagine, could have authored
this poem only with great difficulty. Unless the speaker has in mind debt peonage as a "new slavery," the allusion to Georgia's black folks as a "race of slaves"
engaged in "caroling softly souls of slavery" is both sentimental and anachronistic,

effacing these workers' relation to the political economy of present-day Jim Crow. The measurement of time by nature's diurnal and seasonal cycles further lifts the "epoch" in question out of history. The speaker claims to have encountered these singing folk "in time"—signifying both the timeliness and historicity of his discovery—but he gives little evidence of understanding the historical reasons for their song. Nonetheless, like its companion piece, "Georgia Dusk," "Song of the Son" gives hints of a restless political unconscious. The reference to the "old tree . . . stripped bare" suggests the landscape denuded by the peckerwood mills. The description of rural black folks as "dark ripened plums, / Squeezed, and bursting in the pine-wood air" suggests, once again, a lynching; the imagery glances ahead toward the burning of Tom Burwell. The poem's loose syntax suggests, moreover, the speaker's uncertain hold over his material, indeed, the last two stanzas consist of one long sentence that verges on grammatical incoherence. Who exactly is "[p]assing" and "stripping the old tree bare"—the "Negro slaves" or the singing son? If the "Negro slaves" are the "ripened plums," how can they also be the harvesters of the plums? If the speaker is the tree-stripper and harvester, does he ingest the plum signifying the folk—and then swallow the pit? How does the seed germinate in him, turning him into a "singing tree," without the benefit of soil? It is perhaps significant that the only missing term in the poem's *combinatoire* of images constituting the organic trope is "root": for all its proclamation of a recovered belonging, the poem fails to depict the poet's actual connection with the soil. The biological-cum-botanical imagery in "Song of the Son" recalls the trope of parthenogenesis in Toomer's correspondence with Frank, as well as Toomer's December 1922 letter to Sherwood Anderson in which, enthusing about Sparta, he declared, "my seed was planted in myself down there." Pressed into hard service in the poem's attempt to affirm metonymic nationalism through symbolic action, however, the organic trope assumes a hyper-materiality bordering on the grotesque. Even as the poet declares his oneness with the soil and its folk, a "split-gut song" threatens to heave upward from the poem's depths, scattering its "golden words" through the smoky dusk.[15]

Critics have often remarked on the blending of lyrical nostalgia and social critique in "Georgia Dusk and "Song of the Son." This admixture derives, I suggest, not simply from Toomer's desire to portray what he called, in both "Kabnis" and "The South in Literature," the "pain and beauty of the South," or from his writerly ambition to produce an "image saturated in its own lyricism" that would also convey "extra-artistic significance." The dialectical tension in these poems derives principally from the contradictory pressures of Toomer's felt need to treat Georgia at once as soil and region—inhabited by a folk as entitled as any other group to make a claim to national belonging—and as land and property—inhabited by a peasantry whose labor is the source of profits for those holding possession. In order to be incorporated within the program of Young America, all the folk needed to do was sing and be heard; in order to become actors in modernity, however, the peasantry needed to take steps to free themselves from the yoke of capital.

"O cant you see it?": "Karintha"

Scholarly commentary on the portraits of women in part 1 of *Cane* remains largely divided over the question of point of view: do these sketches participate in a sexist reification of Georgia's female folk, or do they contain a critique of the gendered constraints on their humanity? Do the sketches strain toward a pastoral notion of utopia or an ironic commentary on its impossibility? Routinely at stake in these debates is an assessment of the narratorial presence in the tales: does he stand in for the author of *Cane*, or do his assumptions and opinions invite ironization? I argue that the portraits of women in part 1 play out on the level of narrative the contradictory standpoint that in the lyrics is discernible as the antinomy between "golden words" and "split-gut song"; it is not authorial irony but the arrested dialectic of history that supplies the cognitive dissonance between competing modes of comprehension and representation. While the observing narrator attempts to equate women with the rhythms of the land, thereby restoring them to a pristine state prior to exploitation, his efforts at controlling the terms of their representation—signaled in part by his reliance on spherical form—result not in the recovery of a lost totality but in a denial of history. But as the text moves from the initial portraits—"Karintha," "Becky," "Carma," and "Fern"—to "Esther" and, finally, "Blood-Burning Moon," the exploitative social relations that have been largely occluded in the earlier stories return to the fore. As we shall see, it is no accident that "Esther" features a shopkeeper's daughter who lives across the street from a notions shop, or that the last story situates its climactic action in the ruins of an antebellum cotton factory. Cotton returns to the fore, albeit multiply mediated by its migration through various processes of production and exchange.[16]

In a number of African American magazines of the early twentieth century, covers featuring portraits of women conventionally signaled the politics and aesthetics informing the magazine's editorial stance. The women pictured on *Crisis* covers were predictably middle-class in aura. Even in magazines associated with the political left, such as the *Messenger* and the *Crusader*, the featured women were domestic, charming, unassuming, and pure: model mothers of the race. Toomer's placement of the transgressive Karintha on the front cover of *Cane* signals his critique of the puritanical politics routinely accompanying the depiction of the ideal race-woman. We should recall Nathan and Natalie's performance of "Karintha" in *Natalie Mann*, where—by linking Karintha's murder of her unwanted child with Mertis Newbolt's death from a back-alley abortion—the prose poem underlines the play's feminist call for access to birth control. In both *Natalie Mann* and subsequently in *Cane*, the sketch's nonjudgmental portrayal of Karintha's actions and choices points to the continuing influence of the capital city women who had encouraged Toomer's early literary efforts. The infanticide particularly brings to mind Mary Burrill's treatment of poor rural women's subjection to unwanted pregnancy in "They That Sit in Darkness." Indeed, the assertion that Karintha's premature "ripening" had been affected by her growing up in a two-room cabin where she witnessed her parents' lovemaking specifically recalls the discussion of familial poverty and cramped space that accompanied the publication of Burrill's play in the special issue on Negro women of the *Birth Control Review*. The reference to young men leaving town for college and running stills to give her money indicates, moreover, that Karintha early learned the value of her sexuality as a measure of exchange value; she was not powerless in her interactions with the men hungering to hasten her maturity. And while the race of the father of Karintha's baby can only be guessed, her determination to murder it suggests that its father may well have been white. Running illegal stills could have been undertaken by both blacks and whites, but attending college away from home was not a likely activity for the great majority of Sempter's young men of African descent: Karintha may have been "ripened too soon" by the scion of a wealthy white family. These are not the kinds of characterizing details ordinarily accompanying the portraits of race women in African American magazine culture.[17]

Even as the narratorial presence in "Karintha" gestures toward the contemporaneous social conditions shaping her limited options, however, he—for he is emphatically, if implicitly, male—insists upon equating her with the natural

THE CRUSADER

JANUARY, 1921   *15 CENTS A COPY*

Figure 8. Cover, *Crusader*, January 1921. Image typical of the portrayal of women on the covers of African American periodicals in the 1910s and 1920s.

world. She is compared with a landscape (her skin is "like dusk on the eastern horizon"), a wild creature ("a black bird that flashes in light"), a botanical phenomenon ("innocently lovely as a November cotton flower"; "a growing thing ripened too soon"). In the narrator's imagination, Karintha is removed from history and reprojected as nature—whence she can be re-reprojected yet again as an embodiment of folk culture. Converted into smoke that "curls up and hangs in odd wraiths about the trees . . . and spreads itself out over the valley," her child's burning corpse inspires "[s]ome one" to "make up a song"—to call on the smoke to "rise / And take my soul to Jesus." The sketch's spherical form further encloses Karintha's story within the poet-narrator's substitution of first nature processes occurring beyond human agency for second nature processes stemming from the impress of human labor on the land:

> Her skin is like dusk on the eastern horizon,
> O cant you see it, O cant you see it
> Her skin is like dusk on the eastern horizon
> . . . When the sun goes down.

Although Karintha's life has been plotted through its various phases (childhood, pubescence at age twelve, maternity at age twenty), the poet-narrator's repeated tribute to her beauty contains the tragic diachrony of her experience within the lyrical synchrony of his redemptive vision, which restores her oneness with the rhythms of the cosmos.[18]

As in "Georgia Dusk" and "Song of the Son," however, the poet-narrator's hyper-material lyricism turns back on itself. The "wraithlike" smoke that ascends from Karintha's burning baby at once inspires the folk hymn to Jesus and pollutes the water supply; the baby's burial in the "pyramidal sawdust pile" affirms both its connection with an ancestral past and its anonymous absorption into the detritus of a modern industrial labor process. In this opening sketch of *Cane*, the poet-narrator is looking for a buried culture, one that will link ancient pyramids with southern Negro folk practices and support the claim that this culture—and its practitioners—can participate on equal terms in the project of sectional art. He urges, "O cant you see it?" But he finds, instead, a buried baby, a ruined environment, and a foreclosed future.

Although "Karintha" makes no reference to events occurring beyond a small town in Georgia, its principal images suggest the possibility of broader historical allegory. As we have seen, the association of revolution with pregnancy and birthing, as well as with dawn in the Soviet East, was commonplace in the discourse of both conservatives and leftists. While Winston Churchill had promoted the postwar Allied invasion of the USSR as an attempt to strangle the Bolshevik baby in its cradle, Waldo Frank had written of the Russian Revolution as the "new world [that] had risen . . . in the East where the Old World had first gone down." Babette Deutsch had written in "Petrograd" of the "impatient and impeded birth" of the Russian Revolution. Claude McKay, combining the tropes of parturition and dawn, had written that "[i]n the East the clouds grow crimson with the new dawn that is breaking, / For the new birth rends the old earth and the very dead are waking, / Ghosts are turned flesh, throwing off the grave's disguise." But writers and artists acquainted with the crisis of birthing and nurturing specifically experienced by African American women had continually directed attention to the death-dealing power of racism. In the opening sketch of *Cane*, the narrator's assertion that Karintha's baby "fell out" replicates Layman's statement that Mame Lamkins's baby "fell out" when she was sliced open by her attackers. The narrator's insistence upon seeing in Karintha's beauty a reflection of dusk rather than dawn on the eastern horizon further dissociates her from the genesis of a new phase of history. So long as the fires of lynching and infanticide prevail, the Jim Crow South will not witness the birth of the New Negro, let alone the arrival of the epoch of world revolution; revenging ghosts will not turn flesh. Both the death of Karintha's baby and the coercive pressures of spherical form signal the arrested dialectic of historical process.[19]

"November Cotton Flower," paired with "Karintha" through its echo of the preacher's nickname for Karintha, obliquely invokes the "raw hillside" of history lurking behind the rhetoric of lyrical transcendence. The sonnet's octave describes a waste land: the weevil and the drought have destroyed the land's capacity to bear fruit; dead birds fall into wells and pollute the water supply. The sestet proclaims that, against all odds, an out-of-season blossom appears, equated with a bold and beautiful woman: "Brown eyes that loved without a trace of fear / Beauty so sudden for that time of year." This phrasing suggests that even if the flower will not produce a boll worthy of harvesting, ginning, and baling, its unexpected blossoming is a redemptive gift from the natural world. Yet, on careful scrutiny, the poem reveals that the flower's appearance "assumed . . . significance"; it is "superstition" that imagines the lovely brown eyes and witnesses the appearance of "[b]eauty so sudden for that time of year" (4). The metonymical association of the flower with the woman is, it turns out, an arbitrary invention, not an essence always already embedded in the soil, waiting to be discovered. As in "Karintha," the signifying chain linking woman with land is a fragile one.[20]

Toomer had perhaps an additional motivation for putting on the cover of *Cane* this portrait of a woman "ripened too soon." For the sketch's prominent placement also permits Toomer's "dark sister" Mamie Toomer—at the age of twelve the intended object of premature "ripening" by her adult stepbrother Charles Dickson—to preside over *Cane*'s gallery of female portraits. In *Natalie Mann*, we will recall, the names of Nathan Toomer and Amanda America Dickson haunt the dramatis personae; the words "Nathan" and "kin" are anagrammatically combined in "Karintha." If we add to the mix Toomer's statement that "Kabnis is me," the wordplay associating Karintha with both her creator and his oddly named artist-hero reinforces the assertion, "Nathan is kin." Further connections among "Kabnis," "Karintha," and "November Cotton Flower" are suggested in the resemblance between the woman with the "[b]rown eyes that loved without a trace of fear" and Carrie Kate Halsey, who, on first seeing Lewis, "fearlessly loves" into his eyes. In "Kabnis," Toomer takes care to preserve Carrie Kate's chastity; he keeps her in the cellar of history. But his placing at the very outset of *Cane* this portrait of a violated girl turned into a murdering mother suggests Toomer's abiding preoccupation with the predatory sexual practices, inherited from the era of slavery, that had shaped the tragic outcome of the marriage between Nathan Toomer and Amanda America Dickson. Particularly if Karintha killed her baby because its father was a member of the plantation-owning class, the possible link between Karintha and Mamie becomes more provocative still. As an avatar of Toomer's "dark sister," Karintha embodies a history that hurts—and haunts—but cannot be given direct expression in the text. The reader is teased, however, to look more closely: "Cant you see it?"[21]

"The true word of it": "Becky"

"Karintha" is told from the standpoint of an observer who evades identification as a first-person narrator. Although the text strains under the pressure of its contradictory symbolic acts, the narratorial voice cannot be clearly distinguished from the authorial presence; the text's overdetermined deployment of natural tropes to describe Karintha carries the stamp of authorial author-ity. The next three sketches in Toomer's gallery of female portraits are related by "I"-narrators who play increasingly prominent roles in the tales that they tell. Making his debut in "Becky," this first-person narrator opens and closes with a repeated prose lyric: "Becky was the white woman who had two Negro sons. She's dead; they've gone away. The pines whisper to Jesus. The Bible flaps its leaves with an aimless rustle on her mound." As he unfolds Becky's story, the narrator renders a stark portraiture of southern race relations. "Her eyes were sunken, her neck stringy, her breasts fallen": Becky evidently suffers from pellagra, a disease of the poor that—despite the Georgia Department of Health's denials—had become prevalent in the postwar economic downturn. He replicates the prejudicial language by which she is "cast out" by both whites—who dismiss her as a "[c]ommon, God-forsaken, insane white shameless wench"—and blacks—who view her as a "[p]oor Catholic poor-white crazy woman." The narrator notes that Becky has been placed, in a classically scapegoating gesture, in a flimsy cabin with a brick chimney (contributed by John Stone, who "owned the lumber and the bricks," and built by Lonnie Deacon) on an "islanded," "eye-shaped" piece of ground, between the railroad tracks and the highway, which has been supplied by the "railroad boss." She assumes increasingly magical powers in the eyes of others—people toss "little crumpled slips of paper scribbled with prayer" out of the "blue-sheen God" of the passing train—even though, as the years pass, she disappears from view, the "thin wraith of smoke" above her cabin the only sign of her continuing presence.

The text contains unattributed fragments of prayer—"O pines, whisper to Jesus; tell Him to come and press sweet Jesus-lips against their lips and eyes"—as well as Becky's thoughts on receiving food and snuff from neighbors and old David Georgia's gift of cane syrup: "O thank y Jesus." In the story's climactic scene, the narrator and Barlo, riding past her cabin one Sunday to the "listless and heavy" tolling of the Ebenezer Church bell, see the chimney fall in and think that they hear a groan. Barlo tosses his Bible on the collapsed pile of bricks; when they reach Sempter, "folks crowded round to get the true word of it" (5–7). The text's spherical form suggests at once the reifying social categories to which Becky is confined and the immanent spirituality of a natural world beyond reification.[22]

In its sociological register, "Becky" offers a near-Marxist parable of the role played by raced and gendered scapegoating, as well as religious false consciousness, in maintaining the hegemony of the owning class. The poor-white woman who has transgressed the ultimate racial taboo binds Sempter's residents, black and white alike, to the dominant ideology that would persuade them of her sinfulness. While her impoverished condition is surely shared by others, black and white, her scapegoating precludes a class-based multiracial resistance to the existing social hierarchy. A trans-class and trans-race male bonding further effects Becky's ostracism. The town's white ruling elite supply the materials and land for Becky's cabin; black men associated with organized Christianity build the cabin (the aptly named Lonnie Deacon) and ritually grieve its collapse (Barlo). Folk superstitions—the scribbled prayers, the fears of the "bluesheen god"—reinforce the power of the church; the animistic Jesus of the pines cannot alleviate the distress of Becky and her mixed-race offspring. The original publication of "Becky" in the *Liberator* reinforced its Marxist elements. Giving the name "John Towne" to John Stone, Toomer here emphasizes the suturing role of ideology in the collective scapegoating of Becky. The closing image of the Bible on Becky's living tomb resonates with the magazine's recent publication of Mike Gold's comparison of Lenin with Christ. "The Russian Bolsheviks will leave the world a better place than Jesus left it," wrote Gold. "They will leave it on the threshold of the final victory—the poor will have bread and peace and culture in another generation, not churches and a swarm of lying parasite minister dogs, the legacy of Jesus."[23]

In a reading stressing the critique of ideology in "Becky," the first-person narrator is clearly complicit in Becky's ostracism. Identifying with the town's prejudices, he notes of Becky's sons, "We, who had cast out their mother, could we take them in?" Acceding to local superstitions, he thinks that he hears a "ghost-train" rumble by when Becky's chimney collapses; he appears unaware of the train's role in transporting Sempter's agricultural products to market or migrants to the North. Given his failure to investigate whether or not Becky has survived the collapse of her cabin, the narrator is hardly equipped to deliver the "true word" of her death. His invocation of the whispering pines obfuscates but cannot hide the social reality of Jim Crow, which has descended on her like a ton of bricks.

But the cameo role played by David Georgia makes it difficult to read "Becky" as a consistently materialist critique of ideologically driven scapegoating. While the syrup he bestows on Becky, having little nutritional value, will not cure her pellagra, his gift giving is paralleled, not contrasted, with the cabin building by the town's bosses. His surname, moreover, signals the discourse of sectional art. Just as "Georgia Dusk" proposes that the lumber workers "making folk songs from soul sounds" embody the essence of soil and region, David Georgia, as "genius loci"—"some genius of the South"—embodies the utopian possibility that Sempter, riven as it may be along lines of class and race, can transcend its antagonisms and contribute its folkish mote to the spiritual unity of the nation. "Becky" at once contains a critique of the brutality enacted in Georgia and mutes this critique: just as ideology sutures the community, the ideologeme of sectional art, reinforced by the text's spherical form, mediates between a harsh social reality and the enclosing imagery of whispering pines. There is no clearly articulated "true word of it."[24]

"Time and space have no meaning in a cane field": "Carma"

Like "Karintha" and "Becky," "Carma is framed by a brief lyric:
> Wind is in the cane. Come along.
> Cane leaves swaying, rusty with talk,
> Scratching choruses above the guinea's squawk,
> Wind is in the cane. Come along.

Where the "Karintha" narrator lacks bodily presence and the "Becky" narrator remains largely in the background, the man who paints Carma's portrait is a distinct character in his own story. A northerner seeking belonging in the male peer group gathered around the cane kettle, the narrator in "Carma" tells of a woman with a "mangrove-gloomed, yellow flower face" whose tale, he asserts, is "the crudest melodrama." "Strong as any man," Carma in her wagon is a "[n]igger woman driving a Georgia chariot" down the Dixie Pike; the narrator "leave[s] the men around the stove to follow her with [his] eyes" as the sun "shoots primitive rockets" across her face. He addresses a man "cradled" on a mule as "black boy . . . you are the most sleepiest man I ever seed, Sleeping Beauty"; moved by the voice of a woman who sings a "sad strong song," the narrator fantasizes an archetypal black woman: "Pungent and composite, the smell of farmyards is the fragrance of the woman. She does not sing; her body is a song. She is in the forest, dancing. Torches flare . . . juju men, greegree, witch-doctors . . . torches go out. . . . The Dixie Pike has grown from a goat path in Africa." Once he stops daydreaming and gets back to Carma, the narrator quickly relates her story. Her husband, Bane, temporarily a wage laborer on the railroad, was away; she "had others." He, returning, became jealous; she grabbed a gun and rushed to a cane field, where, the narrator remarks, "Time and space have no meaning." Carma fired the gun; Bane gathered a search party; she was discovered to have faked the attempted suicide; he slashed the man who found her. "Now he's in the gang," comments the narrator. "Who was her husband. Should she not take others, this Carma, strong as a man, whose tale as I have told it is the crudest melodrama?" (10–11). The repeated characterization of Carma's story as "melodrama" calls attention to the voice making this claim: who is he, and what are we to think of his assumptions and assertions?[25]

The "Carma" narrator has invited a range of responses. In one reading, his prophetic assertion that "[t]ime and space have no meaning in a canefield"—at times conjoined with the invocation of "oracular . . . deep-rooted cane" in the epigraph to *Cane*—expresses Toomer's own mysticism. Linked with the chanting workers' "race memories of . . . king and caravan" in "Georgia Dusk," the narrator's association of the invisible singing woman with an imagined woman dancing in the forest, surrounded by flaring torches and "juju men, greegree, witch-doctors," reflects Toomer's own curiosity about the African roots of Negro folk culture. The description of Carma's wagon as a "Georgia chariot" situates her in both premodern transnationalism and present-day American regionalism; the reader is invited to "come along" in forging a vital connection between the Dixie Pike and a "goat path in Africa."[26]

Yet it is difficult to overlook the markedly primitivist view of southern black folks in general, and black women in particular, that is signaled in the spectatorial stance of the "Carma" narrator. His notion that the sun "shoots primitive rockets" after Carma barely disguises his phallic interest; his recognition that she is "strong as any man" does not lead him to be curious about the work she performs. Indeed, along with the men around the stove—who presumably furnish his information about Carma, and who may number among her past lovers—he is an unabashed voyeur. His assertion that the woman dancing in the forest has a "farmyard . . . smell" is all the more remarkable because she exists only in his imagination. His proclamation that Carma has the right to "take others" is belied by his conclusion that Bane's ending up on the gang after slashing another man is "her fault." His penchant for exotic fantasy extends beyond Carma and the forest dancer to the man on the mule, whom he feminizes as a "Sleeping Beauty" presumably awaiting arousal from his feudalistic slumber. The narrator's vision of torchlit "juju men, greegree, witch-doctors," with its incantation of repeated-syllabic words, suggests a "mumbo-jumbo" view African culture even more syncretic than the vision of pyramids, high priests, and juju men in "Georgia Dusk." Although the crisis in Carma and Bane's marriage is precipitated by conditions of wage labor—on the road he presumably works for the same "railroad boss" who paid for the construction of Becky's cabin—the narrator sees only a sleepy man on a mule and calls on his listeners to hear animistic voices in the wind-blown leaves and squawking birds. Indeed, the imitation of Negro dialect in narrator's description of the man on the mule as "the most sleepiest man I ever seed" suggests his rhetorical debt to the plantation school of literature. The discursive assumptions of the narrator of "Carma" are central to both the how and the what of the tale's act of representation.[27]

That the author invites the reader to scrutinize the standpoint from which "Carma" has been told is suggested by the narrator's closing attempt at self-correction: "Should she not take others, this Carma, strong as a man, whose tale *as I have told it* is the crudest melodrama?" (emphasis added). Even the narrator intuits that his account may have imposed popular literary conventions on a tragedy at once personal and social. That Toomer himself did not wholly subscribe to his narrator's view that "time and space have no meaning in a canefield" is indicated, moreover, by his scribbling in his Sparta notebook that he felt "vexed and irritated" that the "wind in the corn" and "dry October leaves talking" confined their "whisperings" to the "now": they "give heed neither to that soil of a past hundred years ago, nor to the rolling land that lost itself far, far to westward. And, of course, in a region where corn is the only voice, for life I had to seek by turns the past and future." Skeptical of the illusion of timelessness, the Toomer who in the fall of 1921 stood in a Hancock Country cornfield—not, we might note, a cane field—appears not to have shared his narrator's rhapsodic view of southern laborers as a beautiful sleeping folk cut off from the economic relations of modernity, in need of awakening by the kiss of the visiting poet-hero. Indeed, the temporal connection that Toomer imagines is not to eternity but to a hundred years before, when bonded African labor would have harvested the corn; while the geographical connection he seeks is not to the cosmos but to the expanding western frontier which, in the previous century, was thought to mark the limitless potential for the extension of slavery throughout the United States. Where the "Carma" narrator thinks in terms of abstract space and time, Toomer—at least in his original encounter with the cornfields of Hancock County—thinks in terms of place and history. The distinction is not a minor one.[28]

For all his ahistorical proclivities, however, the narrator of "Carma" cannot simply be seen as the object of ironic distancing, if only because the notion of irony presupposes a stable scale of values against which a given utterance can be assessed. Like the persona in "Georgia Dusk," he is eager to view Georgia's peasantry as bearers of an African cultural legacy, even if this means ignoring—or at least minimizing—their identity as workers. Like the narrators in "Karintha" and "Becky," he struggles to enclose the contradictions of the tale he tells within the coercive lyricism of spherical form. Preoccupied with the task of creating a sectional art, the Toomer who composed "Carma" in the spring of 1922 was casting around for a set of second-order mediations that would permit him to defuse the antagonism between the peasantry and the owners of the land so prominent in "Kabnis." That the quest for a revised explanatory paradigm required him to reconfigure the terms in which he originally encountered the Deep South is displayed in his subtle reworking of the impressions recorded in his 1921 notebook.

Toomer's avoidance of an encounter with the harsher features of Jim Crow is further indicated in his decision not to develop for inclusion in *Cane* a poetic fragment possibly written in Georgia:

> Beside a gully,
> A grey and red clay gully
> On a Georgia road,
> Convicts, black and white,
> And stripes themselves but for the feet
> They do not alternate
> Convicts, beside a gully
> A grey and red clay gully
> On a Georgia road.

This imagistic fragment portrays the red clay soil as the site of hard labor; the repetition of the phrase "on a Georgia road" points to the role of prison labor in constructing the Deep South's road system. The poem stresses, moreover, the class character of the segregated chain gang system: black and white convicts may not be "alternated," but they are largely indistinguishable in their striped black and white uniforms. In "Carma," Bane's hard labor on the chain gang is left to the imagination. Had this poem—perhaps titled "Convicts"—been added to the cluster of poems in part 1 dealing with labor and the land, the "Carma" narrator's inclination to transcend time and space, and to view Carma and Bane's story as "melodrama," might have met a forcible challenge from the realm of the Real.[29]

"I could hear only her song": "Fern"

Of all the portraits of women featured in part 1 of *Cane*, "Fern" engages in the fullest equation of women with the folk, the folk with the soil, and the soil with the region; the ideologeme of metonymic nationalism patently guides the narrator's retrospective representation of the story's title character. When he introduces Fern's physiognomy, the narrator insistently deploys images of flowing water: "Face flowed into her eyes" in "soft cream foam and plaintive ripples"; the "whole countryside seemed to flow into her eyes"; the "curves of her profile" are "like "mobile rivers" flowing to a "common delta." Signifying her capacity geographically to embody the region where she lives, the fluids that flow through Fern also signify her oneness with its soil and trees. When she goes into a fit during a walk with the narrator down the canebrake to the stream, her body is "tortured with something it could not let out," something like "boiling sap" that "flooded arms and fingers till she shook them as if they burned her." The narrator recalls: "Dusk hid her; I could hear only her song. It seemed to me as though she were pounding her head in anguish upon the ground" (14–17). More completely than any other woman in *Cane*, Fern *is* the South, and the northern narrator's attempt to know her signifies his attempt to connect with the geographical site of his origins.[30]

The word "Georgia" appears more frequently in "Fern" than in any other sketch. Fern's face recalls the "listless cadence of Georgia's South"; the narrator recalls, "I felt strange, as I always do in Georgia, particularly at dusk. . . . It would not have surprised me had I had vision. People have them in Georgia more often than you might suppose." Yet Fern also contains in her genetic heritage that most cosmopolitan of all U.S. ethnic groups, the Jews. Noting that "[h]er nose was aquiline, Semitic," the narrator recalls that "at first sight of her I felt as if I heard a Jewish cantor sing . . . [a]s if his singing rose above the unheard chorus of a folk-song." Her name, we are told at the story's end, is "Fernie May Rosen"—a name that approximates "Fern May-Flower," thereby suggesting at once her foreign roots and her claim to belonging on the nation's soil. Constituting a counter-discourse to the central claims of nativists (churning racial waters being the key trope in Lothrop Stoddard's *The Rising Tide of Color*, and the "Jew" being Mary Austin's *bête noire*), Fern's genealogy and description suggest that she embodies Toomer's revision of Frank's *Our America*, as well as the multiculturalist vision set forth in Randolph Bourne's "Trans-National America."[31]

Even as Toomer's narrator makes a compelling bid for Fern's metonymic nationalist status, however, he betrays the preoccupations of an identity-seeking cultural tourist. Before he has heard her utter a sound, Fern's "Jewish" profile leads him to imagine not just a Jewish cantor singing, but also "the unheard chorus of a folk-song": he is not only conflating culture with biology but also—like the narrator in "Carma"—doing a good deal of listening with the inner ear that he brought to Georgia from points north. When Fern disappoints him with her raspy singing, he shifts to botanical imagery to describe her painful gyrations as her body becomes "flooded" with "boiling sap." His insistence upon viewing Fern through lenses supplied by the organic trope prevents him from seeing that her very rootedness to the ground—her location in the political economy of Jim Crow—is not the remedy but the source of her misery. The song that he hears is cacophonous because it does not conform to his expectations of folk authenticity. Noting her habitual sitting on her porch along the Dixie Pike with her head tilted to avoid the nail driven into a post, he attributes her inactivity to indolence. What he appears not to recognize is that, like another famous Jew, she has been nailed to a cross—in this case the cross of the Real, the history that hurts.[32]

As with the narrators in "Karintha" and "Carma," the "Fern"-narrator's masculinist standpoint cannot be separated from his exotic conception of the folk in relation to the land. What sets "Fern" apart from the other portraits of women, however, is the sketch's foregrounding of its own strategies of mediation. The woman does not merely invite comparison with the land; she *is* the land. The woman is not merely like a flower, a piece of fruit: she *is* a tree. As in "Song of the Son," metonymic nationalism pressures the sketch's hyper-material imagery to the point where "golden words" become coercive, even violent. Small wonder that fire intrudes on the organic trope through the image of boiling sap: the liquid that David Georgia tends with care here burns Fern from within, compelling her utterance of a "split-gut song." Although the narrator's voyeuristic preoccupation with Fern is similar to that exhibited by the narrators of "Karintha" and "Carma," his predatory behavior signals his complicity in Jim Crow sexual mores with a long and oppressive history. He continually asserts "something I would do for her" and expresses concern that she not move to a "southern town where white men are more aggressive" and she could "become a white man's concubine." Yet he appears oblivious to the fact that his own sexually aggressive behavior—"[f]rom force of habit, I suppose, I held Fern in my arms"—is what prompts Fern's presumably incomprehensible outburst. He assumes that the reader he addresses throughout the tale is a man and in closing passes along her name to men both black and white, presumably wishing them better luck in sexual conquest. The ease with which he proposes that Fern is best left where she is—what business would she have in a Harlem tenement, or even married to a northern doctor or a lawyer?—testifies, moreover, to his writerly investment in viewing this woman as an embodiment of the Georgia soil. "Better that she listen to folk-songs by dusk in Georgia, you would say, and so would I," he declares. He does not to want her to become part of the project of modernity that northward migration would entail; he is comfortable with—indeed, comforted by—her position, geographical, historical and symbolic, in the rural dusk. Sufficiently cosmopolitan to valorize Fern's hybridity, the narrator cannot imagine she might herself participate in the formation of a cosmopolitan future. The nail on her porch thus signifies not only the Real, but also the discursive categories through which he has chosen to mediate the Real. Fern is as much a victim of the narrator's fantasies as she is of Georgia's sharecropping economy.[33]

As with the other male narrators encountered in part 1 of *Cane*, however, it is difficult to subject the "Fern" narrator to consistent ironization. In his decision to feature the indolent, sensual Fern as an embodiment of "the South," the narrator is, like his creator, an opponent of the puritanical Negro magazine convention. But where the prophetic voice heard in "Georgia Dusk" chants of giving "virgin lips to cornfield concubines," the "Fern" narrator himself participates in the very pattern of oppressive male behavior that has led Fern to reject the embrace of men and "become a virgin"; his reconfiguration of rejection as a recovery of original virginity takes shape as a distinctly male rationalization. And while the gendered nature of this exploitation is patent, the narrator's narcissistic limitations imply a broader commentary on the limitations of any sectional art that would substitute cultural tourism for an encounter with political economy. Noting that "[a] black woman once saw the mother of Christ and drew her in charcoal on the courthouse wall," the narrator concludes from this incident that "[w]hen one is on the soil of one's ancestors, most anything can come to one." His absorption of the unknown black woman's representational gesture into his own mystical matrix is self-serving: that she may have had other motivations in sketching that picture on that wall is beyond his ken. To the extent that he remains unaware of the dehumanizing effects of his speculative standpoint, then, the narrator embodies the complicity of the North in the continuing subjugation of the South; of art in acceding to an oppressive social order. If *Cane* is to prefigure the contribution of the New Negro to "our America," it will have to feature another kind of consciousness, another kind of practice.

"T give birth t you an me": "Esther"

"Esther" and "Blood-Burning Moon," the two stories in part 1 of *Cane* that Toomer wrote after his trip to South Carolina with Frank in the fall of 1922, constitute a significant formal and thematic departure from the earlier prose sketches. The presence of the artist-narrator is effaced; to varying degrees, the women characters are endowed with thoughts and emotions of their own. The organic trope is increasingly challenged as a means of metonymically proclaiming the linkage of the people with the land; instead, alienated labor is brought to the fore. These two stories are, moreover, distinctly aligned with identifiable national and world events: although the earlier portraits of women have gestured in passing toward contemporaneous social realities, in "Esther" and "Blood-Burning Moon" Sempter enters the world of historical time. Toomer mused to Frank that, of all the pieces in *Cane*, "Karintha" and "Fern" come "nearest to the old Negro, to the spirit saturate with folk-song. . . . the dominant emotion is a sadness derived from a sense of fading, from a knowledge of my futility to check solution. There is nothing about these pieces of the buoyant expression of a new race." While Toomer would postpone his full portrayal of the "new race" to part 2, there is no nostalgia in "Esther" and "Blood-Burning Moon." Modernity has come to the South: the question is, what form is it taking, and what forces is it unleashing?[34]

In "Esther"—the only story in part 1 set wholly in the town of Sempter—the organic trope continues to connect female sexuality with the fruits of the land; here, however, it functions to signal absence, not presence. By contrast with the magnetically sexual Karintha, Carma and Fern, the almost-white Esther has cheeks that are "flat and dead"; at sixteen, she has hair "like the full silk on puny corn ears," and her face "pales until it is the color of the gray dust that dances with dead cotton leaves" (20, 23). When, at twenty-seven, she ventures out on her one and only quest for sexual experience, she fears being aroused by the "peculiar phosphorescent glitter of the sweet-gum leaves" (24). These imagistic comparisons are, however, relatively incidental to the story, which principally traces the denial of emotion and sexuality to commodification and class hierarchy. Going beyond Frank's straightforward association of whiteness with repression and blackness with desire in *Holiday*—which Toomer was reading in manuscript around the time when he wrote "Esther"—the text traces Esther's inner deadness not so much to her "high-yellow" complexion or separation from the soil as to the estrangement resulting from her isolated social status as the daughter of Sempter's richest Negro store owner. Intraracial bigotry and the predominance of the exchange relation are shown to be inseparable.[35]

Fire imagery, up to this point a minor presence in the sketches of part 1, is central to the political analysis embedded in "Esther." The sun that brought out the dusky glow in Fern's and Karintha's skins now reflects off the flaming windows of McGregor's notion shop. When Esther fantasizes that loafing men squirt gallons of tobacco juice onto a raging fire, giving her a "[b]lack, woolly tobacco-juice baby" (22) that she takes to her breast, her repressed sexuality is linked with her repressed identification with the dark-skinned tobacco-chewing masses. In her final encounter with Barlo, the fire of desire is explicitly traced to class guilt: "As if her veins are full of fired sun-bleached southern shanties, a swift heat sweeps them. Dead dreams, and a forgotten resolution are carried upward by the flames" (24). Where Fern is beset by the boiling sap in her veins, the fire burning inside Esther alludes to the sites of rural poverty from which her family earns its income. That the shanties are said to be "fired," too, hints at the collective punishment to which black communities were not infrequently subjected in retaliation for some presumed individual transgression. Social violence on a larger scale lurks in the background.

Although "Karintha" makes mention of its title character at different ages, "Esther" is alone in *Cane* for its division into sections corresponding to different points in Esther's life; these enable the reader to track the trajectories of both Esther and Barlo. Toomer appears to have borrowed from Sherwood Anderson's "Adventure," a short story in *Winesburg, Ohio*, the device of mapping a character's emotional development into distinct phases, but Toomer deploys these for both psychoanalytical and political purposes. The final segment, when Esther is twenty-seven, takes place sometime after the war, during which Barlo had become rich through sales on the cotton market. If we assume that this final segment coincides approximately with Toomer's visit to Sparta in 1921, then, dating backward, we can determine that Esther was born in 1894; the first scene, occurring when Esther is seven, would be set in 1903. In this scene, Barlo—here named "King Barlo"—assumes heroic stature: dominating the town square, he preaches about a "big an black an powerful" African dragged into slavery by "little white-ant biddies": "They led him to th coast, they led him t the sea, they led him across th ocean an they didnt set him free. The old coast didnt miss him, an th new coast wasnt free, he left th old-coast brothers, t give birth t you and me" (21). While arousing envy and fear among the town's elites, "King Barlo" inspires a woman of holy reputation to create a picture of the Black Madonna on the courthouse wall. The next segment, set in 1910 and depicting the sixteen-year-old Esther's fantasy about the black baby, does not involve Barlo directly, although the dream's patent eroticism stems from her yearning to have sex with him. The next passage occurs when Esther is twenty-two, in 1916. Barlo, we learn, is the town's alpha male: the best lover, the best fighter, the best gambler, the best cotton picker for miles around—as well as, still, a "vagrant preacher" (23). In the closing postwar segment, Barlo has metamorphosed into a rich businessman who rides around in a big open car; once again calling himself King Barlo, he patronizes prostitutes at the local speakeasy. Although there is no mention of his having any religious affiliation, this is presumably the same Barlo who tosses his Bible onto the ruins of Becky's cabin.[36]

What are we to make of this careful sequencing of the stages of Esther's development? The text suggestively registers Toomer's historical awareness of religiously inflected black nationalist movements. The King Barlo who appears in 1903, denouncing the "white-ant biddies" and inspiring the courthouse wall artwork, recalls the itinerant proponents of the Black Christ who roamed the South in the late nineteenth and early twentieth centuries. While Garveyism would not be a force in the rural South until the late 1910s, the poetic rhetoric deployed by "King Barlo" in 1903 quite precisely replicates key features of the verses that appeared in Garvey's *Negro World*. In particular, the rhymes in his poem-sermon call to mind the poetry of Ethel Trew Dunlap, whose meditations on the redemption of Africa made frequent use of "sea," "free," and "me." While Toomer the experimental modernist would have had little use for conventional versifying of this kind, Barlo's heroic portrait of the mighty African subdued by "white-ant biddies" indicates Toomer's acquaintance with the Afrocentric poetry typically published in the *Negro World*. Markedly different in tone and implication from the culturalist references to Africa elsewhere in part 1 of *Cane*—goat paths, juju men, greegree bushes, high priests sporting ostrich feathers—this image of the "big an black an powerful" African dragged into enslavement reconfigures Africa as a key site of the primitive accumulation of capital. Esther's desire to be immaculately impregnated with Barlo's child, moreover, suggests Toomer's acquaintance with the Black Madonna in the discourse of Garveyism, where she was figured as the mother of a Black Messiah of pan-Africanist origin. Although the Garvey movement did not explicitly link itself with Christianity, the Black Madonna and the Black Messiah were featured prominently in its formulation of the New Negro. The sanctified woman's act of drawing the Black Madonna on the courthouse wall, treated by the narrator in "Fern" as an instance of inscrutable southern mysticism, in this historical context takes shape as a politically inspired gesture signaling the need for liberation from the supremacy of the "white-ant biddies." This Black Madonna will, perhaps, "give birth t you and me."[37]

But Barlo's subsequent appearances in "Esther" intimate the rise, decline and fall of not just a man but a historical movement. When he appears in 1916, Barlo is a hard worker, high liver, and "vagrant preacher"—just the kind of rank-and-file militant for whom Garveyism had its distinct appeal, in small towns of the South as well as the larger metropoles where the movement rapidly grew. Barlo's final appearance in 1921, however, marks his descent into corruption; he has metamorphosed into a war profiteer and patron of prostitutes. His reasserted pretension to royalty suggests the self-aggrandizing fraudulence surrounding Garvey's public image as he gained in power and notoriety, even as he routinely castigated as "dictie" his critics in other parts of the New Negro Movement. Toomer's critique of the sell-out preacher is reiterated in "Conversion," the poem immediately following "Esther," which describes a man of the cloth who has abandoned his "African guardian of souls" for the "weak palabra / Of a white-faced, sardonic god." During the fall of 1921 the black press was full of reports of Garvey's recent rapprochement with the Ku Klux Klan, with which he shared a commitment to complete racial segregation: the *Messenger* was especially merciless in pointing up Garvey's collusion with both white supremacists and union-busting capitalists. King Barlo has metamorphosed from an opponent of the "white-ant biddies" to their black counterpart; he has aligned himself with the gold-and-blood profiteers depicted in "Ghouls." Although the dialectic of revolution was arrested primarily by ruling-class repression, the New Negro was also betrayed, argued the black Marxists of the day, by the bourgeoisie in its own ranks. As Toomer had noted in "Banking Coal," the furnace of revolution was "banked" by those in "hooded nightcaps" and their various allies, "each in his way" contributing to the extinction of the fire.[38]

Toomer's mapping of Esther's tale into segments corresponding to phases in her psychic development links her blocked sexual desires and emotional needs with the public historical developments signaled in the transformation of Barlo. Her personal decline into madness is connected with her illusion that a Black Messiah will come and save her from her race- and class-based alienation. But this chronological mapping also permitted Toomer to trace a parallel history: his own. For it is a peculiar coincidence that Esther and her creator are exactly the same age. Like Esther, Toomer was born in 1894. Just as Esther is twenty-seven in the last phase of her tale, Toomer was twenty-seven when in 1921, living in Sparta, he visited the barbershop where he began to speculate about his father's prior marriage. In this autobiographical connection, certain details associated with Esther's story take on added resonance, historical, political, and psychological.[39]

In the longer version of "Conversion" that appeared in "Withered Skin of Berries," we will recall, the first stanza linked the treacherous preacher with the "courthouse tower" that served as "bell-buoy" to the "black barges" toiling along the river. Through its association of Barlo with the preacher in "Conversion," "Esther" displays the connections in Toomer's mind between the character of Barlo, organized Christianity, the exploitation of black labor, and the courthouse tower (where Kabnis imagines himself exposed to a mob "juggling justice and a nigger"). The crucial autobiographical link in this signifying chain—possibly suggesting Toomer's reason for making Esther the same age as himself—is the fact that it was Amanda America Dickson, the first wife of Toomer's father, who had funded the construction of the new Hancock County courthouse in a show of gratitude for the court ruling that enabled her to inherit her father's huge estate. Although the full text of the poem that David Teyy chants in "Withered Skin of Berries" does not appear in *Cane*, we can infer that Toomer associated the preacher of "Conversion," whom *Cane* clearly links with Barlo, with the legal system that safeguarded Amanda America Dickson's fortune while subjecting sharecroppers and debt peons to the rigors of post-Reconstruction Jim Crow. At about the same time—and at the same age—that Esther discovers the falsity of the myth she has built up around Barlo, moreover, Toomer was, it is highly probable, discovering the falsity of the myth that he had built up around his father. He was, after all, staying in Sparta, visiting Augusta on the weekends, patronizing the local businesses, and learning of his father's Sparta-based courtship of a wealthy woman of mixed race: as I argue in chapter 4, it is implausible that he did not make further inquiries about his father's second marriage to the famous Amanda America Dickson and follow the trail of thirty-year-old gossip. While Toomer may have modeled the structure of "Esther" on Anderson's "Adventure," his temporal mapping of Esther's psychological conflicts enabled him to limn comparable conflicts of his own.

We recall, too, that Carrie Kate Halsey—whose age associates her with Mamie Toomer—is described at the end of "Kabnis" as a Black Madonna. That a Black Madonna is transgressively sketched on the courthouse wall—in both "Fern" and "Esther"—suggests not only Toomer's interest in the public challenge to white supremacy posed by Afrocentric religion but also his private desires to align himself with his "dark sister" in defacing Sparta's premier monument to Jim Crow state power. It would appear that the troubled and troubling dynamics of class, gender, and race that surrounded Toomer's family romance continued to press on his consciousness as he moved toward the completion of *Cane*.

The expanded historical canvas of "Esther" is accompanied by—indeed, premised on—an expanded conception of the South as a site connected with global capital in its moments of production, consumption, and distribution. Not only has the allusion to the "white-ant biddies" capturing the magnificent African king pointed to the origin of the South's wealth in bonded black labor. In addition, Barlo has become rich through manipulating the machinations of wartime markets, profiting from the high price of cotton when foreign sources of supply were closed off. His car is thus not only a status symbol but a distillation of the congealed labor of Sempter's sharecroppers and tenant farmers. Esther's father, as the wealthiest Negro shopkeeper in town, has made his living from exchanging food commodities for the wages earned by the laborers in the surrounding plantations and sawmills; his profits too arise from the abstraction and exploitation of labor. We are told repeatedly, moreover, that Esther's sexual fantasies are fueled by the fiery glare of the sunset off the windows of McGregor's notion shop, where all the materials needed for sewing clothes—from patterns to thread to the cloth itself—are sold. Her face may be pale as "dead cotton leaves," but the dead labor stored in the cloth produced from those plants has been converted into a means of profitable exchange. The "original virginity" of the cotton picked on the plantations around Sparta has its symbolic analogue in the repressed virginity of the daughter of the town's richest Negro merchant.

"Their songs were cotton-wads to stop their ears": "Blood-Burning Moon"

"Blood-Burning Moon," the last and longest story in part 1 of *Cane*, continues the shift in emphasis, formal and thematic, begun in "Esther." The intrusive male narratorial presence of the earlier stories has disappeared; historical developments shape the characters' actions; the political economy of the South is displayed in its naked exploitation and embedded violence. The explicit description of a lynching—Kabnis's nightmare made flesh—returns the text to the felt immediacy of the closing section of *Cane*.[40]

At first glance the story seems built around a fairly straightforward pastoral dualism, one counterposing a thematic *combinatoire* comprising nature, the folk, and the soil with another comprising the machine, the factory, and white supremacist domination of the land. Louisa, the central female character, is insistently described through botanical images like those deployed in "Karintha," "Carma," and "Fern." Her skin is "the color of oak leaves on young trees in fall"; her breasts are "firm and up-pointed like ripe acorns"; her singing has "the low murmur of winds in fig trees": she is the Georgia countryside, replete with promise for harvest, a growing thing ripened not too soon. Her aura of autumnal fullness is enhanced by the omnipresent scent of boiling cane, which suffuses the landscape from the stove where David Georgia presides over the production of cane syrup as he regales other men with tales "about the white folks, about moonshining and cotton picking, and about sweet nigger gals." Cane has, it seems, the medicinal potential to drain off the burning passions of racism: when Bob Stone, beset by jealousy over Louisa and shame that his sexual competitor is a black laborer, throws himself down and "[digs] his fingers in the ground," the "[c]ane-roots [in the cool earth] [take] the fever from his hands." David Georgia's ritual production of cane syrup can be contrasted with the market-driven production of cotton embodied in Tom's competition with Barlo, as well as in the antebellum cotton factory where Tom meets his violent end. Tom's naturalness can be contrasted with the mob's mechanism: he "seem[s] rooted," whereas the lynch mob approaches in a "taut hum" and, with overwhelming "pressure and momentum . . . flatten[s] the Negroes beneath it."[41]

But a careful survey of the uses of the organic trope in "Blood-Burning Moon" hardly reveals a realm of first nature apart from history and human use. Louisa may have skin "the color of oak leaves" and breasts "like ripe acorns," but the cotton mill too is constructed of "solid hand-hewn beams of oak." Nature is always already material for industrial use and assimilated to the imperatives of private property; we may recall the oak stake separating the lands tilled by different sharecropping families in "Balo." Where the narrator in "Carma" would like to believe that "time and space have no meaning in a canefield," in "Blood-Burning Moon" the land is clearly owned: Tom Burwell longs to have his own farm, while Bob Stone, going to meet Louisa, has to pass through "old Lemon's canefield." Although Tom's destroyers are compared with tautly humming industrial machines, they are also described as a collective river, "divid[ing] and flow[ing]" around the ruins of the old factory: as in "Kabnis"'s revision of "Deep River," in the land of cotton rivers become sites not of transcendence over Jordan but of murder. Meanwhile, Tom's connection to the natural world hardly works to his benefit. As a landless black man working for "ol Stone," he has been bound to the land by terms of sharecropping that have prevented him from ownership of the soil that he tills. While "rooted" in place when the mob approaches, Tom is not a burnt tree trunk after the lynching, but a "blackened stone." As the "stone" walls of the ruined factory reverberate to the cries of his killers, he remains dominated to the end by the Stone family made rich through his labors. Rather than proposing a utopian alternative to the world of Jim Crow, the scent of cane that "drenches" the air becomes mixed with the "[s]tench of burning flesh." The macabre potential surrounding the description of "Negro slaves" in "Song of the Son"—"bursting in the pinewood air"—is realized; the "wraith" of Karintha's dead baby is once again flesh. Requiring the reader to abandon any hope of finding recourse in a realm exempt from social and historical processes, "Blood-Burning Moon" calls into question the naturalizing categories by means of which the narrators have mediated the relationship between people and the land in the first four sketches in *Cane*.[42]

Just as the scent of cane becomes implicated in the smoke rising from the lynching fire, the folk culture that is supposed to supply an antidote to suffering emerges as hardly uncontaminated by dominant ideology. The lyric that continually appears—"Red nigger moon. Sinner! / Blood-burning moon. Sinner! / Come out that fact'ry door"—carries dual signification. On the one hand, this apocalyptic apostrophe signals the religious beliefs enabling African Americans to endure the cruelties of slavery and Jim Crow; accompanied by ominous descriptions of the reddish moon hanging over the town, it invokes spirituals that contemplate the Day of Judgment. "In That Great Getting-Up Morning" contains the refrain,

> You see de world on fire,
> You see de moon a bleedin',
> See de stars a fallin',
> See de elements meltin'.

"Stars in the Elements" describes a time when "the moon drips away in blood, / And the ransomed of the Lord are returning home to God." The repeated address to a "sinner" is a mode of self-address, enabling the singer—like the first speaker featured in "Cotton Song"—to grapple with pain by taking upon himself moral responsibility, trusting in God to deliver cosmic justice in the end. On the other hand, Tom's joining in the chant to the moon indicates his accession to an immobilizing fatalism; while Louisa's participation cannot stave off the madness that overwhelms her upon Tom's death. The songs softly caroled by the townspeople are not just the residue of a slave past but integral to the New South's modernity. The songs are, the narrator observes, "cotton-wads to stop their ears": the crop forming the principal basis for the ongoing exploitation of black labor figures into its ongoing ideological formation. Where in "Georgia Dusk" song figures as an expression of vital communal culture, and in "Balo" it silences materialist critique, in "Blood-Burning Moon" it functions to root the folk in a soil they do not own.[43]

Besides registering a harsher judgment of folk religiosity than has yet been heard in part 1, "Blood-Burning Moon" subjects to scrutiny the male gaze that has been largely uninterrogated in the earlier stories. The heat from the fire that kills Tom is anticipated not just by the moon "[g]lowing like a fired pine-knot" and the "red-hot" coals of jealousy "sizzling up" in Bob Stone, but also by the heat from the cane-boiling stove where Old David Georgia and a cluster of Negro men gather to talk "about the white folks, about moonshining and cotton picking, and about sweet nigger gals." "Nigger gals": the same descriptor preoccupies Bob Stone as he wonders whether he should think of Louisa, whom he loves more than he dares acknowledge, as either "nigger gal," or "just plain gal." It is when Tom overhears the men's gossip about Louisa and Bob that he dashes off to confront his white rival. As in "Becky," a male-dominated culture enables the scapegoating of a woman who has dared to transgress racial and sexual norms. As in "Carma," the men around the stove view African American women as objects of gossip and lust. As in "Fern," a beautiful black woman is viewed as the potential property of either the white riders of Pullman cars or the black riders of Jim Crow cars. In "Blood-Burning Moon," the tragic consequences of gendered fetishistic voyeurism are graphically explored as the haze rising from the cane kettle shrouds and reddens the low-hanging moon. In this last story, however, men's desire for power and possession—which is treated in "Karintha" as simply an inherent attribute of the male sex—is located within a critical analysis of property and ideology. The unremitting imagistic comparisons of Louisa with the land suggest that the dispute between Tom and Bob is not so much over who has control of Louisa's body as over who is to have control of the land and harvest its fruits; while Bob's desire for Louisa is for a "cornfield concubine" on land possessed by his family, Tom's desire is inseparable from his yearning for land of his own. In the ideologeme of metonymic nationalism, the organic trope treats land in its aspect of earth. But in a materialist analysis of the political economy of Jim Crow, land is not just fecund soil but property over which men, black and white, will fight and kill. In its critical commentary on the masculinist ideology that falsely aligns the black men around the kettle with the white owners of the land, "Blood-Burning Moon" not only displays the material consequences of such alignment but also calls into question the reified thinking that equates woman with the land to begin with.[44]

"Portrait in Georgia," the lyric that directly precedes "Blood-Burning Moon," displays the violent consequences of the voyeuristic anatomizing of female beauty. Invoking the Renaissance genre of the blazon, which enumerates the features of the poet-lover's mistress, the poem proposes that the reification of the white woman—

> Hair . . .
> Eyes . . .
> Lips . . .
> Breath . . .

—results in the lynching of the black man. Indeed, the poem suggests that her whiteness—her "slim body" is "white as the ash of black flesh after flame"—is a function of his blackness: as in "Reflections on the Race Riots," "racial differences" are "caused" by violent acts. The poem also starkly features the inadequacy of the organic trope to suture the pain of history: "the last sweet scent of cane" is implicated in the flames of a lynching. Calling into question the capacity of "Georgia" to signify the project of a sectional art that will represent "our America," "Portrait in Georgia" contrasts dramatically with the metonymic nationalist premises of "Georgia Dusk," as well as the various mentions of Georgia in part 1's preceding sketches of women.[45]

The location of Tom's lynching in the ruins of an antebellum cotton factory affords the reader a further glimpse of the social totality limned in this last story in part 1 of *Cane*. The reference to the blood-red moon conjoins the poem's call on the "sinner" and its reference to the Book of Revelations with the line, "Come out that fact'ry door." While some of the peasantry of Sempter—like the first laborer heard in "Cotton Song"—may interpret "sinner" as an allusion to their own transgressions, Toomer's location of the "sinner" at the "fact'ry door" strongly suggests that the real "sinner" is the owner of the factory, fearing the revenge of those workers who, like the second voice heard in "Cotton Song," are not willing to wait until the Day of Judgment to gain the compensation due to them. The "skeleton walls" that echo the yells of the lynching party remind the reader of the dead labor congealed in this generations-old means of production, as well as of the continuity between chattel slavery and the political economy of Jim Crow: the cotton processed for sale in the world market of the nineteenth century continues to be produced by the Tom Burwells laboring on land they do not own. Rather than functioning to enclose the history that hurts within the compass of spherical form, the repeated invocation of the "sinner" standing behind factory door as the Day of Judgment approaches points to the social contradictions driving the action of "Blood-Burning Moon."[46]

The "red nigger moon" referenced in the repeated lyric also invites further scrutiny. For Toomer may intend a play on the phrase "red nigger," in which "red" and "nigger" do not jointly modify "moon," but instead "red" modifies "nigger." During the "red summer" of 1919, when workers engaged in a mass radical upsurge and African Americans defied rampaging racists with armed self-defense, the categories of "red" and "black" overlapped in the government's repressive response. While for radicals like Claude McKay, "black reds" needed to find common ground with antiracist white revolutionaries, for ruling-class figures from Woodrow Wilson to Attorney General Palmer, the conjunction of "red" and "black" was the worst nightmare imaginable. If the nation were to return to Harding-era "normalcy," "red niggers"—militant New Negroes demanding their place in the sun—must be not only prevented from standing for the nation; they must be destroyed. A peasant seeking private ownership of a plot of land, Tom Burwell possesses no conscious left politics; and while the Toomer who defended the revolutions of 1919 and the emergent Soviet state was aware of plans for the socialist collectivization of agriculture, Tom Burwell's aspirations are constrained by his love for Louisa and his desire for private property, as well as his accession to the fatalism produced by the "cotton-wad" songs in his ears. But Louisa figures metonymically as both the soil of the earth and the land of the South; Tom Burwell insists upon his right to have her. In his willingness to use violence to defend his sense of selfhood, Tom Burwell is a New Negro—not in the culturalist mold to be celebrated by Locke in his 1925 anthology, but in the activist mold celebrated in the pages of the *Messenger* and the *Crusader* at the time when Toomer was composing *Cane*. Despite the limitations imposed by his geographical and historical circumstances, Tom Burwell is the Negro in possession of "an essentially new psychology, characterized by a fighting attitude" whom Toomer had described in "Reflections on the Race Riots." He may not be the heir to the tradition of multiracial struggle embodied in John Brown, which, in David Teyy's words, conjoined the "[w]hite red blood" and the "[b]lack red blood" spilled at Harpers Ferry; as has been shown in "Becky," Jim Crow as yet prevents multiracial proletarian unity in lynch-ridden rural Georgia. But Tom Burwell is the Black Christ in vengeful mode; he has inherited the legacy of John Cain. And if he cannot survive his challenge to the social order or spark a new Civil War, he will at least take his enemy with him.[47]

Toomer's gesturing toward the revolutionary horizon in "Blood-Burning Moon" may account for his apparently anomalous placement of this story after "Esther." Located in the postwar years by its reference to Barlo's having become wealthy during the war, the action in "Esther" evidently postdates that in "Blood-Burning Moon," where Barlo is featured as the town's champion cotton picker but does not yet ride around in a big car with prostitutes on his arm. The Barlo who is alluded to in "Blood-Burning Moon" is if anything linked with the "vagrant preacher" of 1903 who celebrates the heroic African dragged into slavery by the "white-ant biddies"—the very term used to describe the lynch mob that swarms over Tom Burwell. Although Toomer was under no obligation to adhere to a tight chronology in ordering his tales, it is noteworthy that he situates the last story in part 1 of *Cane* in a historical space where the heroic figure of the New Negro can be invoked. Better the image of failed defiance than that of corrupt betrayal. Better defeated rebellion than the arrested dialectic of history. Better the common ruin of contending races than the continuing regime of Jim Crow.

The history that hurts in "Blood-Burning Moon" is both general and specific. Toomer's description of the gruesome death of Tom Burwell synthesizes details in accounts of lynchings published in the *Crisis*; there was no such occurrence in Hancock County during Toomer's stay in the fall of 1921. But his deployment of the names of various characters and geographical sites draws on particular features of Sparta, Georgia. "Factory Town" alludes to the ruins of the Montour Factory that were still standing when Toomer visited in 1921. The designation of Louisa's white lover as Bob Stone not only links "Blood-Burning Moon" with "Becky"—where John Stone, Bob Stone's father, pays for the construction of the scapegoated woman's cabin—but also indicates Toomer's awareness of Hancock County's prominent Stone family. While the reader would not be expected to recognize these allusions, they suggest Toomer's felt need to anchor his text in the Real.[48]

Toomer's most significant reference to the Georgia historical record consists, however, in his choice of the name "Tom Burwell" for his sharecropper hero. For Toomer clearly had in mind the Burwell family, formerly slave owners, who had been prominent in Sparta for generations; in 1900 the businessman and politician William Hix Burwell had bought up Factory Town in the hope of erecting a new textile factory on the land. In giving Tom the surname "Burwell" Toomer could, of course, simply have been pointing to the continuing legacy of slavery, which supplied the laborer with the name of the master. But William Hix Burwell was also the businessman who had "fleeced" Nathan Toomer some thirty years before and was most likely the "boss of the town" who was "called nigger behind his back," according to the local barbershop gossip Toomer heard in 1921. Although there were a number of mixed-race branches of wealthy white families in Hancock Country, there was no such—or at least no such acknowledged—branch of the Burwell family. By naming his black hero "Tom Burwell," Toomer challenged the town boss's exclusive right to his name; it was, after all, the labor of the Tom Burwells that generated the capital that had created and sustained the "Burwell" fortune. Besides outing old rumors about the mixed racial background of this pillar of white supremacy, however, Toomer exacted personal revenge. For this was the man whose theft of a significant portion of Nathan Toomer's wealth had precipitated the older Toomer's courtship of Amanda America Dickson, thereby setting in motion the sequence of events that tragically merged the histories of the Dicksons and the Toomers. Although Toomer's retaliation against the "boss" of Sparta was private, it was, we may imagine, sweet.[49]

The *Liberator* of June 1923 published a drawing by Robert Minor featuring black migrants moving northward, shaking their fists at Klan members who have hanged and burned a black man. With its closing indictment of the "sinner" hiding inside the "fact'ry door," "Blood-Burning Moon" not only looks back toward the conditions that made the migration inevitable for hundreds of thousands. It also looks forward to the changed terms of existence that would face the newly proletarianized migrants in the urban neighborhoods and worksites of the North. Even though the Toomer who authored the story in late 1922 was registering skepticism about the capacity of the working class to "bellow, 'We Want Power'"—and in fact was anticipating that race war was more likely than workers' revolution—his gripping representation of lynching at the end of part 1 of *Cane* is guided by his clear understanding of the relationship between Jim Crow violence and class struggle. What Toomer would call the "peasant-adjustment rhythm of the South" in his 1923 essay "The South in Literature" was, *Cane* reveals, continually ruptured by outbreaks of rebellion. The "sleepy southern town" of sectional art featured at the end of "Kabnis" is haunted by the spectre of lynching enacted in "Factory Town." Violence is the principal mediator of the relationship between labor and the land, cotton and capital.[50]

CHAPTER 7

Black and Brown Worlds Heaving Upward
Part 2 of Cane

Becoming is . . . the mediation between past and future. . . . When the
concrete here and now dissolves into a process . . . it is the focus of the
deepest and most widely ramified mediation, the focus of decision and
the birth of the new. Man must be able to comprehend the present as
a becoming. He can do this by seeing in it the tendencies out of whose
dialectical opposition he can *make* the future. Only when he does this will
the present be a process of becoming that belongs to *him.*
—Georg Lukács, *History and Class Consciousness*

A rumble comes from the earth's deep core. It is the mutter of powerful
underground races.
—Jean Toomer, *Cane*

In part 2 of *Cane*, Toomer's critique of capitalist modernity comes to the fore. The
voice heard in his *New York Call* writings of 1919 and 1920 is once again audible,
and the 1919 Washington race riot—for him the key domestic event emerging
from the postwar conjuncture—signals the arrival of the urban New Negro as
history-making proletarian. Situated mostly in the nation's capital, the stories and
poems here call into question the limitations of metonymic nationalism; if the
liberation of the submerged masses is to occur, it will have to be part of a worldwide "heaving upward" of the "underground races" of the globe. Yet the exchange
relation is also shown to dominate each and every human interaction; the very
spaces within which modern city dwellers work, live, and revel are confined and
constrained by a universal commodification that compels critical commentary.
Faced with the task of representing this contradictory modern reality is the figure
of the New Negro as artist: the poetic-narratorial presence struggling to represent the folk/peasantry in "Kabnis" and part 1 here struggles for an avant-garde
aesthetic that can do justice to the complexity of African American life in the
urban capitalist setting.

Whether the New Negro will succeed in this project, however—either as artist or as political rebel—is left open to question. The eruption of antiracist class
struggle along Seventh Street is threatened with absorption into a regime of reification that invades every corner of life. Even as the project of sectional art—and

its accompanying *combinatoire* of metaphors drawn from the organic trope—is clearly incapable of supplying second-order mediations that can account for the sources of urban alienation, the futuristic language of the machine lacks both a coherent iconography and an audience capable of recognizing itself in a new and different system of representations. Toomer's montage in part 2 exhibits the dialectical vision of totality briefly made available in the wake of the global radical upsurge of 1919. But while the text provides glimpses of a possible revolutionary future, the urban section of *Cane* ends up testifying to the arrested dialectic of history: antinomic oscillation between the poles of irony and nostalgia prevails over dialectical negation and sublation.

As with "Kabnis" and part 1, it is useful to bear in mind the order in which the different pieces gathered in part 2 were composed. Most of the poems and short pieces clustered in the first half—from "Seventh Street" through "Calling Jesus"—were written between January and July 1922, more or less simultaneously with the texts that open part 1, from "Karintha" through "Fern." With the exception of "Bona and Paul," the pieces that close part 2 were written more or less simultaneously with "Esther" and "Blood-Burning Moon." The contrast between texts written before and after the fall 1922 trip to Spartanburg with Waldo Frank is, if anything, more pronounced in part 2 than in part 1; in particular, "Box Seat"—the last-written short story in the collection—exhibits the felt need for a revolutionary challenge to the status quo that Toomer experienced in the wake of his re-exposure to the Deep South. The fact that Toomer brackets the urban section of *Cane* with pieces dating from his early attraction to leftist politics— "Seventh Street" recalls his August 1919 essay "Reflections on the Race Riots," while his still earlier introduction to socialism in Chicago in 1916 is in the background of "Bona and Paul"—further indicates that he had by no means ceased yearning for proletarian revolution as he put the final touches on his text. That the text exhibits a sense of diminished possibility does not mean that Toomer had forgotten the lesson learned in the shipyard: "I realized as never before the *need* of socialism, the *need* of a radical change of the conditions of human society."[1]

"'Who set you flowin'?'": "Seventh Street" and the Washington Race Riot of 1919

Although "Seventh Street" is often read as a commentary on the *élan vital* of the African American migrant culture located in the heart of the nation's capital, the sketch's explicit reference to the race riot of July 1919—of which Seventh Street was the hub—invites interpretation in the postwar context. The Washington uprising, one of several dozen occurring in U.S. cities during the summer of 1919, was a response to the current economic and political crisis: the pressure on housing stock as a result of the rapid wartime growth of the black population;

the high rate of postwar unemployment and racialized competition for jobs; white resentment at displays of wealth among blacks who had advanced during the war; simmering black anger at the recent segregation of government offices and the contemplated Jim-Crowing of the city's streetcar system; and rumors of black criminality spread by white anti-prohibitionists eager to prove that dry laws had resulted in an increase in crime. The catalyst was a press campaign of inflammatory headlines and dubious reporting about an alleged series of sexual assaults on white women by black men, culminating in a July 21, 1919, *Washington Post* invitation for a "mobilization" of former servicemen to engage in a "clean-up" of the city.[2]

On the night of July 21, several hundred white veterans convened at the Knights of Columbus Hut at Seventh Street and Pennsylvania Avenue; an additional thousand white civilians joined the mob and, one historian recounts, "proceeded to take over the city from the Capitol to the White House." African American men and women were "mobbed, chased, dragged from streetcars, and beaten within the shadow of the dome of the Capitol and at the very door of the White House." In the Negro neighborhood centered on Seventh Street—which was designated the riot's "bloodfield"—the attackers were repulsed by residents armed with guns that had been rushed into the city by blacks in nearby Baltimore. In the area around Fourteenth and U Streets—just down the block from the apartment that Toomer shared with his grandparents—gunfire "blazed all through the night," according to James Weldon Johnson, who toured the city the next evening. In several instances African Americans—some of them recent veterans—commandeered vehicles and, bearing guns, patrolled the area in self-defense. The riot lasted nearly a week; it was quelled only when a battery of infantrymen and several hundred cavalrymen were brought in from Fort Meade, as well as marines from Quantico, to back up District police. Although the violence had been initiated entirely by whites, they numbered fewer than ten among the more than one hundred persons arrested; the racist nature of state repression was patent.[3]

Throughout these events, the role of the mainstream press was predictable. The NAACP's request that the *Post* be indicted for its incendiary role was ignored. In the riot's wake, the southern press seized the occasion to demonstrate the necessity for Dixie-style discipline in handling African American rebellion. A Mississippi newspaper controlled by the notorious white supremacist and former Senator Ben Vardaman editorialized that "the mob is the only protection of the white man's home" against black returning soldiers who had been "French-women-ruined." Even the *Sparta Ishmaelite* weighed in, exulting that "[n]othing but the presence of the soldiers can be counted on to keep the rioters subdued." The northern white press, if less pleased by the outbreak, evinced little interest in exploring its reasons. The *New York Times* announced that "Angry and Defiant Negroes Roam about Shooting at Whites"; the *New York Globe*, calling the riot a "humiliating and shameful business," admitted, "[W]e make no pretense nowadays of settling

Figure 9. "The 'New Crowd Negro' Making America Safe for Himself," *Messenger*,
September 1919. Cartoon from the African American Socialist press portraying Negro
militancy during the "red summer" of 1919.

the race question; we simply keep it in abeyance." The *Washington Star* opined
that the "unusual spectacle" of rioting in the nation's capital was "enough to shock
the community seriously."[4]

The black press, however, came into its own as the "voice of the Negro" during
the "red summer" of 1919. The *Washington Bee*, ordinarily cautious, commended
the rebels and seconded the NAACP's call for an indictment of the *Post*. James
Weldon Johnson wrote in the *Crisis* that the decision of Washington's blacks "not
to run, but to fight . . . in defense of their lives and homes" had in fact "saved
themselves and saved Washington." The left-wing black press saw the potential for
revolutionary action in the display of black militancy. The *Crusader* declared, "The
long-suffering worm . . . at last had turned upon its persecutors. . . . [Negroes],
in true 'Hell Fighters' style . . . were carrying the war into the 'enemy's country,'
speeding through the streets of the white quarters in improvised tanks and leaving deadly leaden souvenirs behind." The *Messenger* argued that the capitalist-

controlled press had played a major role in sparking and then distorting the riot: "[I]t is apparent that he who controls the bread and butter will also control and shape the ideas." It is only when capitalism is replaced by "industrial democracy," and "no profits are to be made from race friction," Owen and Randolph asserted, that "no one will longer be interested in stirring up race prejudice." We will recall that Toomer's op-ed piece in the *New York Call* was written in the same spirit, asserting that despite the efforts of the "governing classes . . . to keep the masses in constant conflict," the capital city uprising heralded the appearance of a Negro possessing "an essentially new psychology, characterized by a fighting attitude": a new historical subject. The "turning of the worm" in the conjuncture of 1919 was potentially an event, like the Bogalusa strike, with world-historical implications.[5]

"Seventh Street" makes clear reference to the energetic culture—the "unconscious rhythms" alliteratively thrust into the "white and whitewashed wood of Washington"—that the migrants brought northward. But the text's continual querying, "Who set you flowin'?" also invokes the bloodletting that occurred in Seventh Street's "bloodfield" in July 1919. "Whitewash" signifies not just the dominance of white supremacist ideology—epitomized in the recent segregated dedication ceremony at the Lincoln Memorial—but also the press cover-up of state repression during the riot. The added mention of the "blood-suckers of the war" who "would spin in a frenzy of dizziness if they drank your blood" recalls Toomer's portraiture in "Ghouls" of the whirling battlefield death of the monstrous body robber, as well as of capitalists dining on the hearts of wage slaves. Besides alluding to Marx's famous description of capital as a vampire, this linkage of war profiteers with Washington's "whitewash" places the actions of the Seventh Street rebels in the context of the recent imperialist war. That God—even "A Nigger God!"—would "not dare to suck black red blood," and would instead "duck his head in shame and call for the Judgment Day," suggests that it is the Seventh Street rebels—the "black reds"—who will deliver sentences at the Last Judgment, fulfilling the prophecy of the "red nigger moon" in "Blood-Burning Moon." The image of "blood-red smoke" spiraling upward at once summons the image of Tom Burwell's lynching and promises retribution for racist repression; the answer to the question "Who set you flowin'?" is, it would seem, the migrants themselves. No longer imaginable as "non-historical people" living according to the "peasant-adjustment rhythm of the South," these African Americans have emerged as actors on the northern historical stage. Although Toomer's portrayal of their "unconscious rhythms" invokes the rhetoric of primitivism, it also anticipates his formulation of his projected novel about "the black and brown world heaving upward . . . to be symbolic of the proletariat or world upheaval . . . likewise to be symbolic of the subconscious penetration of the conscious mind."

The reworking of the organic trope in "Seventh Street" reinforces the notion that the movement from one mode of production to another has entailed a qualitative rupture with the past of the peasants' belonging on soil they could not own. The narratorial voice declares, "Stale soggy wood of Washington. Wedges rust in

soggy wood . . . Split it! In two! Again! Shred it! . . . the sun. Wedges are brilliant in
the sun; ribbons of wet wood dry and blow away." This is not the voice of the poet-
visitor who saw in Fern a tortured, sap-filled trunk, or of the returning son who
envisioned himself as a "singing tree," preserving the "carols" of a "song-lit race of
slaves." Instead, this voice calls for cutting down Washington's whitewashed tree.
It is not worth preserving; it is waterlogged, rotten: best to shred it and let it blow
away. Seventh Street—the geographical corridor along which African American
migrants expanded their presence in the capital city—is the wedge that has been
positioned by these new agents wielding the ax of history. No longer the victims
of ax-brandishing plantation owners—as was the fate of the Jasper County debt
peons—these proletarianized migrants are clearing the way to urban modernity.
Toomer wrote to Waldo Frank that the denizens of Seventh Street are, in their
energy and purpose, their "health and freedom," quintessentially "American."
The pioneer/puritan theory of U.S. history has been given a new spin: the New
Negro as proletarian migrant is making a bid for a new belonging—a place in
the national sun of "our America."[6]
    Spherical form in "Seventh Street" serves a double function:

> Money burns the pocket, pocket hurts,
> Bootleggers in silken shirts,
> Ballooned, zooming Cadillacs,
> Whizzing, whizzing down the street-car tracks.

This futuristic fragment partakes of none of the soil-soaked lyricism pervading
the lyrics in part 1; dusk, smoke, and cane have been superseded by modern machinery enabling rapid motion from place to place. Although a proposal was afoot
to resegregate the capital city's streetcar system, the bootleggers have evidently
bypassed this problem; like Tome Mangrow in *Natalie Mann*, they live their lives
on their own extralegal terms. Yet the repeated appearance of this short poem—
which, notably, begins with the word "money"—also suggests that the potential
revolutionary energies fueling the Seventh Street uprising may be diverted into
consumerism and status display. The Cadillac-driving bootleggers are not heroic
resisters of racial oppression but agents of commodification, recalling the conversion of Barlo from antiracist rebel to war profiteer in "Esther." Seventh Street is the
hub of both class struggle and assimilation to capitalist hegemony; the "wedge"
of migration splits African American experience into two possible futures. What
politics will accompany the revised meaning of "American"? What retrospective metonymic signification will attach to Seventh Street as time passes? Will
class struggle directed toward eventual socialist transformation—what Toomer
in "Reflections on the Race Riots" called "the substitution of a socialized reality"—emerge from the encounter with capitalist state power? Or does the sketch's
spherical form imply closure within an arrested historical dialectic? We will recall
what Gramsci wrote of the revolutionary postwar conjuncture: "The point is to see

whether in the dialectic of revolution/restoration it is the element of revolution or of restoration that prevails, since it is certain that in the movement of history there can be no turning back ever." Whichever result occurs, one thing is certain: these migrants won't go home again.[7]

"Shredded life-pulp": Nostalgia and Reification in "Rhobert" and "Calling Jesus"

The bootleggers of Seventh Street, their pockets loaded with money, experience freedom of movement along the city's streets. For the average law-abiding migrant, however, inclusion within the brave new world of capitalist modernity entails the twin burden of wage labor and debt, accompanied by a blinkered consciousness preventing awareness of its sources. The consequence of this alienation is a retreat to the enclosed domain of the isolated self, as well as a lyrical longing for a pastoral South that never existed.

"Rhobert" is a bitter satire on the emotional price paid by the upwardly mobile migrant city dweller who substitutes the cash nexus for human connection. The central trope of the sketch is the surreal image of Rhobert's house as a "monstrous diver's helmet." Beset by the pressures of mortgage and respectability, Rhobert, a "banty-bowed, shaky, ricket-legged man"—whose curved legs probably developed as a result of a rural childhood of malnutrition—has displaced his life onto his house, which, "stuffed . . . with shredded life-pulp," weights him down into the mud. He has ceased to think about his situation: "Like most men who wear monstrous helmets, the pressure it exerts is enough to convince him of its practical infinity. And he cares not two straws as to whether or not he will ever see his wife and children again." Reminding himself that suicide is wrong—"It is sinful to have one's own head crushed"—he worships a god he imagines as "a Red Cross man with a dredge and a respiration-pump who waits at the periphery." Having twice warned, "Brother, life is water that is being drawn off," the narrator closes by proposing an honorific funeral:

> Lets build a monument set in the ooze where he goes down. A
>   monument of hewn oak, carved in nigger-heads. Lets open our
>   throats, brother, and sing "Deep River" when he goes down.
> Brother, Rhobert is sinking.
> Lets open our throats, brother,
> Lets sing Deep River when he goes down. (40–41)[8]

"Rhobert" conveys a searing critique of what Marx called "the silent compulsion of economic relations." The grotesque helmet of Rhobert's mortgage, rather than affording him the comfort and status of a "family man," both precludes participation in family life and persuades him of the immutability—the "practical infinity"—of his circumstances. The work he performs that earns him the

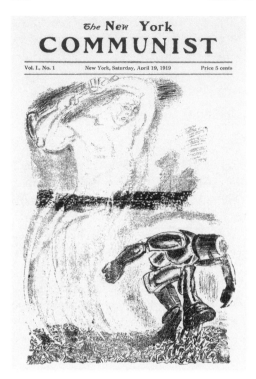

Figure 10. Cover, *New York Communist*, April 1919. Image from the Communist press depicting the "robotic" worker's inability to recognize the need for revolution.

wage enabling him to pay his mortgage is never featured; he lives his conscious life at the level of consumption and debt. There is an eerie resemblance between Toomer's Rhobert and the robotic creature featured in Robert Minor's cover for the April 1919 issue of the *New York Communist*: a mechanized creature with a metallic head is mired in mud, unable to look up and see the vision of revolutionary possibility that hovers above. The term "robot," too, had recently come into cultural currency in Karol Čapek's popular 1920 play *R.U.R. (Rossum's Universal Robots)*, in which the Czech term for "serf," *robota*, features prominently in a critique of modern industrial dehumanization. Rhobert's authoritarian religion only compounds his helplessness, teaching him that his despair is "sinful" and that God helps only those who help themselves. His vision of the deity as a "Red Cross man" indicates his acceptance of the jingoistic wartime propaganda that equated purchasing Red Cross-sponsored Liberty Bonds with "100% Americanism"—as well as of the Red Cross's support for the Allied invasion of the Soviet Union and its early 1920s involvement in the growth of the Ku Klux Klan. Ever ready to engage in wordplay, Toomer creates an ironic anagram—"brother" / "Rhobert"—that suggests the homeowner's imperviousness to the narrator's call for comradely succor. While Sam Raymon, one of the "death farm" victims, drowns as a result of murderous coercion, Rhobert drowns in what Lukács called the "mire of immediacy"; in the urban North, reification is a matter more of ideology than of overt repression.[9]

Although the binary oppositions around which "Rhobert" is constructed might suggest that the remedy to Rhobert's distress consists in a therapeutic return to his roots, the organic trope provides no folk-based antidote to the capitalist marketplace. Instead, it designates the industrial process by which the wood pulp created by the sawmill workers of Sempter/Sparta, mediated via a series of labor processes, reappears as the dead labor embedded in the newspapers and magazines shaping the migrants' consciousness. For the matter that constitutes the "live stuffing" in the "dead house" of Rhobert's head is "shredded life-pulp": wood pulp converted into newsprint advertising the commodities to which Rhobert has bonded over his humanity. The migrants in "Seventh Street" may have split and dispersed the "stale soggy . . . white and whitewashed wood of Washington." But the "monument of hewn oak carved in niggerheads," apparently offering an alternative to the metallic surface of Rhobert's helmet, is constructed of the same material used in the beams of the factory in "Blood-Burning Moon" and the property stake in "Balo." Indeed, the term "Niggerhead"—most commonly referring to a cigar or cigar butt—was invoked in early twentieth-century racially derogating magazine advertisements for Rastus Cigars: Rhobert's middle-class aspirations have not saved him from second-class citizenship.[10]

The narrator's call on the unspecified "brother" to mourn Rhobert's death-in-life—"Lets sing Deep River when he goes down"—invokes folk spirituality as a counter-discourse to Rhobert's pseudoscientific view of life as "murky, wiggling, microscopic water." As "Kabnis" demonstrates, however, "Deep River" does not offer an escape from the "rivering" of the workers on Georgia's "death farm"; Rhobert's mortgage, a northern urban version of Jim Crow debt peonage, cannot be effaced through prayer. The narrator's hope that folk culture will supply an alternative to urban alienation is futile: while his final words—"goes down"—echo the testament to Karintha's dusky beauty, recourse to a lyrical celebration of natural processes beyond human agency cannot compensate for a history—now marked by the hegemony of the exchange relation—that hurts. The narrator's repeated injunction to "open our throats, brother, and sing 'Deep River' when he goes down" sets up an echo chamber in which spherical form displays both Rhobert's enclosure within a fragmented consciousness and the chanter's enclosure within an impotent longing.

In the two lyrics that follow "Rhobert," natural imagery continues to be used in descriptions of urban modernity. "Beehive" displays the impotence of pastoral nostalgia in contesting the regime of the exchange relation: analogizing alienated urbanites with inhabitants of a beehive producing wealth for the "world-comb" of global capital, the poem features a persona who, "drunk" on the "silver honey" of money, longs for the peace of a "farm-yard flower" (48). But the poem's rhetorical premise—which ostensibly counterposes city with countryside, the world of the market with the world of nature—actually describes both zones of experience by means of a single trope, the beehive. The binary opposition essential to pastoral critique collapses; as carrier of a critique of market-dominated social relations, the governing image is itself reified. "Storm Ending," when read in isolation from "Beehive"—as in its original publication in the *Double Dealer*—simply evokes the passing of a thunderstorm. When juxtaposed with the imagery in preceding poem, however "Storm Ending" asks to be read as historical allegory. The suggested equation of the flowers with "full-lipped" African Americans, "[b]itten by the sun / Bleeding rain / Dripping rain like golden honey," links the migrants' present-day position in the urban North with their flight from the violence of the rural South. And although the poem's title proposes that the "storm" of Jim Crow has "ended," the altered trope in the last line, where flowers give way to the "sweet earth flying from the thunder," merges the plants growing in the soil with the soil itself. By contrast with "Seventh Street," which heralds the migrants' qualitative break with both the soil and its products, "Storm Ending" suggests that the "earth" of southern violence follows the fleeing workers to the city (49). The urban riots of 1919 are continuous with the regime of rural Jim Crow; the "earth" of the entire nation, south and north, is suffused in coercion.[11]

Of all the texts in part 2 of *Cane*, "Calling Jesus" contains perhaps the most pointed critique of rural nostalgia as ideological compensation. Portraying a lonely nameless woman whose soul is compared with "a little thrust-tailed dog" that has been left whimpering at night in a cold vestibule, the sketch is built on the stark contrast between images of urban enclosure and a spiritualized rural southern landscape. The woman dreams that "some one . . . eoho Jesus . . . soft as a cotton boll brushed against the milk-pod cheek of Christ . . . soft as the bare feet of Christ moving across bales of southern cotton" will cover the shivering dog and "carry it to her where she sleeps: cradled in dream-fluted cane." We hear an echo of "Cotton Song," where the first speaker thinks of the bales that he heaves as "the fleecy way / Weary sinner's bare feet trod, / Softly, softly to the throne of God." But the woman's memory of the South has repressed the labor process and social conditions under which cotton is produced; she seems not to have heard the objection of "Cotton Song"'s second speaker, who insists, "'We aint agwine t wait until th Judgment Day!'" Her fantasy of a "milky-cheek[ed]" Christ shows that she accepts the "white-faced sardonic god" advocated by the treacherous preacher in "Conversion." The Black Messiah is absent from her dreams; she is not about to etch a Black Madonna on any of the whitewashed walls of Washington. Where Rhobert has closed off thought of anything beyond the immediate pressures of urban life, the protagonist of "Calling Jesus," like the persona in "Beehive," thinks only of escaping those pressures. All, however, are confined in the vestibule of ideology. These migrants have not taken up the mantle of the New Negro as revolutionary; the promise potentially embedded in "Seventh Street" is receding.[12]

"I recited some of my own things to her":
"Avey" and the Artist of the Beautiful

The commentary on reification embedded in "Rhobert" and "Calling Jesus" is explicitly addressed in a series of short stories featuring male artist-heroes. If working-class and upwardly aspiring migrants have not answered the challenge of the radical New Negro, what will the artists do? The narrator in "Avey," which was composed at the same time as the cluster of female portraits appearing toward the beginning of part 1, recalls previous first-person narrators bent on viewing African American women as embodiments of the soil. Where they were gathering information for future projects, however, the "Avey" narrator is a practicing literary artist, one who self-consciously creates binary oppositions between rootlessness and belonging, urban and rural, North and South, organicism and enclosure. From the outset, where he describes his childhood attempts to free young trees from the boxes binding their roots, the narrator associates urbanized black people with rootbound plants and congratulates himself on his youthful compassion: "I like to feel that something deep in me responded to the trees, the young trees that whinnied like colts impatient to be let free" (42). The sensual Avey, to whom he has been drawn from childhood onward, is said to be "as silent as those great trees whose tops we looked down upon"; when she rebuffs his youthful love-making, he consoles himself by observing that she "was no better than a cow"—an impression confirmed when he "felt an udder in a Wisconsin stock-judging class" (44–45). This young man comes supplied with natural tropes enabling him at once to proclaim his own sensitivity and explain away its failure to gain appreciation.[13]

Consisting of a series of vignettes describing the narrator's encounters with Avey over the years, the tale concludes with his meeting her as an adult and discerning that she has become a prostitute. Taking her to "a spot in Soldier's Home to which I always go when I want the simple beauty of another's soul," he muses, "When the wind is from the South, soil of my homeland falls like a fertile shower upon the lean streets of the city." Under the influence of his nostalgic mood, he "wanted the Howard Glee Club to sing 'Deep River' and started to hum a folk-tune." Taking it upon himself to explain Avey to herself, he "traced [his] development from the early days up to the present time" and "described her own nature and temperament . . . point[ing] out that in lieu of proper channels, her emotions had overflowed into paths that dissipated them." Washington, he advises her, is "incapable . . . of understanding [her] need . . . for a larger life." He recalls, "I talked, beautifully I thought, about an art that would be born, an art that would open the way for women the likes of her. I asked her to hope, and build up an inner life against the coming of that day. I recited some of my own things to her." When Avey falls asleep listening to him, he tells us, "I wanted to get up and whittle at the boxes of young trees. . . . I saw the dawn steal over Washington. The Capitol dome looked like a gray ghost ship drifting in from sea. Avey's face was pale, and her eyes were heavy. She did not have the gray crimson-splashed beauty of the dawn" (45–47).[14]

The narrator in "Avey" combines the self-conscious lyricism of the "Fern" narrator with some of the least appealing qualities of Nathan Merilh and David Teyy, who also go around reciting their own poetic works and instructing young women about self-development; it is tempting to conclude that Toomer invites an unequivocally ironic response to the "Avey"-narrator. But these parallels with other quasi-autobiographical characters, along with the text's replication of a number of Toomer's own experiences and attitudes—from attending agronomy classes at the University of Wisconsin to working in a shipyard to asserting his superiority over his provincial Washington, DC, acquaintances—make it difficult to argue that Toomer intends us to dislike his narrator actively. The would-be writer featured in "Avey" is evidently associated with, if not identical to, the master of "golden words" who creates the gallery of female portraits in part 1. These earlier narrators are in the process of culling the impressions that will subsequently be worked up as literary texts; the first-person narrator in "Avey" is now back home in the North, sketching his own self-portrait of the New Negro artist as a young man. Having apparently forgotten about "rivering," he yearns to hear "Deep River"; removed from the terrain where women are deflowered, raped, and turned back into virgins, he is engaged in the process of creating a sectional literature that will align region with nation, contributing to the project of Young America.[15]

The "Avey" narrator appears partially aware, however, that his recuperative project cannot quite work. An experienced stage manager, he sets up the situation in which Avey can play the role he has imagined for her; he has apparently previously engaged in spiritual pioneering into the souls of other women on the grounds of the Old Soldiers Home. He speaks to her—beautifully, he thinks—of his mission to free northern African Americans from their deracinated state. But when she falls asleep listening to his patter, he cannot acknowledge her existence apart from his perception of her as an inhabitant of nature, not of history. If she does not have "the gray crimson-splashed beauty of the dawn"—if she does not coincide with the requirements of his tableau—then she has no meaningful past: she is an "orphan-woman." The narrator in the opening sketch in *Cane* equates Karintha's skin with "dusk on the eastern horizon" and urges, "Cant you see it?" The narrator in "Avey" concludes that there is nothing to see.[16]

In Avey herself, perhaps. But in a remarkable closing conceit, the narrator describes the Capitol dome as a "gray ghost ship floating in from the sea." Recalling the allusion to the "whitewash of Washington" in "Seventh Street," this image equates the presumed seat of U.S. democracy with a ship of state that has lost its bearings—perhaps, even, a slave ship. The would-be poet is bent on creating a signifying chain that metonymically links woman with tree with soil with folk with region with nation. But he appears uncertain about how to use the *combinatoire* of images associated with the ideologeme that guides his project: if his notion that the "soil of my homeland" can descend in a fertilizing shower on the North turns out to be based on faulty assumptions—if the roots of the boxed trees cannot be released into the ground—then what is the Capitol, the final element in the signifying chain, but a floating signifier? The narrator's attempt to incorporate Avey into his schema, along with his troubled closing vision of the Capitol dome—in whose shadow the race riot had transpired—indicates the limits of metonymic nationalism as both a political and an artistic project. Even as betrayed promises of democracy haunt the nation, the ghostlike Capitol, like Sempter's courthouse tower, haunts the text, revealing the continuing pressures of a political unconscious that can be silenced but not stilled.[17]

"The walls press in, singing": "Theater" and Mass Culture

In his December 1922 letter to Frank describing the arc of *Cane*, Toomer wrote that, after "plung[ing]" into "Kabnis" and "emerging" in "Karintha," the text "swings upward" into "Theater" and "Box Seat." Composed around the same time as "Esther" and "Blood-Burning Moon," these two stories were to culminate *Cane*'s urban section. Based loosely on Toomer's two-week job as assistant manager of the Howard Theater, which was managed by his uncle, "Theater" is explicitly about representation: both John, the "dictie" manager's brother who observes a line-up of chorus dancers in rehearsal, and Dorris, the most talented dancer in the group, are aware of their roles as consumers and producers of staged performance. This impression is enhanced by Toomer's construction of the story as a quasi-drama, in which, as in "Kabnis," the characters' thoughts, spoken or unspoken, are often preceded by a colon. Although "Theater" is mainly John's story, this technique supplies access to Dorris's ambitions and desires; as in "Blood-Burning Moon," the female object of male longing is supplied with a degree, however slight, of interiority. As in "Esther," sexual repression is traceable to class-based alienation, here conveyed through the trope of walls, which signal both the external constraints confining the theater and the internal constraints inhibiting John's sexuality. His artistic process entails transparent procedures of sublimation: "John's body is separate from the thoughts that pack his mind" (50). As he watches the women dancing, he "tries to trace origins and plot destinies"; as he voyeuristically focuses on Dorris, he imagines her in a setting of untrammeled collective sensuality: "Glorious songs are the muscles of her limbs. And her singing is of canebrake loves and mangrove feastings" (53). In his subsequent sexual fantasy, the walls of the theater collapse into the walls of her vagina:

> [Dorris's] face is tinted like the autumn alley. Of old flowers, or of a southern canefield. . . . They glide off with footfalls softened on the leaves, the old leaves powdered by a million satin slippers. . . .

They are in a room. John knows nothing of it. Only, that the flesh and blood of Dorris are its walls. Singing walls. . . .

John reaches for a manuscript of his, and reads. Dorris, who has no eyes, has eyes to understand him. He comes to a dancing scene. The scene is Dorris. She dances. (53)

The fantasy's presentation in small type indicates not just its dreamlike quality but also its irrelevance to the walled urban world inhabited by both characters.[18]

John is another aspiring (and more than slightly narcissistic) male artist of a now familiar type. Like the "Avey" narrator, John denies the subjectivity of the woman he presumes to represent: "Dorris, who has no eyes, has eyes to understand him" (53). Like the authenticity-seeking narrators of "Carma" and "Fern," he situates his fantasies about cornfield concubines amid canebrakes and lush plant life; the organic trope is his central device for imagining the relationship between women and the soil, the folk and the nation. Familiar with the current marketing of Negro popular culture, John fancies himself a critic of its commodification. Alluding most probably to the revue "Shuffle Along"—which began its 474-performance Broadway run in May 1922—he thinks, "Soon the director will herd you, my full-lipped, distant beauties, and tame you and blunt your sharp thrusts in loosely suggestive movements, appropriate for Broadway. (O dance!) Soon the audience will paint your dusk faces white, and call you beautiful" (50). But he also longs to connect through his art to "the mass-heart of the black audience"—a phrasing that links his aspirations not so much to literary nationalism as to the emerging genre of literary proletarianism. As the Communist critic Mike Gold had recently declared in his 1921 Liberator manifesto, "Towards Proletarian Art," the longings of the "masses" could not be voiced in an art nurtured in the "hothouse" of the bourgeoisie, but only in an art that speaks to the site of the "tenement," the collective experience of the working class. While John's position as the manager's brother links him with the exploiters of African American culture, his desire to write for the masses suggests his felt need for an alternative class alignment. It is not difficult to see in John an authorial self-portrait, half critical, half laudatory.[19]

"Theater" makes no explicit reference to an immediate geographical or historical context. Contemporaneous readers of Cane familiar with Washington, however, would have known that the Howard Theater was located at the intersection of Seventh and T Streets: the site where "black-skinned [people] dance and shout above the tick and trill of white-walled buildings" (50) was at once the cultural heart of migrant Washington and the "bloodfield" of the 1919 race riot. That there was no firewall between the left press's commentary on world affairs and its promotion of the migrants' mass culture was signaled by the appearance of the advertisement for the nearby Republic Theater as "America's finest colored movie house—Walter Pinchback, Manager"—in the August 1921 issue of the Crusader. Toomer's own uncle evidently had no qualms about featuring one of the theaters that he managed in the premier black Communist periodical of the day, which had heralded the militants of 1919 who "in true 'Hell Fighters' style [carried] the war into the 'enemy's country.'" Situated in the "white-walled" Howard Theater along the principal urban corridor where black rebels had faced off against the power of the state, "Theater" invokes the trope of enclosure not only in its treatment of the protagonist's repressed social and sexual needs but also in its consideration of the kind of art best suited to reflect the consciousness of the newly proletarianized migrants from the Deep South. That John is, like the narrator in "Avey," not up to the task of creating this art does not render its production any the less urgent.[20]

"A new-world Christ is coming up":
"Box Seat" and the World Revolution

Dan Moore, the protagonist of "Box Seat," makes explicit the call for a revolutionary art that is adumbrated in "Theater." After "Kabnis" the longest piece in *Cane*, this story was the last to be written, and by Toomer's account the one that posed him the greatest challenge. Writing to Frank that "my novel is already shaping itself in my mind," Toomer continually revised his conception of Dan Moore. "Sensitive, but weak" in early versions of "Box Seat," the hero "expanded," gaining "new energy" and "greater strength," leading his creator to wonder whether the "ego and consciousness of the new Dan" would allow him at the end to "slough off up the alley." Toomer complained, "I dont see how I can channel [the new energy . . . ragged dynamic, perhaps vicious] into the first rounded form." While Toomer was realizing the limitations of the "rounded" (spherical) form he had inherited from Frank, his soon-to-be-former mentor was intuiting that Toomer's art was taking a new direction. After reading a revision that made Dan a more forceful character, Frank warned, "You must learn the economy of art . . . which is that each state of soul and mind has its own Body, and if you muddle them, you're lost. . . . Don't spoil your book by putting into it bits of your next book and your next mood. Already in your revision of Box-seat, though you doubtless lifted the whole thing up, you have introduced things that are forced, formless, alien. Are you sure you arent DONE with *Cane*, and really ready for something else? Look out!" Frank was onto something: more than any other piece in *Cane*, "Box Seat" displays Toomer's growing preoccupation with the notion of "black and brown worlds heaving upward" that was to inform the novel already gestating in his mind. The "upward swing" of the arc of *Cane* replicated Toomer's continuing preoccupation with the upsurge of global revolutionary movements in the wake of the Great War.[21]

Dan Moore is the most messianic, the most class-conscious—and also, it seems, the blackest—of Toomer's artist-heroes: the play on "Moore" / "moor" in his name is not to be missed. "Born in a canefield," he is not only an aspiring poet but also "a poor man out of work." While northward migration was motivated for African Americans in large part by the anticipation of steady and better-compensated work, capitalism—as Toomer well knew from personal experience—relies on a sizeable reserve army of the unemployed; Dan is one such soldier. The economic system also relies on racist violence in word and deed: while Dan's fear of being seen as a burglar (or, worse still, a "Jack the Ripper" or "[b]aboon from the zoo") might seem somewhat paranoid, it is a plausible reaction to the press scare about rampaging black rapists and criminals that sparked the 1919 race riot. In fact, his yearning to "[b]reak into an engine-house [and] steal a thousand horse-power fire truck" indicates his identification with the Seventh Street rebels who commandeered municipal vehicles and defended their neighborhood from the rioting white ex-servicemen (56). The 1919 race riot—as both repression and resistance— is evidently in recent, and still traumatized, memory. Where the "Avey" narrator appears content to breathe the poetic dust borne on the winds from the South, and John of "Theater" dreams about writing to the "mass-heart" of the migrants but can only fantasize about Dorris at a "mangrove-feasting," Dan is unable to sublimate his rage. He is the New Negro militant whose firsthand acquaintance with migration is not readily mediated through the language of lyrical nostalgia; he cannot easily square his experience of Seventh Street's "bloodfield" with its conversion into a site of mass-cultural consumption.[22]

Dan's courtship of the schoolteacher Muriel is constrained by the surveillance of her landlady, Mrs. Pribby, who, like Rhobert, draws her identity from ownership of a house and her ideas from newspaper propaganda: "Her eyes . . . are bluish and watery from reading newspapers. The blue is steel. It gimlets Dan" (57). An exemplar of sexual repression and petty bourgeois respectability, Mrs. Pribby resembles the older generation in *Natalie Mann*; her "bolted down" house recalls the ethics and values of the Newbolt family. Dan's anger at Washington's petty bourgeoisie is unfocused: his desire to "[g]rab an ax and brain em" uncannily replicates Layman's description of the "death farm" murders in "Kabnis." But his rage at the upwardly mobile pretensions of Muriel and her friend Bernice—a "cross between a washerwoman and a blueblood lady" (61)—expresses his despair at their willing submission to the dictates of capitalist consciousness. As Muriel, from her box seat, applauds the blood-soaked battle royal that she and Bernice witness on the stage of the Lincoln Theater, her "claps are steel fingers that manacle her wrists and move them forward to acceptance" (66). When Dan rises from his seat and shouts, "JESUS WAS ONCE A LEPER!" (62), he condemns the occupants of the theater for their refusal to acknowledge their oneness with less assimilated members of the migrant community, such as the old former slave on the street outside the theater who was wheeled away by the police. The African American audience may freely gather in the "Lincoln" Theater, but in critical respects they remain boxed in, enslaved; as in "Rhobert" and "Calling Jesus," the trope of enclosure signifies ideological containment. That Dan's response recalls the violence of both the 1919 race riot and the 1921 Jasper County murders reveals that the struggle for liberated consciousness in the North is continuous with—and no less urgent than—the struggle for simple survival in the Deep South.[23]

Dan is an artist-prophet—at least in the making—who seeks to inspire Washington's migrants to overcome shame about their peasant origins. "Shake your curled wool blossoms, nigger," declares the narrative voice that replicates his thoughts. "Open your liver lips to the lean, white spring. Stir the root-life of a withered people. Call them from their houses, and teach them to dream" (56). Invoking the motif of desiccated rootlessness informing T. S. Eliot's newly published *The Waste Land* (1922), Dan's call is for more than a revival of folk consciousness. For a "passing streetcar and something vibrant from the earth" make him hear a "rumble [that] comes from the earth's deep core. It is the mutter of powerful underground races. Dan has a picture of all the people rushing to put their ears against walls, to listen to it. The next world-savior is coming up that way. Coming up. A continent sinks down. The new-world Christ will need consummate skill to walk upon the waters where huge bubbles burst" (57). In a presumed reference to Soviet Asia—the "continent" that has generated the seismic shift liberating "powerful underground races" elsewhere on the earth—Dan's vision suggests that the messiah of revolution (the "next world-savior") will challenge the current hegemony of the savior imagined by white supremacy, pictured as walking atop cotton bales in "Calling Jesus." Indeed, even this "new-world Christ" will have trouble walking on the oceans where the "huge bubbles" generated by the earthquake of revolution have exploded. A modern avatar of the biblical prophet Daniel, Dan calls for the new messiah to "wake the nations underground," rendering concrete the prophecy in the spiritual "My Lord, What a Morning." That a "passing streetcar" accompanies this "rumble" indicates the relevance of the postwar global upsurge to the continuing struggle against Jim Crow segregation in the nation's capital: the occupants of the Jim-Crowed Washington theater need to rush to the walls to listen. Notably, however, this messiah, while evidently a partisan of the "underground races," is not specified as black; the "new-world Christ" of the world revolution is beyond racial classification.[24]

In its direct allusions to the postwar global upsurge, "Box Seat" complicates some of the key tropes informing *Cane*. The text's deployment of the organic trope implies that Dan, like many of the text's characters and narrators, seeks reconnection with the soil of the South. As Dan anguishes next to a "portly Negress" in one of the Lincoln Theater's rows of bolted-down seats, however, the motif of rootedness signifies a belonging that is more than regional and national:

> A soil-soaked fragrance comes from her. Through the cement floor her strong roots sink down. They spread under the asphalt streets. Dreaming, the streets roll over on their bellies, and suck their glossy health from them. Her strong roots sink down and spread under the river and disappear in blood-lines that waver south. Her roots shoot down. Dan's hands follow them. Roots throb. Dan's

heart beats violently. He places his palms upon the earth to cool them. Earth throbs. Dan's heart beats violently. He sees all the people in the house rush to the walls to listen to the rumble. A new-world Christ is coming up. Dan comes up. He is startled. The eyes of the woman dont belong to her. They look at him unpleasantly. From either side, bolted masses press in. He doesnt fit. The mass grows agitant. (62)

Dan's surreal vision of the woman's roots shooting beneath the theater as "blood-lines that waver South" links the sectional experience of the migrants to the body politic, and the destiny, of the nation: the theater is named after the Great Emancipator. But Dan imagines the metonymic chain extending from soil to folk to region to nation to world: the "new-world Christ" carries a message from the other side of the globe. It is this connection between the Washington theater, the South, and rest of the world that enables Dan to imagine himself "plac[ing] his palms upon the earth to cool them"; the gesture that yielded no comfort to Bob Stone in "old Lemon's canefield" here may yield some solace.

In order to move from theory to praxis, however, the needed action must be a collective one. It would seem that the woman and the rest of the "bolted masses" are unaware of the role they are scripted to play in the world-historical drama of their time. Although they are part of the "masses" of the world, these modern-day African Americans are unprepared to "rush to the walls to listen to the rumble" of world revolution. They are, instead, passive spectators to the play placed before them; their eyes, like the newspaper-weakened eyes of Mrs. Pribby, are not their own. The wood produced under conditions of extreme exploitation by the sawmill workers of Georgia, converted into wood pulp and then newspaper, locks these theater-going migrants, like Rhobert, into a new regime of reification. That this regime remains within the circuit of capital is further indicated by the continuing presence of King Cotton in their lives. Bernice is a laundress, earning the price of her theater ticket by washing the clothes of the wealthy; while Muriel cannot take off her coat for fear that her orange dress—the product of factory waged labor—will clash with the crimson drapery of the box seat that establishes her prominence and individuality. Dan's awareness of the "blood-lines that waver south" emanating from the woman next to him signals a recognition that rootedness is not only cultural but also economic: the members of the audience will not be free from their northern urban manacles until they acknowledge the continuity between the rural realm of Jim Crow and the world of segregated Washington.[25]

The incorporation of products of the soil into a universal process of commodification is further shown in Mr. Barry's symbolic seduction of Muriel with a blood-spattered white rose to the accompaniment of a "sentimental love song." It is the parody of courtship in Mr. Barry's falsetto serenade that drives Dan's imagining of sexual intercourse in brutally mechanistic terms: "Me, horizontally above her. / Action: perfect strokes downward oblique" (64). After repudiating

Muriel and denouncing the inhabitants of the theater, however, Dan last appears "as cool as a green stem that has just shed its flower" in an alley "heavy with the scent of rancid flowers and with the scent of fight" (67). Rather than embodying the nostalgic promise of folk reconnection with the land, the organic trope is stripped of interpretive power: the streets of Washington may turn over and suck the soil for sustenance, but the city's denizens have chosen to forget their rural origins. Dan's reduction to a flowerless green stem amid foul-smelling blossoms signals, however, a kind of relief: he is at least no longer burdened with the task of creating symbolic acts that suture contradictions rather than explode them. Where the narrator in "Avey" and John in "Theater" persist in nostalgically recuperating the language of the countryside to explain life in the city, Dan is aware of the need for a new iconography to meet new needs.

While the principal target of Toomer's satirical commentary in "Box Seat" is the false consciousness of the upwardly mobile black working and middle classes, this target extends to an implied commentary on the audience's receptivity to the propaganda accompanying the recent war. For the dwarves fight one another without any ostensible reason: they resemble the "little people" of the world who were propelled into the mass slaughter, even as those who protested the war were manacled and silenced. Mr. Barry's "high-pitched, sentimental" voice as he gives the blood-spattered white rose to Muriel recalls the wartime role of vaudeville shows in melding ferocious militarism with fervent patriotism and romance. Since the Ku Klux Klan was self-designated as the Order of the White Rose, Mr. Barry's offering the rose, and Muriel's accepting it, become more grotesque still. That an African American audience is shown cheering this performance suggests the formidable barriers to their hearing the world's "underground races" rumbling beyond the walls that enclose them. Indeed, the combat staged in the Lincoln Theater, resulting in Mr. Barry's emergence as "the champion" (65), may allude obliquely to the Civil War as well. While the old former slave on the street outside may have seen such world-historical personages as Grant, Lincoln, or Whitman, the audience sees only the bloody victor of a staged battle royal; both the Great War and the Civil War haunt the vaudevillian stage of "Box Seat."[26]

As in other sketches in part 2, the predominant trope in "Box Seat" is one of claustrophobic enclosure. Rather than supplying a formalistic counterpoint to the natural realm, however, images connoting confinement undergo substantial development in the course of the story, challenging the limits of the thematically fused "rounded form" advocated by Waldo Frank. "Houses" are initially described by the narrator as "shy girls whose eyes shine reticently upon the dusk body of the street" (56). But for Dan, Washington's houses are "sharp-edged, massed, metallic"; Mrs. Pribby's house is "bolted to endless rows of metal houses" (57). The seats in the theater are also "bolted houses," each one "a bolt that shoots into a slot, and is locked there" (61). When Dan, refusing to remain silent, shouts out his condemnation of the parody of courtship taking place on the stage and is challenged to fight another patron, the audience becomes "the house," which "tumultuously stirring, grabs its wraps and follows the men" to see them fight in the alley (67). The collective noun signifies that the "mass" that has grown "agitant" is not, as Mike Gold would have it, collectively yearning for revolution, but instead, as "the house," collectively hungering for spectacle. That the spectacle includes a vaudeville battle royal in which two black men beat each other to a pulp to the cheers of a black audience only heightens the irony of the situation. Although the story ends with the narrator's repetition of the opening words—"Eyes of houses, soft girl-eyes, glow reticently upon the hubbub and blink out"—spherical form here produces not reiteration but reversal (67). The "house" of individual property ownership has produced the "house" of mob consciousness: "Box Seat" displays what happens when the mortgage-burdened Rhobert goes out for an evening of entertainment and joins the crowd.

More central to the imagistic matrix of "Box Seat," and to the glimpsed revolutionary horizon in *Cane*, is the startling set of symbols and metaphors briefly sketched in Dan's fantasized act of rebellion: "I am going to reach up and grab the girders of this building and pull them down. The crash will be a signal. Hid by the smoke and dust Dan Moore will arise. In his right hand will be a dynamo. In his left, a god's face that will flash white light from ebony. I'll grab a girder and swing it like a walking-stick. Lightning will flash. I'll grab its black knob and swing it like a crippled cane" (65). A latter-day Samson—or Christ in the temple of the money lenders—Dan yearns to bring down the regime of capitalist white supremacy. The tools he will use to dismantle the master's house are drawn not from the nostalgic *combinatoire* of the organic trope but from the arsenal of industrial modernity. In one hand he (the use of the third person is provocative) will wield a dynamo: a mechanism for creating and storing electrical energy that, for the conservative Henry Adams, signified technological change run rampant but that, for the Soviet futurists, referenced liberated forces of production in a workers' state. In the other hand the poet-rebel will hold a black flashlight, presumably powered by the dynamo: endowed with a "god"-like capacity to extract whiteness from blackness, this lighting mechanism—capable of generating "lightning"—exhibits the power of modern technology, in combination with revolutionary will, to negate and transcend a social order based on racial binaries. The realization that race and racism are functions of capitalist social relations—adumbrated in Toomer's 1919 "Reflections on the Race Riots" and in his program for the capital city discussion group—is here suggestively linked with futuristic artistic practice. Aware, moreover, that steel, not wood, is the medium needed to contest the hold of mind-forged manacles and bolted-down houses in the urban world of the present, Dan will seize one of the girders that have upheld the theater of representation; he will swing it "like a walking stick . . . like a crippled cane." The wooden ideological supports of the past have been superseded by the steel instruments of modernity; the sawmill product that has generated the wood pulp of newspapers is here linked not with vibrant migrant energy ("Stale soggy wood of Washington. . . . Split it! . . . Shred it!") but with status consciousness (the "walking-stick") and senescence (the "crippled cane"). This last image warrants particular note: the cane attributed with prophetic powers in the epigraph to the text—"oracular, deep-rooted cane"—here takes shape as a less than adequate means of penetrating to deeper meanings.[27]

Dan's chosen symbols for communicating his revolutionary desires convey Toomer's continuing preoccupation with power: his statement to Munson that "great art" must have "great substance, great power"; his desire to hear "the workers bellow, 'We Want Power'" in order to "make the walls of capitalism collapse." But Dan's embrace of the dynamo, flashlight, and steel girder, along with his rejection of the walking stick and crippled cane, call on the reader to consider not only a new ideologeme—world revolution—but also a new interpretive process, one requiring cognition of new forms of symbolic action rather than re-cognition of familiar ones. Alone among the many artist figures peopling the pages of *Cane*, Dan Moore is a practitioner of—or at least an aspirant to—Proletkult; he has presumably been reading the *Liberator*. His peasant origin—he was "born in a canefield"—conjoined with his experiences of racial violence and unemployment upon arriving in the capital city, is what supplies him with his subversive standpoint. Indeed, the dynamo and the crippled-cane-shaped steel girder that he imagines in his grasp suggest that his artistic motivation derives from his embrace of a U.S. variant on the Soviet hammer and sickle. Discerning the impotence of symbols burdened with the weight of tradition, he draws his poetry from the future; alone among the protagonists portrayed in *Cane*, Dan Moore at least glimpses what Lukács called "the present as a becoming." Embodying Toomer's closest approximation to the "standpoint of the proletariat," Dan's epistemic positioning enables him to "see in [the present] the tendencies out of whose dialectical opposition he can *make* the future" (original emphasis).[28]

Yet—to continue the quotation from Lukács—"the present cannot be a process of becoming, that belongs to *him*" (original emphasis), insofar as Dan lacks access to a public capable of grasping his message. The audience in the Lincoln Theater may see themselves in the mirror that Mr. Barry shines into their eyes; but they will not grant the prophetic status of the present-day Daniel who wishes to tear down the old and proffer the new. When Dan does speak, he can only invoke the Jesus who moved among the poor; his confinement to the Bible shows that he is, like the rest of the audience, constrained by the walls of the Lincoln Theater. His cry of protest becomes one more voice in the vaudevillian mix. We are reminded that, in the same journal entry where Toomer expressed his longing to hear "the workers" proclaim their desire for "Power," he acknowledged his awareness that "the masters know that little or nothing that I will ever say will have much effect upon the masses. The masters know . . . my solitude." Dan's isolation creates a state of alienation that morphs over into misanthropy—indeed, into misogyny when he imagines himself sexually dominating Muriel with "perfect strokes downward oblique." Divested of its liberatory potential for the collective, the machine can become an instrument of individual dehumanization.[29]

Dan's situation at the end of "Box Seat" hardly supplies grounds for optimism about the fate awaiting the revolutionary artist-rebel in the United States. But the poem "Her Lips Are Copper Wire," which is strategically situated between "Theater" and "Box Seat," suggests, if whimsically, that emotional richness is also accessible through the futurist vision. Relying exclusively on mechanical imagery to describe a moment of passionate embrace, "Her Lips" is noteworthy, among the multiple portraits of male-female alienation throughout *Cane*, for its playful depiction of fulfilled romantic love. The organic trope, used near obsessively by the male poet-narrators elsewhere in *Cane* to describe desired women, is here altogether absent; instead, images from urban life—streetlights, telephones, power-houses, advertising billboards, electrical wires—constitute the poem's signifying *combinatoire*. The metaphor comparing sexual energy with a powerhouse—"telephone the powerhouse / that the main wires are insulate"— here enacts on a personal scale the revolutionary role attributed to the dynamo in "Box Seat." Although Dan Moore's sexual impulses, blocked by Muriel's prudish resistance, turn into mechanized rape-fantasy, the persona in "Her Lips" enjoys an "incandescent" kiss. When the "power-house" is accessible to ordinary men and women, a new ideologeme, workers' power, makes accessible—or at least imaginable—a new range of emotional experiences describable in a new set of tropes and images.[30]

Dan Moore's seething resentment toward the black petty bourgeoisie bears a provocative relationship to Toomer's private feelings of anger and resentment at his own family's position in the "blue-veined" hierarchy, in both the Deep South and the capital city. Notably, Toomer's "dark sister" is absent from the urban section of *Cane*; but his male relatives are, if obliquely, present. As an impeccably dressed man about town, wearing a different suit every day of the week and often sporting a diplomatic cutaway coat, P. B. S. Pinchback routinely carried a stylish walking-stick. The only items of personal property that Toomer inherited from his father, Nathan Toomer, were "some beautiful silk handkerchiefs, a set of small diamond shirt studs, and a slender ebony cane with a gold head." In his decision to feature Dan Moore comparing a black-knobbed steel girder with a "crippled cane," Toomer may have not only pledged his allegiance to an art based in industrial modernity but also declared his independence from both his father and his grandfather. The gold head of the walking stick is converted to black steel; the "slender ebony cane"—suggestively a phallic symbol—is "crippled." As he contemplated a future-perfect art and political practice that would relegate the plantation source of Nathan Toomer's acquired wealth to a social order buried in the past, Toomer took steps to free himself from the burden of shame associated with his father's "parasitic" way of life. With his peasant origins, "liver lips," and hair of "curled wool blossoms," Dan Moore is a far cry from such light-skinned alter-ego characters as David Teyy, Nathan Merilh, and Ralph Kabnis. Toomer's impassioned identification with Dan's mission supplied him with a means of moving past and beyond his father's derivation of easy living from bonded black labor, as well as his grandfather's prominent status among the capital city's elite Negro Four Hundred. Embodying Toomer's notion of the New Negro as both artist and proletarian, this rough-hewn protagonist enabled the son to defeat both versions of the father in his tangled family romance. Social revolution would have purging effects both general and particular.[31]

Finally, "Box Seat" subtly signals Toomer's growing detachment from the aesthetics and politics of Waldo Frank, a surrogate father of a different kind. In some respects, "Box Seat" manifests the strong influence of Frank; *City Block* appears especially to have been on Toomer's mind as he wrote the story. Mr. Barry bears a marked resemblance to "John the Baptist"'s Caesar Dott, the mysterious Negro dwarf whom the tale's protagonist, Karl Loehr, encounters in a park: Dott is "wide as a hogshead," with an "iron bar toothed and clamped . . . in the obscene mass of black flesh." Dan's neighbor in the theater is supplied with a fantasized rootedness comparable to that assigned to Clara, the Negro housekeeper whose unqueried faith steadies the vacillating Karl. She is pictured as "a naked woman, tall and firm, and glowing like red earth. Her hands were above her head. . . . There was a tree above her. And her long bare feet, with the straight toes, were somehow intertwined with the tree's roots." The resemblance between Clara and the woman with the southward-extending roots in "Box Seat" is hard to miss.[32]

The very convergence between Toomer's characterizations in "Box Seat" and Frank's in *City Block* indicates all the more, however, the increasing divergence between the projects of the two writers. Frank's heavily racialized Negro characters remain inarticulate grotesques whose only function is to counter the deracinated alienation of Karl Loehr. They are "non-historical people," destined to foster the psychological development of whites but having no role to play in the cultural and political destiny of the nation, let alone the globe. Caesar Dott's imprisoned flesh is "obscene" in its powerlessness, while the passive Clara simply blends into the natural world. In "Box Seat," by contrast, Mr. Barry takes shape as a purposive agent in the forming of mass consciousness; while the "portly Negress" sitting next to Dan steadfastly refuses to acknowledge the organic connection with the soil which Frank automatically assigns to Clara. Although Toomer's characters remain fixed—bolted down—in the parts they play, they have the option of listening to the "underground races" clamoring to be heard through the walls of the Lincoln Theater; they can be actors in history if they choose. That Dan Moore shouts aloud his condemnation of their refusal to identify with the "leprous" masses outside the theater disrupts their portrayal as figures in a static tableau. Frank may have complained that Dan's outburst was "forced, formless, alien"; but Dan has to cry out, even if he fumbles in his attempt to find an audience and teach it to dream.

"I fear knowledge of my hunger":
"Harvest Song," "Prayer," and the Crisis
of the Organic Trope

While "Box Seat" is situated at the acme of the curve that rises in part 2, it also sets forth the limits past which Toomer could not move. In his description of the circular form of *Cane*, Toomer remarked to Frank that, after the text "swings upward into Theater and Box Seat," it "ends (pauses) in Harvest Song." As Toomer noted in a draft letter—probably written to Frank—some ten months later, however, this "pause" was hardly restful: *Cane* had been "distilled from the most terrible strain I have ever known. . . . 'Harvest Song,' better than any other of the book's contents, gives an idea of my state at that time."[33]

"Harvest Song" offers an allegory of the process of literary creation; arguably, of the process of writing *Cane* itself. The poem's title, recalling "Cotton Song," parallels the labors of writerly and agricultural production. In theme and imagery, "Harvest Song" gestures toward works by Robert Frost—"After Apple Picking," "A Tuft of Flowers"—that analogize the depression and ambivalence of a reaper after bringing in the harvest with the psychic exhaustion of the poet after completing a literary work. The writer's "cradled . . . oats" signify the pieces of his text; the act of binding, their final collation and organization (69). The poet has abandoned the spectatorial stance of "Reapers"; he is a harvester in his own right, working within shouting distance of other workers similarly employed. The writer who continually used botanical metaphors to describe his various schemes for ordering the poems and sketches of his book-in-progress has finally culled the fruits of his labors.

But the poem hardly celebrates this achievement. The speaker's closing words betray a recognition that the production of literary texts, however exhausting, cannot be fully analogized with manual labor:

> O my brothers, I beat my palms, still soft, against the stubble of my harvesting. (You beat your soft palms, too.) My pain is sweet. Sweeter than the oats or wheat or corn. It will not bring me knowledge of my hunger.

That the speaker's palms—and those of his fellow writers—are "soft" suggests his awareness of the difference between the labor of writing books and that of working in a field or on a loading dock (or, indeed, in a shipyard). While he shares with the workers featured in "Reapers" the experience of toil, class privilege intrudes on the otherwise easy analogy between producing texts and culling crops. Even though the reapers are most likely sharecroppers who will receive little compensation for their toil, they are engaged in a collective activity; by contrast, even though he owns the fruits of his labor, he works alone. Indeed, the poem attests to the speaker's lack of solidarity with the other "soft-palmed" workers; he evinces empathy with fellow writers who are "dust-caked and blind" like himself but also resents the "stack'd field of other harvesters" who have worked more rapidly than he. Signaling the writer's ambivalent relation to the community of artists under conditions of capitalist competition, the poem also suggests Toomer's tenuous relationship to the modernist circles to which he hungered to belong. At the same time, the speaker's repeated referring to the other harvesters as "brothers" and uttering of the word "eoho" recall the tenor of Toomer's letters to Frank, in which both words figured frequently and prominently. One can plausibly read into the divided consciousness of the speaker in "Harvest Song" the complex amalgam of gratitude, envy, and resentment that increasingly characterized Toomer's feelings toward his mentor, who had played such an important role in the cradling, gathering, and binding of the parts of Toomer's book.[34]

Arguably, however, more than class guilt, postproduction blues, or even envious resentment of a more accomplished fellow writer is conveyed through the anguished consciousness recorded in "Harvest Song." Where "Box Seat" strains against the confines of spherical form, this poem enacts spherical form with a vengeance. The beginnings of all the stanzas except for the last one constitute near mirror images of one another. The first and penultimate stanzas begin "I am a reaper"; the third and fifth-from-last begin, "My eyes are caked" and "My ears are caked"; the fourth and fourth-from-last begin, "It would be good to see them" and "It would be good to hear their songs"; and so forth. The poet is entrapped within a chiasmatic verbal net, an arrested dialectic, of his own making; he is blinded and deafened by the redundancy of his own words. By contrast with the technological images that signal Toomer's embrace of the political and aesthetic avant-garde in "Box Seat," moreover, the exclusive use of images drawn from agrarian production renders "Harvest Song" strangely anomalous, especially in the context of the urban modernity portrayed throughout the rest of part 2. The hyper-materiality of the poem's repeated images—the reaper cannot taste the grain he cracks in his mouth; he hungers and thirsts; his eyes and his ears are caked with dust; his throat is dry—suggests that he in fact now nearly chokes on the organic trope. The poem reverberates with echoes from "Song of the Son," where the speaker pledged to become a "singing tree" transmitting the culture of generations of African-descended laborers. But the literalism of "Harvest Song"— its insistence upon the physical reality underlying its dominant tropes—suggests that the fruits of the poet's labor possess little nourishing power. "Harvest Song" displays not the triumphant capacity of the organic trope to assert the connection between the Negro folk and the nation, but instead the *combinatoire*'s reification of the very images meant to contest the objectification of the folk. As in "Kabnis," the poet's yearning for "golden words" ends up in a "split-gut song."[35]

The writerly dilemma presented in "Harvest Song" is illuminated by the situation of the speaker in the immediately preceding poem, "Prayer." Although Frank found "Prayer" weak and urged its elimination, Toomer—who acceded to almost all Frank's other suggestions regarding cuts—in this case objected: "I know it is an imperfect realization," he wrote. "But its idea is essential to the spiritual phase of Cane. And it is the companion piece, the only companion piece to Harvest Song. I am almost willing to sacrifice the artistic to the spiritual curve in this instance."[36]

Since Toomer may indeed have sacrificed his book's artistic curve—"Prayer" is murky and confusing—his insistence upon its inclusion is provocative. The speaker laments not only that mind and body are "opaque to the soul" but also that the soul itself cannot escape its entrapment within the physical world: its "flesh-eye" has a "closed lid." While he hopes that the soul is "but a little finger" of the "Spirits" to whom he is praying, he admits that he has confused the body with its soul as well as with its little finger (68). In obsessively settling on fragmented body parts to explore the seemingly unbridgeable gulf between consciousness and material reality, the speaker addresses concerns that are simultaneously ontological and epistemological. He proclaims the tyranny of the concrete over the abstract: when the concrete is divested of a larger interpretive context, all that remains is the realm of immediacy. The little finger is part of the body, but it cannot function as its metonymic equivalent. The soul thinks of itself as independent but relies on its "flesh-eye" for location in the body. No single part of an entity contains the meaning of the whole; yet the whole cannot be known separately from the parts that it comprises. In the absence of a felt connection with the social totality, the fragmentation of consciousness is inevitable.[37]

Read in connection with "Harvest Song," "Prayer" locates the poet's dilemma of assigning meaning not so much in the dualism of body and spirit as in the mistaken way in which he has been positing the relationship of the part to the whole. The poem's very abstraction points to the fact that Toomer experienced the crisis in metonymic nationalism at a high level of generality. In "Avey," the narrator encounters a crisis in locating the ending of the metonymic chain; in "Prayer," the very process of articulating the links is called into question.

"Crimson Gardens. Hurrah!": "Bona and Paul" and the Limits of Cultural Pluralism

In the description of Cane's circular form that designates "Harvest Song" as the text's "pause," Toomer noted that "the curve really starts with Bona and Paul (awakening)" before it "plunges into Kabnis." This view of "Bona and Paul" as an "awakening" corresponds both with events in Toomer's life and with the compositional history of Cane. Drawing on Toomer's experiences at Chicago's American School of Physical Culture in the mid-1910s, the story was probably drafted as early as 1918 or even 1917. It was revised twice, however: once in October 1922, after Toomer showed it to Lola Ridge, and then again in early 1923, when Toomer was preparing Cane for publication. It is important to bear this history in mind, for "Bona and Paul" is probably the text to which Toomer decided to add, at Ridge's advice, the "flare of poetry" that would dispel its former "sterile, aloof, disillusioned note." While we can only guess where this "flare of poetry" was inserted, Toomer was evidently aware that much of his writing continually wavered between affirmation and irony, and that a single brushstroke could shift the balance in one direction or another.[38]

While the other stories in part 2 either specifically reference Washington, DC, or suggest a generalized city setting, "Bona and Paul" is situated in Chicago— a choice of setting potentially supporting a reading of the story affirming the doctrines of cultural pluralism and literary nationalism. This city was, after all, featured in Frank's *Our America* as the quintessential early modernist site of the "turning of the soil"; Paul, as poet in the making, can be seen to inherit the mantle of Carl Sandburg and Edgar Lee Masters. Paul's thoughts as he looks south over the El tracks position him as the future creator of "Song of the Son": "Paul follows the sun to a pine-matted hillock in Georgia. He sees the slanting roofs of gray unpainted cabins tinted lavender. A Negress chants a lullaby beneath the mate-eyes of a southern planter. Her breasts are ample for the sucking of a song. She weans it, and sends it, curiously weaving, among lush melodies of cane and corn. Paul follows the sun into himself in Chicago" (71). This passage can be read as a counter to the portrayal of Kabnis as failed artist that appears in the following section of *Cane*. While Kabnis, in his hilltop cabin, anguishes over his "bastard" origins, Paul presumably draws artistic inspiration from the biracial source of the song that warms his life in Chicago; bloodlines can, it seems, waver north. The conjunction of the tropes of parturition and organicism in the creation of the song suggests that the offspring of the "Negress"—evidently impregnated by the planter—will supply the basis for a sectional art with national implications. Anticipating the final image of "Kabnis"—the song arising over the treetops at dawn in the "sleepy southern town"—this vision can be seen to assert the continuing relevance of the organic trope to the representation of social relations, rural and urban, south and north. Indeed, it can be read as compensation for the failed connections between women and men that have crowded the pages of *Cane*. Not only does Bona's comparison of Paul's complexion with a "harvest leaf" and an "autumn moon" (70) suggest that the kinds of images Toomer's male narrators used to portray the South's women of color retain their valence in the North. It also shows that women can use these tropes in their perceptions of men: as in "Esther," "Blood-Burning Moon," and "Theater," the reader is exposed to the thoughts of characters of both sexes. When Paul and Bona, Art and Helen walk to dinner along a Chicago boulevard, moreover, they "move along an island-like far-stretching strip of leaf-soft ground" (74). Although in Sempter the scapegoated Becky was isolated on an "eye-shaped piece of ground between the road and the railroad tracks," in Chicago the median strip affords a site of leisure—and love—exempt from racial categorization.

The closing scene at the Crimson Gardens, too, can be read as reinforcing this portrayal of utopian possibility. The blood that ran down Tom Burwell's face in "Blood-Burning Moon" reappears as the fused sexual energy of the dancing Bona and Paul, "a dizzy blood clot on a gyrating floor" (77): in Chicago, interracial romance is not the catalyst to murder. The mixed-race Paul's attainment of integrated selfhood is, furthermore, described in Whitmanesque terms: "Suddenly he knew that people saw, not attractiveness in his dark skin, but difference. Their stares, giving him to himself, filled something long empty within him, and were like green blades sprouting in his consciousness" (75). When he plans to leave the club in Bona's company, Paul's closing words to the doorman at once affirm his own Negro identification and proclaim the belonging of the Negro in Young America's cultural pluralist project. "I came back to tell you, brother, that white faces are petals of roses," Paul declares. "That dark faces are petals of dusk. That I am going out and gather petals. That I am going out and know her whom I brought here with me to these Gardens which are purple like a bed of roses would be at dusk" (78). Even if Bona has decided to leave, according to this line of interpretation, Paul has attained an insight that is not only personally therapeutic but also instrumental in limning the concepts of race, nation and representation guiding Toomer's composition of *Cane*.[39]

Ample evidence invites this kind of affirmative reading of "Bona and Paul," and a number of critics have responded to this call. But the story's near-complete enmeshment within the dominant tropes of *Cane* requires the reader to contemplate the equally plausible possibility of ironic subversion. Paul's vision of the Negress's baby-as-song wending its way northward through "lush melodies of cane and corn" is countered by the memory of the smoke rising from Karintha's buried infant. The image of the lullaby-singing Negress—invoking the figure of the Mammy Monument then under debate in Washington, DC—would soon take on horrific overtones in "Kabnis," where the mammy becomes the murderer of the infant in her charge. The "island-like" piece of ground where the students walk is enclosed by stone mansions that "overshadow" working-class clapboard houses; these in turn resemble "Negro shanties in some southern alley" (74). Both the songs and the buildings signify not only the U.S. class divide but also the continuing prevalence of the myth of Dixie in the apparently freer North. Bona's exoticized conception of Paul as an "autumn leaf" and a "harvest moon" does not, moreover, rule out her viewing him as a "nigger" and abandoning him at the story's end.

Above all, the Crimson Gardens, the presumed site of utopian transcendence, invites critical interrogation. The narrator's insistence that a good time is being had by all—the phrase "Crimson Gardens. Hurrah! So one feels" appears repeatedly—becomes increasingly frenetic with each iteration. The breakneck pace of the popular song "Little Liza Jane" in the background enhances the hysterical mood: everyone in the Crimson Gardens is required to have fun. But the cabaret's pretension to democracy is specious: it may welcome college students and stockbrokers, but it is guarded by a doorman, himself African American, endowed with the godlike power to exclude people too markedly of African descent. Looking at Paul, the patrons wonder, "What is he, a Spaniard, an Indian, an Italian, a Mexican, a Hindu, or a Japanese?" (74). That he may be a Negro is beyond contemplation. By contrast with the garden of life imagined in Georgia Douglas Johnson's "Fusion"—which produces hybrids "[m]ore gorgeous and more beautiful / Than any parent portion"—the Crimson Gardens of "Bona and Paul" is a Jim-Crowed cultural pluralist Eden; petals of different hues may be culled, but there will be no grafting of plants. Art's complexion varies from pink to blue to purple, but it never shades into yellow, brown, or black, even in shadow.[40]

The prevalence throughout the sketch of pastel colors, especially pink, suggests that Paul is seeing whiteness through glasses that favor rose- and purple-tinted blends of red, white, and blue. These tints darken ominously to "a spot . . . in the purple" that "comes furiously toward him" as the "face of the black man" (78) hired to defend the racial purity of the Crimson Gardens. We recall the purple plums bursting in the pinewood air of "Song of the Son," as well as Kabnis's curse on the "whole damn purple country"; the petals of cultural pluralism morph readily into bruised flesh. As in Randolph Bourne's "Trans-National America" and Waldo Frank's *Our America*, even for the more advanced cultural pluralists the nation's "e pluribus unum" is not extended to the dark-skinned people of the nation or the world. Paul's Whitmanesque vision that "giv[es] him to himself" is, moreover, ambiguous: the recognition that the revelers at the Crimson Gardens see in "his dark skin . . . not attractiveness . . . but difference" is described as not "leaves" but "blades" of grass: the truth that "sprou[ts] in his consciousness" supposedly gives him "fullness, and strength and peace," but it may cut into his flesh as well. When Paul finally announces to the doorman that he is gathering blossoms of various hues, we are thus reminded that—as at the end of "Box Seat"—removing blossoms from their stems kills them. That the "flare of poetry" that Toomer inserted is probably either Paul's "blades of grass" realization or his "petals of roses" / "petals of dusk" proclamation—these are, after all, the story's two apparently utopian moments—suggests the fragility of his achieved sense of self: both moments hinge on Paul's perception of how he is perceived. Just as the organic trope is working overtime, its hyper-materiality yoked with the frenetic declaration "Hurrah! So one feels," Paul is, arguably, protesting too much. His declaration of achieved psychological harmony is as much a defensive act of ideological suturing as a positive declaration of national belonging.[41]

For all its pink decor, the signature color of the Crimson Gardens is red—bloodred. Chicago had been the site of even more bloodletting than Washington during the "red summer" of 1919; the "dizzying clot of blood" of Paul and Bona's wild dancing does not dispel the "frenzy of dizziness" experienced by the "blood suckers of the War" upon tasting the blood of the migrants. Despite the absence of official policies of Jim Crow, moreover, many Chicago public facilities—including nightclubs like the Crimson Gardens—were routinely segregated. As in

Washington, where black migrants who wished to "dance and shout above the tick and trill of white-walled buildings" were restricted to the segregated area around Seventh Street, Chicago's African Americans lived and partied—and retained their connection with the culture of the South—in black neighborhoods on the South Side. In the whites-only Crimson Gardens, "crimson" blood-thinking intrudes on the "garden" of cultural pluralist innocence. With its pastel petals, the nightclub is at best a "hothouse," one that—as Mike Gold put it in his sardonic commentary on the literature of liberalism—precludes the growth of an art that grows from "the soil of the masses." This is not a place where the "mass-heart" of the nation's proletariat, black, white, or whatever, can be heard beating.

In "Bona and Paul," there are simply too many oblique allusions to the blood and bruising that pervade *Cane* to allow for a wholly affirmative reading. Toomer's own protestation notwithstanding, the story can be read as Paul's achievement of an identity beyond racial dualism only if one ignores the cognitive dissonance embodied in its imagery and action. But neither, I propose, can the stick be bent too far in the direction of irony. When Toomer was putting the finishing touches on the story in early 1923, he was experiencing increasing doubts about the depth and breadth of Frank's commitment to a racially expanded notion of "our America"; but he was by no means disillusioned with either the man or the program. Toomer was well aware, moreover, that Frank and his allies were under attack by nativists like Lothrop Stoddard and Mary Austin; "America" remained a contradictory ideologeme calling for continuing contestation. "Bona and Paul" is, like "Box Seat," best read symptomatically as Toomer's response to a historical situation in which the possibilities for radical social change were rapidly receding. Where the closing story in part 2 of *Cane* differs from "Box Seat," however, is in its confinement of this response within the realm of the nation. Dan Moore's imagined seizure of the dynamo, flashlight, and girder are inspired by the hope that Washington's working class will at some point hear and join the uprising of the "underground races" of the world; his rage and frustration with the audience in the Lincoln Theater are proportional to his awareness that the walls of U.S. capitalism are not about to collapse. Paul's hopes—more personal, more modest, more bound to a Whitmanesque vision of the nation—occasion less mourning when they are dashed.[42]

That a white woman in Chicago is portrayed as the agent of Paul's failed attempt to cull blossoms of different colors, however, warrants special note. For Chicago was, we should recall, the site of Toomer's own political awakening. Along Chicago's wide boulevards, their grassy centers filled with summer revelers at night, he had felt that "the workers' revolution had already taken place and that the city belonged not to the few but to the many." At the American School of Physical Culture—the site of Bona's flirtation with Paul—Farrell had catechized the young Toomer about the need for socialism. And in his friendship with the white Eleanor Davis, Toomer had first discovered a woman whose attraction to philosophy and political radicalism meshed with his own. "Bona and Paul" is semiautobiographical not only in its basis of Paul in Toomer, but also in its basis of Art in Toomer's friend Harry Karstens and, especially, of Bona in Eleanor Davis. In the story, however, Toomer retains the mutual attraction between Bona and Paul but effaces her enthusiasm for leftist theory and practice. Although Art describes Bona to Paul as "[t]all, not puffy and pretty, more serious and deep—the kind you like these days," the content of this seriousness and depth is not explored; she is portrayed as psychologically probing and sexually curious, but hardly critical of capitalism. Moreover, whereas Eleanor Davis had resisted the attempt by her guardian to turn her against Toomer on the basis of his racial ancestry, Bona is portrayed as casually but irremediably racist. Toomer retains in "Bona and Paul" the utopian space of a Chicago boulevard in the summer, but he divests it of its political valence; it is a site where interracial love and friendship can find a momentary stay against confusion, but the surrounding environment cannot, it seems, be transformed.

Toomer was, of course, under no obligation to reproduce in "Bona and Paul" the tenor, emotional or political, of his relationship with a girlfriend from his time in college some seven years previously. But we need to bear in mind that a crucial element in his 1923 vision of the "proletariat or world upheaval" was the connection between the revolt of the "whole black and brown world heaving upward" and white people. The upsurge would heave "against" some whites, while with others it would "mix"—the "mixture" being, however, "insufficient to absorb the heaving, hence it but accelerates and fires it." In this complicated formulation, which recalls in part the imagery of "Banking Coal," white people figure as either impediments or accelerants to the process of world revolution: precisely because their participation will be too limited to "absorb" the movement of the "underground races," this participation, when it occurs, will "fire" the movement all the more, creating conditions of dramatically uneven development.

Toomer was hardly alone among radicals of his day in having no roadmap for charting the course of the proletarian revolution; like many others, black and white, he hoped for class-based multiracial unity, even as he doubted whether the working class, especially the white working class, could work its way through and past its racist socialization. Given the formative role of his experiences in Chicago in "accelerating" his own radicalization, however—and especially his positive experiences with at least some whites who sparked and shared his enthusiasm for socialism—it is telling that Toomer chose in *Cane*'s final short story not to raise the possibility of consummated interracial union. Alone among the stories in *Cane*, "Bona and Paul" features in its title both a man and a woman; that this apparent equality in their gendered roles is not matched by a reciprocity in their racialized roles speaks volumes about the constrained possibilities for social and political change that Toomer envisioned as he put the finishing touches on his text. Racism is central to the arrested dialectic of history in *Cane*.

Coda

Black Super-Vaudeville:
History and Form in Cane

In the dark times
Will there also be singing?
Yes, there will also be singing
About the dark times.
—Bertolt Brecht, "Motto" (1938)

Cane is black vaudeville. It is black super-vaudeville out of the South.
—Jean Toomer, publicity sketch for *Cane* (1923)

We now turn to a brief consideration of the relationship between history and form in *Cane*. Given the wide range of interpretations of the text's parts, it comes as no surprise that critics have offered dramatically differing interpretations of the whole. Some have discerned a progression toward resolution and synthesis; others a suspended state of fragmentation and division; still others a triumphant achievement of polyphony and hybridity. With a few noteworthy exceptions, however, commentaries on *Cane* have largely overlooked the text's engagement with history. They may address *Cane*'s representation of the present as an outgrowth of the past, its connection with contemporaneous racial discourses and practices, or its placement within literary experimentalism; but they do not generally treat the text's form as itself an enactment of the historical contradictions shaping the time and place of its creation.

In *The Political Unconscious*, Fredric Jameson proposes that it is primarily at the level of form—of genre—that a text displays its relationship to the shifting and clashing modes of production in the world from which it arises. "Cultural revolution," he writes, designates "that moment in which the coexistence of various modes of production becomes visibly antagonistic, their contradictions moving to the very center of political, social, and historical life." As we have seen, *Cane*'s poems and sketches, as well as their ordering within and among the text's sections, bear out this formulation of its dramatically variegated nature. The text's movement from South to North to South exhibits the changing social practices and modes of consciousness accompanying the starkly uneven development of capitalism in the early twentieth-century United States. The divergent outcomes to interracial sexual relationships in "Blood-Burning Moon" and "Bona and Paul" point to qualitatively different manifestations of Jim Crow in rural Georgia and urban Illinois; the fates of Sam Raymon and Rhobert exhibit the workings of hegemony in markedly varying admixtures of ideology and coercion; and "Portrait in Georgia" and "Her Lips Are Copper Wire" represent conditions of human possibility that are, to all appearances, worlds apart. Moreover, Toomer's skilful maneuvering between and among his kaleidoscopic array of themes, images, and styles permits the reader to see all these texts as mediations of a socioeconomic system that rests on not one but many modes of abstracted labor: the cotton that supplies the basis of open racist terrorism against debt peons in "Kabnis" is remediated as exchangeable goods in "Esther" and then again as pastoral nostalgia in "Calling Jesus." At the same time, the reader catches glimpses of the various modes of resistance to which reification gives rise: Mame Lamkins's defiance of her lynchers in "Kabnis"; the cotton baler's unwillingness to wait for Judgment Day in "Cotton Song"; the migrants' rejection of "whitewash" in "Seventh Street"; Dan Moore's messianic call to Washington, DC, theatergoers to join the revolt of the world's submerged masses in "Box Seat."[1]

Toomer's ability to capture all these voices, moods, and scenes in a single text derives in no small measure, I argue, from the vision of possibility that opened up in the wake of the Russian Revolution and the class struggles of 1919: the text's formal embodiment of "cultural revolution" hinges largely on its emergence from a revolutionary conjuncture in one part of the world that promised, for many, to become a transformative event on a global scale. *Cane*'s attention to uneven geographical and historical development, both global and national, is largely what permits Toomer to draw together poetry, prose, and drama in an experimental collage without precedent in U.S. literary history. His description of *Cane* as "black super-vaudeville out of the South" conveys this aspect of the text's performance. Stipulating both the South and blackness—routinely viewed as backward—as the sources of inspiration, Toomer proposes that his text, like a vaudeville performance, has something for everyone. Indeed, its "super-" quality derives from its ability to stage a range of possible destinies, thereby mediating the multiple contradictions of its historical moment. Alluding to the only text in *Cane* directly featuring a vaudeville performance, "Box Seat," Toomer's description of the book as "black super-vaudeville" gestures not only toward the centrality of this story to the key images and ideas in *Cane* but also to the choices that Dan Moore imagines himself holding out to the audience in the Lincoln Theater. The phrase "black super-vaudeville" suggests the ability of a popular artistic form to gesture toward both the past and the future embedded in the present.

If *Cane* registers the impact of the postwar revolutionary upsurge at the meta-level of genre, however, its constitutive texts project the confusion and disappointment that, for many, followed the failure of 1919 to generate expanding revolutionary possibilities in the United States. The bloody repression of the "red summer," the Palmer Raids, the rise of the new Ku Klux Klan, the defeat of the Dyer Anti-Lynching Bill, the proposed retelling of history through the Mammy Monument and Heyward Shepherd memorials, the failure of the labor movement to carry forward the spirit of Bogalusa: these reversals of historical potentiality are refracted through the characters, actions, and images of *Cane*. At the level of symbolic action, the reader catches only glimpses of an alternative paradigm. Every gesture toward liberation is contested by its dialectical counterpart: folk soil-rootedness by peasant bondage to the land; the flames of revolution by the bonfires of lynching. At the level of ideologeme, the text's guiding concepts are beset by ambiguity: sectional art is riven by the contradiction between Georgia's beauty and its violence; the New Negro cannot decide whether to cower or rebel; and the United States is multiply signified by Sempter's courthouse tower, Washington's Capitol dome, and Chicago's Crimson Gardens. The doctrine of metonymic nationalism, promising a fusion of the New Negro Movement with the aspirations of Young America, cannot heave upward against the weight of tradition to supply a new paradigm for theory and praxis.

The trope in *Cane* that more than any other conveys the text's encounter with historical aporia is the figure of the Black Madonna, whose fate—whether as murdering/murdered mother or as perpetual virgin—simultaneously signals the failed birth of revolution and the grounding of this failure in the Real of Jim Crow, South and North. The function of the black woman as an index to historical stillbirth, I have proposed, takes on particular intensity because of the experiences of Toomer's own family; his knowledge of the fate of his "dark sister," repressed into the text's political unconscious but clamoring for expression, energizes *Cane*'s larger exploration of exploitation and halted potentiality. Yet while Toomer offers a searing critique of the regime of capital and its second-order ideological and institutional mediations, this critique oscillates between the poles of antinomy rather than moving toward negation and sublation. Toomer's designation of his text as "black super-vaudeville out of the South" points toward his text's confinement within discourses familiar to its audience. Even as its vaudevillian inclusion of multiple acts registers the conflicting forces constituting the postwar social formation, displaying a stunning comprehension of totality, its circular form indicates its enclosure within an arrested historical dialectic: *Cane* enacts, in Walter Benjamin's teasingly paradoxical formulation, "dialectics at a standstill."

That *Cane* fails to chart a course beyond the limits of its time and place should not, however, strike us as especially strange. After all, Dan Moore's call on the inhabitants of the Lincoln Theater to heed the rumbling of the world's underground races is of necessity a "futuristic" gesture so long as a new and different future does not emerge from the present, creating an audience capable of hearing the message of the prophet. Jameson argues that "cultural revolution" is not limited to "so-called 'transitional' periods, during which social formations dominated by one mode of production undergo a radical restructuration in the course of which a different 'dominant' emerges." Rather, every text bears witness to a "perpetual cultural revolution" derived from a "permanent struggle between the various co-existing modes of production." What *Cane* reveals, however, is that "cultural revolution" rests at the level of the "merely" cultural in the absence of such "radical restructuration"; in order for a text to do its work as the bearer of an alternate future, it needs to be articulated with a corresponding project at work in the realm of the Real. The text's relationship to the history that hurts remains a largely symptomatic one to the extent that its encounter with this history remains lodged in its political unconscious, unable openly to call people from their houses and teach them to dream.[2]

Yet *Cane* also reveals that there is a historically specific reason for this text's inability to project a collective subject capable of transforming a conjuncture into an event—namely, the force and prevalence of racism in the United States as both a psychological and a material phenomenon. Toomer sought, in both his writing and his life, to find a way through and past the barriers mounted by race-based reification. Only at our peril do we imagine that such barriers no longer exist. While much has changed since the time when Toomer wrote *Cane*, much has not: the forces producing an arrested historical dialectic in our own time may not be all that different from those with which Toomer grappled in the production of his 1923 masterwork.

NOTES

Abbreviations

AGP	Angelina Grimké Papers, Moorland-Spingarn Research Institute, Howard University
Brother	Jean Toomer, *Brother Mine: The Correspondence of Jean Toomer and Waldo Frank*, ed. Kathleen Pfeiffer (Urbana: University of Illinois Press, 2010)
Cane, Norton 2	Jean Toomer, *"Cane": Authoritative Text, Contexts, Criticism*, 2nd ed., ed. Rudolph P. Byrd and Henry Louis Gates Jr. (New York: Norton, 2011)
JT	Jean Toomer
JTP	Jean Toomer Papers, James Weldon Johnson Collection, Beinecke Library, Yale University
JTTAH	Charles Scruggs and Lee VanDemarr, *Jean Toomer and the Terrors of American History* (Philadelphia: University of Pennsylvania Press, 1998)
Letters	*Letters of Jean Toomer*, ed. Mark Whalan (Knoxville: University of Tennessee Press, 2006)
O'Daniel	Therman B. O'Daniel, ed., *Jean Toomer: A Critical Evaluation* (Washington, DC: Howard University Press, 1988)
Wayward	*The Wayward and the Seeking: A Collection of Writings by Jean Toomer*, ed. Darwin T. Turner (Washington, DC: Howard University Press, 1980)

Introduction

1. Barbara Foley, *Spectres of 1919: Class and Nation in the Making of the New Negro* (Urbana: University of Illinois Press, 2003).

2. Antonio Gramsci, *Selections from the Prison Notebooks*, ed. and trans. Quintin Hoare and Geoffrey Nowell Smith (New York: International, 1971), 178, 219–20; William H. Sewell Jr., *Logics of History: Social Theory and Social Transformation* (Chicago: University of Chicago Press, 2005), 218; Alain Badiou, *The Communist Hypothesis*, trans. David Macey and Steve Corcoran (London: Verso, 2010), 219. Gramsci further noted, "The demonstration in the last analysis only succeeds and is 'true' if it becomes a new reality, if the forces of opposition triumph" (178). For more on Gramsci's notion of conjuncture, see Peter D. Thomas, *The Gramscian Moment: Philosophy, Hegemony, and Marxism* (Chicago: Haymarket Books, 2009), 294–97.

3. Richard B. Moore, "Bogalusa," *Emancipator*, 13 March 1920, 4; Walter Benjamin, *The Arcades Project*, ed. Rolf Tiedemann, trans. Howard Eiland and Kevin McLaughlin (New York: Belknap Press, 2002), 463; Gramsci, *Selections from the Prison Notebooks*, 276. For

more on "arrested dialectic," see Marcial González, "Jameson's 'Arrested Dialectic': From Structuralism to Postmodernism," http://clogic.eserver.org/2–2/gonzalez.html, accessed 31 October 2013; and E. P. Thompson, *The Romantics: England in a Revolutionary Age* (New York: New Press, 1997), 37. For the argument that modernity and modernism are marked by the trauma of lost hope in social revolution, see Marianne DeKoven, *Rich and Strange: Gender, History, Modernism* (Princeton, N.J.: Princeton University Press, 1991); Jonathan Flatley, *Affective Mapping: Melancholia and the Politics of Modernism* (Cambridge, Mass.: Harvard University Press, 2008); and Seth Moglen, *Mourning Modernity: Literary Modernism and the Injuries of American Capitalism* (Stanford, Calif.: Stanford University Press, 2007).

4. Lothrop Stoddard, *The Rising Tide of Color against White World-Supremacy* (New York: Scribner's, 1920). The term "non-historical people," derived from Hegel, strongly influenced the theory and practice of the Second International. See G. W. F. Hegel, *Philosophy of History*, trans. A. V. Miller (New York: Dover, 1956), 142–62; and Mark Pittenger, *American Socialists and Evolutionary Thought, 1870–1920* (Madison: University of Wisconsin Press, 1993).

5. Paul U. Kellogg, "The Negro Pioneers," in Alain Locke, *The New Negro: An Interpretation* (1925; rpt. New York: Simon and Schuster, 1992), 271–77; Foley, *Spectres of 1919*, 159–97. For more on the postwar connections among regionalism, nationalism, and racism, see Susan Hegeman, *Patterns for America: Modernism and the Concept of Culture* (Princeton, N.J.: Princeton University Press, 1999); and Leigh Anne Duck, *The Nation's Regions: Southern Modernism, Segregation, and U.S. Nationalism* (Athens: University of Georgia Press, 2006).

6. William K. Wimsatt Jr. and Monroe C. Beardsley, "The Intentional Fallacy," in *The Verbal Icon: Studies in the Meaning of Poetry*, ed. William K. Wimsatt Jr. (Lexington: University of Kentucky Press, 1967), 3–18; Michel Foucault, "What Is an Author?," in *Aesthetics, Method and Epistemology: Essays of Michael Foucault*, ed. Richard Faubion (New York: New Press, 1998), 205–19.

7. Karl Marx, *The Eighteenth Brumaire of Louis Bonaparte* (New York: International Publishers, 1969), 15. For more on the methodology of "reading forward" specifically in connection with textual revision, see Barbara Foley, *Wrestling with the Left: The Making of Ralph Ellison's "Invisible Man"* (Durham, N.C.: Duke University Press, 2010).

8. Fredric Jameson, *The Political Unconscious: Narrative as a Socially Symbolic Act* (Ithaca, N.Y.: Cornell University Press, 1981), 102, 35, 76, 81–87. Useful summaries of Jameson's theoretical schema are supplied by William C. Dowling, *Jameson, Althusser, and Marx: An Introduction to the Political Unconscious* (Ithaca, N.Y.: Cornell University Press, 1984); Ian Buchanan, *Fredric Jameson: Live Theory* (London Continuum, 2006); and Adam Roberts, *Fredric Jameson* (London: Routledge, 2000). For more on "structured silences," see Pierre Macherey, "The Spoken and the Unspoken," in *A Theory of Literary Production*, trans. Geoffrey Wall (London: Routledge and Kegan Paul, 1978), 85–89; and Jameson, *Political Unconscious*, 66–67.

9. Jameson, *Political Unconscious*, 79. For criticism of Jameson's notion of social formation, see Sean Homer, *Fredric Jameson: Marxism, Hermeneutics, Postmodernism* (New York: Routledge, 1998), 68; and James Seaton, "Marxism without Difficulty: Fredric Jameson's *The Political Unconscious*," *Centennial Review* 28–29 (fall–winter 1984–85): 122–42.

10. Fredric Jameson, "Third World Literature in the Era of Multinational Capital" (1986; rpt. in *The Jameson Reader*, ed. Michael Hardt and Kathi Weeks [Oxford: Blackwell, 2000],

315–39); Fredric Jameson, "Interview," *Diacritics* 12, no. 3 (autumn 1982): 72–91, quoted 84. The term *ideologeme* derives from M. M. Bakhtin, *The Formal Method in Literary Scholarship: A Critical Introduction to Sociological Poetics*, trans. Albert J. Wehrle (Baltimore, Md.: Johns Hopkins University Press, 1985), 21. See also William Marling, "The Formal Ideologeme," *Semiotica* 98 (1994): 277–99.

11. This positing of different "layers" of the political unconscious is to be differentiated from the methodological paradigm based on a psychological mapping of the conscious/preconscious/unconscious. See Claudia Tate, *Psychoanalysis and Black Novels: Desire and the Protocols of Race* (New York: Oxford University Press, 1998).

12. Georg Lukács, *History and Class Consciousness: Studies in Marxist Dialectics*, trans. Rodney Livingstone (Cambridge, Mass.: MIT Press, 1971), 100. For criticisms of Jameson's emphasis on reification, see Cornel West, "Fredric Jameson's Marxist Hermeneutics," *boundary 2*, 11 (autumn 1982–winter 1983): 177–200; Terry Eagleton, "The Politics of Style," *Diacritics* 12, no. 3 (autumn 1982): 14–22; and Timothy Bewes, *Reification; Or, the Anxiety of Late Capitalism* (London: Verso, 2002), 19–21.

13. *JTTAH.*

14. According to Toomer's friend Gorham Munson, by the 1930s Toomer had developed the habit of "lying, lying" about many features of his past, not just his racial background (Indice M. Watterson, interview with Gorham B. Munson, 27 June 1969, Amistad Research Center, Tulane University, New Orleans, La.). See also Kathleen Pfeiffer, *Race Passing and American Individualism* (Amherst: University of Massachusetts Press, 2003), 90. For more on autobiography and mendacity, see Timothy Dow Adams, *Telling Lies in Modern American Autobiography* (Chapel Hill: University of North Carolina Press, 1990).

15. JT to Waldo Frank, 12 December 1922, *Letters*, 101.

16. Paul Ricoeur, *Freud and Philosophy: An Essay on Interpretation*, trans. Denis Savage (New Haven, Conn.: Yale University Press, 1970). For critiques of Jamesonian "depth" reading from the standpoint of "surface" reading, see Stephen Best and Sharon Marcus, "Surface Reading: An Introduction," *Representations* 108 (fall 2009): 1–21; and Mary Crane, "Surface, Depth, and the Political Imaginary: A Cognitive Reading of *The Political Unconscious*," *Representations* 108 (fall 2009): 76–97. My articles on Toomer include "Jean Toomer's Sparta," *American Literature* 67, no. 4 (December 1995): 747–75; "Jean Toomer and the Politics of Class: From 'Blue Veins' to Seventh-Street Rebels," *Modern Fiction Studies* 42, no. 2 (1996): 289–321; and "'In the Land of Cotton': Economics and History in Jean Toomer's *Cane*," *African American Review* 32, no. 2 (summer 1998): 181–98.

Chapter 1. Touching Naked Reality

1. *JTTAH.* See also George Hutchinson, "Identity in Motion: Placing *Cane*," in *Jean Toomer and the Harlem Renaissance*, ed. Geneviève Fabre and Michel Feith (New Brunswick, N.J.: Rutgers University Press, 2001), 38–56; and Seth Moglen, *Mourning Modernity: Literary Modernism and the Injuries of Capitalism* (Stanford, Calif.: Stanford University Press), 2007. Early biographical studies minimized Toomer's leftist politics. See Nellie Y. McKay, *Jean Toomer, Artist: A Study of His Literary Life and Work, 1894–1936* (Chapel Hill: University of North Carolina Press, 1984); and Cynthia Kerman and Richard Eldridge, *The Lives of Jean Toomer: A Hunger for Wholeness* (Baton Rouge: Louisiana State University Press, 1987). The introduction to the 2011 Norton edition of *Cane* continues to efface Toomer's connections with political radicalism. See Rudolph P. Byrd and Henry Louis

Gates Jr., "Introduction: 'Song of the Son': The Emergence and Passing of Jean Toomer," in *Cane*, Norton 2, xix–lxxix. I use "Socialist" and "Communist" to refer, respectively, to the Socialist Party of America (SPA) and the Communist Party of America (CPUSA); "socialist" and "communist" refer to more general political affinities and movements.

2. See *Wayward*. Toomer wrote several versions of autobiography, covering his family background and childhood in "Earth-Being" (late 1920s) and "Incredible Journey" (late 1930s/early 1940s); his young adulthood in "The Outline of an Autobiography" (1931), "On Being an American" (1934); "Book X" (1935); and an untitled handwritten version (1936); his Gurdjieff years in "From Exile into Being," later retitled "The Second River" (1944). For more on Toomer and Gurdjieff, see Paul Beekman Taylor, *Shadows of Heaven: Gurdjieff and Toomer* (York Beach, Maine: Samuel Weiser, 1998); Robert C. Twombly, "A Disciple's Odyssey: Jean Toomer's Gurdjieffian Career," in *Prospects: An Annual of American Cultural Studies*, ed. Jack Salzman (Burt Franklin, 1976): 2:437–62; Rudolph P. Byrd, *Jean Toomer's Years with Gurdjieff: Portrait of an Artist, 1923–1936* (Athens: University of Georgia Press, 1990); and Jon Woodson, *To Make a New Race: Gurdjieff, Toomer, and the Harlem Renaissance* (Jackson: University of Mississippi Press, 1999).

3. JT, "The Outline of an Autobiography," box 20, folder 514, JTP. Toomer variously referred to this text as "Outline of the Story of the Autobiography" and "Outline of the Autobiography."

4. JT, "The Outline of an Autobiography." The sociologist Lester Ward, best known for his *Dynamic Sociology* (1883), was a critic of laissez-faire capitalism.

5. JT, "The Outline of an Autobiography"; *Wayward*, 111–12. Critical commentaries on Toomer's shipyard experience that rely on the 1931 and 1934 autobiographies often deploy tropes having to do with illness, religious faith, and flirtation. Charles Larson writes that Toomer was "cured . . . of his flirtation with socialism" (*Invisible Darkness: Jean Toomer and Nella Larsen* [Iowa City: University of Iowa Press, 1993], 9). Darwin Turner refers to Toomer's "abortive crusade in the shipyard (*In a Minor Chord: Three Afro-American Writers and Their Search for Identity* [Carbondale: Southern Illinois University Press, 1971], 10). Michael Krasny opines that Toomer "lost an ephemeral infatuation for socialism" ("Jean Toomer's Life Prior to *Cane*: A Brief Sketch of the Emergence of a Black Writer," in O'Daniel, 41–46 quoted 43). See also Nellie McKay, *Jean Toomer, Artist*, 28, and Kerman and Eldridge, *Lives of Jean Toomer*, 71.

6. JT, "On Being an American," box 20, folder 513, JTP. Ernst Haeckel was a German biologist who sought to graft the doctrines of Darwin onto those of Lamarck.

7. JT, "Book X," box 11, folder 364, JTP. Kerman and Eldridge note that in the mid-1930s "[t]he wave of literature friendly to Marxism and the atmosphere in New York stirred [Toomer's] interest in social issues. . . . That spring of 1935 he had so many discussions with advocates of communism, fascism, monarchy, and Social Credit that he felt bombarded, overwhelmed, and exhausted" (*Lives of Jean Toomer*, 223).

8. JT, untitled 1936 autobiography, box 22, folder 559, JTP. The Cooper Union offered free education to working-class students. Both the SPA-affiliated Rand School and the settlement houses were viewed by the New York State government as dangerous hotbeds of radical activity. See *Revolutionary Radicalism* (Albany, N.Y.: J. B. Lyon, 1920), 1:66–78, 1:1112–22, 1:1450–75. Working alongside Toomer at the East Side settlement were the leftist experimental playwright Elmer Rice; Harry Best, author of *The Men's Garment Industry of New York and the Strike of 1913* (New York: University Settlement Society, 1914); and Clara Hildeman Ehrlich, who would later author *Tribal Culture in Crow Mythology* (1937). The last is probably the "Clara" fondly addressed in a 1920 unidentified letter by Toomer (*Let-*

ters, 11–12). On the postwar *Dial*, see Adam McKible, *The Space and Place of Modernism: The Russian Revolution, Little Magazines, and New York* (New York: Routledge, 2002), 59–77. For Toomer's early—and largely unsuccessful—attempt to form a friendship with Mumford, see Toomer to Mumford, 9 March 1920 and n.d. [March 1921], *Letters*, 10, 20–21.

9. JT, untitled 1936 autobiography, box 22, folders 559, 560, JTP. None of the mimeographed letters from this Ellenville period—from December 1918 to May 1919—has survived. Shaw's *New York American* series was published on 19, 22, 26, and 29 January and on 2 February 1919. Toomer evidently informed Lide Goldsmith of his mixed racial identity (see Goldsmith-Toomer correspondence, 25 July and 22 December 1923, box 3, folder 89, JTP). For Goldsmith's support of "the enfranchisement of the American colored woman," see Lide Goldsmith, letter to the *Nation* 112 (2 March 1921): 341. The mountain to which Toomer and the Goldsmiths hiked through the snow was probably Cragsmoor, the site of a women's art colony (Guy Goldsmith interview, 15 October 2010).

10. JT, untitled 1936 autobiography, box 22, folder 560, JTP. Toomer's comments on boss-worker relations suggest his familiarity with the leftist psychoanalyst André Tridon's discussion of alienation: "Those who assemble the parts had no share in the producing of those parts. . . . Nothing but a direct share in the shaping of their political and economic destiny will satisfy them" *(Psychoanalysis: Its History and Practice* [New York: B. W. Huebsch, 1919], 100. In his correspondence with Lewis Mumford, Toomer mentioned having read Tridon (9 March 1920, *Letters*, 10).

11. JT, untitled 1936 autobiography, box 22, folder 560, JTP. An advocate of social democracy, Childs was the author of *Sweden: The Middle Way* (1936). Toomer's reference to his work suggests that his mid-1930s revived leftist politics were overlaid upon his recall of his 1919 experiences.

12. Claude McKay, "Birds of Prey," *Messenger* 2 (December 1919): 23; rpt. in Claude McKay, *Complete Poems*, ed. William J. Maxwell (Urbana: University of Illinois Press, 2004), 174. In the version of "Birds of Prey" published in *Harlem Shadows*, the parenthetical phrase designating the races of the workers was omitted (*Harlem Shadows* [New York: Harcourt, Brace, 1922], 76). For more on the Toomer-McKay connection, see Wolfgang Karber, "Black Modernism?: The Early Poetry of Jean Toomer and Claude McKay," in *Jean Toomer and the Harlem Renaissance*, ed. Fabre and Feith, 128–41.

13. JT, untitled 1936 autobiography, box 20, folder 560, JTP.

14. Ibid.

15. Ibid. Toomer's choice of metaphor may suggest his awareness that "the worm has turned" was used in postwar New Negro writings to signify a qualitative development in militancy. For *Crusader* editor Cyril Briggs, the Washington race riot showed that "the long-suffering worm that at last had turned upon its persecutors" ("The Capital and Chicago Race Riots," *Crusader* 2, no. 1 [September 1919]: 3–6, quoted 4). The November 1919 issue featured a two-part cartoon titled "The Worm Turns," showing first a lynching, then an African American chasing a plantation owner to the Capitol over the dead body of a white rioter (*Crusader* 2, no. 3 [November 1919]: 1). See also the use of the metaphor in Carrie Williams Clifford, "Silent Protest Parade (On Fifth Avenue, New York, Saturday, July 28, 1917, protesting against the St. Louis riot)," in *The Widening Light* (Boston: Walter Reid, 1922), 16–18.

16. David Montgomery, *The Fall of the House of Labor: The Workplace, the State and American Labor Activism, 1865–1925* (Cambridge: Cambridge University Press, 1987); Theresa S. McMahon, "The Strike in Seattle," *Survey*, 8 March 1919, 821–23.

17. For the political struggle within the SPA in 1919, see Theodore Draper, *The Roots of*

American Communism (New York: Viking, 1957), 139–66. The left wing's critique of the right wing is epitomized in Art Young's cartoon depicting the U.S. Socialist Party hesitantly sticking its toe into the sea of revolution (*Liberator* 2 [July 1919]: 6). See also Crystal Eastman's denunciation of the SPA for "tak[ing] refuge in pre-Marxist documents like the Constitution and the Declaration of Independence," making them "part of old-fashioned Americanism" ("The Socialist Party Convention," *Liberator* 3 [July 1920: 24–29], quoted 25).

18. For more on wartime discrimination against black workers in the shipyards, see Philip Foner, *Organized Labor and the Black Worker, 1619–1981* (New York: International, 1980), 133–34. See also "Anise" (Anna Louise Strong), "The Negro Worker," *Messenger* 2 (August 1919): 22. The *New York Call*, issued by the New York branch of the SPA—which was more alert to the need for antiracism than was the rest of the SPA—noted the influx of 15,000 Negro workers into shipyards and the need for multiracial unity (24 June 1918 and 12 June 1919). For more on racism and antiracism in the SPA, see Philip Foner, *American Socialism and Black Americans: From the Age of Jackson to World War II* (Westport, Conn.: Greenwood Press, 1977); and Barbara Foley, *Spectres of 1919: Class and Nation in the Making of the New Negro* (Urbana: University of Illinois Press, 2003), 70–121.

19. In "The Outline of an Autobiography," Toomer specifies that he left home for New York on "the 20th or 21st of December" and two days later obtained "a little room on 9th Street near Fifth Avenue" (box 20, folder 514, JTP). For more on the Palmer Raids in New York, see the *New York Times*, 3 January 1920; Julian F. Jaffe, *Crusade against Radicalism: New York during the Red Scare, 1914–1924* (Port Washington, N.Y.: Kennikat Press, 1972); and Draper, *Roots of American Communism*, 203–6.

20. Editorial, "Self-Government and Decentralization," *Nation* 108 (29 March 1919): 463.

21. JT, "Present-Day Socialism," *Nation* 108 (17 May 1919): 792; rpt. in *Letters*, 1–2. Toomer probably refers to John Spargo and George Louis Arner's *Elements of Socialism*, where it is written that "a centralized state is not implied" (*Elements of Socialism* [New York: Macmillan, 1912], 232–33). An opponent of the SPA's antiwar stance, Spargo would emerge as a leader of the SPA's right wing. See John Spargo, *Americanism and Social Democracy* (New York: Harper and Bros., 1918); and John Spargo, *Bolshevism: The Enemy of Political and Industrial Democracy* (New York: Harper and Bros., 1919). See also Donny Gluckstein, *The Western Soviets: Workers' Councils Versus Parliament 1915–1920* (London: Bookmarks, 1985).

22. JT, "Ghouls," *New York Call*, 15 June 1919; rpt. in *JTTAH*, 225–26. Toomer inaccurately referred to "Ghouls" as "Profiteers" in the 1923 publicity sketch for *Cane* (box 26, folder 611, JTP).

23. Scott Nearing, "War Shouters and War Contracts," *Messenger* 2 (January 1918): 2; Karl Marx, *Capital: A Critique of Political Economy*, trans. Ben Fowkes (New York: Penguin, 1976), 342; W. E. B. Du Bois, "The African Roots of War," *Atlantic Monthly* 115 (May 1915): 707–14; A. Philip Randolph and Chandler Owen, *Terms of Peace and the Darker Races* (New York: Poole Press, 1917). For more on the Paris Peace Conference, see Yuichiro Onishi, "The New Negro of the Pacific: How African Americans Forged Solidarity with Japan," in *Escape from New York: The New Negro Renaissance beyond Harlem*, ed. Davarian L. Baldwin and Minkah Makalani (Minneapolis: University of Minnesota Press, 2013), 127–56.

24. JT, "Reflections on the Race Riots," *New York Call*, 2 August 1919; rpt. in *JTTAH*, 226–28, quoted 226–27; A. Philip Randolph, "Lynching: Capitalism Its Cause; Socialism Its Cure," *Messenger* 2 (March 1919): 9–12. The *New York Call* article expands on Toomer's earlier response to a *Nation* editorial that had criticized the "'fighting' psychology of the Negro" (*Nation* 109 [12 July 1919]: 44). Toomer wrote, "Led for the most part by 'leaders'

whose vision is circumscribed by the color line, and embittered by opposition and disillusionment, the Negroes, if their 'fighting psychology' of today is to be translated into
action, would be likely to direct the conflict not so much against the iniquities of the white
race, as against the white race itself" (Toomer to the *Nation*, 29 June 1919; rpt. in *Letters*,
2–3).

25. JT, "Reflections on the Race Riots," 227–28.

26. Ibid., 227–28. Toomer's August 1919 *New York Call* article anticipated a number of
the arguments appearing a month later in Randolph and Owen's editorial, "The Causes
of and Remedy for Race Riots" (*Messenger* 2 [September 1919]: 14–21).

27. Toomer's criticisms of electoral politics resemble those by SPA left-winger—and
Communist (Workers) Party founder—John Reed in "Political Democracy Must Go!,"
New York Communist 1 (1919): 4.

28. *JTTAH*, 53–54; JT, untitled 1936 autobiography, box 22, folder 560, JTP.

29. For more on "Americans and Mary Austin" and "The South in Literature," see chapter
3. Toomer is addressed as "Comrade" in the *New York Call* correspondence. See David
Karsner to JT, 2 October 1920, n.d., box 6, folder 191, JTP; John Crawford to JT, 1 October
1923, box 1, folder 24, JTP; and Edwin Seaver to JT, 16 October 1923, box 6, folder 191, JTP.
Karsner quit his editorial post in 1923 because, according to the *Liberator*, "[h]e had an
awkward time trying to swallow a new policy of aggressive communist-baiting which the
governing board of the *New York Call* laid down for him to swallow" ("Anti-Red Hootch,"
Liberator 6 [May 1923]: 7).

30. Editorial, *Liberator*, 1 (March 1918): 3; Claude McKay, *A Long Way from Home* (1937;
rpt. New York: Arno and the New York Times, 1969), 109; Toomer to Floyd Dell, 22 November 1921 ("from box 55, Sparta GA"), box 4, folder 145, JTP. The version of "Georgia
Night" that Toomer submitted to *Liberator* has disappeared.

31. Claude McKay to JT, 27 June 1922, box 4, folder 145, JTP; JT to Claude McKay, 23
July 1922, *Letters*, 48.

32. Toomer to the *Liberator*, 19 August 1922, *Letters*, 70–71.

33. Mike Gold (Irwin Granich), "Toward Proletarian Art," *Liberator* 36 (March 1921):
20–22.

34. Joseph Freeman, *An American Testament: A Narrative of Rebels and Romantics*
(New York: Farrar and Rinehart, 1936), 260. Subsequent letters from the *Liberator* editors to Toomer (12 September and 1 November 1922, box 4, folder 145, JTP) presumably
had counterparts from Toomer to the *Liberator* in the journal's destroyed files. The May
1926 *New Masses* list of contributing editors shows Toomer in notable company, including Sherwood Anderson, Floyd Dell, Max Eastman, Waldo Frank, Claude McKay, Lewis
Mumford, Lola Ridge, and Art Young. The *Workers Monthly* briefly filled the gap between
the *Liberator* and the *New Masses*.

35. JT, 1922–23 Journal, box 60, folder 1411, JTP.

36. A 1921 *Crusader* editorial declared that the SPA "has rejected not only the Third
Internationale, but all international affiliations as well. It has cast from it the banner of
International Labor and taken up that of One Hundred Per Cent Americanism" ("The
Socialist Surrender," *Crusader* 4, no. 6 [August 1921]: 8–9, quoted 9). By mid-1923 the
SPA-affiliated *Messenger* took a sharp turn to the right as the SPA came under increasing
attack from the left. See editorial, "The Menace of Negro Communists," *Messenger* 5 (Au-
gust 1923): 784, 792–94. For more on the IWW's reputation for antiracism, see Theodore
Kornweibel, "Ultra Radical Negro Bolsheviki," in *Seeing Red: Federal Campaigns against
Black Militancy, 1918–1925* (Bloomington: Indiana University Press, 1998), 155–73; and

Mark Ellis, "J. Edgar Hoover and the 'Red Summer' of 1919," *Journal of American Studies* 28 (April 1994): 39–59.

37. Domingo quoted in *Revolutionary Radicalism* 2 (1920): 1510, 1504; Claude McKay, "Birthright," *Liberator* 5 (August 1922): 15–16; Karl Marx, *Manifesto of the Communist Party*, trans. Eugene Kamenka (New York: Penguin, 1983), 204.

38. Toomer to Naumberg, 2 August 1923, *Letters*, 168–69. Margaret Naumberg, a progressive educator and founder of the Walden School, was married to Waldo Frank from 1916 to 1924; starting in the summer of 1923, she and Toomer were lovers for several years.

39. JT, "Banking Coal," *Crisis*, 24 (June 1922): 65; rpt. in *The Collected Poems of Jean Toomer*, ed. Robert B. Jones and Margery Toomer Latimer (Chapel Hill: University of North Carolina Press, 1988), 20. Although John Chandler Griffin asserts that "Banking Coal" was left out of *Cane* at the advice of Waldo Frank, he offers no documentation to support this claim (*The Uncollected Works of American Author Jean Toomer 1894–1967*, ed. John Chandler Griffin [Lewiston, N.Y.: Edwin Mellen Press, 2003], 3). Notably, Toomer never mentions "Banking Coal"—or his other pre-*Cane Crisis* publication, "Song of the Son"—in any of his known letters to Frank.

40. John Reed, "Triumph of the Bolsheviki," *Liberator* 1 (April 1918): 14; John Reed, "Soviet Russia Now," *Liberator* (December 1920): 17; editorial, *Messenger* 2 (September 1920): 86; Theresa McMahon, "The Strike in Seattle," *Survey*, 8 March 1919, 821–23, quoted 822; Claude McKay, *Complete Poems*, 177, 178; Lola Ridge, "Reveille," in *Sun-Up and Other Poems* (New York: B. W. Huebsch, 1920), 86–87. In 1935 Toomer expressed admiration for Ridge's continuing "perception of the spirit of fire awake in revolution" (review of Lola Ridge, *Dance of Fire*, *New Democracy* 4 [15 May 1935]: 105). See also *Gitlow v. New York* (1925), where the prosecution justified the suppression of political speech on the ground that "a single revolutionary spark may kindle a fire that, smoldering for a time, may burst into a sweeping conflagration" (http://www.digitalhistory.uh.edu/disp_textbook.cfm?smtID=3&psid=4070, accessed 12 February 2013).

41. *JTTAH*, 57–58; the authors also suggest a connection between "Banking Coal" and Robert Frost's "The Bonfire" (261 n6). It is noteworthy that in 1919 some 400,000 coal miners went on strike and faced a repressive injunction; accusations were bandied about that the strike had been organized by Lenin and Trotsky. See "The Coal Strike of 1919" (http://www.lib.iup.edu/spec_coll/articles/coalstrike1919.html, accessed 7 November 2013). See also Du Bois's 1907 poem, "The Song of the Smoke," in which the smoke declares, "I whiten my black men—I blacken my white!" (*Creative Writings of W. E. B. Du Bois: A Pageant, Poems, Short Stories, and Playlets*, ed. Herbert Aptheker [White Plains, N.Y.: Kraus-Thompson, 1985], 11).

42. Editorial, *Messenger* 3 (July 1921): 210. For more on the East St. Louis and Tulsa riots, see W. E. B. Du Bois and Martha Gruening, "The Massacre of East St. Louis," *Crisis* 14 (September 1917): 219–38; and Tim Madigan, *The Burning: Massacre, Destruction, and the Tulsa Race Riot of 1921* (New York: Thomas Dunne Books, 2001).

43. Toomer to Gorham Munson, 31 and 8 October 1922, *Letters*, 92, 83; Toomer to Mae Wright, 4 August 1922, *Letters*, 62; JT, "Richard Aldington's 'The Art of Poetry,'" in *Jean Toomer: Selected Essays and Literary Criticism*, ed. Robert B. Jones (Knoxville: University of Tennessee Press, 1996), 3–5, quoted 4. Toomer was responding to Aldington's formalist manifesto, "The Art of Poetry," where Aldington declared, "[T]he old cant of a poem's 'message' is now completely discredited" (*Dial* 69 [1920]: 251–58, quoted 251).

44. Toomer to Horace Liveright, 27 February 1923, *Letters*, 137; Toomer to Waldo Frank, n.d. (mid-March 1923), *Letters*, 138. In the letter to Frank, Toomer added, "Great guns,

brother! Whenever I get a real glimpse of the thing, a terrific emotion sweeps me." Darwin Turner asserts that Toomer "proposed to write a collection of stories about communistic influences on Afro-American life" but offers no documentation in support of this claim (introduction to *Cane* [New York: Liveright, 1975], xxiii).

45. Editorial, "The Arkansas Challenge," *Crusader* 2, no. 5 (January 1920): 5–6, quoted 6; editorial, "Bolshevism's Menace: To Whom and to What?" *Crusader* 2, no. 6 (February 1920): 1–2; editorial, "The Rising Wave," *Crusader* 2, no. 6 (February 1920): 8–9; Ben E. Burrell, "The Coming Conflict," *Crusader* 2, no. 12 (August 1920): 6.

46. Interview with Bela Kun, *Liberator* 3 (March 1920): 16–21, quoted 19; Melville J. Herskovits, "Anthropology Since Morgan," *Liberator* 6 (February 1923): 29–30, quoted 29; editorial, "Africa and the White Proletariat," *Crusader* 4, no. 2 (April 1921): 10–11. While the *Crusader* occasionally flirted with the notion that people of African descent had a "race genius" that "leaned toward Communism," their principal arguments drew on economics, history, and anthropology, not notions of biological essentialism. See editorial, "The Salvation of the Negro," *Crusader* 4, no. 2 (April 1921): 8–9, quoted 8. For more on the postwar anticolonial upsurge, see A. S. Kanya-Foster, "The War, Imperialism, and Decolonization," in *The Great War and the Twentieth Century*, ed. Jay Winter, Geoffrey Parker, and Mary R. Habeck (New Haven: Yale University Press, 2000), 231–62.

47. For assessments of psychoanalysis and "Freudianism" by Greenwich Village cultural radicals and Socialists and Communists, see Joseph Freeman, review of André Tridon's *Psychoanalysis and Love, Liberator* 5 (October 1922): 31; and William Gropper's cartoon, "A Freudian Session" *Liberator* 5 (September 1922): 28.

48. For more on Toomer's sketch of the post-*Cane* novel, see chapter 3.

49. JT, "Race Problems in Modern Society," in *Problems of Civilization*, ed. Baker Brownell (New York: Van Nostrand, 1929); rpt. in *Jean Toomer: Selected Essays and Literary Criticism*, ed. Jones, 60–76, quoted 63, 74. For a critique of Toomer's developing interest in eugenics, see Diana I. Williams, "Building the New Race: Jean Toomer's Eugenic Aesthetic," in *Jean Toomer and the Harlem Renaissance*, ed. Fabre and Feith, 188–201.

50. JT, journals, box 51, folder 1108, JTP. For instances of Toomer's continuing hostility to the capitalist marketplace, see his untitled article on George Bernard Shaw (journals, box 61, folder 1108, JTP), and "Letter from America," trans. Victor Llona, *Bifur* 1 (May 1929): 105–14, rpt. in *Jean Toomer: Selected Essays and Literary Criticism*, ed. Jones, 77–85.

51. JT, journals, box 51, folders 1116 and 1125, JTP. Traces of Marxist influence are displayed in some of Toomer's post-*Cane* fictional and dramatic works. In "A Certain November," a satirical short story commenting on politics and race in the United States, a character observes to another, "[W]e may as well know that bloodsuckers are abroad, abstractions which we permit to bleed us. Race, Nation, Class, the Government, the State, Business, Art, Sciences, and I've heard tell that we are bled by God. . . . You've been sitting there like one of the men Karl Marx wrote about—'the tradition of all dead generations weighs like a nightmare on the brains of the living'" (*Dubuque Dial* 4 [1 November 1935]: 107–12, quoted 107). Besides referencing Marx's famous comparison of capital with a vampire, the speaker directly quotes from *The Eighteenth Brumaire*. The critique of capitalist alienation in *The Sacred Factory*, Toomer's 1927 expressionist drama, echoes such radical plays as Elmer Rice's *The Adding Machine* (1923) and Karel Čapek's *R. U. R. (Rossum's Universal Robots)* (1920). See *The Sacred Factory: A Religious Drama of Today*, in *Wayward*, 327–410. For more on Čapek's play, see chapter 7.

52. JT, journals, box 62, folder 1446, JTP. For more on Toomer's dreams about racial passing, see chapters 2 and 4.

Chapter 2. The Tight Cocoon

1. The term "blue veins" refers to a "skin light enough to review one's blue veins" (Willard B. Gatewood, *Aristocrats of Color: The Black Elite, 1880–1920* [Bloomington: Indiana University Press, 1990], 153). For the increase in black-white binarism in the 1920s, see Naomi Zuck, *Race and Mixed Race* (Philadelphia: Temple University Press, 1993); Matthew Guterl, *The Color of Race in American 1900–1940* (Cambridge, Mass.: Harvard University Press, 2001), 154–83; F. James Davis, *Who Is Black? One Nation's Definition* (University Park: Pennsylvania State University Press, 1991); and Werner Sollors, *Neither Black Nor White Yet Both: Thematic Explorations of Interracial Literature* (New York: Oxford University Press, 1997). For useful summaries of Toomer's conceptions of race from the *Cane* period onward, see Lara Vetter, *Modernist Writings and Religio-Scientific Discourse: H.D., Loy, and Toomer* (New York: Palgrave Macmillan, 2010), 134–57; Gino Michael Pellegrini, "Jean Toomer and Cane: 'Mixed-Blood' Impossibilities," *Arizona Quarterly* 64 (winter 2008): 1–20; George Hutchinson, "Jean Toomer and American Racial Discourse," *Texas Studies in Language and Literature* 35 (summer 1993): 226–50; and Tania Friedel, "*Cane*'s Betrayal and Jean Toomer's Untethered Universalism," in *Racial Discourse and Cosmopolitanism in Twentieth-Century African American Writing* (New York: Routledge, 2008).

2. To John McClure of the *Double Dealer*, Toomer wrote, "Viewed from the world of race distinctions, I take the color of whatever group I at the time am sojourning in" (JT to John McClure, 30 June 1922, *Letters*, 40). Samuel Pessin of *Prairie* received a similar message. "Racially my bloods are mixed to the extent that it is stupid and absurd to call me anything other than an American," wrote Toomer. "When I live with the blacks I'm a Negro. When I live with the whites, I'm white, or, better, a foreigner. . . . My concern is with the art of literature. Call me what you like" (JT to Samuel Pessin, 25 March 1923, *Letters*, 154).

3. For a summary of the changing meaning of "New Negro" from the early to mid-1920s, see Henry Louis Gates Jr., "The Trope of a New Negro and the Reconstruction of the Image of the Black," *Representations* 24 (fall 1988): 129–56.

4. JT, "The Outline of an Autobiography," box 20, folder 514, JTP. The sculptor was "probably May Howard Johnson, a Philadelphia-born sculptor who later taught at Howard" (Mark Whalan, *Letters*, 18). When Toomer explained his idea of an "American race" to Ken, his friend responded that such a notion was possible for Toomer only because he looked white (JT, "Outline of an Autobiography"). Darwin Turner notes that "[i]n the extant fragment of his autobiographical novel . . . Harry Kenton [Henry Kennedy], an Afro-American who is darker in color than Eugene Stanton (Toomer's self-portrait), curses America: 'My family has been here for generations. But they're colored. They're not Americans yet. Any cockeyed louse with a white skin can come over here from lousy Europe and become an American. I can't'" ("Jean Toomer—Exile," in *In a Minor Chord: Three Afro-American Writers and Their Search for Identity* [Carbondale: Southern Illinois University Press, 1971], 12). Ken appeared in at least one dream about passing that Toomer recorded during his psychoanalysis many years later (JT, Journal, box 62, folder 1444, JTP).

5. JT to Alain Locke, 26 January 1921, *Letters*, 19–20.

6. Clarissa Scott Delany (1901–1927) was a Dunbar graduate and taught there from 1923 to 1926; Angelina Grimké elegized her after her premature death in the poem, "Dusky Answer" (Lorraine Elena Roses and Ruth Elizabeth Randolph, *Harlem's Glory: Black Women Writing 1900–1950* [Cambridge, Mass.: Harvard University Press, 1996], 188–91).

E. C. Williams was the principal of the M Street/Dunbar High School from 1909 to 1916. For more on the M Street/Dunbar, see Gatewood, *Aristocrats of Color*, 260; Henry S. Robinson, "The M Street High School, 1891–1916," *Records of the Columbia Historical Society of Washington, DC* 51 (1984): 119–42; and Jervis Anderson, "A Very Special Monument," *New Yorker* 54 (20 March 1978): 97–107. Gerri Majors observes that the study of foreign languages was emphasized at Dunbar so that its students and graduates might "launch into French or Spanish if challenged by a store clerk, a waiter, or a theatre usher" (Gerri Majors, with Doris E. Saunders, *Black Society* [Chicago: Johnson Publishing, 1976], 259).

7. On the Washington, DC, Negro intelligentsia, see Ronald M. Johnson, "Those Who Stayed: Washington Black Writers of the 1920s," *Records of the Columbia Historical Society* 50 (1980): 484–99; and George B. Hutchinson, "Jean Toomer and the 'New Negroes' of Washington," *American Literature* 63 (December 1991): 683–92.

8. H. G. Wells, *The Outline of History, Being a Plain History of Life and Mankind* (New York: Macmillan, 1920); Thomas R. R. Cobb, *An Historical Sketch of Slavery, from the Earliest Period* (Philadelphia: T. and J. W. Johnson, 1858), 278; Captain Theodore Canot, *Adventures of an African Slaver*, ed. Brantz Meyer (1854; rpt. New York: Dover, 1969); "A Selected List of Books Dealing with the Negro Problem," *Crisis* 21 (January 1921): 96. For criticism of Wells's racism, see William Pickens, *The Vengeance of the Gods and Three Other Stories of Real American Color Line Life* (1922; rpt. New York: AMS, 1975), 7. Floyd Dell published a mixed review of Wells's book, noting that, despite his reformism, Wells was "a magnificently destructive influence" who "made people quit believing in capitalism" ("Wells the Destroyer," *Liberator* [January 1921]: 27, 33).

9. Jessie Redmon Fauset to JT, 17 February 1922, box 1, folder 34, JTP. For more on Fauset's career at the *Crisis*, see Cheryl Wall, *Women of the Harlem Renaissance* (Bloomington: Indiana University Press, 1995), 53–62.

10. JT to Georgia Douglas Johnson, 7 January, 20 February, and 7 June 1920, *Letters*, 5–7, 13. Toomer wrote of Johnson to John McClure, "[H]er faculty of expression is not up to her sensibilities. Nor is she sufficiently conscious. I do not think she will ever be. The inhibitions and taboos and life-limitations she labors under make even her modest achievement remarkable" (JT to John McClure, 22 July 1922, *Letters*, 47). See also JT to Waldo Frank, 2 August 1922, *Letters*, 59. Du Bois similarly condescended to Johnson, stating in his preface to *Bronze* that "[h]er word is simple, sometimes trite, but it is singularly sincere and true" (foreword, *Bronze*, 1922; rpt. in *The Selected Works of Georgia Douglas Johnson*, ed. Claudia Tate [New York: G. K. Hall, 1997], 85). Editor Claudia Tate conjectures that, in Johnson's short story "The Smile," the young man with whom the older female protagonist falls in love is based on Toomer (lxiii).

11. Johnson's "Song of Courage" appeared in the *Liberator* next to a drawing of Red soldiers with the caption, "Before Us—The Communist Order!" In the mid-1930s Johnson published two proletarian short stories—"Tramp Love" and "Gesture"—in the black Marxist journal *Challenge* under the pseudonym Paul Tremaine (*Selected Works of Georgia Douglas Johnson*, 417–28). See also Judith L. Stephens, "Art, Activism, and Uncompromising Attitude in Georgia Douglas Johnson's Lynching Plays," *African American Review* 39, nos. 1–2 (2005): 87–102. For more on Johnson's role in Washington literary circles, see Elizabeth McHenry, *Forgotten Readers: Recovering the Lost History of African American Literary Societies* (Durham, N.C.: Duke University Press, 2002), 251–95; and Jeffrey C. Stewart, "Alain Locke and Georgia Douglas Johnson, Washington Patrons of Afro-American Modernism," *Washington Studies* 12 (July 1986): 37–44.

12. Georgia Douglas Johnson, foreword to *Bronze*, "To John Brown," *Selected Works of Georgia Douglas Johnson*, 81, 165; Thomas Dixon, *The Man in Gray: A Romance of North and South* (New York: D. Appleton and Co., 1921). For the Harpers Ferry controversy, see Mary Johnson, "An 'ever present bone of contention': The Heyward Shepherd Memorial," *West Virginia History* 56 (1997): 1–26. The proposed dedication of the monument to the "Faithful Slave" overlooked the fact that Shepherd had been free.

13. Georgia Douglas Johnson, "The Octoroon," "Fusion," and "Cosmopolite," *Selected Works of Georgia Douglas Johnson*, 36, 60, 59.

14. Georgia Douglas Johnson, "Maternity" and "Black Woman," *Selected Works of Georgia Douglas Johnson*, 118, 119. For more on plays addressing lynching and black motherhood, see Daylanne English, *Unnatural Selections: Eugenics in American Modernism and the Harlem Renaissance* (Chapel Hill: University of North Carolina Press, 2004), 117–39.

15. Mary Burrill, "To a Black Soldier Fallen in the War," *Liberator* 1 (December 1918): 11; Mary Burrill, "Aftermath," *Liberator* 2 (April 1919): 10–14, quoted 13, 14.

16. Mary Burrill, "They That Sit in Darkness," and Blanche Schrack, "Editorial Comment," both in *Birth Control Review: Dedicated to Voluntary Motherhood* 3 (September 1919): 5–8 and 3–4. See also Anne Stavney, "'Mothers of Tomorrow': The New Negro Renaissance and the Politics of Maternal Representation," *African American Review* 32, no. 4 (1998): 533–61.

17. Angelina Grimké, letter, *Messenger* 2, no. 11 (December 1919): 29. Among Grimké's papers are two love sonnets followed by the typed initials "G.J.D."; in style these resemble poems by Georgia Douglas Johnson. One ends, "'Tis better not to drop the seed at all / Than be afraid to taste the fruits that fall" (n.d., box 38-2, AGP). On the Grimké family, see Mark Perry, *Lift Up Thy Voice: The Grimké Family's Journey from Slaveholders to Civil Rights Leaders* (New York: Viking, 2001).

18. Angelina Grimké, "Goldie," *Birth Control Review* 4 (November 1920): 7–11, and 4 (December 1920): 10–14, rpt. in *Selected Works of Angelina Grimké*, ed. Carolivia Herron (New York: Oxford University Press, 1991), 282–306, quoted 302; Angelina Grimké, "The Closing Door," *Birth Control Review* 3 (September 1919), rpt. in *Selected Works of Angelina Grimké*, 252–81.

19. Carrie Williams Clifford, "Little Mother (Upon the Lynching of Mary Turner)," in *The Widening Light* (Boston: Walter Reid, 1922), 19; Anne Spencer, "White Things," *Crisis* 25 (March 1923): 204. On Fuller's statue, see Phyllis Jackson, "Re-Living Memories: Picturing Death," *Ijele: Art Ejournal of the African World* 5 (2002). Grimké's other narratives based on the death of Mary Turner are "Blackness," in *Selected Works of Angelina Grimké*, 218–51, and "The Waitin'," box 38, folder 12, AGP. When Grimké sent "Blackness" to the *Atlantic Monthly*, she explained that it was "based on fact" in the Mary Turner lynching (n.d., box 38-2, folder 28, AGP; rpt. in *Selected Works of Angelina Grimké*, 417). She may have submitted a version of "Goldie" to the *Liberator*, since Crystal Eastman returned a manuscript that she thought "remarkable" but "too long" (Crystal Eastman to Angelina Grimké, 11 September 1920, box 38-2, folder 44, AGP). For more on representations of the Mary Turner lynching, see Julie Buckner Armstrong, *Mary Turner and the Memory of Lynching* (Athens: University of Georgia Press, 2011).

20. Micki McElya, "Commemorating the Color Line: The National Mammy Monument Controversy of the 1920s," in *Monuments to the Lost Cause: Women, Art, and the Landscapes of Southern Memory* (Knoxville: University of Tennessee Press, 2009), 203–18. Du Bois responded to earlier efforts to construct the Mammy Monument in "The Black Mother," *Crisis* (December 1912): 78. The UDC won the senate's support in early 1923, but

the project was so controversial that it was dropped. Chandler Owen wrote: "We favor [a monument] erected to the 200,000 Negro soldiers who fought to wipe out slavery . . . to the New Negro, who is carving a new monument in the hearts of our people. . . . to the Negro women who have risen above insult, assault, debauchery, prostitution and abuse, *to which these unfortunate 'black mammies' were subjected*" ("Black Mammies," *Messenger* 5 [April 1923]: 676, original emphasis).

21. Karl Marx, *Capital: A Critique of Political Economy*, trans. Ben Fowkers (New York: Penguin, 1976), 916. Babette Deutsch, "Petrograd," *Liberator* 2, no. 8 (August 1919): 10; Claude McKay, "Exhortation: Summer, 1919," in *Complete Poems*, ed. William J. Maxwell (Urbana: University of Illinois Press, 2004), 175; ; Chireton W. Rice, "Easter," *Liberator* 2, no. 8 (August 1919): 50; Langston Hughes, "Advertisement for the Waldorf-Astoria" (1931), rpt. in *The Collected Poems of Langston Hughes*, ed. Arnold Rampersad (New York: Random House, 1994), 146. Gold's novel ends with these words: "O workers Revolution, you brought hope to me, a lonely, suicidal boy. You are the true Messiah. . . . O great beginning!" (*Jews without Money* [1930; rpt. New York: Carroll and Graf, 1996], 309).

22. Anonymous, "Lament," *Liberator* 5 (January 1922): 6; Winston Churchill quoted in Ronald E. Powaski, *Toward an Entangling Alliance: American Isolationism, Internationalism, and Europe, 1901–1950* (Westport, Conn.: Greenwood Press, 1991), 18. Churchill's words have been reported retrospectively in various forms, but the notion of strangling the baby of Bolshevism figures in all versions.

23. JT to Mae Wright, 22 July and 4 August 1922, *Letters*, 45, 60–62; JT to Waldo Frank, n.d. [early January 1923], *Letters*, 117–18. Toomer complained to Mae Wright that members of the writers' group interrupted his reading of a poem by teasing him about "what had happened to me at the Ferry" (JT to Mae Wright, 29 July 1922, *Letters*, 56–57). For more on Mae Wright, see Therman B. O'Daniel, "An Interview with Mae Wright Peck," in O'Daniel, 25–40.

24. JT to Waldo Frank, 29 September 1923, *Letters*, 177; "*Messenger* Editors Receive Ovation," *Messenger* 2 (March 1920): 13; Wallace V. Jackson, "The Theatre-Drama," *Messenger* 5 (1923): 746–47.

25. Advertisement for "Republic Theatre—Walter Pinchback, Mgr., America's Finest Colored Movie House," *Crusader* 4, no. 6 (August 1921): 2. The *Crusader* also sponsored an anti-KKK meeting at the Metropolitan Baptist Church in February 1921; located at 1225 R. Street N.W., the church was two blocks from the apartment where Toomer lived with his grandparents (*Crusader* 4, no. 2 [April 1921]: 23).

26. M. Franklin Peters, review of *Darkwater*, *Crusader* 3, no. 3 (November 1920): 911; W. E. B. Du Bois, *The Negro* (1915; rpt. Millwood, N.Y.: Kraus-Thomson, 1975). Several of the pieces in *Darkwater* allude to the Black Messiah: "The Riddle of the Sphinx," 53–55, "The Second Coming," 105–8, "Jesus Christ in Texas" (123–33), and "The Call," 161–62 (1920; rpt. Millwood, N.Y.: Kraus-Thomson, 1975). *Crisis* articles invoking the Black Jesus include "Jesus Christ in Georgia," *Crisis* 3 (December 1911): 70–74; "The Gospel According to Mary Brown," *Crisis* 19 (December 1919): 41–43; and "The Sermon in the Cradle," *Crisis* 23 (December 1921): 58–59. For a discussion of Du Bois's writings on the Black Messiah, see Eric J. Sundquist, *To Wake the Nations: Race in the Making of American Literature* (Cambridge, Mass.: Harvard University Press, 1993), 592–625.

27. JT to Jesse E. Moorland, 28 July and 4 October 1922, *Letters*, 54–55, 81–82.

28. Moorland wrote to President R. S. Wilkinson of the State Agricultural and Mechanical College, Orangeburg, South Carolina, that Toomer—whom he referred to as "Eugene Pinchback Toomer"—was the "grandson of the late Governor Pinchback" and wanted to

reach "correct and scientific conclusions." He added, "This young man has, to my mind, a very big contribution to make" (Jesse E. Moorland to R. S. Wilkinson, 31 July 1922, Jesse Edward Moorland Papers, Moorland-Spingarn Research Institute, Howard University).

29. Leonard Harris and Charles Molesworth opine that it was Locke, and not Fauset, who arranged for the publication of "Song of the Son" and "Banking Coal" in the *Crisis* (*Alain Locke: Biography of a Philosopher* [Chicago: University of Chicago Press, 2008], 171–75).

30. Alain Locke to JT, n.d., box 5, folder 151, JTP; JT to Alain Locke, n.d. [late August 1920], *Letters*, 15–16. They were discussing a recent article by the educator Marion Hawthorne Hedges titled "The Teacher's Real Dilemma," *Nation* 111 (21 August 1920): 214–15. Hedges was also the author of the novel *Iron City* (New York: Boni and Liveright, 1919), a satiric treatment of college campus life that had been critically reviewed in the *New York Call* (16 November 1919, 11).

31. Toomer had attended the University of Wisconsin at Madison, the University of Massachusetts, the American College of Physical Culture in Chicago, the University of Chicago, City College of New York, New York University, and Columbia University.

32. JT to Alain Locke, 8 and 24 November 1921, *Letters*, 27–28.

33. For more on Locke's changing views on politics and culture 1916–25, see Barbara Foley, *Spectres of 1919: Class and Nation in the Making of the New Negro* (Urbana: University of Illinois Press, 2003), 198–249 and 205–12.

34. JT to Alain Locke, 1 August 1922, *Letters*, 58; Alain Locke to JT, 17 October 1922, and 4 January and 1 July 1923, box 5, folder 151, JTP. The three novels to which Locke refers are Hubert Anthony Shands's *White and Black* (New York: Harcourt, Brace, 1922), T. S. Stribling's *Birthright* (1922; rpt. Delmar, N.Y.: Scholars' Facsimiles & Reprints, 1987), and Clement Wood, *Nigger: A Novel* (New York: E. P. Dutton, 1923). For more on the misspelling of "Cane" as "Cain," see chapter 3.

35. JT, "On Being an American," box 20, folder 513, JTP.

36. JT, "The Negro Emergent," handwritten draft, box 51, folder 1114, JTP. The usual dating of this essay in 1924 is clearly incorrect. On the making of the *Survey Graphic* issue on the New Negro, see Foley, *Spectres of 1919*, 217–37; and Anne Elizabeth Carroll, *Word, Image, and the New Negro: Representation and Identity in the Harlem Renaissance* (Bloomington: Indiana University Press, 2005), 122–55.

37. JT, "The Negro Emergent," in *Jean Toomer: Selected Essays and Literary Criticism*, ed. Robert B. Jones (Knoxville: University of Tennessee Press, 1996), 48, 51, 54; Alain Locke, "Enter the New Negro," *Survey Graphic* 53 [1 March 1925]: 631, 634. Toomer's description of the psychological "emergence" of the New Negro resonates with his statement to his Ellenville host Lide Goldsmith, soon after *Cane* appeared, that "[it] seems as though one's personality is a compound of false and bad habits. As one gradually breaks these habits, one's personality seems to dissolve. . . . Mine—my false personality—the gestures and ways that have been peculiar to me—is going" (JT to Lide Goldsmith, 22 December 1923, *Letters*, 184).

38. Alain Locke, "Harlem," *Survey Graphic* 53 (1 March 1925), 629; Alain Locke, "Youth Speaks," *Survey Graphic* 53 (1 March 1925): 660; JT, "The Negro Emergent," 49. Toomer's critique of the "exotic" treatment of the folk may have been influenced by the anthropologist Edward Sapir's "A Symposium of the Exotic," *Dial* 73 (July–December 1922): 568–71.

39. Locke, "Enter the New Negro," 633; JT, "The Negro Emergent," 50; W. E. B. Du Bois, "The Souls of White Folk," *Darkwater*, 29–52, quoted 29–30 and 43.

40. JT, "The Negro Emergent," draft.

41. Locke, "Youth Speaks," 660; William Stanley Braithwaite, "The Negro in American Literature" in *The New Negro: An Interpretation* (1925, rpt. New York: Simon and Schuster, 1997), 44.

42. Alain Locke, "Negro Youth Speaks," in *The New Negro*, 51.

43. For a comparative discussion of the role played by "soul" and "soil" in Russian and African American cultural nationalisms, see Dale E. Peterson, *Up from Bondage: The Literatures of Russian and African American Soul* (Durham, N.C.: Duke University Press, 2000).

44. For more on the reception of *Cane*, see chapter 3. For the argument that Toomer knowingly participated in the racialized publicity for *Cane*, see Vera M. Kutzinski, "Unseasonal Flowers: Nature and History in Plácido and Jean Toomer," *Yale Journal of Criticism* 3, no. 2 (spring 1990): 153–79.

45. JT to Lola Ridge, n.d. [late January/early February 1923], *Letters*, 125; JT to Sherwood Anderson, 29 December 1922, *Letters*, 106; JT to Claude Barnett, 29 April 1923, *Letters*, 159–60. Writing to Ella H. Elbert, a patron of the arts recommended by Alain Locke, Toomer referred to himself as "the grandson of the late P. B. S. Pinchback" and wrote of his desire "to lay the foundations for a literary magazine (how we need one!) the first issue of which should appear next fall" (JT to Ella H. Elbert, 18 October 1922, *Letters*, 87).

46. JT to the Hotel Theresa, 15 September 1922, box 3, folder 96, JTP; Indice M. Watterson, interview with Gorham B. Munson, 27 June 1969, Amistad Research Center, Tulane University, New Orleans, Louisiana. George Hutchinson notes that "Ethel Ray Nance (Charles S. Johnson's assistant at *Opportunity* magazine) remembered [Toomer's] visiting the Harlem apartment she shared with Regina Anderson in 1924 or 1925, when prominent black writers often dropped by. Moreover, well after *Cane* appeared, black friends such as Dorothy Peterson and Aaron Douglas continued to visit him at his home on East 10th Street, according to his second wife" ("Jean Toomer and the 'New Negroes' of Washington," 691–92). Access to Toomer's letters to Dorothy Peterson at Yale University's Beinecke Library is prohibited by the Peterson family. For more on race in Toomer's Gurdjieffian period, see Jon Woodson, *To Make a New Race: Gurdjieff, Toomer, and the Harlem Renaissance* (Jackson: University Press of Mississippi, 1999); and Badia Sahar Ahad, *Freud Upside Down: African American Literature and Psychoanalysis Culture* (Urbana: University of Illinois Press, 2012), 60–81.

47. JT to Alain Locke, 17 August 1923, *Letters*, 169–70; Albert Rosenthal to JT, 5 May 1924, box 6, folder 221, JTP; JT to Albert Rosenthal, n.d. (early May 1924), *Letters*, 198; Ernestine Rose to JT, 19 March 1924, box 6, folder 191, JTP; Geneviève Taggard, ed., *May Days: An Anthology of Verse from the Masses-Liberator* (New York: Boni and Liveright, 1925), 139; Alain Locke, ed., *Four Negro Poets* (New York: Simon and Schuster, Pamphlet Poets Series, 1927); Charles Johnson to JT, 6 March 1924, box 4, folder 115, JTP; *Who's Who in Colored America: A Biographical Dictionary of Notable Living Persons of Negro Descent in America* (New York: Who's Who in Colored America Corp., 1927). The five poems from *Cane* that appeared in Locke's 1927 anthology are "Song of the Son," "Reapers," "Face," "November Cotton Flower," and "Georgia Dusk" (12–14). The publisher's preface notes, "Grateful acknowledgment is hereby made to the poets represented in this pamphlet, and their publishers to reprint as follows: . . . Boni & Liveright—*Cane* by Jean Toomer" (3). In his introductory comment, titled "The Poetry of Negro Life," Locke writes, "To Toomer, slavery, once a shame and stigma, becomes a spiritual process of growth and transfiguration, and the tortuous underground groping of one generation the maturing and high blossoming of the next. . . . Jean Toomer's probing into the sub-soil of Southern

life is only a significant bit of the same plowing under of Reconstruction sentimentalism that has yielded us a new realistic poetry of the South" (6). Nowhere in his autobiography does Toomer make mention of Locke's 1927 reprinting of poems from *Cane*, apparently with Toomer's permission.

48. JT, journal, 20 September 1929, box 61, folder 1420, JTP; JT to James Weldon Johnson, 11 July 1930, box 20, folder 482, JTP; JT to Nancy Cunard, 8 February 1932, box 3, folder 24, JTP. While in Chicago, Toomer wrote in his journal that he was engaged in "destroying . . . [the] pictures and impressions [that] tended to hinder my work" (box 51, folder 1122, JTP). The French impression of Toomer as a "black poet" may have been influenced by the fact that the only poems of Toomer's that had been translated into French—by Leopold Senghor—were "Song of the Son," "Georgia Dusk," and "Harvest Song," a choice that "limited [Toomer's] to being a poetry of the soil, the South, and the African heritage" (Michel Fabre, "The Reception of *Cane* in France," in *Jean Toomer and the Harlem Renaissance*, ed. Geneviève Fabre and Michel Feith [New Brunswick, N.J.: Rutgers University Press, 2001], 202–14, quoted 210). Toomer's résumé altered considerably over the years, often effacing the *Crisis*, *Liberator*, and/or *New York Call* as early publishing venues (autobiographical sketches 1931–43, n.d., box 11, folder 343, JTP).

49. Victor Francis Calverton, ed., *Anthology of American Negro Literature* (New York: Modern Library, 1929), 21–26, 202–3, introduction quoted vii; *The Negro Caravan: Writings by American Negroes*, ed. Sterling Brown, Arthur P. Davis, and Ulysses Lee (New York: Citadel Press, 1941), 41–54, 355–57; "As the Eagle Soars," *Crisis* (41, no. 4 [April 1932]: 116). Toomer had been invited by Du Bois to submit work to the *Crisis* the previous year (W. E. B. Du Bois to JT, 20 May 1931, box 1, folder 37, JTP). Louis Untermeyer included "Song of the Son" and "Georgia Dusk" in the fifth edition of *Modern American Poetry*; although his introductory sketch did not mention Toomer's race directly, it referred to the publication of "Fern" in Calverton's anthology, which had contained only works by African Americans (*Modern American Poetry*, 5th rev. ed. [New York: Harcourt, Brace, 1936], 529–31).

50. *Baltimore Afro-American*, 1 December 1934, 1; marriage certificate, Portage Wisconsin, 28 October 1931, box 60, folder 1404, JTP; JT, "Thus May It Be Said," box 51, folder 1122, JTP. There was no miscegenation law in Wisconsin that would have prevented the interracial Toomer-Latimer marriage. The racist publicity surrounding the marriage is described in Cynthia Kerman and Richard Eldridge, *The Lives of Jean Toomer: A Hunger for Wholeness* (Baton Rouge: Louisiana State University Press, 1987), 201–4. For more on Toomer's 1942 draft registration, see Rudolph Byrd and Henry Louis Gates Jr., "Jean Toomer's Racial Self-Identification: A Note on the Supporting Materials," in *Cane*, Norton 2, lxvi–lxxix.

51. JT, "The Second River," box 22, folder 553, JTP. Toomer's insistence upon his sense of belonging in the "shining ground" of the folk has its dystopian counterpart in an undated poem in which he portrays himself as rootless: "I am a tree, uprooted. / Soil, still clinging to my sap-roots, / Dries in the wind. / I have sucked the moisture from my smallest rootlet; / My great trunk is dying. . . . The sun upon my roots is torture. / My leaves, the teeth of my voice, / Are falling. / A sound scratches against the hollow winds / It is my call for soil to cover me" (untitled poem, box 48, folder 1002, JTP).

52. JT, Journal, box 62, folders 1446 and 1443, JTP; see folders 1442–47 for a series of dream recollections from 1949 to 1950. That Toomer had experienced disturbing dreams about his racial identity many years before is indicated in a dream that he recorded in

his journal in January 1924: "I fly. I go up, Negroes from apartment windows jeer at me. Negroes from the roofs of buildings jeer at me. At an ultimate height, a gargoyle-Negro face on a pole grins. . . . The Negro scene is curiously stagey and artificial. It seems to be an act from some play. I am not myself; some actor is" (Notes, box 60, folder 1413, JTP).

53. Alain Locke to JT, 1 July 1923, box 5, folder 151, JTP; JT to Alain Locke, 17 August 1923, *Letters*, 169; JT, 1922–23 Journal, box 60, folder 1411, JTP. For commentaries on "Balo," see Michael J. Krasny, "Design in Jean Toomer's 'Balo,'" in O'Daniel, 355–57; Nellie Y. McKay, *Jean Toomer, Artist: A Study of His Life and Work* (Chapel Hill: University of North Carolina Press, 1984), 60–68; and Frederik Rusch, "Jean Toomer's Early Identification," *MELUS* 13 (spring–summer 1986): 115–29. Continuing his narrative of Locke's presumed betrayal in publishing parts of *Cane* in *The New Negro*, Toomer wrote, "Later on Locke again used without my consent one of pieces for a new book of his. Years ago I had submitted this sketch, 'Balo,' one of my early attempts, to Locke and Gregory when they were running the Howard University Players. They had done nothing with it. Imagine my surprise, then, and my anger years later suddenly to see this naive attempt appearing in a collection" (JT, "Thus May It Be Said," box 51, folder 1122, JTP).

54. JT, "Balo," in *Plays of Negro Life: A Source-Book of Native American Drama*, ed. Alain Locke and Montgomery Gregory (Westport, Conn.: Negro University Press, 1927), 271–72.

55. Ibid., 276.

56. Ibid., 276. Before their trip south in 1922, Toomer wrote to Frank of the Negro church, "When they overflow in song, there is no singing that has so touched me. Their theology is a farce (Christ is so immediate): their religious emotion, elemental, and for that reason, very near the sublime" (JT to Waldo Frank, 21 August 1922, *Letters*, 73).

57. JT, "Balo," 280, 284.

58. Ibid., 275, 277, 282. Aside from Du Bois's *The Souls of Black Folks* (1903; rpt. Boston: Bedford Books, 1997), other sources on African American song available to Toomer were Hampton Normal and Agricultural Institute, *Religious Folk Songs of the Negro as Sung on the Plantation*, rev. ed. (Hampton, Va.: Institute Press, 1909); and Henry Edward Krehbiel, *Afro-American Folksongs: A Study in Racial and Notational Music* (New York: Schirmer, 1914). Krehbiel's book was included in the January 1921 *Crisis*'s list of recommended readings.

59. JT, "Balo," 285–86. Robert B. Jones comments, "As the curtain descends . . . [the] embrace [of Uncle Ned and Balo] symbolizes the union of past and present in a shared recognition of spiritual harmony" (*Jean Toomer and the Prison-House of Thought: A Phenomenology of the Spirit* [Amherst: University of Massachusetts Press, 1993] 30).

Chapter 3. *The Experiment in America*

1. Waldo Frank, *Our America* (New York: Boni and Liveright, 1919), 14, 45, 179, 209. Frank wrote to Toomer in December 1922, "I have been busy with a series of lectures at the Rand School on the Rev. in Art and Lit" (Waldo Frank to JT, n.d. [late December 1922], in *Brother*, 87). For more on Frank's place in U.S. cultural history, see Paul J. Carter, *Waldo Frank* (New York: Twayne, 1967); Lewis Mumford, "Waldo Frank: The Ego and His Own," in *My Works and Days: A Personal Chronicle* (New York: Harcourt Brace Jovanovich, 1979), 512–25; and Cary Nelson Blake, *Beloved Community: The Cultural Criticism of Randolph Bourne, Van Wyck Brooks, Waldo Frank, and Lewis Mumford* (Chapel Hill: University of North Carolina Press, 1990).

2. Frank, *Our America*, 82–83, 205, 226–27, 4, 93–116, 227, 203, 198–200, 320–32. Gorham Munson adjudged *Our America* a "remarkable manifesto" written from "a consciously socialist point of view" (*The Awakening Twenties: A Memoir-History of a Literary Period* [Baton Rouge: Louisiana State University Press, 1985], 54, 67). Kathleen Pfeiffer observes that *Our America* "lauded the revolutionary potential of blending such systems as Freudian psychoanalysis, spiritual mysticism, and communism" (introduction to Waldo Frank, *Holiday* [1923; rpt. Urbana: University of Illinois Press, 2003], xiii).

3. Frank, *Our America*, 226, 201, 134, 135, 209, 228. For the critique of Frank's manifesto as "a gallant effort to give young and lonely idealists a background," see Floyd Dell, review of *Our America*, *Liberator* 3 (January 1920): 43–44, quoted 44.

4. Frank, *Our America*, 179, 172, 136, 229.

5. JT, "The Critic of Waldo Frank: Criticism, an Art Form," *S4N* 30 (January 1924), rpt. in *Jean Toomer: Selected Essays and Literary Criticism*, ed. Robert B. Jones (Knoxville: University of Tennessee Press), 27. "S4N" stood for "Space for Name." See Walker Rumble, "'Space for Name': Printing a 1920s Little Magazine," *Massachusetts Review* 48, no. 2 (summer 2007): 257–72. Gorham Munson considered *Our America* "an inspired psychological history of a pioneer-puritan-industrial civilization" (*Waldo Frank: A Study* [New York: Boni and Liveright, 1923], 20). For more on Frank and psychoanalysis, see Leslie Fishbein, "Freud and the Radicals: The Sexual Revolution Comes to Greenwich Village," *Canadian Review of American Studies* 12 (fall 1981): 173–89.

6. Frank, *Our America*, 107, 48. For more on Frank's "buried cultures," see Susan Hegeman, *Patterns for America: Modernism and the Concept of Culture* (Princeton, N.J.: Princeton University Press, 1999), 103–16; and Walter Benn Michaels, *Our America: Nativism, Modernism, and Pluralism* (Durham, N.C.: Duke University Press, 1995), 135–42.

7. John Dewey, "Americanism and Localism," *Dial* 68 (June 1920): 684–88; Frederick Jackson Turner, "Sections and Nation" (1922), in *Rereading Frederick Jackson Turner: "The Significance of the Frontier in American History" and Other Essays*, ed. John Mack Faragher (New York: Henry Holt, 1994), 181–200, quoted 200. For more on regionalism, nationalism and modernism, see Leigh Anne Duck, *The Nation's Region: Southern Modernism, Segregation, and U.S. Nationalism* (Athens: University of Georgia Press, 2006); Carrie Tirado Bramen, *The Uses of Variety: Modern Americanism and the Quest for National Distinctiveness* (Cambridge, Mass.: Harvard University Press, 2000), 115–98; and C. Barry Chabot, *Writers for the Nation: American Literary Modernism* (Tuscaloosa: University of Alabama Press, 1997).

8. Mary Austin, "New York: Dictator of American Criticism," *Nation* 111 (July 1920): 129–30; JT, "Americans and Mary Austin," *New York Call*, 10 October 1920, rpt. in *JTTAH*, 228–31. For more on Austin and anti-Semitism, see Esther Lanigan Stineman, *Mary Austin: Song of a Maverick* (New Haven, Conn.: Yale University Press, 1989), 121.

9. JT, "Americans and Mary Austin," 229, 230, 231.

10. Ibid., 228, 231.

11. V. I. Lenin, "Critical Remarks on the National Question" (1913), trans. Bernard Isaacs and Joe Fineberg, *Collected Works*, vol. 20, 4th English ed. (Moscow: Progress Publishers, 1964), 29–30. The term "dictator" did not take on uniformly negative associations until after World War II. Compare the first *Liberator* editorial applauding the Soviet Union for bringing into being "economic or real democracy. . . . It is the working-class who will accomplish it by establishing a dictatorship, overt and uncompromising" ("The Russian Dictators," *Liberator* 1 [March 1918]: 6).

12. For more on the multiple valences of the melting-pot metaphor, see Philip Gleason, *Speaking of Diversity: Language and Ethnicity in Twentieth-Century America* (Baltimore, Md.: Johns Hopkins University Press, 1992), 1–46.

13. Waldo Frank to JT, 21 October 1920, in *Brother*, 26; JT to Waldo Frank, 24 March 1922, *Letters*, 32. "The First American" has disappeared.

14. Waldo Frank to JT, n.d. [late April 1922], in *Brother*, 36; JT to Gorham Munson, 31 October 1922, *Letters*, 90. For positive assessments of the relationship between Frank and Toomer, see Mark Helbling, "Jean Toomer and Waldo Frank: A Creative Friendship," in O'Daniel, 85–97; Kathleen Pfeiffer, introduction to *Brother*, 1–23; and Kathleen Pfeiffer, *Race Passing and American Individualism* (Amherst: University of Massachusetts Press, 2003), 82–106. For negative evaluations, see Charles R. Larson, *Invisible Darkness: Jean Toomer and Nella Larsen* (Iowa City: University of Iowa Press, 1993), 18–21; and Kathryne V. Lindberg, "Raising *Cane* on the Theoretical Plane: Jean Toomer's Racial Personae," in *Cultural Difference and the Literary Text: Pluralism and the Limits of Authenticity in North American Literatures*, ed. Winfried Siemerling and Katrin Schwenk (Iowa City: University of Iowa Press, 1996), 49–74.

15. Waldo Frank to JT, n.d. [April 1922], in *Brother*, 36; JT to Waldo Frank, 26 April 1922, n.d. [early May 1922], and 2 August 1922, *Letters*, 37, 38, and 59.

16. JT to Waldo Frank, 2 August 1922, n.d. [April 1923], and n.d. [early to mid-March, 1923], *Letters*, 59, 157, 138; JT to Gorham Munson, 14 March 1923, *Letters*, 140; JT to Jane Heap, 12 January 1923, *Letters*, 119; JT to Ridge, 20 August 1922, *Letters*, 72. For more on Toomer's management of his relationships with various "little magazines," see Matthew Christian Luskey, "Modernist Ephemera: Little Magazines and the Dynamics of Coalition, Passing and Failure," PhD diss., University of Oregon, 2003. John McClure's New Orleans–based *Double Dealer* proclaimed its commitment to portray "the raw stuff, cleared of the myths of glamor-throwers and Utopia-weavers. . . . [W]e mean to deal double, to show the other side" (editorial, *Double Dealer* 1, no. 1 [January 1921]: 2–3). Although claiming to transcend the "treacly sentimentalities" of southern representations of the Negro, the journal chided Du Bois's *Darkwater* as a "bitter book" that was insufficiently grateful for the good will toward the Negro exhibited by white Southerners ("Southern Letters," *Double Dealer* 1 [June 1921]: 214; review of W. E. B. Du Bois's *Darkwater*, *Double Dealer* 1, no. 6 [June 1921]: 254–55, quoted 254). The journal also viewed the Russian Revolution as a "barbarian invasion," its "theory of equality" papering over a reality of "mob-mastery" (editorial, *Double Dealer* 1, no. 3 [March 1921]: 86).

17. JT to John McClure, 22 July 1922, *Letters*, 46; JT to Waldo Frank, 5 May 1922, n.d. [early to mid-December 1922], 12 December 1922, and n.d. [early to mid-January 1922], *Letters*, 39, 99, 101, 115; JT to Gorham Munson, 19 March 1923, *Letters*, 144.

18. Waldo Frank to JT, n.d. [April 1922], in *Brother*, 34–37.

19. JT to Waldo Frank, 5 May 1922, n.d. [mid-January 1923], 20 September 1922, and n.d. [late January/early February 1923], *Letters*, 39, 121, 78, 126.

20. JT to Sherwood Anderson, 18 December 1922, *Letters*, 101–2; Sherwood Anderson, "Out of Nowhere into Nothing," in *The Triumph of the Egg* 1921; rpt. New York: Four Walls Eight Windows, 1988), 171–231. Anderson praised *Cane* as "the first negro work I have seen that strikes me as really negro" (quoted in Darwin Turner, "An Intersection of Paths: Correspondence between Jean Toomer and Sherwood Anderson," in O'Daniel, 99–110). Toomer complained to Frank that Anderson, while "doubtless [having] a very deep and beautiful emotion by way of the Negro," nonetheless "limits me to Negro" (JT to Waldo

Frank, n.d. [early January 1923], *Letters*, 113). For more on Anderson's influence, see Mark Helbling, "Sherwood Anderson and Jean Toomer," in O'Daniel, 111–20; and Mark Whalan, *Race, Manhood, and Modernism in America: The Short Story Cycles of Sherwood Anderson and Jean Toomer* (Knoxville: University of Tennessee Press, 2007).

21. Waldo Frank, "A Note on the Novel," in *Salvos: An Informal Book about Books and Plays* (New York: Boni and Liveright, 1924), 223–31, quoted 227–30; Waldo Frank to JT, 3 April 1922, in *Brother*, 30. Frank's essay was originally titled "The Major Issue" when it appeared in the *New Republic Spring Literary Supplement* 32 (3 May 1922): 9–12.

22. JT to Waldo Frank, 10 April 1922, *Letters*, 34. For Kenneth Burke's criticism of Frank, see "Enlarging the Narrow House," *Dial* 73 (September 1922): 346–48, and "The Consequences of Idealism," *Dial* 73 (October 1922): 450–51. See also Charles Scruggs, "Jean Toomer and Kenneth Burke and the Persistence of the Past," *American Literary History* 13 (spring 2001): 41–66.

23. Gorham Munson, "The Mechanics for a Literary Secession," *S4N* [November 1922], rpt. in Gorham Munson, "A Comedy of Exiles," *Literary Review* 12 [fall 1968], 53); JT to Gorham Munson, 20 December 1922, *Letters*, 103; JT to Lola Ridge, n.d. [late December 1922/early January 1923], *Letters*, 111. *Secession* claimed to be "a group organ" dedicated to publishing "the unknown path-breaking artist," having "swerved aside and shot ahead of its American contemporaries—straight into the dangerous rapids of modern letters. It disdains life-belts" (*Secession* 1, no. 2 [April 1922]: 32, 33). Toomer's experiments with Dada are exemplified in "Sound Poem (I)," "Sound Poem (II)," "Skyline," and "Gum," in *Collected Poems of Jean Toomer*, ed. Robert B. Jones and Margery Toomer Latimer (Chapel Hill: University of North Carolina Press, 1988), 15–18. For more on the "machine aesthetic," see Jayne E. Marek, ed., *Women Editing Modernism: "Little" Magazines and Literary History* (Lexington: University Press of Kentucky, 1995); and Dickran Tashjian, *Skyscraper Primitives: Dada and the American Avant-Garde, 1910–1925* (Middletown, Conn.: Wesleyan University Press, 1975).

24. JT to Gorham Munson, 20 December 1922, *Letters*, 103; Vladimir Lenin, "Our Foreign and Domestic Position and Party Tasks," in *Collected Works*, trans. Julius Katzer, 4th English ed. (Moscow: Progress Publishers, 1965), 31:408–26, http://www.marxists.org/archive/lenin/works/1920/nov/21.htm, accessed 27 January 2013. Toomer expressed his requirement of "extra-artistic consciousness" several times: see JT to Gorham Munson, 8 October and 4 November 1922, *Letters*, 83 and 93; and JT to Waldo Frank, 22 October 1922, *Letters*, 89. For more on Toomer's attempted synthesis of the programs of Munson and Frank as constituents of "triangular culture," see JT to Waldo Frank, n.d. [early to mid-March 1921], *Letters*, 138; and JT, "The Critic of Waldo Frank: Criticism, An Art Form," *S4N* 30 (January 1924), rpt. in *Jean Toomer: Selected Essays and Literary Criticism*, ed. Jones, 24–31.

25. JT to Gorham Munson, 19 March 1923, *Letters*, 144; JT to Lola Ridge, n.d. [late January 1923], *Letters*, 123.

26. JT to Rex Fuller, 19 February 1923, *Letters*, 132; JT to Margaret Naumberg, n.d. [summer 1923], *Letters*, 165–66; JT, "General Ideas and States to Be Developed," box 48, folder 1002, JTP.

27. Waldo Frank, "Foreword to the 1923 Edition of *Cane*," rpt. in *Cane*, Norton 2, 117–19.

28. JT to Waldo Frank, n.d. [late February 1923], *Letters*, 133–34; *Wayward*, 126. Turner's text of *The Wayward and the Seeking* is drawn from the typed version in box 20, folder 513, JTP. One handwritten version, interpolated after the words "the world of American literature," reads as follows: "How explain Frank's behavior? I cannot believe ['believe' is crossed out: 'credit' is substituted] that he failed to understand me, in this respect. I cannot believe

that, in the fact of knowing me, in the face of having seen my ['obviously white' is crossed out] family, in the face of having heard ['my explanations' is crossed out; 'my statements' is substituted], he deliberately misrepresented me." Toomer then crossed out "Some motive, of which he himself was not aware, must . . ." and continued, "Then what? It wasn't necessary that he mention race at all—I mean theoretically it wasn't. But if he felt compelled to, then certainly he could have told the truth—again theoretically. Some motive was at work. I have my guesses. Perhaps he himself will one day tell us what it was" (box 20, folder 511, JTP). Georgia Douglas Johnson recalled Toomer bringing Frank to a gathering of African American writers at her house in the fall of 1922 (Elizabeth McHenry, *Forgotten Readers: Recovering the Lost History of African American Literary Societies* [Durham, N.C.: Duke University Press, 2002], 274). For Frank's memories of having been introduced by Toomer to "the most conscious community of American Negroes" for whom "[t]o be colored was a trauma they all suffered together," see Waldo Frank, *Memoirs of Waldo Frank*, ed. Alan Trachtenberg (Amherst: University of Massachusetts Press, 1973), 106–07.

29. Waldo Frank to JT, n.d., in *Brother*, 94; JT to Waldo Frank, n.d. [early January 1923], and n.d. [late February 1923], *Letters*, 117 and 133–34; JT to Montgomery Gregory, 2 January 1924, *Letters*, 187. In his review of *Cane*, Gregory had approvingly cited Frank's statement that *Cane* is the "'aesthetic equivalent' of the Southland," indeed, "IS the South" (Gregory quoted in JT, *Cane*, Norton 2, 179).

30. Horace Liveright to JT, 29 August 1923, box 1, folder 16, JTP; JT to Horace Liveright, 5 September 1923, *Letters*, 171–72; Rudolph P. Byrd and Henry Louis Gates Jr., "Introduction: 'Song of the Son': The Emergence and Passing of Jean Toomer," in *Cane*, Norton 2, lx–lxi. Toomer wrote to Liveright on the acceptance of *Cane*: "I am so glad to be in the fold. There is no other like it. The American group with Waldo Frank, Gorham B Munson, TS Eliot—well, it simply cant be beaten" (JT to Horace Liveright, 11 January 1923, *Letters*, 118). For more on Liveright and the avant-garde, see Tom Dardis, *Firebrand: The Life of Horace Liveright* (New York: Random House, 1995). Kathleen Pfeiffer concludes that the letters between Toomer and Frank "provide no evidence whatsoever that Toomer felt betrayed by Frank's foreword" (introduction, *Brother*, 3). On Toomer's interactions with both Liveright and Frank, see Michael Nowlin, "The Strange Literary Career of Jean Toomer," *Texas Studies in Language and Literature* 53 (summer 2011): 207–35.

31. JT, publicity sketch for *Cane*, box 26, folder 611, JTP. There are three drafts of the sketch, two of which contain interpolations and corrections in Toomer's handwriting.

32. For the argument that someone at Boni and Liveright, not Toomer, authored the entire publicity sketch, see Michael Soto, "Jean Toomer and Horace Liveright: Or, A New Negro Gets 'Into the Swing of It,'" in *Jean Toomer and the Harlem Renaissance*, ed. Geneviève Fabre and Michel Feith (New Brunswick, N.J.: Rutgers University Press, 2001), 162–87. For more on the alternatively modernist and racist meanings of the phrase "black super-vaudeville out of the South," see Rachel Farebrother, *The Collage Aesthetic in the Harlem Renaissance* (London: Ashgate, 2009), 90; Michael North, *The Dialect of Modernism: Race, Language, and Twentieth-Century Literature* (New York: Oxford University Press, 1998), 168–69; and Geoffrey Jacques, *A Change in the Weather: Modernist Imagination, African American Imaginary* (Amherst: University of Massachusetts Press, 2009), 110–47. Many of the reviews of *Cane* are gathered in box 26, folder 60, JTP. Henry Louis Gates Jr. discusses the reception of *Cane* in *Figures in Black: Words, Signs, and the "Racial" Self* (New York: Oxford University Press, 1987), 199–219.

33. JT to Waldo Frank, 29 September 1923, *Letters*, 176; JT, review of Waldo Frank's *Holiday*, *Dial* 75 (October 1923): 382–86, rpt. in *Jean Toomer: Selected Essays and Literary Criticism*,

ed. Jones, 7–10. For Frank's hurt response, see Waldo Frank to JT, n.d., in *Brother*, 157–58. Frank originally intended to call the novel "Carnival" and to feature a black-on-white rape leading up to the lynching; he omitted the rape in the published text. See Christine Pfeiffer, introduction to *Holiday* (1923; rpt. Urbana: University of Illinois Press, 2003), vii–xl.

34. JT, "The South in Literature," in *Jean Toomer: Selected Essays and Literary Criticism*, ed. Jones, 12–15. Calling Toomer's article "a humdinger," Liveright wrote that "Ryan Walker of the Call . . . I know will be glad to print it. Of course, as you say, we'll have to sign it with a faked name" (Horace Liveright to JT, 27 September 1923, box 1, folder 16, JTP). Reviewing *Cane* and *Holiday* together for the *Survey*, Bruno Lasker had asserted that Toomer and Frank were one and the same—namely, Frank: "[I]s not 'Jean Toomer' a polite fiction?" ("Doors Opened Southward," *Survey Graphic* 4 [November 1923]: 190–91). For Toomer's angry response, see JT to the editor of the *Survey Graphic*, 12 November 1923, *Letters*, 182–83. Other reviews compared—but did not equate—Toomer with Frank. See P.H.J., "Ambitious Verse and Negro Tales by Jean Toomer," *Philadelphia Public Ledger*, 12 January 1924; Alice Beal Parsons, "Toomer and Frank," *World Tomorrow* 7 (March 1924): 96; and Anonymous, *Dial* 76 (January 1924): 92.

35. JT, "The South in Literature," 11–15.

36. Waldo Frank to JT, 17 July 1922, in *Brother*, 44; JT, "The South in Literature," 16.

37. Scholars proposing that Toomer's assessment of Frank changed during the writing of *Cane* include Charles Scruggs, "Jean Toomer and Kenneth Burke and the Persistence of the Past"; *JTTAH*, 98–100; Mark Whalan, *Race, Manhood, and Modernism in America*, 139–47; and Daniel Terris, "Waldo Frank, Jean Toomer, and the Critique of Racial Voyeurism," in *Race and the Modern Artist*, ed. Heather Hathaway, Josef Jarab, and Jeffrey Melnick (New York: Oxford University Press, 2003): 92–114. Terris also proposes that "[a]n unavoidable erotic undercurrent runs through [Frank and Toomer's] correspondence, especially after their return from the South. . . . Although there is no evidence to suggest that they explicitly thought of themselves as lovers, the intensity with which they approached their shared writing suggests a form of displacement" (106). Both Toomer and Frank subsequently gave erroneous accounts of the Spartanburg trip. Toomer would state that he had sent the manuscript of *Cane* to Liveright before the trip; Frank, conversely, wrote in his memoir that it was Toomer, not he, who first proposed the trip.

38. JT to Waldo Frank, n.d. [mid-March 1923], *Letters*, 143. For more evidence of Toomer's growing reservations about Frank's writerly abilities, see JT to the *New Republic* critic Robert Littell, 23 October and 5 November 1923, *Letters*, 179 and 181. The earlier letter, more harshly critical, was never sent.

39. JT to Waldo Frank, 19 July 1922, *Letters*, 43. Toomer began work on "Withered Skin of Berries" in early May 1922 and sent it to the *Dial* in June 1922 (JT to John McClure, 30 June 1922, *Letters*, 41). Toomer contemplated including the story in a collection of shorter pieces that would also have contained the play *Natalie Mann* and an untitled "third long piece that I'm forming in my mind" (JT to Waldo Frank, n.d. [early to mid March 1923], *Letters*, 138). See also JT to Ella H. Elbert, 18 October 1922, *Letters*, 87. Storer College at Harpers Ferry was a favorite vacation spot of the capital city's African American elite. See Mary Church Terrell, *A Colored Woman in a White World* (1940; rpt. Salem, N.H.: Ayer, 1986), 239.

40. JT, "Withered Skin of Berries," in *Wayward*, 139–65, quoted 139 and 165.

41. Ibid., 155, 141; JT to Lillie Buffum Chace Wyman, 24 January 1922, *Letters*, 30. Henry Lincoln Johnson, husband of Georgia Douglas Johnson, wrote that "[ever since] President Wilson was inaugurated, . . . the persistent aim of the Democratic Party has been to eliminate and humiliate the Negro" (*The Negro under Wilson* [Washington, DC: Republican

National Committee, 1916], 4). Johnson's list of African American Republicans who had been replaced by whites included Johnson himself, Toomer's grandfather P. B. S. Pinchback, and the Pinchbacks' family friend Whitefield McKinlay (8–11) (see my chapter 4). For more on the impact of Wilsonian segregation on the postwar polarization of racial categories, see Joel Williamson, *The Crucible of Race: Black-White Relations in the American South since Emancipation* (New York: Oxford University Press, 1984), 111–39. Scruggs and VanDemarr note that the Masonic Temple was "a venue for racist speakers, particularly Southern politicians" such as Senator James. K. Vardaman of Mississippi (*JTTAH*, 282 n8).

42. JT, "Withered Skin of Berries," 139–40, 153–54.

43. Ibid., 142–44, 147.

44. Ibid., 147. Carl may be based on an unnamed former fellow student of Toomer's at the University of Wisconsin, a bigot "prejudiced against everyone who was not white, bourgeois and Christian . . . I had the pleasure of hating him a little more than he hated me" (JT, box 20, folder 513, JTP). For readings of the story's treatment of sexuality, see Siobhan Somerville, *Queering the Color Line: Race and the Invention of Homosexuality in American Culture* (Durham, N.C.: Duke University Press, 2000), 146–49; and Peter Christensen, "Sexuality and Liberation in Jean Toomer's 'Withered Skin of Berries,'" *Callaloo* 11 (1988): 616–26.

45. JT, "Withered Skin of Berries," 152.

46. Ibid., 151.

47. Ibid., 141. The Tomb of the Unknown Soldier in Arlington National Cemetery was dedicated 21 November 1921.

48. JT, "Withered Skin of Berries," 161. The poem is an extended version of "Conversion" in part 1 of *Cane*. Toomer frequently included suspension points in his writings, both poetry and prose. Here and in subsequent quotations, these suspension points are reproduced as unspaced dots.

49. JT, "Withered Skin of Berries," 155. The hyper-masculine and hyper-talented David Teyy reappears as Nathan Merilh in *Natalie Mann* and as Nathan Antrum in Toomer's 1929 novella, "York Beach" (*New American Caravan*, ed. Alfred Kreymborg, Lewis Mumford, and Paul Rosenfeld [New York: Macaulay Co., 1929], 12–83). For a discussion of cars as sites of rebirth in the discourse of futurism, see Marjorie Perloff, *The Futurist Moment: Avant-Garde, Avant Guerre, and the Language of Rupture* (Chicago: University of Chicago Press, 2003), 86–87.

50. JT, "Withered Skin of Berries," 145–46, 143.

51. Ibid., 158. The rhetoric of the "rising tide of color" was confronted and revised in radical black postwar poetry. See, for example, Andy Razaf, "The Rising Tide," *Negro World* (1920), rpt. in Tony Martin, *African Fundamentalism: A Literary and Cultural Anthology of Garvey's Harlem Renaissance* (Dover, Mass.: Majority Press, 1991), 173–74; and Claude McKay, "America," *Liberator* 4 (December 1921): 9, rpt. in Claude McKay, *Complete Poems*, ed. William J. Maxwell (Urbana: University of Illinois Press, 2004), 153.

52. JT, "Withered Skin of Berries," 159, 162, 163–64; Brown quoted in W. E. B. Du Bois, *John Brown*, rev. ed. (New York: International, 1972), 271.

53. Claude McKay, "Exhortation: Summer, 1919," *Complete Poems*, 175. Toomer noted the "strain of Indian blood" in the population around Harpers Ferry (JT to Waldo Frank, 19 July 1922, *Letters*, 43).

54. For a more on "Withered Skin of Berries" in relation to contemporaneous racist discourses, see Barbara Foley, "The Color of Blood: John Brown, Jean Toomer, and the New Negro Movement," forthcoming, *African American Review* 46, 2 [Summer 2013].

Chapter 4. All the Dead Generations

1. JT, *The Collected Poems of Jean Toomer*, ed. Robert B. Jones and Margery Toomer Latimer (Chapel Hill: University of North Carolina Press, 1988), 49. Jones concludes that the poem was written between 1934 and 1940; he observes, "In its interpretation of what is ostensibly ancestral consciousness, the poem is curiously haunting" (108).

2. See Sigmund Freud, "Family Romances" (1909), *Collected Papers*, vol. 5, trans. and ed. James Strachey [New York: Basic Books, 1959], 74–78. Freud's gender-biased formulation of the family romance stressed the male identity of its creator, as well as the high social rank of the child's fantasized alternative parents. See also Johanna Krout Tabin, "The Family Romance: Attention to the Unconscious Basis for a Conscious Fantasy," *Psychoanalytic Psychology* 15, no. 2 (1998): 287–93.

3. For the argument that miscegenation is the hidden secret in *Cane*, see *JTTAH*, 135–58. For more on the racialized Gothic in American literature, see Teresa A. Goddu, *Gothic America: Narrative, History, and Nation* (New York: Columbia University Press, 1997).

4. JT, "The Outline of an Autobiography" (1931), box 20, folder 514, JTP; JT, "On Being an American" (1934), rpt. in *Wayward*, 84–85. The typical followers of Gurdjieff are described in Paul Beekman Taylor, *Shadows of Heaven: Gurdjieff and Toomer* (York Beach, Maine: Samuel Weiser, 1998).

5. JT, "Book X," quoted in Isaac Johnny Johnson III, "The Autobiography of Jean Toomer: An Edition" (PhD diss., Purdue University, 1982), 64. For the argument that Toomer's autobiographies inaccurately portray the lives of the capital city's mixed-race aristocracy as being largely free of the strictures of Jim Crow, see Rudolph P. Byrd and Henry Louis Gates Jr., "Introduction: 'Song of the Son': The Emergence and Passing of Jean Toomer," in *Cane*, Norton 2, xix–xli.

6. JT, "Incredible Journey," box 18, folders 487, 490, and 491, JTP. Toomer's discussion bears a marked resemblance to Marx's discussion of "Large-Scale Industry and Agriculture" in *Capital: A Critique of Political Economy*, trans. Ben Fowkes (New York: Penguin, 1976), 1:636–39.

7. JT, "Incredible Journey," box 18, folder 491, JTP. Coxey's Army was a march of the unemployed on Washington, DC, in 1894. The Paris Commune of 1870–71 was held up by Marx and Lenin as a possible precursor of socialist revolution.

8. JT, "Book X," box 11, folder 359, JTP; JT, "On Being an American," box 20, folder 513, JTP; JT, "Incredible Journey," box 19, folder 498, JTP. In his interview with Marjorie Content Toomer, Toomer's second wife, John Chandler Griffin reports her saying, in relation to Pinchback's self-identification as a Negro, that "Jean felt that P. B. S. did that merely to get elected, to use that period in history when Blacks were supposed to be on their way up." She is also reported to have stated, with regard to Pinchback's mother, Eliza, that Toomer "thought Eliza might have been Indian or West Indian. Actually, he said he didn't know." See John Howard Griffin, "A Chat with Marjorie Content Toomer," *Pembroke Magazine* 5 (1974): 14–27, quoted 16; and "Jean Toomer: American Writer (A Biography)," PhD diss., University of South Carolina, 1976. W. E. B. Du Bois stated that Pinchback was, in appearance, "[t]o all intents and purposes . . . an educated, well-to-do, congenial white man with but a few drops of Negro blood" (*Black Reconstruction: An Essay toward a History of the Part Which Black Folk Played in the Attempt to Reconstruct Democracy in America, 1860–1880* [New York: Harcourt, Brace and Co., 1935], 469). For more on Pinchback's activism and stature, see Philip Dray, *Capital Men: The Epic Story of Reconstruction through the Lives of the First Black Congressmen* (Boston: Houghton Mifflin, 2008).

9. JT, authorial sketch, box 26, folder 610, JTP. Toomer would continue to shadowbox with Pinchback years after his grandfather's death. See JT, "Meditations: JT and PB: Make Good," *New Mexico Literary Sentinel*, 20 July 1937, 6–7.

10. JT, "Incredible Journey," box 18, folders 491 and 487, JTP.

11. Divorce decree quoted in Maria Onita Estes-Hicks, "Jean Toomer: A Biographical and Critical Study," PhD diss., Columbia University, 1982, 56–57; JT, "Incredible Journey," box 18, folder 487, and box 19, folder 499, JTP. See also Nina Pinchback Toomer to Nathan Toomer, 8 July 1897, box 6, folder 262, JTP. For press coverage of the Pinchbacks' social activities—including "Col. Toomer's" appearance in Washington—see *Washington Bee*, 30 December 1893, Social Page; 3 February 1894, 1; 18 August 1894, 1; and 3 August 1895, City Brevities. The Toomer-Pinchback wedding took place at the Fifteenth Street Presbyterian Church, where the abolitionist Henry Highland Garnet had presided years before.

12. JT, "Incredible Journey," box 18, folder 487, JTP. Nathan Toomer wrote to Whitefield McKinlay, "Have you seen the Little Colonel? . . . I have some clothes and other things for him, but I don't know his name or how to send anything to him" (10 May 1898). Two years later, Nathan Toomer wrote that he had left various articles with "my child's mother," including "1 small gold headed walking cane 1 heavy gold ring 2 silver cups 1 set diamond shirt buttons 1 large picture" (quoted in Willard B. Gatewood Jr. and Virginia Kent Anderson Leslie, "'This Father of Mine . . . a Sort of Mystery': Jean Toomer's Georgia Heritage," *Georgia Historical Quarterly* 77 [winter 1993]: 804, 805).

13. JT, "Incredible Journey," box 18, folder 491, JTP. Nathan Toomer settled in Houston County, Georgia, in 1870; one section of Byron, Georgia, was designated Toomerville after the black Toomers (Estes-Hicks, "Jean Toomer," 52). Toomer was also a prominent name among the county's plantation-owning class (Bobbe Smith Hickson, *A Land So Dedicated: Houston County, Georgia* [Houston County Library Board, 1976]).

14. JT, "On Being an American," box 20, folder 513, JTP; JT, "Incredible Journey," box 19, folder 498, and box 18, folders 488 and 487, JTP. Referring to Toomer's 1913 conversation with Pinchback, Rudolph Byrd has written that "when Toomer visited Macon during his term as acting-principal of Sparta's Normal and Industrial Institute, he verified this biographical information by speaking with the town's black and white residents" ("Jean Toomer and the Afro-American Literary Tradition," *Callaloo* 24 [1985]: 310–19, quoted 313). But Byrd cites no evidence of this Macon trip.

15. JT, "Incredible Journey," box 19, folder 508, JTP.

16. Toomer, "Incredible Journey," box 18, folder 487, JTP. Although Cynthia Kerman and Richard Eldridge (*The Lives of Jean Toomer: A Hunger for Wholeness* [Baton Rouge: Louisiana State University Press, 1987], 285) assert that Toomer looked into his family background for the first time only when he began work on "Incredible Journey," the contradictions within and among his various autobiographies indicate that he had begun searching for this information many years before. His open admission to mixed racial ancestry at various points in "Incredible Journey" squares with his option to register for the draft in 1942 as a "Negro." See *Cane*, Norton 2, lxvii; and my chapter 2.

17. JT, "Incredible Journey," box 18, folder 487, JTP.

18. JT, "Incredible Journey," box 18, folder 491, and box 19, folder 508, JTP. Toomer's writing "three" instead of "two" is a slip of the pen—perhaps a classically Freudian one, but a slip nonetheless. Scruggs and VanDemarr rely on the first version of the barbershop visit in "Incredible Journey" (*JTTAH*, 21), as do Byrd and Gates (*Cane*, Norton 2, xxx).

19. JT, "Incredible Journey," box 18, folder 489, and box 19, folder 508, JTP.

20. Virginia Kent Anderson Leslie, *Woman of Color, Daughter of Privilege: Amanda*

America Dickson, 1849–1893 (Athens: University of Georgia Press, 1995), 57. See also H. William Rice, "Searching for Jean Toomer," *American Legacy* 3, no. 3 (fall 1997): 17–22. Amanda Dickson and Charles Eubanks would not have been able to marry in Georgia, where antimiscegenation laws had been reinstated after the Civil War (Leslie, *Woman of Color*, 58). For Dickson's groundbreaking achievements as a planter and ambiguous social status, see Chester Destler, "David Dickson's System of Farming and the Agricultural Revolution in the Deep South, 1850–1885," *Agricultural History* 31 (1957): 30–39. For more on the procedures of changing racial designation in New Orleans, see Virginia R. Dominguez, *White by Definition: Social Classification in Creole Louisiana* (New Brunswick, N.J.: Rutgers University Press, 1986).

21. Leslie, *Woman of Color*, 79, 124; *New York Times*, 15 July 1892, 3, quoted in Gatewood and Leslie, "'This Father of Mine,'" 790; Jonathan Bryant, "Race, Class and Law in Bourbon Georgia: The Case of David Dickson's Will," *Georgia Historical Quarterly* 71, no. 2 (summer 1987): 226–42. See also Adele Alexander, *Ambiguous Lives: Free Women of Color in Rural Georgia, 1789–1879* (Fayetteville: University of Arkansas Press, 1991), 183–91.

22. Bryant, "Race, Class and Law in Bourbon Georgia," 239–40. One of the Dickson family lawyers, "show[ing] that the future of the Anglo-Saxon, the traditions of the past, the hopes of the future" were at stake in the case, "finally overwhelmed the court; the Chief Justice put his head down upon the docket before him and wept like a child" (Nathaniel E. Harris, *Autobiography: The Story of an Old Man's Life and Reminiscences of Seventy-Five Years* [Macon, Ga.: J. W. Burke, 1925]), 487–93, quoted 491).

23. Destler, "David Dickson's System of Farming and the Agricultural Revolution," 36–38, quoted 38. Bryant notes Dickson's political connections: "Every fall, arson was a common form of economic revenge for sharecroppers and tenants who felt cheated by their landlords, with gin-house burnings across Georgia adding up to more than one hundred per season." When several Sparta area gins were burned in 1884, Dickson's property was the only case in which the governor offered a $250 reward for identifying the arsonist (232).

24. Bryant, "Race, Class and Law in Bourbon Georgia," 241; Clarence Bacote, "Some Aspects of Negro Life in Georgia, 1880–1908," *Journal of Negro History* 43 (1958): 194–95.

25. "The Richest Colored Woman: Amanda Eubanks Dickson Married to Nathan Toomer," *New York Times*, 15 July 1892, 3; Leslie, *Woman of Color*, 105–17.

26. Leslie, *Woman of Color*, 117–33. Although Nathan Toomer brought legal charges against Charles Dickson for his role in the events surrounding the abduction of Mamie, Dickson offered a competing narrative, "stat[ing] that the girl's father [Nathan Toomer] offered to give him her hand in marriage for $15,000. This he states that he was unwilling to do as the love is mutual between his step-sister and himself. The only draw-back to an early wedding, he states, is that he formed an unhappy alliance at the age of seventeen years. Proceedings are now going on in the courts of Georgia, which, he says, will free him in a short time" ("A Georgia Case," *Atlanta Constitution*, 29 April 1893, 2).

27. JT, "Incredible Journey," box 19, folder 508, JTP.

28. Forrest Shivers, *The Land Between: A History of Hancock County, Georgia to 1940* (Spartanburg, S.C.: Reprint Co., 1990), 253, 286, 315; Burwell quoted 286. Shivers is the source of the description of Burwell as a "windbag politician" (telephone conversation with the author, 20 April 1993).

29. While in "Incredible Journey" Toomer mentions going to Augusta only on his way home from Sparta (box 18, folder 487, JTP), his 1921 memorandum book refers to

a Mrs. Hattie Foster living in Augusta (box 60, folder 1410, JTP). Marcellus P. Foster (d. 1897) was the name of Nathan Toomer's white lawyer in Augusta (Gatewood and Leslie, "'This Father of Mine,'" 802 n40); Dr. W. H. Foster had been Amanda America Dickson Toomer's physician during her final illness (Leslie, *Woman of Color*, 123). A letter from "Evelyn" living in Sparta addressed to "Mary Alice" and "Emma Lue" in Augusta asks them to "make it pleasant" for Toomer on his way home (25 November 1921, box 9, folder 287, JTP). Toomer was evasive about his father's connections with Augusta, writing that, in his "life lived around Macon and Atlanta [Augusta is crossed out], Nathan Toomer was "lordly . . . a dreamer and perhaps also a schemer" (box 18, folder 487, JTP). In 1900 Nathan Toomer went to live with his daughter Martha in Macon, where his 1906 death certificate is recorded.

30. Nathan Toomer wrote to Whitefield McKinlay, "Caty Dickson has just gotten a divorce from Charley Dickson. In the wreck the court gave her and her three children four hundred acres of poor land and $1800 in money. Her lawyer took from her one thousand in cash and has left Cathy [*sic*] almost nothing—poor woman. She was and is today a good girl—after all Charley's bad treatment to her, he having on several occasions worn a buggy whip nearly out on her and taken a shot at her, and did his best to kill her." Regarding his own affairs, he wrote on 6 July 1900: "I have sued Julian Dickson for a large amount and have him held under bond of several thousand dollars. Charley is a perfect drunk in every way" (28 August 1900, quoted in Gatewood and Leslie, "'This Father of Mine,'" 806). Charles Dickson moved to California sometime after his divorce from Kate Holsey, passed as white under the name of Fred V. Carlyle, and died in his forties of Bright's disease (Leslie, *Woman of Color*, 133).

31. That the marriage of Nathan and Amanda continued to haunt Toomer is suggested in a "very significant" dream in relation to "my strange white Negro difficulty" that he recalled when undergoing Jungian psychoanalysis in 1949–50: "I am not passing, so I can't be penalized . . . I will tell them how my own father lived right here in Georgia. What I am doing was done by my ancestor with the affirmation of all concerned. . . . I pass by a fine-looking well set up Negro woman, a person of natural dignity and some richness of life. As we pass we smile in greeting" (Journal, 10 March 1950, box 62, folder 1446, JTP).

32. In 1951, Toomer conveyed some thoughts about paternal lineage to the fatherless young Paul Beekman Taylor: "Blood strain is an accident which binds people together long enough for them to decide whether they like each other or whether they've had enough of each other. This 'father' of yours is a ghost. Looking for the flesh only puts you in the position of wanting to get away from the ghost. The flesh only disappoints the thought. You have a father in you. Do you want to risk losing the father you have for the chance of finding a father whose person will not only destroy that image, but will lay a claim on your conception of fatherhood? . . . Don't lack for claims on yourself and the worst to seek and the hardest to quit is the claim of blood. . . . Reclaim yourself for yourself" (Taylor, *Shadows of Heaven*, 201).

33. JT, *Natalie Mann: A Play in Three Acts*, in *Wayward*, 243–325, quoted 247. The typescript of the play is dated February 1922 (box 45, folder 935, JTP).

34. Waldo Frank to JT, n.d. [spring 1922], in *Brother*, 34; JT, *Natalie Mann*, 324–25. For commentary on *Natalie Mann*, see Nellie Y. McKay, *Jean Toomer, Artist: A Study of His Literary Life and Work, 1894–1936* (Chapel Hill: University of North Carolina Press, 1984), 68–78; Rudolph P. Byrd, *Jean Toomer's Years with Gurdjieff: Portrait of an Artist, 1923–1936* (Athens: University of Georgia Press, 1990), 131–36; Jeffrey C. Stewart, "Alain Locke and

Georgia Douglas Johnson, Patrons of Afro-American Modernism," *GW Washington Studies* 12 (July 1986): 37–44; Darwin Turner, *In a Minor Chord: Three Afro-American Writers and Their Search for Identity* (Carbondale: Southern Illinois University Press, 1971), 11–14; and Susan Edmunds, *Grotesque Relations: Modernist Domestic Fiction and the U.S. Welfare State* (Oxford: Oxford University Press, 2008), 65–70, 79–84.

35. JT, *Natalie Mann*, 257–58.

36. Ibid., 279–80.

37. Ibid., 307–8.

38. Ibid., 300–301. In the preface to *Man and Superman*, Shaw writes that "virtue and courage" consist in "identifying with the purpose of the world"; the best art is intellectually challenging and didactic, propagating "opinions" rather than "grievances" (George Bernard Shaw, "Epistle Dedicatory," *Man and Superman: A Comedy and a Philosophy* [1903; rpt. Baltimore, Md.: Penguin Books, 1952], xxxii).

39. Toomer's treatment of feminism and sexual liberation in *Natalie Mann* may have been influenced by André Tridon, who cited Shaw at length in his discussion of "The New Woman and Love" (*Psychoanalysis and Love* [1922; rpt. Whitefish, Mont.: Kessinger Publishing, 2007], 275–90).

40. For a discussion of Karintha as the object of an aestheticizing gaze, see Daniel Terris, "Waldo Frank, Jean Toomer, and the Critique of Racial Voyeurism," in *Race and the Modern Artist*, ed. Heather Hathaway, Josef Jarab, and Jeffrey Melnick (New York: Oxford University Press, 2003): 92–114.

41. JT, *Natalie Mann*, 318–19; W. E. B. Du Bois, "The Damnation of Women," *Darkwater: Voices from within the Veil* (1920, rpt. Millwood, N.Y.: Kraus-Thomson, 1975), 163–86.

42. Toomer noted, "I inherited from my grandfather not only my liking for words but the tendency to give certain people close to me all sorts of strange, funny, vivid, and sometimes apt names" (box 19, folder 499, JTP). Toomer also combined syllables to make odd new words; the title of his unpublished story "Caromb," for example, was drawn from "*Car* from Carmel, *omb* from somber" (JT to Melville Cane, n.d., box 1, folder 27, JTP).

43. Toomer may have had in mind an association between David *Teyy* of "Withered Skin of Berries" and *Etty* Beal.

Chapter 5. In the Land of Cotton

1. JT, Liveright publicity sketch, box 26, folder 611, JTP; JT to Waldo Frank, 21 December 1922, *Letters*, 101. While the final section of *Cane* has no title, Toomer routinely referred to it as "Kabnis," and it was published in *Broom* under this title. Toomer submitted the play to the Provincetown Playhouse producer Kenneth Macgowan in early 1923; he was indignant that Macgowan rejected the play on the grounds that it "is a study in character and not a dramatic narrative" (JT to Margaret Naumberg, 24 September 1923, *Letters*, 174–75).

2. For the argument that *Cane*'s montage defies thematic or sequential patterning of any kind, see Joel B. Peckham, "Jean Toomer's *Cane*: Self as Montage and the Drive toward Integration," *American Literature* 72, no. 2 (2000): 275–90; and Rachel Farebrother, *The Collage Aesthetic in the Harlem Renaissance* (Farnham, UK: Ashgate, 2001): 79–110.

3. JT to Waldo Frank, n.d. [November 1922], *Letters*, 94. "Kabnis" appeared in *Broom* 5 (August 1923): 12–16, and *Broom* 5 (September 1923): 83–94. The first segment comprises section 1 of the *Cane* version; the second comprises sections 5 and 6. See JT to Lola Ridge, n.d. [late January/early February 1923], *Letters*, 127.

4. Georg Lukács, *History and Class Consciousness: Studies in Marxist Dialectics*, trans. Rodney Livingstone (Cambridge, Mass.: MIT Press, 1971), 100. For more on the relationship between immediacy and mediation in the thought of Hegel, see Theodor W. Adorno, *Hegel: Three Studies*, trans. Shierry Weber Nicholsen (Cambridge, Mass.: MIT Press, 1993), 57–59.

5. István Mészáros, *Beyond Capital: Towards a Theory of Transition* (London: Merlin Press, 1995), 108–9; C. J. Arthur, *Dialectics of Labour: Marx and His Relation to Hegel* (Oxford: Basil Blackwell, 1986), http://chrisarthur.net/dialectics-of-labour/chapter-01.html, accessed 8 November 2013. For more on de-mediation and re-mediation, see Steven Vogel, *Against Nature: The Concept of Nature in Critical Theory* (Albany: State University of New York Press, 1996); and Richard Gunn, "Marxism and Mediation," *Common Sense* 2 (July 1987), http://richard-gunn.com/pdf/5_marxism_mediation.pdf, accessed 8 November 2013.

6. JT, *Cane* (1923; rpt. New York: Liveright, 1975), 84; subsequent quotations are cited parenthetically in the text; JT to Waldo Frank, n.d. [November 1922], *Letters*, 94.

7. *New York Call*, 1 January 1919, 1; National Association for the Advancement of Colored People (NAACP), *Thirty Years of Lynching in the United States, 1889–1918* (1919; rpt. New York: Arno and the New York Times, 1969); "Lynchings in the United States," *Crisis* 23 (February 1922): 165; Lynching Record, *Crisis* 19 (November 1919): 349; "Lynching 'Wake' at Washington, Ga.," *Augusta Chronicle*, 6 October 1919, 1, 7; Forrest Shivers, *The Land Between: A History of Hancock County, Georgia, to 1940* (Spartanburg, S.C.: Reprint Co., 1990), 287. For the use of the term "American Congo" to describe the Deep South, see William Pickens, "The American Congo—The Burning of Henry Lowery," *Nation* 109 (23 March 1921): 426–28; and Herbert Seligmann, *The Negro Faces America* (New York: Clarence S. Nathan, 1920), 218–52. For more on the fall 1919 Arkansas massacre of African Americans involved in organizing the Progressive Farmers and Household Union, at which as many as 856 deaths may have occurred, see Grif Stockley, *Blood in Their Eyes: The Elaine Race Massacres of 1919* (Fayetteville: University of Arkansas Press, 2001); and Robert Whitaker, *On the Laps of Gods: The Red Summer of 1919 and the Struggle for Justice That Remade a Nation* (New York: Crown Publishers, 2008). For more on lynching in connection with the Great Migration, see Fitzhugh Brundage, *Lynching in the New South: Georgia and Virginia, 1880–1930* (Urbana: University of Illinois Press, 1981); and S. Tolnay and J. Massey, "Black Flight: Lethal Violence and the Great Migration, 1900–1930," *Social Science History* 14 (1989): 347–70.

8. "Tarheels Lynch Negro for Attack on White Girl," *Augusta Chronicle*, 15 August 1921, 1; editorial, "Sheriff Plunkett and the Vengeance Mob from South Carolina," *Augusta Chronicle*, 17 August 1921, 6.

9. "Three Dead, 9 Wounded in Shooting Affray When Lone Negro Runs Amuck; No Race Riot," *Augusta Chronicle*, 17 August 1921, 1; "Mass Meeting of Officials and Citizens Says No Race Riot in Augusta; Denounces Mobs," *Augusta Chronicle*, 18 August 1921, 1.

10. Walter White, "The Work of a Mob," *Crisis* 16 (September 1918): 221–23, quoted 222.

11. Christopher C. Meyers, "'Killing Them by the Wholesale': A Lynching Rampage in South Georgia," *Georgia Historical Quarterly* 90, no. 2 (summer 2006): 214–35.

12. "Death Dealt to Man and Wife," *Savannah Morning News*, 20 May 1918, 1.

13. Editorial, "The Hun in America," *Messenger* 2 (July 1919): 5. A *Nation* editorial noted of the murder of Mary Turner, "This was not in Belgium or Serbia, but in Christian America" ("Rewards to Catch Lynchers," *Nation* 107 [31 August 1918]: 219). Another possible source of Toomer's revised version of the baby's death is Theodore Canot's *Adventures*

of an African Slaver (1854; rpt. New York: Dover, 1969, 384–85), which Toomer read with the Washington study group.

14. *Atlanta Constitution*, 14 March–15 April 1921; "Slayer's Graphic Story of Wholesale Murders Unshaken by Withering Fire of Cross-Examiners—Sack Chained to Bodies," *Atlanta Constitution*, 7 April 1921, 2. See Pete Daniel, *The Shadow of Slavery: Peonage in the South, 1901–1969* (Urbana: University of Illinois Press, 1972), 110–31; and Douglas A. Blackmon, *Slavery by Another Name: The Re-Enslavement of Black People in America from the Civil War to World War II* (New York: Doubleday, 2008), 360–64. Blackmon estimates that between 100,000 and 200,000 African Americans were transferred from county jails into forced debt peonage labor camps during the Jim Crow era (7). Jasper County, which described itself as "strictly a white man's county" (advertisement, *Sparta Ishmaelite*, sect. 3, 22 August 1921, 6), had an especially brutal reputation even before the "death farm" became notorious ("Social Progress," *Crisis* 21 [February 1921]: 178).

15. Daniel, *Shadow of Slavery*, 122–23. The Williams trial was moved to Newton County because several government officials in Jasper County, including the sheriff and chief prosecutor, were being investigated for debt peonage. While widely practiced throughout the South in the early twentieth century, as a form of involuntary servitude, debt peonage had been illegalized in 1867. For more on the role of chain gangs in constructing the South's modern infrastructure, see Alex Lichtenstein, *Twice the Work of Free Labor: The Political Economy of Convict Labor in the New South* (London: Verso, 1996).

16. "Race Riot Plots Up to Grand Jury—Postpone Williams Trial," clippings, box 38-16, folder 274, AGP; "Georgia's Death Farm," *Literary Digest* 16 (21 April 1921): 13–14; Hugh Dorsey, *The Negro in Georgia* (Atlanta: N.p., 1921), 24–25; Du Bois, editorial, *Crisis* 22 (June 1921): 5; editorial, "The New Slavery," *Crusader* 4 (May 1921): 8; Esau Jones, "Georgia Saves Her Reputation," *Liberator* 4 (May 1921): 30. See also Chandler Owen, "Peonage, Riots, and Lynching," *Messenger* 3 (August 1921): 233. The *Negro World* published a series of poems about the "death farm" in its "Poetry for the People" column: Leonard Braithwaite's "In Covington, Georgia" (23 April 1921, 6) and "Georgia" (7 May 1921, 6); and Ethel Trew Dunlap's "The Peonage Horrors" (23 April 1921, 6).

17. David Oshinsky, *Worse than Slavery: Parchman Farm and the Ordeal of Jim Crow Justice* (New York: Free Press, 1997); "Southern Race Savagery Punishing Itself," *Atlanta Constitution*, 14 April 1921, 8. Williams and his sons were subsequently charged with several more murders of workers ("18 Deaths Now Laid to Williams Family," *Atlanta Constitution*, 15 April 1921, 1, 5).

18. Guardians of Liberty quoted in Daniel, *Shadow of Slavery*, 128; *Crisis* quoted in NAACP, *Thirty Years of Lynching*, 165; Stephen Graham, *The Soul of John Brown* (New York: Macmillan, 1920), 266–67. The *Nation* editorialized, "The case of John Williams should be a warning to the South. . . . The white Czars once thought the Russian serfs would never rise. Twice now have the serfs set themselves free" (editorial, *Nation* 112 [6 April 1921]: 496).

19. W. E. B. Du Bois, "Georgia: The Invisible Empire State," *Nation* 120 (21 January 1925): 67; "Financial Status of Klan Is Told/Klan Membership 126,000," *Houston Home Journal* (Houston County, Ga.), 20 October 1921, 1. The *New York World* published an exposé of the KKK (6–20September 1921); this was syndicated in eighteen other newspapers. For more on the growth of the Klan in the early 1920s, see Nancy Maclean, *Behind the Mask of Chivalry: The Making of the Second Ku Klux Klan* (New York: Oxford University Press, 1994); Kathleen M. Blee, *Women of the Klan: Racism and Gender in the 1920s* (Boulder: University of Colorado Press, 1991); and Wyn Craig Wade, *The Fiery Cross: The Ku Klux Klan in America*

(New York: Simon and Schuster, 1987). Six months before Toomer's arrival the Klan held an organizing meeting in Sparta (*Sparta Ishmaelite*, 25 February 1921, 1).

20. JT, poems, box 56, folder 1309, JTP.

21. Shivers, *Land Between*, 160–61; Adele Alexander, *Ambiguous Lives: Free Women of Color in Rural Georgia, 1789–1879* (Fayetteville: University of Arkansas Press, 1991), 133. In March 1996 I interviewed Katy Hunt, the 106-year-old granddaughter of Spencer Beasley, who with a proud twinkle referred to her grandfather as a "bad Negro." In some versions of African American folk legend, the biblical Cain was turned white as a consequence of his fratricidal crime (Lawrence W. Levine, *Black Culture and Black Consciousness: Afro-American Folk Thought from Slavery to Freedom* [New York: Oxford University Press, 1977], 85). For more on *Cane*/Cain, see Charles W. Scruggs, "The Mark of Cain and the Redemption of Art: A Study in Theme and Structure of Jean Toomer's *Cane*," *American Literature* 44, no. 2 (May 1972): 276–91.

22. JT to Kenneth Macgowan, 15 March 1923, *Letters*, 141; JT to Waldo Frank, n.d. [early to mid-January 1923], and 2 August 1922, *Letters*, 116, 58. The racial particularity of Kabnis's fears is illuminated by Toomer's comments on Eugene O'Neill's *The Emperor Jones*: "[T]he contents of the unconscious not only vary with individuals; they are differentiated because of race, by social conditions due to race. . . . [Brutus Jones's] fear becomes a Negro's fear, recognizably different from a similar emotion, modified by other racial experience" ("Negro Psychology in *The Emperor Jones*" [1921], in *Jean Toomer: Selected Essays and Literary Criticism*, ed. Robert B. Jones [Knoxville: University of Tennessee Press, 1996], 6). For more on lynching and group social trauma, see Daniel J. Martin, "Lynching Sites: Where Trauma and Pastoral Collide," in *Coming into Contact: Explorations in Ecocritical Theory and Practice*, ed. Annie Merrill Ingram et al. (Athens: University of Georgia Press, 2007), 93–110.

23. JT to Kenneth Macgowan, 15 March 1923, *Letters*, 141; JT, "The South in Literature," in *Jean Toomer: Selected Essays and Literary Criticism*, 15.

24. For commentaries on Kabnis's terrorized alienation, see Ignacio Ortiz-Monasterio, "Jean Toomer's 'Kabnis' and the Language of Dreams," *Southern Literary Journal* 38, no. 2 (spring 2006): 19–39; Mary Battenfeld, "'Been Shapin Words T Fit M Soul': *Cane*, Language, and Social Change," *Callaloo* 25, no. 4 (2002): 1238–49; Tom Marvin, "Jean Toomer's 'Kabnis,'" *Explicator* 67, no. 1 (fall 2008): 43–45; John M. Reilly, "The Search for Black Redemption: Jean Toomer's *Cane*," *Studies in the Novel* 2, no. 3 (fall 1970): 312–24; Jennifer D. Williams, "Jean Toomer's *Cane* and the Erotics of Mourning," *Southern Literary Journal* 40, no. 2 (spring 2008): 87–101; and Raphael Comprone, *Poetry, Desire, and Fantasy in the Harlem Renaissance* (Lanham, Md.: University Press of America, 2006), 51–107. A slang expression for masturbation is "choking the chicken." For more on Toomer's youthful anxieties about masturbation, see Mark Whalan, *Race, Manhood, and Modernism in America: The Short Story Cycles of Sherwood Anderson and Jean Toomer* (Knoxville: University of Tennessee Press, 2007), 174–82. For an Afrocentric reading of the ritual killing of the hen, see Chikwenye Okonjo Ogunyemi, "From a Goat Path in Africa: Roger Mais and Jean Toomer," *Obsidian* 5 (winter 1979): 7–21.

25. For more on the opposition of "golden" to "split-gut" words in "Kabnis," see Michael North, *The Dialect of Modernism: Race, Language, and Twentieth-Century Literature* (New York: Oxford University Press, 1994), 162–74; and Karen Jackson Ford, *Split-Gut Song: Jean Toomer and the Poetics of Modernity* (Tuscaloosa: University of Alabama Press, 2005), 118–43.

26. JT, Liveright publicity sketch, box 26, folder 611, JTP. Lewis has been variously characterized and identified. Gorham Munson dubbed Lewis "a clear-headed radical

black" (*Destinations: A Canvass of American Literature Since 1900* [New York: J. H. Sears, 1928], 180). Kathryne Lindberg views Lewis as a stand-in for Waldo Frank ("Raising *Cane* on the Theoretical Plane: Jean Toomer's Racial Personae," in *Cultural Difference and the Literary Text: Pluralism and the Limits of Authenticity in North American Literatures*, ed. Winfried Siemerling and Katrin Schwenk [Iowa City: University of Iowa Press, 1996], 58). Mark Whalan identifies Lewis as a northern ethnographic observer (*Race, Manhood, and Modernism in America*, 163). Jerome E. Thornton argues that Lewis is homosexual ("'Goin' on de muck': The Paradoxical Journey of the Black American Hero," *CLA Journal* 31 [March 1988]: 261–80); as does Siobhan B. Somerville (*Queering the Color Line: Race and the Invention of Homosexuality in American Culture* [Durham, N.C.: Duke University Press, 2000]: 131–65). Lewis D. Moore argues that Lewis "exemplifies the male in his inability to both confront and defeat convention and desire" and, in his impotence, is to be compared with the mules outside ("Kabnis and the Reality of Hope: Jean Toomer's *Cane*," *North Dakota Quarterly* 54, no. 1 [winter 1986]: 35).

27. JT to Lola Ridge, n.d. [late January/early February 1923], *Letters*, 124–25. Toomer was responding to Ridge's criticism that, in an early draft, Lewis is "not convincing," seeming "to have been yanked into your story from some source entirely without your own experience" (Lola Ridge to JT, n.d., box 1, folder 18, JTP).

28. Emmett J. Scott writes that the wartime Great Migration from Georgia and Alabama was influenced by the fact that "hundreds believed that God had cursed the land when he sent droughts and floods and destructive pests to visit them" (*Negro Migration during the War* [New York: Oxford University Press, 1920], 40).

29. James Weldon Johnson, *Along This Way: The Autobiography of James Weldon Johnson* (New York, Viking, 1933), 333–34; Walter White, *A Man Called White: The Autobiography of Walter White* (New York: Viking, 1948), 46–50.

30. For discussions valorizing Lewis's position on racial identity, see Chester Fontenot, "W. E. B. Du Bois's 'Of the Coming of John,' Toomer's 'Kabnis,' and the Dilemma of Self-Representation," in *The Souls of Black Folk One Hundred Years Later*, ed. Dolan Hubbard (Columbia: University of Missouri Press, 2003), 130—60; Jennifer Wilks, "Writing Home: Comparative Black Modernism and Form in Jean Toomer and Aimé Césaire," *Modern Fiction Studies* 51 (winter 2005): 801–23; and Tace Hedrick, "Blood-Lines That Waver South: Hybridity, the 'South,' and American Bodies," *Southern Quarterly: A Journal of the Arts in the South* 42, no. 1 (fall 2003): 39–52. For a negative assessment of Lewis's racial position vis à vis Kabnis, see Charles Harmon, "*Cane*, Race, and 'Neither/Norism,'" *Southern Literary Journal* 32, no. 2 (2000): 90–101.

31. For more on the ironic invocation of "Deep River" in "Kabnis" and elsewhere in *Cane*, see T. Austin Graham, "O Cant: Singing the Race Music of Jean Toomer's *Cane*," *American Literature* 82 (December 2010): 725–52.

32. Toomer may have been familiar with Aleline F. Ries's "Mammy," a story describing a slavery-era mother who murders the white child in her charge when her own daughter is sold away ("Mammy," *Crisis* 13 [January 1918]: 117–18). For more on the songs in "Kabnis," see Geneviève Fabre, "Dramatic and Musical Structures in 'Harvest Song' and 'Kabnis': Toomer's *Cane* and the Harlem Renaissance," in *Jean Toomer and the Harlem Renaissance*, ed. Geneviève Fabre and Michel Feith (New Brunswick, N.J.: Rutgers University Press), 109–27; and Ford, *Split-Gut Song*, 118–43.

33. "Rock-a-Bye Your Baby with a Dixie Melody," http://www.metrolyrics.com/rockabye -your-baby-with-a-dixie-melody-lyrics-rufus-wainwright.html, accessed 2 November 2013.

34. Lola Ridge, "Lullaby," *The Ghetto and Other Poems* (New York: B. W. Huebsch, 1918), 80. See also Nancy Berke, *Women Poets on the Left: Lola Ridge, Geneviève Taggard, Margaret Walker* (Gainesville: University Press of Florida, 2001), 47. Mark Ellis has proposed that the East St. Louis riot was the "decisive event . . . in the wartime experience of black Americans [that] shaped the New Negro" ("Federal Surveillance of Black Americans during the First World War," *Immigrants and Minorities* 12 [March 1993]: 1–20, quoted 11).

35. "Lamkins," in Francis James Child, *The English and Scottish Popular Ballads*, 5 vols. (New York: Dover, 1965), 2:322. There are twenty-two versions of the ballad, listed as A through V (320–42). It is designated as both "Lamkins" and "Bo Lamkins."

36. For interpretations of the Black Madonna as a dehistoricizing figure, see Vera M. Kutzinski, "Unseasonal Flowers: Nature and History in Plácido and Jean Toomer," *Yale Journal of Criticism* 3, no. 2 (spring 1990): 153–79; and Adam McKible, *The Space and Place of Modernism: The Russian Revolution, Little Magazines, and New York* (New York: Routledge, 2002), 71–77. For commentary on the "curious absence of the Southern black maternal feminine" throughout *Cane*, see Yolanda Manora, "'She was in th family-way': The Dialectics of Modernity and Maternity in Jean Toomer's *Cane*," *Obsidian 3: Literature in the African Diaspora* 8 (spring/summer 2007–9): 51–67, quoted 56.

37. JT to unnamed, n.d., quoted in *Cane: An Authoritative Text, Backgrounds, Criticism*, ed. Darwin T. Turner (New York: www.Norton, 1988), 156.

38. JT, "On Being an American," box 20, folder 513, JTP. For readings of "Kabnis" stressing the search for a father/ancestor, see Ann Douglas, *Terrible Honesty: Mongrel Manhattan in the 1920s* (New York: Farrar, Straus and Giroux, 1995), 270–71; Ortiz-Monasterio, "Jean Toomer's 'Kabnis' and the Language of Dreams"; and Farah Jasmine Griffin, *"Who Set You Flowin'?": The African-American Migration Narrative* (New York: Oxford University Press, 1995), 147–54. Critics who discern in "Kabnis" particular allusions to Toomer's family history include Nathan Grant, *Masculinist Impulses: Toomer, Hurston, Black Writing, and Modernity* (Columbia: University of Missouri Press, 2004), 77–91; and Maria Onita Estes-Hicks, "Jean Toomer: A Biographical and Critical Study," PhD diss., Columbia University, 1982. For a description of Pinchback's oratory, see Nicholas Lemann, *Redemption: The Last Battle of the Civil War* (New York: Farrar, Straus and Giroux, 2006), 196–97.

39. Bishop L. H. Holsey, *Autobiography, Sermons, Addresses, and Essays* (Atlanta, Ga.: Franklin Publishing, 1898), 10. Several members of the Holsey family were living in Sparta at the time of Toomer's visit; one, a local brick mason, is a possible model for Toomer's Halsey (Estes-Hicks, "Jean Toomer," 156). See also See Mark Schultz, "Interracial Kinship Ties and the Emergence of a Rural Black Middle Class: Hancock County, Georgia, 1865–1920," in *Georgia in Black and White: Explorations in the Race Relations of a Southern State, 1865–1950*, ed. John C. Inscoe (Athens: University of Georgia Press, 1994), 141–72. One of the mixed-race branches of the Holsey family renamed itself "Halsey" (Forrest Shivers, interview with the author, 20 April 1993). Halsey's direct prototype was most likely the blacksmith William Henry Ingram, a graduate of the Paine Institute who was at the time of Toomer's visit in 1921 the proprietor of the Old Rock Shop, a Sparta wagon-making and repair establishment. The description of Halsey's shop in *Cane* closely resembles that of the Old Rock Shop in Elizabeth Wiley Smith, *The History of Hancock County, Georgia*, 2 vols. (Washington, Ga.: Wilkes Publishing Co., 1974), 1:59. For more identification of local landmarks in *Cane*, see my "Jean Toomer's Sparta," *American Literature* 67, no. 4 (December 1995): 747–75. Varying estimates of Lucius Holsey and Paine Institute are supplied by George Esmond Clary Jr., "The Founding of Paine College—A Unique Ven-

ture in Inter-Racial Cooperation in the New South, 1882–1903," EdD thesis, University of Georgia, 1965; John Brother Cade, *Holsey—The Incomparable* (New York: Pageant Press, Ann Arbor: University Microfilms, 1982); Othal Hawthorne Lakey, *The History of the CME Church* (Memphis, Tenn.: CME Publishing House, 1985); and Glenn T. Eskew, "Black Elitism and the Failure of Paternalism in Postbellum Georgia: The Case of Bishop Lucius Henry Holsey," *Journal of Southern History* 58, no. 4 (November 1992): 637–65. Eskew states that "Blacks disliked the Paine Idea so much that in order to get students Holsey had to pay them to attend class" (651).

40. For more on the reception of *The Birth of a Nation*, see Michelle Faith Wallace, "The Good Lynching and *The Birth of a Nation*: Discourses and Aesthetics of Jim Crow," *Cinema Journal* 43, no. 1 (fall 2003): 85–104.

41. For discussion of possible word-plays on "Kabnis," see Nathan Grant, *Masculinist Impulses*, 78–79; Chezia Thompson Cager, *Teaching Jean Toomer's 1923 "Cane"* (New York: Peter Lang, 2006), 72, 106; and Linda Wagner-Martin, "Toomer's *Cane* as Narrative Sequence," in *Modern Short Story Sequences: Composite Fictions and Fictive Communities*, ed. J. Gerald Kennedy (Cambridge: Cambridge University Press, 1995), 19–34. For affirmative readings of the roles of Father John and Carrie Kate, see Sally Bishop Shigley, "Recalcitrant, Revered, and Reviled: Women in Jean Toomer's Short Story Cycle, *Cane*," *Short Story* 9, no. 1 (2001): 88–98; Alain Solard, "The Impossible Unity: Jean Toomer's 'Kabnis,'" in *Myth and Ideology in American Culture*, ed. Régis Durand (Villeneuve d'Ascq: Université de Lille, 1976), 175–94; Patricia Chase, "The Women in *Cane*," in O'Daniel, 389–402; and Houston Baker, *Afro-American Poetics: Revisions of Harlem and the Black Aesthetic* (Madison: University of Wisconsin Press, 1988): 102–3. For an analysis of Carrie Kate as a figure comprising the Virgin Mary, Mary Magdalene, and Martha, see Farah Jasmine Griffin, *"Who Set You Flowin'?,"* 153–54.

42. Several critics have argued that "Kabnis" ends with the emergence of its protagonist as artist, making *Cane* a Kunstlerroman. See Catherine L. Innes, "The Unity of Jean Toomer's Cane," in O'Daniel, 153–67; Bowie Duncan, "Jean Toomer's *Cane*: A Modern Black Oracle," in O'Daniel, 237–46; Susan Blake, "The Spectatorial Artist and the Structure of *Cane*," in O'Daniel, 195–212; and Baker, *Afro-American Poetics*, 39–44. For the possible influence on Toomer of Hart Crane's depiction of "[t]he black man forlorn in the cellar" in "Black Tambourine," see Victor A. Kramer, "The 'Mid-Kingdom' of Crane's 'Black Tambourine' and Toomer's *Cane*," in O'Daniel, 121–31.

43. JT to Montgomery Gregory, 2 January 1924, *Letters*, 188; Montgomery Gregory, review of *Cane*, *Opportunity* 1 (December 1923): 374–75. For ironic readings of the ending of "Kabnis," see Moore, "Kabnis and the Reality of Hope"; Battenfeld, "'Been Shapin Words T Fit M Soul'"; Wilks, "Writing Home"; Ford, *Split-Gut Song*; Robert B. Jones, *Jean Toomer and the Prison-House of Thought: A Phenomenology of the Spirit* (Amherst: University of Massachusetts Press, 1993), 118–43; and Alan Golding, "Jean Toomer's *Cane*: The Search for Identity through Form," *Arizona Quarterly* 39, no. 3 (autumn 1983): 197–214. Toomer's emphasis on Father John's struggle to speak may refer to Waldo Frank's view of the nation as "a turmoiled giant, [with] tied . . . tongue," waiting to be "lift[ed] into self-knowledge" by revolutionary art (*Our America* [New York: Boni and Liveright, 1919], 4–5). Arguably, however, "Kabnis" displays the artist's limited potency.

44. Waldo Frank to JT, n.d. [April 1922], in *Brother*, 35; JT to Waldo Frank, 26 April 1922, *Letters*, 36. As late as February 1923, Toomer still had different versions of "Kabnis" in mind, for he wrote to Frank that "I still have enough stuff in me to judge the merits of

the two Kabnises. (?) In the one I have on hand there is no essential alteration. Nor will there be any" (JT to Frank, n.d. [late February 1923], *Letters*, 134).

45. Lola Ridge to JT, n.d., box 1, folder 18, JTP; JT to Lola Ridge, n.d. [late January/ February 1923], *Letters*, 128–29.

46. JT to Waldo Frank, 22 October 1922, *Letters*, 89. The final paragraph's imagery may have been influenced by Frank's finale to *The Unwelcome Man*, which stresses the failure of the protagonist, Quincy Burt, to attain a healthy maturity: "A dawn came to Quincy. Was this not another climax, another ecstasy to be shunned? . . . The rising sun flamed into his room. He pulled down the blind, shutting out the sun. Then he went to bed in the made, swart shadows, and fell asleep" (Waldo Frank, *The Unwelcome Man: A Novel* [Boston: Little Brown, 1917], 369). Toomer was putting the finishing touches on *Cane* when he read Frank's novel (JT to Waldo Frank, n.d. [mid-December 1923], *Letters*, 98).

Chapter 6. Georgia on His Mind

1. JT to Waldo Frank, 22 July 1922, *Letters*, 49; JT, "The Outline of an Autobiography," box 20, folder 514, JTP. Texts composed (or drafted) before Toomer's 1921 trip to Sparta include "Face," "Bona and Paul," "Evening Song," "Storm Ending," and "Her Lips Are Copper Wire." Lola Ridge singled out "Face" as "fine, best of group" in a cluster of portraits that Toomer sent to her the previous year (Lola Ridge to JT, 12 October 1920, box 1, folder 18, JTP).

2. For more on the repression of social and historical contradictions in the genre of the pastoral, see Robert Bone, *Down Home: Origins of the Afro-American Short Story* (New York: Columbia University Press, 1988); Lucinda H. MacKethan, *The Dream of Arcady: Place and Time in Southern Literature* (Baton Rouge: Louisiana State University Press, 1980); Nathaniel Mackey, "Sound and Sentiment, Sound and Symbol," *Callaloo* 10 (winter 1987): 29–54; and Maria Farland, "Modernist Versions of Pastoral: Poetic Inspiration, Scientific Expertise, and the 'Degenerate' Farmer," *American Literary History* 19, no. 4 (September 2007): 905–36.

3. The terms "first nature" and "second nature" are explored in Neil Smith, *Uneven Development: Nature, Capital, and the Production of Space*, 3rd ed. (Athens: University of Georgia Press, 2008).

4. Edward E. Lewis, *The Mobility of the Negro: A Study in the American Labor Supply* (New York: Columbia University Press, 1931), 24; Forrest Shivers, *The Land Between: A History of Hancock County, Georgia, to 1940* (Spartanburg, S.C.: Reprint Co., 1990), 295; "Hancock County Cotton Report for 1921," *Sparta Ishmaelite*, 21 October 1921, 1. The 1919 Elaine massacre was in response to the unionizing farmers' demand for a larger share of the profits from high-priced wartime-era cotton. See also Fabian Lange, Alan L. Olmstead, and Paul W. Rhode, "The Impact of the Boll Weevil, 1892–1932," *Journal of Economic History* 69 (September 2009): 685–718.

5. "Ingraham Returns from Trip through North," *Sparta Ishmaelite*, 4 November 1921, 3. For more on the economic decline of Hancock County, see John Rozier, *Black Boss: Political Revolution in a Georgia County* (Athens: University of Georgia Press, 1982), 1–19.

6. "Several Saw Mills Shut Down in County," *Sparta Ishmaelite*, 13 May 1921, 1; William P. Jones, *The Tribe of Black Ulysses: African American Lumber Workers in the Jim Crow South* (Urbana: University of Illinois Press, 2005), 15–42; John C. Howard, *The Negro in the Lumber Industry*, Wharton School of Finance and Commerce, the Racial Policies of

American Industry, Report No. 19 (Philadelphia: University of Pennsylvania Press, 1970), 12–13; Vernon H. Jensen, *Lumber and Labor* (1945; rpt. New York: Arno, 1971), 71–98; Stephen H. Norwood, "Bogalusa Burning: The War against Biracial Unionism in the Deep South, 1919," *Journal of Southern History* 63 (August 1997): 591–628. For a discussion of the temporary revival of Georgia's lumber industry in the mid-1920s, see Arthur Raper, *A Preface to Peasantry: A Tale of Two Black Belt Counties* (1936; rpt. New York: Arno Press, 1971); and David G. Nicholls, *Conjuring the Folk: Forms of Modernity in African America* (Ann Arbor: University of Michigan Press, 2000).

7. JT, *Cane* (1923; rpt. New York: Horace Liveright, 1975), v; subsequent quotations are cited parenthetically in the text. For a discussion of cane as commodity, see Wesley Beal, "The Form and Politics of Networks in Jean Toomer's *Cane*," *American Literary History* 24, 4: 658–79. Rupert B. Vance, *Human Factors in Cotton Culture: A Study in the Social Geography of the American South* (Chapel Hill: University of North Carolina Press, 1929); Shivers, *Land Between*, 198–99. Like the cotton and lumber industries, the sugar industry underwent a postwar slump: "In the spring of 1921, Negro laborers readily accepted field work at $1 per day, and the autumn harvesting wages rarely exceeded $1.25 per day" (J. Carlyle Sitterson, *Sugar Country: The Cane Sugar Industry in the South, 1753–1950* [Lexington: University Press of Kentucky, 1953], 357). For more on the differences between sorghum and sugar cane, see Joseph S. Wall and William M. Ross, eds., *Sorghum Production and Utilization: Major Feed and Food Crops in Agriculture and Food Series* (Westport, Conn.: Avi Publishing Co., 1970).

8. JT, memorandum notebook, box 60, folder 1410, JTP.

9. Ibid. Charles Scruggs and Lee VanDemarr propose that the last two lines read, "Mules pulling a mowing machine fill [needs] / A rat with belly close to ground / A matter medicinal" (*JTTAH*, 278). For more on the pastoral/anti-pastoral dialectic in "Reapers," see J. Martin Favor, *Authentic Blackness: The Folk in the New Negro Renaissance* (Durham, N.C.: Duke University Press, 1999), 66; Farland, 96; Karen Jackson Ford, *Split-Gut Song: Jean Toomer and the Poetics of Modernity* (Tuscaloosa: University of Alabama Press, 2005), 44–45; and Patricia E. Chu, *Race, Nationalism and the State in British and American Modernism* (Cambridge: Cambridge University Press, 2006), 140–44. While horse-drawn mowers were invented in the late nineteenth century, they did not come into widespread use in the United States until the 1930s. See http://www.farmcollector.com/implements/history-of-hay-equipment-mower.aspx?PageId=4#axzz2mQmtcck1, accessed 5 December 2013.

10. Given the 1921 collapse of the cotton market, it is unlikely that Toomer heard many cotton heavers at work. "Cotton Song" may draw on Frederick Law Olmsted's 1851 description of the chant by a "loading gang of Negroes" in *A Journey in the Seaboard Slave States*. See Udo Jung, "Spirit Torsos of Exquisite Strength: The Theme of Individual Weakness vs. Collective Strength in Two of Toomer's Poems," in O'Daniel, 329–35. Toomer may also have read Sherwood Anderson's 1922 description of the chants of New Orleans dock laborers in the *Double Dealer*. See Sherwood Anderson, "New Orleans, the *Double Dealer* and the Modern Movement in America," in *Sherwood Anderson: The Writer at His Craft*, ed. Jack Salzman, David D. Anderson, and Kichinosake Ohashi (Mamaroneck, N.Y.: Paul P. Appel, 1979), 287–88.

11. "Georgia Dusk" first appeared in the *Liberator* 5 (September 1922): 25.

12. Toomer's possible sources of information about juju included Theodore Canot, *Adventures of an African Slaver*, ed. Brantz Mayer (1854; rpt. New York: Dover, 1969),

270; and John H. Harris, *Africa: Slave or Free?* (New York: E. P. Dutton, 1920), 220–21. The Washington study group, we will recall, read Canot's book (see my chapter 2).

13. The draft poem reads in part, "Barking of hounds and shouts / A possum hunt under the quarter moon" (JT, memorandum book, box 60, folder 1410, JTP). For readings of "Georgia Dusk" as a lynching poem, see Carolyn A. Mitchell, "Henry Dumas and Jean Toomer: One Voice," *Black American Literature Forum* 22 (summer 1988): 297–309; and Susan Edmunds, *Grotesque Relations: Modernist Domestic Fiction and the U.S. Welfare State* (New York: Oxford University Press, 2008), 67.

14. In the *Crisis* version of "Song of the Son," "caroling" was spelled "carrolling" and the second to last line read, "All that they were, and that they are to me" (*Crisis* 23 [April 1922]: 261). This issue of the *Crisis* also contained the obituary of P. B. S. Pinchback (269). For differing views on the poem as a testament to recovered racial authenticity, see Gorham Munson, *Destinations: A Canvass of American Literature Since 1900* (New York: J. H. Sears, 1928), 181–82; Charles T. Davis, "Jean Toomer and the South: Region and Race as Elements within a Literary Imagination" (1974; rpt. in *The Harlem Renaissance Re-examined*, ed. Victor A. Kramer [New York: AMS, 1987], 185–199); Favor, *Authentic Blackness*, 61–63; and Paul Stasi, "A 'Synchronous but More Subtle Migration': Passing and Primitivism in Toomer's *Cane*," *Twentieth-Century Literature* 55 (summer 2009): 145–48.

15. For readings of "Song of the Son" as a lynching poem, see Charles Scruggs, "Jean Toomer and Kenneth Burke and the Persistence of the Past," *American Literary History* 13, no. 1 (spring 2001): 49; Vera M. Kutzinski, "Unseasonal Flowers: Nature and History in Plácido and Jean Toomer," *Yale Journal of Criticism* 3, no. 2 (spring 1990): 153–57; and Edmunds, *Grotesque Relations*, 67. For analyses of the poem's tonal shifts and echoes of spirituals, see Marisa Parham, *Haunting and Displacement in African American Literature and Culture* (New York: Routledge, 2009), 65–71; and Paul Allen Anderson, *Deep River: Music and Memory in Harlem Renaissance Thought* (Durham, N.C.: Duke University Press, 2001), 67.

16. For readings ironizing *Cane*'s male narrators, see Thomas Fahy, "The Enslaving Power of Folksong in Jean Toomer's *Cane*," in *Literature and Music*, ed. Michael J. Meyer (Amsterdam: Rodopi, 2002), 47–63; Nathan Grant, *Masculinist Impulses: Toomer, Hurston, Black Writing, and Modernity* (Columbia: University of Missouri Press, 2004), 20–48; Sally Bishop Shigley, "Recalcitrant, Revered, and Reviled: Women in Jean Toomer's Short Story Cycle, *Cane*," *Short Story* 9 (spring 2001): 88–98; and Jessica Hays Baldanzi, "Stillborns, Orphans, and Self-Proclaimed Virgins: Packaging and Policing the Rural Women of *Cane*," *Genders Online Journal* 42 (2005). For readings stressing the portraits' conformity to sexist conventions of representation, see Donald B. Gibson, "Jean Toomer: The Politics of Denial," in *The Politics of Literary Expression: A Study of Major Black Writers* (Westport, Conn.: Greenwood Press, 1981), 155–81; J. Michael Clark, "Frustrated Redemption: Jean Toomer's Women in *Cane*, Part One," *CLA Journal* 22 (June 1979): 319–34; Laura Doyle, *Bordering on the Body: The Racial Matrix of Modern Fiction and Culture* (New York: Oxford University Press, 1994), 81–109; and Janet M. Whyde, "Mediating Forms: Narrating the Body in Jean Toomer's *Cane*," *Southern Literary Journal* 26 (fall 1993): 42–53.

17. "Karintha" first appeared in *Broom* 4 (January 1923): 83–85. On the African American magazine cover convention, see Anne Stavny, "'Mothers of Tomorrow': The New Negro Renaissance and the Politics of Maternal Representation," *African American Review* 32, no. 4 (winter 1998): 533–61; and Anne Elizabeth Carroll, *Word, Image, and the New Negro: Representation and Identity in the Harlem Renaissance* (Bloomington: Indiana University Press,

2005). Du Bois, no stranger to the convention, wrote approvingly of Toomer's treatment of female sexuality in "The Younger Literary Movement," *Crisis* 27 (February 1924): 161–63. For the argument that Karintha's baby is of mixed race, see *JTTAH*, 136–37; Gino Michael Pellegrini, "Jean Toomer and *Cane*: 'Mixed-Blood' Impossibilities," *Arizona Quarterly* 64 (winter 2008): 10; and Daphne Lamothe, "Jean Toomer's Gothic Black Modernism," in *The Gothic Other: Racial and Social Constructions in the Literary Imagination*, ed. Ruth Bienstock Anolik and Douglas L. Howard (Jefferson, N.C.: McFarland, 2004), 54–71.

18. Toomer sketched fragments of the imagery in "Karintha" in his Sparta memorandum book: "The smoke curls up from the sawdust pile, curls up / Above the pines, then settles down" (notebook, box 60, folder 1410, JTP).

19. For the argument that *Cane*'s "aborted acts of conception stress the impossibility of . . . mending the ruptures that modernity has wrought," see Jennifer Williams, "Jean Toomer's *Cane* and the Erotics of Mourning," *Southern Literary Journal* 40, no. 2 (spring 2008): 87–101, quoted 92.

20. "November Cotton Flower" first appeared in *Nomad* 2 (summer 1923): 4. For Toomer's use of the sonnet form, see Kutzinski ("Unseasonal Flowers," 169) and Ford (*Split-Gut Song*, 40–43).

21. For more on Toomer's wordplay with "Karintha" in connection with Kabnis, Nathan, and Carrie K—as well as the "paedophilic" aspect of Karintha's sexual objectification—see Monica Michlin, "'Karintha': A Textual Analysis," in *Jean Toomer and the Harlem Renaissance*, ed. Geneviève Fabre and Michel Feith (New Brunswick, N.J.: Rutgers University Press, 2001), 96–108, quoted 106. Gayl Jones notes the haunting effect of the positioning of "Karintha" at the beginning of *Cane* ("Blues Ballad: Jean Toomer's 'Karintha,'" in *Liberating Voices: Oral Tradition in African American Literature* [Cambridge, Mass.: Harvard University Press, 1991], 70–78).

22. "'Famine' in the South in a So-called 'Restricted Sense,'" *Augusta Chronicle*, 18 August 1921, 4; "10,000 Reported Dying in South from Starvation," *Sparta Ishmaelite*, 22 July 1921, 3. In 1996 two elderly residents of Sparta recalled that a white woman with two black children lived in the space between the railroad and the Culverton ("Pulverton") road (author interviews with Katy Hunt and George "Snap" Ingram, 14 March 1996). During his visit Toomer recorded fragments of local speech, one of which ("Thank y Jesus, Thank y Jesus") he used in "Becky" (memorandum notebook, box 60, folder 1410, JTP). For Toomer's reconstruction of vernacular language, see Joshua L. Miller, *Accented America: the Cultural Politics of Multilingual Modernism* (New York: Oxford University Press, 2011), 198–210.

23. JT, "Becky," *Liberator* 5 (October 1922): 30; Mike Gold, "The Jesus Thinkers," *Liberator* 5 (October 1922): 8–9, quoted 9. For more on "Becky" and Gothic conventions, see *JTTAH*, 143–46; and Lamothe, "Jean Toomer's Gothic Black Modernism," 67.

24. In "The South in Literature," Toomer wrote that the story "tells of how the conventions ruled [a white woman who had two Negro sons] out of social friendship, and all the while the human instincts in both white and black folk fed her and cared for her more tenderly than if she had been permitted to continue living in the town" ("The South in Literature," in *Jean Toomer: Selected Essays and Literary Criticism*, ed. Robert B. Jones [Knoxville: University of Tennessee Press, 1996], 14).

25. "Carma" first appeared in the *Liberator* 5 (September 1922): 5. Sources on "greegree" available to Toomer included Canot, *Adventures of an African Slaver*, 431; Sarah J. Hale, *Liberia; or, Mr. Peyton's Experiments* (New York: Harper & Brothers, 1853), 231–32; Mary A. Kingsley, *West African Studies* (1899; rpt. London: Frank Cass, 1964), 96–131; George W.

Ellis, "Negro Social Institutions in West Africa," *Journal of Race Development* 3 (October 1913): 168–88; and George W. Ellis, *Negro Culture in West Africa* (New York: Neale, 1914), 53–56. "Dixie" was an African American neighborhood on the fringe of Sparta (Elizabeth Wiley Smith, *The History of Hancock County, Georgia*, 2 vols. [Washington, Ga.: Wilkes, 1974], 1:57). See also Barbara Foley, "Jean Toomer's Sparta," *American Literature* 67 (December 1995): 747–75.

26. Commentaries stressing mysticism and primitivism in "Carma" include Rafael A. Cancel, "Male and Female Interrelationship in Toomer's *Cane*," in O'Daniel, 417–27; and William M. Ramsey, "Jean Toomer's Eternal South," *Southern Literary Journal* 36 (fall 2003): 74–89. For the argument that the tonal oscillations in "Carma" are integral to its collage technique, see Rachel Farebrother, *The Collage Aesthetic in the Harlem Renaissance* (Farnham, UK: Ashgate, 2009), 85–88.

27. Vachel Lindsay notoriously wrote that "Mumbo-Jumbo will hoo-doo you" in "The Congo (A Study of the Negro Race)" (*Collected Poems* [1914; rpt. New York, Macmillan, 1925], 178–84).

28. An early draft reads "Wind is in the corn," not "Wind is in the cane"; corn suggests a cash-based (as opposed to barter-based) agricultural economy (JT, memorandum notebook, box 60, folder 1410, JTP).

29. JT, untitled poem, box 60, folder 1411, JTP. The poem may have been inspired by George Bellows's satirical lithograph, "Benediction in Georgia," which featured a preacher gesticulating heavenward before a group of group of black and white prisoners dressed in stripes and shackled together. *Masses* 9, 7, (May 1917): 22–23.

30. "Fern" was not included in the batch of writings Toomer sent to Frank in April 1922; it first appeared in the *Little Review* 9 (autumn 1922): 25–29. For more on the shifts in tone and perspective in "Fern," see Jürgen E. Grandt, *Shaping Words to Fit the Soul: The Southern Ritual Grounds of Afro-Modernism* (Columbus: Ohio State University Press, 2009), 40–44.

31. Frank, "The Chosen People," *Our America* (New York: Boni and Liveright, 1919), 78–92. Randolph Bourne played on the word "Mayflower," noting that most U.S. immigrants not only missed the Mayflower but, "when they did come," did so "upon a 'Maiblume,' a 'Fleur de Mai,' a 'Fior di Maggio,' a 'Majblomst'" ("Trans-National America," in *War and the Intellectuals: Essays by Randolph S. Bourne 1915–1919*, ed. Carl Resek [New York: Harper and Row, 1964], 108).

32. For an analysis of Jewishness and hybridity in "Fern," see Michael Yellin, "Visions of Their America: Waldo Frank's Jewish-Modernist Influence on Jean Toomer's 'Fern,'" *African American Review* 43 (summer/fall 2009): 427–42.

33. For contrasting views of Fern's status as a symbol of intercultural communion, see Fahy, "Enslaving Power of Folksong in Jean Toomer's *Cane*"; and William Boelhower, "No Free Gifts: Toomer's 'Fern' and the Harlem Renaissance," in *Temples for Tomorrow: Looking Back at the Harlem Renaissance*, ed. Geneviève Fabre and Michel Feith (Bloomington: Indiana University Press, 2001), 193–209.

34. JT to Waldo Frank, n.d. [early to mid-January 1923], *Letters*, 116.

35. "Esther" first appeared in the *Modern Review* 1 (January 1923): 50–54. For a discussion of the class-based critique contained in "Esther," see *JTTAH*, 151–55.

36. On the Andersonian influences on "Esther," see Charles Scruggs, "Textuality and Vision in Jean Toomer's *Cane*," *Journal of the Short Story in English* 10 (1988): 93–114; *JTTAH*, 280; and Chidi Ikonné, *From Du Bois to Van Vechten: The Early New Negro Literature, 1903–1926* (Westport, Conn.: Greenwood Press, 1981), 141.

37. A "fraudulent back-to-Africa preacher" named Ben Gaston appeared in Sparta in the 1890s, according to the Hancock County historian Forrest Shivers (*Land Between*, 267). On images of the Black God and Black Christ, see *Respect Black: The Writings and Speeches of Henry McNeal Turner*, comp. and ed. Edwin S. Redkey (New York: Arno Press and the New York Times, 1971); and Randall K. Burkett, *Garveyism as a Religious Movement: The Institutionalization of a Black Civil Religion* (Metuchen, N.J.: Scarecrow Press and the American Theological Library Association, 1978). For more on the base of Garveyism in the rural South, see Mary Gambrell Robinson, "The Universal Negro Improvement Association in Georgia: Southern Strongholds of Garveyism," in *Georgia in Black and White: Explorations in the Race Relations of a Southern State, 1865–1950*, ed. John C. Inscoe (Athens: University of Georgia Press, 1994), 202–24; and Steven Hahn, *A Nation under Our Feet: Black Political Struggles in the Rural South from Slavery to the Great Migration* (Cambridge, Mass.: Belknap Press of Harvard University Press, 2003): 470–74. For contemporaneous commentary on Dunlap's poetry, see Tony Martin, comp. and ed., *African Fundamentalism: A Literary and Cultural Anthology of Garvey's Harlem Renaissance* (Dover, Mass.: Majority Press, 1991), 68, 175, 179–81.

38. "Conversion" first appeared as one of three "Georgia Portraits" in *Modern Review* 1 (January 1923): 81. For more on "dictie," see Willard Gatewood, *Aristocrats of Color: The Black Elite, 1880–1920* (Bloomington: Indiana University Press, 1990), 321. For highly critical African American reactions to Garvey's meeting with the Klan, see editorial, "Garvey Upholds the Klan!" *Crusader* 5 (October 1921): 9–10; Claude McKay, "Garvey as a Negro Moses," *Liberator* 5 (April 1922): 6–7; and editorial, "Marcus Garvey! The Black Imperial Wizard Becomes Messenger Boy of the White Ku Klux Kleagle," *Messenger* 3 (July 1922): 437.

39. For contrasting views on the narrator's relationship to Esther, see Megan Abbott, "'Dorris Dances . . . John Dreams': Free Indirect Discourse and Female Subjectivity in *Cane*" (1997; rpt. in *Cane*, Norton 2, 340–56); and Charles Harmon, "*Cane*, Race, and 'Neither/Norism,'" *Southern Literary Journal* 32 (spring 2000): 77–100.

40. Toomer wrote to Frank that "Box Seat" and "Blood-Burning Moon" were both written "at the very end of my rush to get CANE off" (n.d. [mid-January 1923], *Letters*, 121. The story first appeared in *Prairie* (March-April 1923): 18–24. Although Toomer referred to the story in a letter to Munson as "distinctly minor" (23 March 1923, *Letters*, 151), it was reprinted in *The Best Short Stories of 1923*, ed. Edward J. O'Brien (Boston: Small, Maynard, 1924).

41. For mythic/religious readings of "Blood-Burning Moon," see Alain Solard, "Myth and Narrative Fiction in *Cane*: 'Blood-Burning Moon,'" *Callaloo* 8 (fall 1985): 551–62; Clyde Taylor, "The Second Coming of *Jean Toomer*," *Obsidian* 1 (1975): 37–57; and Charles-Yves Grandjeat, "The Poetics of Passing in Jean Toomer's *Cane*," in *Jean Toomer and the Harlem Renaissance*, ed. Fabre and Feith, 64.

42. For more on the machine-like description of the lynch mob, see Farah Jasmine Griffin, *"Who Set You Flowin'?": The African-American Migration Narrative* (New York: Oxford University Press, 1995), 26–27.

43. Du Bois quoted these words from "Stars in the Elements" in the chapter on "The Sorrow Songs" in *The Souls of Black Folk* (1903; rpt. New York: Bedford Books, 1997), 192. See also "In That Great Getting-Up Morning," reprinted in J. B. T. Marsh, *The Story of the Jubilee Singers: With Their Songs* (New York: S. W. Green's Sons, 1883), 240.

44. For more on the economics of lynching in "Blood-Burning Moon," see Trudier Harris, *Exorcising Blackness: Historical and Literary Lynching and Burning Rituals* (Bloomington: Indiana University Press, 1984), 81; and Kimberly Banks, "'Like a Violin for the Wind to

Play': Lyrical Approaches to Lynching by Hughes, Du Bois, and Toomer," *African American Review* 38 (autumn 2004): 451–65. Banks contests my earlier reading of the story's imagery in "In the Land of Cotton: Economics and Violence in Jean Toomer's *Cane*," *African American Review* 32 (summer 1998): 181–98. I have come around to Banks's view.

45. "Portrait in Georgia" was the second of three "Georgia Portraits" that appeared in the *Modern Review* 1 (January 1923): 81; the others were "Face" and "Conversion." For the argument that the whiteness of the woman in "Portrait in Georgia" is both a cause and a consequence of the burning of the black man, see Walter Benn Michaels, *Our America: Nativism, Modernism, and Pluralism* (Durham, N.C.: Duke University Press, 1995), 61.

46. A possible source for Toomer's consideration of the continuity between slavery- and Jim Crow-era cotton production was Broadus Mitchell, *The Rise of Cotton Mills in the South* (1921; rpt. Gloucester, Mass.: Peter Smith, 1966).

47. For more on the figure of the Black Christ as resister of oppression, see Kelly Brown Douglas, *The Black Christ* (Maryknoll, N.Y.: Orbooks, 1994).

48. On the Montour factory, see Shivers, *Land Between*, 210, 258; and Smith, *History of Hancock County, Georgia*, 1:101, 122–23. For more on the Stone family of Hancock County, see Smith, *History of Hancock County, Georgia*, 2:161.

49. Regarding Toomer's choice of the given name "Tom," it bears noting that "Tom" can be read as an abbreviated version of "Toomer," and that Toomer also played with his name in the designation of Nathan Merilh's working-class companion in *Natalie Mann*'s "Tome Mangrow" (see chapter 4). Toomer may have wrestled with the "boss" of Sparta through both the names he gives to his sharecropper protagonist.

50. For more on the continuity between "Blood-Burning Moon" and "Seventh Street," the opening sketch in part 2 of *Cane*, see Ralph Reckley Sr., "The Vinculum Factor: 'Seventh Street'; and 'Rhobert' in Jean Toomer's *Cane*," *CLA Journal* 31 (June 1988): 484–89.

Chapter 7. Black and Brown Worlds Heaving Upward

1. Toomer was inaccurate when he later wrote, in "On Being an American," that "the middle section of *Cane* was . . . manufactured" after he had written "a hundred typed pages . . . about Georgia" in order to have "enough for a book" (*Wayward*, 125).

2. *Washington Post*, 21 July 1919, 1. "Seventh Street" first appeared in *Broom* 4, no. 1 (December 1922): 3. For commentaries stressing the sketch's celebration of migrant culture, see Donald A. Petesh, *A Spy in the Enemy's Country: The Emergence of Modern Black Literature* (Iowa City: University of Iowa Press, 1989), 201; and Farah Jasmine Griffin, *"Who Set You Flowin'?": The African-American Migration Narrative* (New York: Oxford University Press, 1995), 65. For more on the causes of the riot, see Constance McLaughlin Green, *The Secret City: A History of Race Relations in the Nation's Capital* (Princeton, N.J.: Princeton University Press, 1967), 191–94; and Lee E. Williams II, *Post-War Riots in America, 1919 and 1946: How the Pressures of War Exacerbated American Urban Tensions to the Breaking Point* (Lewiston, N.Y.: Edwin Mullen, 1991).

3. Williams, *Post-War Riots in America*, 26; *New York Times*, 23 July 1919, 2; James Weldon Johnson, "The Riots: An N.A.A.C.P. Investigation," *Crisis* 18 (September 1919): 241–43, quoted 243. The historian Carter G. Woodson, who happened to be shopping for a book in downtown Washington when the riot broke out, barely escaped serious injury.

4. Ben Vardaman, *New York Globe* and *Washington Star* quoted in "Our Own Subject Race Rebels," *Literary Digest* 62 (2 August 1919): 25; *Sparta Ishmaelite*, 1 August 1919, 2, and 8 August 1919, 2; *New York Times*, 22 July 1919, 1.

5. Robert Kerlin, *Voice of the Negro: 1919* (1920; rpt. New York: Arno and the New York Times, 1968), 76–79; *Washington Bee*, 26 July 1919, 1, and 2 August 1919, 1; Johnson, "The Riots," 243; Cyril V. Briggs, "The Capital and Chicago Race Riots," *Crusader* 2 (September 1919): 4; editorial, "The Cause of and Remedy for Race Riots," *Messenger* 2 (September 1919): 14–21, quoted 19, 21. A woman writing to the *Crisis* anticipated the language of Claude McKay's "If We Must Die": "The Washington riot gave me the thrill that comes once in a lifetime. . . . At last our men had stood like men, struck back, were no longer dumb, driven cattle" ("A Letter from a Southern Colored Woman," *Crisis* 19 [November 1919]: 339). See also Frederick G. Detweiler, *The Negro Press in the United States* (1922; rpt. College Park, Md.: McGrath Publishing, 1968).

6. JT to Waldo Frank, n.d. [early to mid-January 1923], *Letters*, 116. Regarding the sketch's style, Toomer wrote to the *Broom* editor Lola Ridge, "I think my own contribution will curiously blend the rhythm of peasant[r]y with the rhythm of machines. A syncopation, a slow jazz, a sharp intense motion, subtilized, fused to a terse lyricism" (n.d., [late January 1923], *Letters*, 123). For Langston Hughes's 1927 declaration of allegiance to the "dark working people" of Seventh Street, see "Our Wonderful Society: Washington," *Opportunity* 5 (August 1927): 226–27, quoted 227.

7. For more on struggles over streetcar segregation in Washington, DC, see Blair L. M. Kelley, *Right to Ride: Streetcar Boycotts and African American Citizenship in the Era of Plessy v. Ferguson* (Chapel Hill: University of North Carolina Press, 2010).

8. JT, *Cane* (1923; rpt. New York: Liveright, 1975), 40–41; subsequent quotations are cited parenthetically in the text. "Rhobert" was not published in any magazine before it appeared in *Cane*. Its draft is dated July 1922 (box 59, folder 1371, JTP).

9. Karl Marx, *Capital: A Critique of Political Economy*, trans. Ben Fowkes (New York: Penguin, 1976), 1:899; Robert Minor, cover, *New York Communist* (April 1919); Karel Čapek, *R.U.R. (Russum's Universal Robots): A Fantastic Melodrama in Three Acts and an Epilogue*, trans. Paul Selver and Nigel Playfair (New York: S. French, 1923); Georg Lukács, *History and Class Consciousness: Studies in Marxist Dialectics*, trans. Rodney Livingstone (Cambridge, Mass.: MIT Press, 1971), 163. Although Čapek's play did not appear in English translation until 1923, it garnered international fame soon after its 1920 staging in Czech. For more on the Red Cross and the KKK, see Nancy MacLean, *Behind the Mask of Chivalry: The Making of the Second Ku Klux Klan* (New York: Oxford University Press, 1994). For more on the anti-Bolshevik activities of the American Red Cross head Raymond Robins, see Art Young's cartoon, "Will Raymond Robins Please Come Out?," *Liberator* 1 (December 1918): 17. See also John Hutchinson, *Champions of Charity: War and the Rise of the Red Cross* (Boulder, Colo.: Westview Press, 1996), 271–75.

10. Toomer's treatment of wood pulp may have been influenced by Waldo Frank's description of the business world as an "unending blight of magazines and journals—made from the crushing of fair forests into woodpulp!" (Waldo Frank, *The Unwelcome Man: A Novel* [1917], quoted in Paul J. Carter, *Waldo Frank* [New York: Twayne, 1967], 30). For the advertising of Rastus Cigars, see www.streetswing.com/histmai2/d2king_rastus_brown.htm, accessed 26 November 2013. For definitions of "niggerhead," see http://www.urbandictionary.com/define.php?term=niggerhead, accessed 11 November 2013. Janet Farebrother discerns in Rhobert's sinking an allusion to the "'drowning' soldier . . . in 'Dulce Et Decorum Est,'" Wilfred Owen's famous 1917 antiwar poem (*The Collage Aesthetic in the Harlem Renaissance* [Farnham, UK: Ashgate, 2009], 92).

11. For more on the political commentary embedded in "Beehive," see David G. Nicholls, "Jean Toomer's *Cane*, Modernization, and the Spectral Folk," in *Modernism, Inc.: Body,*

Memory, Capital, ed. Jani Scandura and Michael Thurston (New York: New York University Press, 2001), 163; and J. Martin Favor, *Authentic Blackness: The Folk in the New Negro Renaissance* (Durham, N.C.: Duke University Press, 1999), 73. Toomer may have had in mind Marx's discussion of Bernard de Mandeville's 1728 *Fable of the Bees* in his analysis of capital accumulation (*Capital* 1:765). "Storm Ending" appeared in the *Double Dealer* 4 (September 1922): 118. For historicized commentaries on "Storm Ending," see Nellie Y. McKay, *Jean Toomer, Artist: A Study of His Literary Life and Work, 1894–1936* (Chapel Hill: University of North Carolina Press, 1984), 133; and Karen Jackson Ford, *Split-Gut Song: Jean Toomer and the Politics of Modernity* (Tuscaloosa: University of Alabama Press, 2005), 77.

12. "Calling Jesus" was published as "Nora" in the same issue of the *Double Dealer* in which "Storm Ending" appeared (4 September 1922: 132). Sherwood Anderson's encounter with "Nora" sparked his interest in Toomer. For a possible connection between Toomer's sketch and Henrik Ibsen's *A Doll's House*—where the protagonist is named "Nora"—see Udo O. H. Jung, "'Nora' Is 'Calling Jesus': A Nineteenth-Century Dilemma in an Afro-American Garb," in O'Daniel, 293–96.

13. "Avey" was not published separately before it appeared in *Cane*. The image of trees in boxes in Meridian Hill Park appears in an autobiographical prose fragment titled "Meridian Hill" (box 59, folder 1365, JTP), as well as in JT to Waldo Frank, n.d. [early May 1922], *Letters*, 38.

14. The only revision Toomer made in the typescript was to change "pinchbeck" to "pinch-beck" in the description of Avey's mother as a "jerky-gaited creature" (45). See box 58, folder 1365, JTP. The resemblance between "pinchbeck" and "Pinchback," the name of Toomer's maternal grandfather, is provocative; as a child Toomer—who was given the surname "Pinchback"—was nicknamed "Pinchy." See chapter 4.

15. Describing to Frank a recent girlfriend, Toomer displayed qualities not unlike those of the "Avey" narrator: "I share with her my deepest thoughts, that is, I talk to myself in her presence!" (JT to Waldo Frank, n.d. [mid-May 1923], *Letters*, 163).

16. For alternative assessments of the "Avey" narrator, see Nathan Grant, *Masculinist Impulses: Toomer, Hurston, Black Writing, and Modernity* (Columbia: University of Missouri Press, 2004), 52–57; and Burney J. Hollis, "Central Conflict between Rural Thesis and Urban Antithesis in Jean Toomer's 'Avey,'" in O'Daniel, 277–86.

17. For more on the Capitol dome as a slave ship, see *JTTAH*, 168–69. Charles Scruggs also links the image with both the slave ship in Melville's "Benito Cereno" and Melville's portrayal of the Capitol dome in his 1866 poem "The Conflict of Convictions" ("The Photographic Print, the Literary Negative: Alfred Stieglitz and Jean Toomer," *Arizona Quarterly* 53, no. 1 [spring 1997]: 61–89).

18. JT to Waldo Frank, 12 December 1922, *Letters*, 101. Although Toomer tried to persuade Gorham Munson to publish "Theater" in *Secession*, the story first appeared in *Cane* (JT to Gorham Munson, 31 October 1922, *Letters*, 90–92). Toomer viewed "Theater" and "Box Seat" as his finest stories; see JT to Gorham Munson, 1 March 1923, *Letters*, 144; and JT to Kenneth Macgowan, 21 March 1923, *Letters*, 150. For more on the story's narrative point of view, see Megan Abbott, "'Dorris Dances . . . John Dreams': Free Indirect Discourse and Female Subjectivity in *Cane*," in *Cane*, Norton 2, 344–56.

19. Mike Gold, "Toward Proletarian Art," *Liberator* 4 (February 1921): 20–22, quoted 21. For more on "Theater" in relation to popular culture, see Paul R. Gorman, *Left Intellectuals and Popular Culture in Twentieth-Century America* (Chapel Hill: University of North Carolina Press, 1996), 53–82. Charles Scruggs reads "Theater" as a critique of Frank's short

story "Hope" in *City Block* ("Jean Toomer and Kenneth Burke and the Persistence of the Past," *American Literary History* 13 [spring 2001]: 41–66).

20. For more on the Howard Theater, the center of the capital city's "Black Broadway," see Blair A. Ruble, *Washington's U Street: A Biography* (Baltimore, Md.: Johns Hopkins University Press, 2010), 140–44.

21. JT to Waldo Frank, n.d. [February 1923], *Letters*, 129; Frank to JT, n.d., box 3, folder 84, JTP, quoted in *Letters*, 130. See also Waldo Frank to JT, n.d., in *Brother*, 113.

22. It bears noting that Karl Marx's nickname was "Moor" (*Mohr*) given to him by friends on account of his dark complexion. Another possible source for Dan Moore's self-designation as a "baboon from the zoo" is Eugene O'Neill's *The Hairy Ape* (1922), which treats the love-hate relationship between a working-class (white) man and a higher-status woman.

23. For more on the connections between "Box Seat" and *Natalie Mann*, see Sandra Hollin Flowers, "Solving the Critical Conundrum of Jean Toomer's 'Box Seat,'" *Studies in Short Fiction* 25 (summer 1988): 301–5. For contemporaneous advice on women's conduct, from dress to sexual behavior, see Edward S. Green, *National Capital Code of Etiquette* (Washington, DC: Austin Jenkins, 1920); and E. Azalia Hackley, *The Colored Girl Beautiful* (Kansas City, Mo.: Burton, 1916). The Lincoln Theater had just opened when Toomer composed "Box Seat." See Robert K. Headley, *Motion Picture Exhibition in Washington, D.C.: An Illustrated History of Parlors, Palaces, and Multiplexes in the Metropolitan Area, 1894–1997* (Jefferson, N.C.: McFarland & Company, 1999).

24. "My Lord, What a Morning." http://www.akh.se/lyrics/my_lord_what_a_morning. htm, accessed 11 November 2013. References to "submerged races" and "submerged classes" were prominent in the discourse of New Negro radicalism. See Barbara Foley, *Spectres of 1919: Class and Nation in the Making of the New Negro* (Urbana: University of Illinois Press, 2003), 21–22 and 210–11.

25. For the argument that in "Box Seat" Toomer affirms the connections between the South, a "usable past," and American nationalism, see Tace Hedrick, "'Blood-Lines That Waver South': Hybridity, the 'South,' and American Bodies," *Southern Quarterly* 41 (fall 2003): 39–52.

26. For more on wartime musical propaganda, see Glenn Watkins, *Proof through the Night: Music and the Great War* (Berkeley: University of California Press, 2003). See also Claude McKay's sonnet, "The Little Peoples," which references the hypocrisy of the Paris Peace Conference in not granting self-determination to peoples of color ("The Little Peoples," *Liberator* 2 [July 1919]: 21; rpt. in Claude McKay, *Complete Poems*, ed. William J. Maxwell [Urbana: University of Illinois Press, 2004], 136). Despite his evident attraction to futurism, Toomer's antipathy to militarism is sharply at odds with the glorification of war in Filippo Tomaso Marinetti's "The Founding and Manifesto of Futurism," trans. R. W. Flint, in *Documents of 20th Century Art: Futurist Manifestos*, ed. Umbro Apollonio (New York: Viking Press, 1973), 19–24.

27. See Henry Adams, "The Dynamo and the Virgin," in *The Education of Henry Adams: An Autobiography*, 2 vols. (1918; rpt. New York: Time Inc. 1964), 2:161–73. Mark Whalan stresses Toomer's interest in technology as a means to liberation: "[I]t is the transformative capacity of the dynamo that converts Dan's seething resentment against the black bourgeoisie into the focused action of resistance" (*Race, Manhood and Modernism in America: The Short Story Cycles of Sherwood Anderson and Jean Toomer* [Knoxville: University of Tennessee Press, 2007], 191). See also Claude McKay's treatment of Samson as

a present-day black revolutionary ("Samson," *Workers Dreadnought* [10 January 1920]: 1602; rpt. in McKay, *Complete Poems*, 139).

28. Lukács, *History and Class Consciousness*, 204.

29. Ibid., 204. For an alternative reading of Dan's gesture, see Catherine Gunther Kodat, "'To Flash White Light from Ebony': The Problem of Modernism in Jean Toomer's *Cane*," *Twentieth-Century Literature* 46 (spring 2000): 1–19.

30. This poem first appeared in *S4N* 26 (May–August 1923): n.p. The *S4N* editor Norman Fitts translated the poem into Italian and sent it to Marinetti, describing it as "one of the first attempts to write machinery" in the United States (Norman Fitts to JT, Good Friday 1923, box 3, folder 79, JTP). The only other text in *Cane* depicting fulfilled romantic love is "Evening Song" in part 1 (19). Notably, both poems portray a kiss.

31. For more on Pinchback's aristocratic lifestyle, see Willard B. Gatewood, *Aristocrats of Color: The Black Elite, 1889–1920* (Bloomington: Indiana University Press, 1990), 42–44; and Cynthia Kerman and Richard Eldridge, *The Lives of Jean Toomer: A Hunger for Wholeness* (Baton Rouge: Louisiana State University Press, 1987), 24–25.

32. Waldo Frank, "John the Baptist," *City Block* (Darien, Conn.: Waldo Frank, 1922), 139–65, quoted 159, 148.

33. JT to unnamed, in JT, *"Cane": An Authoritative Text, Backgrounds, Criticism*, ed. Darwin T. Turner (New York: W. W. Norton, 1988), 156. This letter was never sent; Turner opines, not unreasonably, that it was addressed to Frank. "Harvest Song" first appeared in the *Double Dealer* 4 (December 1922): 258.

34. "Brother" is the common salutation in the Toomer-Frank correspondence in 1922–23. For Toomer's use of "Eoho!" to announce his texts' acceptance for publication, see JT to Waldo Frank, n.d. [late 1922], and JT to Waldo Frank, n.d. [early to mid-November 1922], *Letters*, 96–97.

35. Karen Jackson Ford, noting the position of "Harvest Song" as the last complete poem in the volume, proposes that "the end of lyric in *Cane* is rightly represented by a poem about the failure of poetry" (*Split-Gut Song*, 143).

36. Waldo Frank to JT, n.d., in *Brother*, 103; JT to Waldo Frank, n.d. [mid-January 1923], *Letters*, 121.

37. "Prayer" may display the influence on Toomer of the mystic P. D. Ouspensky, who wrote, "[W]e study always not the whole but the part . . . by studying the little finger of man we cannot discover his reason" (quoted in Catherine Innes, "The Unity of Jean Toomer's *Cane*," in O'Daniel, 315). Toomer may also have had in mind the words of Fanny Luve in Waldo Frank's novel *Rahab*: "I am a broken curve, a splintered part of a Circle I cannot see. . . . My thoughts a finger feeling from the line of my brokenness for a Roundness beyond me" (*Rahab* [New York: Boni and Liveright, 1922], 33).

38. For more on the "flare of poetry" letter, see chapter 5. Toomer wrote to Frank in January 1923 of the haste in which he had written "Blood-Burning Moon" and the first draft of "Box Seat" in his "rush to get CANE off." He continued, "All of my stuff gains in the second trial. When my mind clears up, I'll see what I can do. Likewise Bona and Paul" (JT to Waldo Frank, n.d. [mid-January 1923], *Letters*, 121). For more on Toomer and physical culture, see Whalan, *Race, Manhood, and Modernism in America*, 171–208.

39. For affirmative readings of Paul's realization of his mixed-race identity, see Charles-Yves Grandjeat, "The Poetics of Passing in Jean Toomer's *Cane*, in *Jean Toomer and the Harlem Renaissance*, ed. Geneviève Fabre and Michel Feith (New Brunswick, N.J.: Rutgers University Press, 2001), 57–63; and *A Jean Toomer Reader*, ed. Frederik Rusch (New York:

Oxford University Press, 1993). Rusch writes, "In transforming the negative self-consciousness of being stared at and thought odd and out of place into a positive understanding of himself and an embracing of others, in a harmonious rose garden of human diversity, Paul embodies the desire of his creator" (xii).

40. Monica Michlin proposes that Paul's presumed experience of "fullness and strength" resulting from the "racist gaze" of the revelers in the Crimson Gardens is a "strained epiphany reflecting Toomer's own contradictions and denials" ("'Karintha': A Textual Analysis," in *Jean Toomer and the Harlem Renaissance*, ed. Fabre and Feith, 98–99).

41. For more on the coincidence of racism with cultural pluralism, see Walter Benn Michaels, *Our America: Nativism, Modernism, and Pluralism* (Durham, N.C.: Duke University Press, 1997); and Werner Sollors, *Beyond Ethnicity: Consent and Descent in American Culture* (New York: Oxford University Press, 1986). Given that the principal metaphor for pluralism favored by Horace Kallen—an early and influential advocate of cultural pluralism—was the orchestra, to which each instrument contributes its distinct timbre, it bears noting that the instruments in the Crimson Gardens orchestra are compared with nursery rhyme creatures ("Hi diddle diddle, the cat and the fiddle"). See Horace Kallen, "Democracy Versus the Melting-Pot," *Nation* 100 (1915): 219–20.

42. Toomer wrote to Georgia O'Keeffe, "Most people cannot see this story because of the inhibitory baggage they bring with them. When I say 'white,' they see a certain white man, when I say 'black,' they see a certain Negro. . . . So that at the end, when Paul resolves these contrasts to a unity, my intelligent commentors [*sic*] wonder what its all about" (JT to Georgia O'Keeffe, 13 January 1924, *Letters*, 191).

Coda

1. Fredric Jameson, *The Political Unconscious: Narrative as a Socially Symbolic Act* (Ithaca, N.Y.: Cornell University Press, 1981), 95.

2. Ibid., 96–97.

INDEX

BARBARA FOLEY is Distinguished Professor of English at Rutgers University-Newark. She is the author of *Spectres of 1919: Class and Nation in the Making of the New Negro.*

The University of Illinois Press
is a founding member of the
Association of American University Presses.

———————————————————

Typeset in 10.5/13 Adobe Minion
Composed by Lisa Connery
at the University of Illinois Press
Manufactured by Sheridan Books, Inc.

University of Illinois Press
1325 South Oak Street
Champaign, IL 61820-6903
www.press.uillinois.edu